DESIGNING SUSTAINABLE RESIDENTIAL AND COMMERCIAL INTERIORS

FAIRCHILD BOOKS

Fairchild Books
An imprint of Bloomsbury Publishing Inc

1385 Broadway   50 Bedford Square
New York   London
NY 10018   WC1B 3DP
USA   UK

www.bloomsbury.com

First published 2015

Library of Congress Cataloging-in-
Publication Data
A catalog record for this book is available
from the Library of Congress
2014001097

ISBN: PB: 978-1-60901-479-7

Typeset by Precision Graphics
Text Designer Evelin Kasikov
Cover Design Sarah Silberg and
Eleanor Rose
Printed and bound in China

DESIGNING SUSTAINABLE RESIDENTIAL AND COMMERCIAL INTERIORS

APPLYING CONCEPTS AND PRACTICES

LISA M. TUCKER

*Virginia Polytechnic Institute
and State University*

Fairchild Books, An Imprint of Bloomsbury Publishing Inc.
New York

Table of Contents

Extended Table of Contents

4   Corporate Projects   117

5   Hospitality Projects   152

6   Cultural, Civic, and Institutional Projects   187

7   Adaptive Reuse Projects   241

8   Single-Family Residential Projects   270

Preface

Although the title *Designing Sustainable Commercial and Residential Interiors: Applying Concepts and Practices* might imply that answers can be found within this book's pages, in many ways (and more importantly, perhaps) this book was written to raise questions.

In my opinion, we are currently at a crossroads. Doing things as they have always been done is insufficient—perhaps even bankrupt. This book will propose ideas and approaches from many different people. While some of these will provide answers, it is more important to question and delve into new and different ways of considering design responses to the world. Thus, while this book is obviously full of information, it is also full of provocations to professional designers, students, and faculty alike.

Sustainable design can range from specifying a "green" material or finish, to rethinking an entire method of building. The initial idea for this book was that it would be a studio guide that designers could have at the ready to assist them with the complexities of sustainable design. It has evolved into a speculative project that seeks to demonstrate the many ways people think about sustainable building and design in an effort to move us further along the path toward a fair, equitable, and beautiful solution to the survival of our own species—along with every other living thing on the planet.

Humanity's ability to satisfy our own needs and desires could be the very thing that leads to our demise. As designers, we need to question the difference between wants and needs—both our own and those of our clients.

It is my sincere hope that this book begins an exploration along the spectrum of sustainable solutions. It strives to raise as many questions as it answers and seeks to challenge all readers to find a meaningful and fulfilling path toward a kinder way of living on our planet.

The book is organized into nine chapters. Chapter 1 introduces many of the concepts discussed in the context of the other chapter-specific project types. Among other topics, it includes descriptions of the latest developments in sustainable design, with a discussion of net-zero buildings, design for disassembly, and material reuse in addition to what is now the commonly accepted LEED approach to buildings. The Appendix provides numerous checklists and guidelines (created by the author and others) that help to demonstrate how to include this new approach into the design of sustainable projects.

Chapters 2 through 9 use specific project types to present issues encountered in the various facets of the design market. Current sources for research and sustainability initiatives are included for several of the most common types of design projects: retail;

healthcare; corporate; hospitality; cultural, civic, and institutional; and residential. In addition to describing current research, trends, and initiatives, each chapter also features projects by both students and firms highlighting how to solve the design problem of each project type using a variety of sustainability approaches.

This book is really intended to be a studio companion for those wanting inspiration and guidance for sustainable project design. Thousands of ideas by hundreds of designers are included to illustrate the wide range of thinking on these issues. As previously mentioned, this is not a book of answers; it is a book to challenge designers to think beyond the norm about how to solve the issues of sustainable design by continuing to innovate in their design solutions.

The discussion questions at the end of each chapter ask students and instructors alike to explore some of the biggest design issues of our time. Designers are trained in creative problem solving—and sustainable design and the sustainability of the planet is a huge design problem. Focusing designers with this special skill set on this issue will help to create the solutions needed in today's world—and for the future viability of our planet.

Acknowledgments

I would like to extend my sincere gratitude to the many people who made it possible for me to write this book. To my husband Jim, thank you for your patience. I also want to thank Olga Kontzias for always thinking I have good ideas and for being a friend and mentor for the last several years. Thank you to Joe Miranda for being easy to work with! A special thanks to Anna Rae Dutro, one of my PhD students who painstakingly worked with me on organizing the images for the book—making them all the right size and keeping them in the right chapters through many changes.

I would also like to extend thanks for the many students and professionals who allowed me to use their work to demonstrate the ideas presented herein. Thank you to Scott Bergstrom and Deborah Lucking with Fentress Architects, Tama Duffy Day at Perkins + Will, Hansoo Kim and Tabatha Thompson at Gensler, Lenore Duncan with Spectrum Design, Chris Good at KSA Interiors, Dean Kawamura at WATG, Keith Switzer of INTEC, Carin Whitney at Kieran Timberlake, Peter Masters, and Jason Moskowitz and Susan Walter at Wilmot Sanz. I give thanks for all of the students I am fortunate enough to teach and learn from every day. They all contributed on some level to this book over the last several years. I have included their names with their works throughout.

I am also grateful for the constructive criticism of proposal and manuscript reviewers: Erin Speck, George Washington University; Meghan Woodcock, Savannah College of Art and Design; Jennifer Blanchard Belk, Winthrop University; Grace F. Baker, Cazenovia College; Ronald E. Dulaney Jr., West Virginia University; Nisha A. Fernando, University of Wisconsin-Stevens Point; Maruja Torres-Antonini, University of Florida; Angela Stephens-Owens, Central Piedmont Community College; Adair Bowen, Baylor University; Matthew Ziff, Ohio University; Anu Thakur, California State University-Northridge; Kathleen Sullivan, Chatham University; Zenaida Espinosa, Palm Beach State College; and Kent Hikida, Parsons New School.

OVERVIEW OF SUSTAINABLE PROJECT APPROACHES

Objectives

- Students will be able to describe a variety of approaches to sustainable design.

- Students will have a better understanding of how various designers contend with sustainability in their own work.

- Students will be able to recognize key components and strategies of sustainable design in the context of interiors.

Overview

Once thought to be only a trend, sustainable design has become the way top designers approach their work. These approaches vary from firm to firm and designer to designer. This chapter provides an overview of the various project approaches that are included as case studies in this text. Although an integrated approach to project delivery and sustainable design are embraced by many firms, the manner in which this has been accomplished varies widely. Through the use of case studies, this chapter presents some of the many approaches toward sustainable design used by a variety of well-known firms as well as by interior design students. One key factor contributing to the success of a sustainable project is the use of an **integrated project delivery**. An integrated approach to project delivery involves all team members from the beginning of a project and helps members to make sure they have agreed-upon goals for the sustainability outcomes of the project, as will be seen through many examples. From the application of sustainable surface materials to the design for net-zero buildings, the way in which commercial and residential interiors are designed is rapidly changing in response to sustainability initiatives and requirements.

In order to better understand the various approaches that designers take toward solving the problem of sustainable interiors, it is first necessary to define the terms used to describe this type of work. Sustainable design, more than any other type of design, can be seen as an umbrella concept with a plethora of terms that are used interchangeably by some, but the definitions can differ between designers. For example, internationally known architect William McDonough describes the process of following nature as a model in terms of a "cradle to cradle" approach where waste equals food. All things in nature and man-made materials can, theoretically, be infinitely recycled in this view and used for a new purpose. Meanwhile, British architect Michael Pawlyn speaks of biomimicry in architecture as a way in which waste becomes an opportunity. Both ideas are quite similar, although the name for each approach is different.

While terminology differs, so do fundamental beliefs underlying an approach to sustainability. In 2001, Simon Guy and Graham Farmer wrote an extremely useful article titled "Reinterpreting Sustainable Architecture: The Place of Technology" that outlined six approaches to the sustainable built environment. What is important to note is that there is both overlap and contradiction in the various approaches. Guy and Farmer referred to the paradigms as "competing" logics. While many new developments have since taken place in building technology, the basic strategies outlined by Guy and Farmer have not changed substantially. What these six paradigms point out is the many ways designers have approached sustainable design as seen in Table 1.1.

Designers have struggled to find the best way to design sustainable buildings for humankind. While many seek scientific answers, others look to simplify and return to basics.

Logic	Image of space	Source of environmental knowledge	Building image	Technologies	Idealized concept of place
Eco-technic	Global	Scientific	Modern/future oriented	Integrated energy/high tech/intelligent	Urban vision/compact and dense city
Eco-centric	Fragile	Systemic ecology	Polluter	Renewable/recyclable	Harmony with nature
Eco-aesthetic	Alienating	Sensual/postmodern	Iconic architecture	Pragmatic/non-linear	New in light of new knowledge
Eco-cultural	Regional	Phenomenological	Authentic/harmonious	Local low tech	Adapted buildings to local bioregion
Eco-medical	Polluted	Medical ecology	Healthy living	Passive non-toxic	Environment that ensures health
Eco-social	Social context	Social ecology	Democratic	Flexible and participatory	Organic, non-hierarchical

Source: Guy and Farmer, adapted from Table 1, p. 141

Table 1.1 Paradigms for Sustainable Design

Net Zero, Zero Carbon, Carbon Neutral, Zero Energy

The first set of terms used interchangeably includes net-zero, zero-carbon building, carbon-neutral building, and zero-energy architecture. All of these efforts enlist the use of science to improve building technology and energy performance (**eco-technic**). The specific differences between each of these terms can cause confusion and often debate among designers. Canadian Roger Brayley created the "Challenge Series" concept for the Southeast False Creek Olympic Village in Vancouver. Published over a series of eight months, the chapters posted on the Challenge Series website focus on creating a net zero complex for the Olympics.

Net Zero

Bayley (2012) defines **net zero** as a building that generates as much energy as it consumes. For example, on-site solar panels might generate the amount of electricity needed to power the building. Glumac,

a full-service engineering firm focused on sustainability, provides a summary of the state of net-zero building design in "Engineering for a Sustainable Future." Engineers at Glumac propose that the awareness about net-zero buildings has increased in response to the Architecture 2030 Challenge, the U.S. Green Building Council (USGBC)'s Living Building Challenge, and by the extraordinary level of sustainability and energy reduction that a net-zero building can achieve. Further, net zero can be defined in many ways based on site, source, cost, or carbon. Carbon dioxide emissions have been identified as a key contributor to global warming. A site approach uses a method by which one can determine an energy budget for a net-zero building that includes multiplying the square footage of the entire site by an energy use factor (5,000–10,000 kwh/sf) and then using this to determine photovoltaic (PV) array placement. A PV array consists of multiple solar cells combined on panels and installed in large numbers. The array can be adjusted to follow the angle of the sun throughout the day and year to maximize solar energy collection. While the average energy use of a commercial building following the latest energy standards is 70,000 btu/sf/year (existing buildings consume more on the order of 90,000 btu/sf/year) according to Glumac, the average for a net-zero corporate building is less 20,000 btu/sf/year.

Established in the 1970s, the National Renewable Energy Lab (NREL) is the only federal laboratory focused on renewable energy development and implementation. According to NREL, Net Zero is a building classification system based on the use of a renewable energy supply. The organization's specific definition is as follows:

> A net-zero energy building (NZEB) is a residential or commercial building with greatly reduced energy needs. In such a building, efficiency gains have been made such that the balance of energy needs can be supplied with renewable energy technologies. (Pleass and Torcellini 2010, iii).

Within this building type there are four variations (NZEB: A, B, C, and D), which refer to the location of the renewable energy source—whether on-site or off. Thus, the net-zero building is one that creates as much energy as it consumes, and this energy source might be on- or off-site. More information can be found in Tables 1.2 and 1.3.

Zero-Carbon Building

While very similar to a net-zero building, a zero-carbon building focuses on achieving net-zero energy use on a yearly basis by averaging energy used with energy produced. The Zero Carbon Hub in the United Kingdom, focused primarily on home design and construction, defines the **zero-carbon** home in a 111-page document, "The Definition of Zero Carbon Homes and Non-Domestic Buildings"

Table 1.2 NZEB Renewable Energy (RE) Supply Option Hierarchy

0	Reduce site energy through energy efficiency and demand-side renewable building technologies.
1	Use RE sources available within the building footprint and connected to its electricity and hot/chilled water distribution system.
2	Use RE sources available at the building site and connected to its electricity and hot/chilled water distribution system.
3	Use RE sources available off-site to generate energy on-site and connected to its electricity and hot/chilled water distribution system.
4	Purchase recently added off-site RE sources, as certified from Green-E (2009) or other equivalent REC programs. Continue to purchase the generation from this new source to maintain NZEB status.

Source: NREL, "Sustainable NREL," *NREL.gov,* p. 10, http://www.nrel.gov/sustainable_nrel/pdfs/44586.pdf

Table 1.3 NZEB Classifications

A	Generate and use energy through a combination of energy efficiency and RE collected within the building footprint.
B	Generate and use energy through a combination of energy efficiency and RE generated within the site.
C	Use the RE strategies as described for NZEB A and/or NZEB B to maximum extent feasible.
D	Use the RE strategies as described for NZEB A, NZEB B, and/or NZEB C buildings. On-site renewable strategies are used to the maximum extent feasible.

Source: NREL, "Sustainable NREL," *NREL.gov,* p. 15, http://www.nrel.gov/sustainable_nrel/pdfs/44586.pdf

(2008). The concise definition is as follows:

> *Building a Greener Future* (July 2007) set out that all new homes are to be built from 2016 in such a way that, after taking account of:
> - emissions from space heating, ventilation, hot water, and fixed lighting,
> - expected energy use from appliances,
> - exports and imports of energy from the development (and directly connected energy installations) to and from centralised [sic] energy networks,
>
> the building will have net-zero carbon emissions over the course of a year.

This approach considers net emissions (including those from appliances) over the course of a year. Thus, according to the Department for Communities and Local Government's 2008 publication, zero-carbon homes should:

- be built with high levels of energy efficiency.
- achieve at least a minimum level of carbon reductions through a combination of energy efficiency, on-site energy. supply, and/or (where relevant) directly connected low carbon or renewable heat.
- choose from a range of (mainly off-site) solutions for tackling the remaining emissions (10).

Therefore, zero carbon in this context specifically refers to eliminating carbon released into the atmosphere from the burning of fossil fuels as calculated on a yearly basis.

Carbon Neutral

Carbon neutral describes a process by which organizations and people can purchase **carbon offset** credits, thus reducing their carbon footprint. Carbon offsets can be purchased to offset carbon emissions in fulfillment of a company's or an individual's carbon reduction goals. Carbon offsets can be purchased from TerraPass and a variety of other sources. It is important to research the seller and make sure their carbon-reducing projects meet all industry standards. The National Resources Defense Council provides an excellent source of information. An example of this in use is included in one of the above-mentioned classifications of net-zero building that includes such a provision as a way to achieve net zero (see Tables 1.1 and 1.2). The basic purpose behind carbon neutrality is to measure, reduce, and offset carbon emissions. In their online publication, the authors of *The Carbon Neutral Building: How to Achieve Carbon Neutrality* (2012) define the carbon-neutral building as one that balances any carbon dioxide released into the atmosphere in one place by lowering emissions somewhere else.

Zero-Energy Buildings

A **zero-energy building** is, according to the U.S. Department of Energy (DOE), one that produces as much energy as it uses over the course of a year. The DOE says in 2013 there are only 10 buildings that do this in the United States: the Aldo Leopold Legacy Center in Baraboo, Wisconsin; the Audubon Center at Debs Park in Los Angeles, California; the Challengers Tennis Club, also in Los Angeles; the Environmental Center at Sonoma State University in Rohnert Park, California; the Hawaii Gateway Energy Center, Kailua-Kona, Hawaii; the IDeAs Z2 Design Facility in San Jose, California; the Net Zero House in Charlotte, Vermont; Oberlin College's Lewis Center, Oberlin, Ohio; the Science House at the Science Museum in St. Paul, Minnesota; and the TD Bank-Cypress Creek Store in Ft. Lauderdale, Florida. (DOE) What distinguishes this approach from the previous ones mentioned is the emphasis on all energy being produced on site and for the building to be completely self-contained. This is the most restrictive label in terms of overall energy use of all the approaches described. While similar to net zero, this approach does not permit the purchase of carbon offsets or allow for energy production off-site.

Architecture 2030

One of the driving factors behind many of these energy initiatives is the visionary organization Architecture 2030. Founded in 2002 by Santa Fe Architect Edward Mazria, **Architecture 2030** is a nonprofit organization focused on responding to climate change. The mission of Architecture 2030 is to "rapidly transform the US and global building sector from a major contributor of [greenhouse] gas emissions to a central part of the solution." The Architecture 2030 Challenge consists of the following milestones, as mentioned on the organization's website:

> Buildings are the major source of global demand for energy and materials that produce by-product greenhouse gases (GHG). Slowing the growth rate of GHG emissions and then reversing it is the key to addressing climate change and keeping global average temperature below 2°C above pre-industrial levels (2010).
>
> To accomplish this, Architecture 2030 issued The 2030 Challenge asking the global architecture and building community to adopt the following targets:
> - All new buildings, developments, and major renovations shall be designed to meet a fossil fuel, GHG-emitting, energy consumption performance standard of 60% below the regional (or country) average for that building type.
> - At a minimum, an equal amount of existing building area shall be renovated annually to meet a fossil fuel, GHG-emitting, energy consumption performance standard of 60% of the regional (or country) average for that building type.
> - The fossil fuel reduction standard for all new buildings and major renovations shall be increased to:
>   - 70% in 2015
>   - 80% in 2020
>   - 90% in 2025
>   - Carbon-neutral in 2030 (using no fossil fuel, GHG-emitting energy to operate)
>
> These targets may be accomplished by implementing innovative sustainable design strategies, generating on-site renewable power and/or purchasing (20% maximum) renewable energy.

While not completely quantifiable, the increasing focus on sustainability is evident in the literature of professional organizations such as the American Institute of Architects (AIA), the American Society of Interior Designs (ASID), and the International Interior Design Association (IIDA). Adopters of the Architecture 2030 challenge include roughly 80,000 members of the American Institute of Architects, the Association of Collegiate Schools of Architecture, the American Society of Interior Designers, the U.S. Conference of Mayors, and many others. Design firms that have registered their commitment to meeting the 2030 challenge include the Smith Group, Perkins + Will, HOK, Cannon Design, NBBJ, Mancini Duffy, Little, and many others.

The U.S. Green Building Council and LEED

One of the earliest organizations to focus on the need for change in the building industry is the U.S. Green Building Council (USGBC), developer of the LEED (Leadership in Energy and Environmental Design) Green Building Rating Systems. The rating systems focus on energy efficiency (eco-technic), indoor environmental quality (**eco-medical**), and have more recently added regional design credits (**eco-cultural**) to the rating systems. Located in Washington, DC, the USGBC is a member organization with the goal of having all people working and living in a green building within this generation. As of 2013, 35,000 projects are participating in the LEED System constituting more than 4.5 billion square feet. According to the USGBC, there are 170,000 LEED professional credential holders, and LEED has recently introduced a tiered credentialing system. A LEED Accredited Professional (LEED AP) is a credential holder who has passed the LEED exam. Current LEED Accredited Professionals (APs) can choose to be accredited in one of the categories such as Building Design and Construction or Interior Design and Construction. Long-standing leaders in the field can be nominated to Fellow status, indicating their prominence as an industry leader, and those just beginning their careers with sustainable building can take an entry-level test and become LEED GA, or LEED Green Building Associate. This designation indicates that the person has a general knowledge of sustainability and the LEED processes and rating systems.

Research Within the Design Firm

Many of the best-known and largest interior design and architecture firms are engaged in research for sustainability. The reasons why people agree to donate their time are as diverse as the firms and designers themselves but are underscored by a desire to give back to the community. The various projects represent three elements of the sustainability equation: social equity, environmental concerns, and economic issues.

Social Equity Project

John Peterson founded Public Architecture in 2002 with the goal of demonstrating a new model for architectural practice whereby architects work for the public good through grants and donations. This allows for design services for those who might not otherwise be able to benefit from such a service. Launched in 2005, "The 1% Pledge" asks all architects to donate 1 percent of their time to the public good. Firms that have committed to the 1 percent challenge include SHoP Architects (NY), Studio Gang Architects (Chicago), Gensler, HOK, and Perkins + Will. This is an example of an eco-social effort toward sustainability.

Public Architecture publications include *The Power of Pro Bono*, which profiles 40 pro bono projects; *Design for Reuse Primer*, which addresses barriers to material reuse; and *Lights on Main Street*, an effort to revitalize areas in San Francisco.

One example of a public architecture project is Scrap House in San Francisco. Constructed from street signs and shower doors, the Scrap House was built in conjunction with World Environment Day 2005 to demonstrate recycling and how to reuse the more than 100 million tons of waste produced by the construction industry each year. The Scrap House temporary demonstration facility was located on Civic Center Plaza in front of the San Francisco City Hall. The entire house was built in six weeks by volunteers and was on display from June 1 through 5, 2005. Award-winning documentarian Anna Fitch filmed the process, and the documentary was aired on National Geographic Channel in September 2006.

Environmental Projects

Several firms have initiated large-scale environmental projects in partial fulfillment of their commitment to a more sustainable world.

SOM

Skidmore, Owings, and Merrill, LLP (SOM) is an internationally renowned

Figure 1.1 Scrap House: Made from found materials as a part of Public Architecture built in conjunction with World Environment Day, 2005
Source: Public Architecture

Figure 1.2 Scrap House, with San Francisco City Hall in the background
Source: Public Architecture

architecture firm and an excellent example of an organization engaging in a large environmental issue. They devoted research money toward a comprehensive study of the Great Lakes region beginning in 2009. The firm selected the Great Lakes not only because it was near to their Chicago headquarters office but also because 21 percent of the world's fresh water supply is located in the Great Lakes, with more than 40 million people dependent upon the water source. The study's recommendations propose solutions to energy and air quality issues, water pollution, and improving or creating the necessary surrounding infrastructure. Proposals include high-speed rail between the major hubs surrounding the Great Lakes, the introduction of wind power and other renewable energy sources to replace fossil fuel–based plants and nuclear facilities, and strategies for the removal of invasive species such as Asian Carp and superweed *Hydrilla verticillata* that are upsetting the current ecosystem of the Great Lakes. (SOM, 2010) This project is an excellent example of an eco-technic approach to solving a sustainability problem.

Gensler

Gensler is a large international design firm with 35,000 professionals practicing in 43 locations across the world. Gensler's Global Seawater Initiative includes strategies for the use of seawater to generate renewable energy in the Middle East. By reversing the flow of water and eroded soil, seawater can provide the necessary nutrients to enhance depleted desert soil. Ultimately, the use of seawater will replace the need to use food as fuel (for example, biofuels) and help to address global warming by reducing carbon emissions. Nutrients from seawater include algae bivalves, finfish, mangroves, wetlands, and salt. The resultant salicornia can be used to fuel diesel and jet engines. **Salicornia** is a salt-tolerant wetlands perennial plant found in the coastal areas of South Africa, North America, and South Asia. The water flow reversal allows for this to be created and sustained, thus improving the soil.

The United Arab Emirates and the New Nile Company have constructed a representative seawater energy generation (eco-technic) project. (Gensler 2010)

Sustainable Materials and Resources

Several firms have realized that solving the many environmental problems we face today and the role of buildings and design in these issues will require the free sharing of information between firms and designers. In response, several leading architecture and design firms have published new materials, either as free downloadable files or for purchase through booksellers.

HOK

HOK is an international design firm with 16,000 professionals in 24 offices located on three continents. HOK has provided leadership in sustainable methods and has made its knowledge available to other practitioners through a series of publications, including *Zero Carbon: Onward to Zero*. The downloadable PDF is available at http://www.hok.com/. Other resources are *The Green Workplace* and *The HOK Guidebook to Sustainable Design*.

In addition to its print materials, HOK has aligned itself with the AIA 2030 commitment, with Biomimicry 3.8, and is working on net zero projects. Additional online and publically available documents include step-by-step instructions for sustainable processes and 10 steps toward a sustainable design.

HOK is one of the first firms to partner with the Biomimcry Guild, founded in 1998 by biologists Janine Benyus and Dayna Baumeister. The Biomimicry Guild allows for practitioners (designers) and scientists to jointly solve environmental issues using nature as model. It offers educational workshops and recently published *Biomimicry 3.8* and guidebook. The guidebook includes eco-technic, eco-centric, eco-cultural, and eco-aesthetic approaches toward sustainable building design.

Perkins + Will Material List

Perkins + Will has recently added a "transparency" section to its website (http://transparency.perkinswill.com/Main) where the firm shares information to encourage the material health of the built environment. This area of the site includes information about precautionary materials (those thought to be toxic), asthma triggers and asthmagens, flame retardants, and news, media, and additional research. The precautionary list is further segmented by searchable units such as alphabetical, category, health effect, and Construction Specification Institute (CSI) Division. The transparency list falls into the eco-medical category.

INTRODUCING THE NEW

TRANSPARENCY.PERKINSWILL.COM

⊕ ⊕ ⊕ ⊕ Encouraging material health in the built environment.

Building Technology Research

Many firms are exploring the use of integrated technology, building information modeling, and the relationship between design and fabrication in an effort to reduce errors in coordination and waste.

Kieran Timberlake

Kieran Timberlake, an internationally renowned and award winning firm, focuses their research on the relationship between manufacturing methods and the building industry. The firm funnels 3 percent of its annual income toward ongoing research. In 2003, the firm published its approach to design in *Refabricating Architecture*. Using the methods of mass production and assembly of kit parts, Keiran Timberlake seeks to

revolutionize the way in which designers work and buildings are constructed. Through the use of Building Information Modeling, waste during production of the parts of a building is nearly eliminated as it is incorporated into the building materials, thus producing a highly sustainable end product (or building, in this case). This represents an eco-technic approach, while the aesthetic of the final project could arguably be considered eco-aesthetic as well. The process, as used in the Loblolly House, is the subject of another of the firm's publications. The Loblolly House, located in Taylors Island, Maryland, was constructed in 2006 and has since received multiple awards and accolades for the firm.

Materials Research

Blaine Brownell, assistant professor in the School of Architecture at the University

Figure 1.4 Kieran Timberlake's Loblolly House, inspired by the surrounding pine trees and made using a kit of parts processed using Building Information Modeling to reduce waste during construction
Photo credit: Peter Aaron

of Minnesota and writer for *Architect Magazine*, has created a series of edited books on revolutionary new materials, *Transmaterial: A Catalog of Materials that Redefine our Physical Environment* (numbers 1–3). In addition to the three-book series, there is an online site containing the most current information about new transmaterials, http://transmaterial.net/. A **transmaterial** is one that redefines the physical environment (thus eco-technic/eco-aesthetic). It can be either a new material or one used in a new way and application. The site includes information about biomaterials, ceramics, metals, and polymers as well as categories for digital, lighting, and features.

Economy: Financial Implications of Sustainability

According to American businessman, environmentalist, and researcher Greg Kats, a green building costs on average about 2 percent more than one of conventional construction. Additionally, after a study of 150 green buildings, Kats reported that the average reduction in energy use was 33 percent. The criterion used for the selection of the 150 buildings was that each was already certified or anticipated LEED Certification or the equivalent. (Kats 2009) The National Resources Defense Council (NRDC) produced a report, "Costing Green: A Comprehensive Cost Database and Budgeting Methodology" (2004), which studied 61 LEED green buildings and also concluded that the average additional first costs totaled 2 percent for buildings meeting the LEED Green Building Rating System.

Matthiessen and Morris of Davis Langdon, an AECOM Company, focused on sustainable construction, were among the first to recommend life-cycle costing as a part of the cost equation rather than simply first cost approaches. **Life-cycle costing** takes into account the life

of a building including all energy and maintenance costs incurred over time.

Life-Cycle Costing

The *Whole Building Design Guide* provides the following formula for calculating life cycle costs:

Calculation Formula:

LCC = I + Repl − Res + E + W + OM&R + O

LCC = Total LCC in present-value (PV) dollars of a given alternative

I = PV investment costs (if incurred at base date, they need not be discounted)

Repl = PV capital replacement costs

Res = PV residual value (resale value, salvage value) less disposal costs

E = PV of energy costs

W = PV of water costs

OM&R = PV of non-fuel operating, maintenance and repair costs

O = PV of other costs (e.g., contract costs for ESPCs or UESCs)

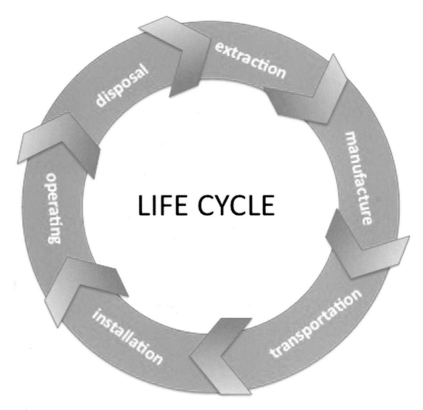

Figure 1.5 Diagram of life cycle

Design for Obsolescence

In a consumer-driven economy such as the one in the United States, planned obsolescence for products is a marketing strategy. Trendy, new, fashion-driven interiors and furniture are in this category and are the antithesis of sustainability. Examples can be found throughout the marketplace.

Sustainable Furniture, Fixtures, and Equipment

Sustainable furniture, fixtures, and equipment are subjected to a variety of rating systems in relation to the environment. The most common ones are SMaRT, SCS, Cradle to Cradle, FSC, GreenGuard, Good Environmental Choice Label, and EnergyStar. There are also several others in use. Each rating system provides a slightly different approach to certifying or rating a product. The need to provide sustainable choices for LEED Buildings has encouraged manufacturers to rate and certify their products. Many of the rating systems for materials fall into the eco-medical category because they test Volatile Organic Compound off-gassing and other indoor air quality issues.

SMaRT

SMaRT is a consensus sustainable product standard developed by the Institute for Market Transformation to Sustainability (MTS). The MTS is ANSI (American National Standards Institute) accredited and includes four rating levels: sustainable, sustainable silver, sustainable gold, and sustainable platinum. A nonprofit group developed the rating system.

SCS, Scientific Certification Systems

SCS, Scientific Certification Systems, provides multilevel attribute certifications for green furniture and is a Business and Institutional Furniture Manufacturer's Association (BIFMA) sustainability standard. This system assesses the entire life cycle of the product and provides a numeric rating between one and three, with three as the highest or most sustainable.

Figure 1.6
Computers: An example of designing for obsolescence

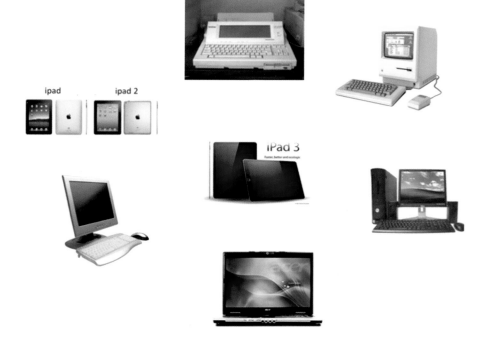

C2C

Although not a new concept, the principle of cradle-to-cradle, as applied to materials and design, was presented in the 2004 book by William and McDonough and Michael Braungart titled *Cradle to Cradle: Remaking the Way We Make Things*. One outcome of the book was the formation of MBDC, a company that seeks to promote cradle-to-cradle in the marketplace, including working with manufacturers to certify their products. The Cradle to Cradle Products Innovation Institute is a spin-off company from MBDC and administers the Cradle to Cradle Certified Program, a third-party certification founded by architect William McDonough and chemist Michael Braungart in 2005. Certified products are classified according to three categories: building materials, interior design, and personal and home care products. Furniture is categorized in the interior design classification.

GreenGuard

GreenGuard certification focuses on reducing human exposure to indoor air pollutants. Certification types include GreenGuard Gold (for sensitive individuals such as children and the elderly) and GreenGuard Certification. Products must meet stringent chemical emissions requirements to be certified. Underwriters Laboratory (UL) acquired GreenGuard in 2011.

FSC

Formed following the 1992 Earth Summit in Rio de Janeiro to stop deforestation, the Forest Stewardship Council (FSC) seeks to control deforestation through 10 principles and 57 criteria for sustainable forest management around the world. FSC-certified wood provides a credible system for tracking the life cycle of the wood from harvest to delivery; it is a recognized system used in more than 80 countries. Unlike many of the other rating systems, the FSC has an eco-centric/eco-social approach. The

FSC focuses its efforts on sustainable forestry at the local level as well as on a cooperative process for documentation.

EnergyStar

EnergyStar is a U.S. Environmental Protection Agency voluntary government-backed program intended to improve the indoor environment through economical and energy-efficient products and practices. The program was established in 1992 under the authority of the Clean Air Act, Section 103 (g). The emphasis is on increased energy efficiency and includes products meeting EnergyStar requirements in all of the following categories: appliances, building products, computers, electronics, battery chargers, heating and cooling units, and water heaters.

Good Environmental Choice Label (Australia)

One example of a non-U.S.-based rating system is GECA. The Good Environmental Choice of Australia (GECA) is a nonprofit program that seeks to assist customers through an eco-labeling program. The labeling program identifies products that meet International Organization for Standardization (ISO) standard 14024:1999. **ISO 14024:1999** addresses standards for environmental labeling and declarations. These standards are reviewed every five years, most recently in 2009.

Recycled Furniture

One area of industry growth within the sustainable furnishings area has been around the idea or recycling office furniture as a way of meeting sustainability goals. One of the first companies to attempt this approach is Creative Business Interiors. This company works to provide sustainable solutions for office furniture, including previously used and refurbished furniture, factory overruns, and as-is furniture instead of furniture with recycled content as the only sustainable solution to outfitting a new office. http://creativebusiness.com/

Figure 1.7 Smithfield by Peter Masters: Demonstrating a recycled interior made from cardboard tubes
Photo credit: Peter Masters

New Ways of Considering Recycling

Other artists and designers are exploring the use of recycled materials or of recycling materials into a new application. An example of this is the 100-percent-recycled cardboard interior featured in an article by Lea Stewart (2009), a Chicago-based industrial designer and writer for Inhabit.com. This retail interior was completed for British menswear company Smithfield, which teamed with furniture designer Peter Masters. Masters is an award-winning furniture designer form the United Kingdom. He strives to use unusual objects and stays away from complex manufacturing techniques in his designs. Examples can be seen here http://mrmasters.co.uk/retailInteriors.php#smithfield.

Additional examples of installations that use frequently discarded everyday materials include a table made from egg cartons, "Auto-Cannibalistic Table," by Atema Architecture and Tara Donovan's cup ceiling art installation from Styrofoam cups. Although pristine new materials are used in both cases, the theoretical exploration of the materials shows the inherent beauty of recombining

Figure 1.8 Smithfield
Photo credit: Peter Masters

everyday objects in a refreshing new way that would not otherwise have happened. This project suggests the use of everyday used objects in new ways to recycle and divert them from the landfill.

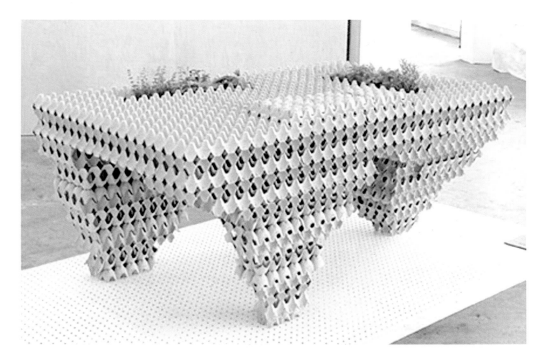

Building for Disassembly/ Design for Disassembly

Designing for disassembly (DfD) is a new way of thinking about building design and construction. The premise behind DfD is that the most sustainable building is one that is flexible and convertible, as well as easily added to and subtracted from to meet ever-changing needs. It is a forward-looking approach that takes a long-term view of the impact of new construction.

The foundations of this approach can be summarized in 10 basic principles, according to the King County, Wash., guidelines. These guidelines were based upon the Scottish Ecological Design Association guidelines, "Design and Detailing for Deconstruction" (2005), and were reviewed by well-known sustainable design advocates such as Lance Hosey of McDonough and Partners and Elizabeth Kahley at the University of Virginia. The 10 principles are as follows:

1. Document materials and methods for deconstruction.
2. Select materials using the precautionary principle (no known toxins).
3. Design connections that are accessible.
4. Minimize or eliminate chemical connections.
5. Use bolted, screwed, and nailed connections.
6. Separate mechanical, electrical, and plumbing systems (MEP).
7. Design to the worker and labor of separation.
8. Simplicity of structure and form
9. Interchangeability
10. Safe deconstruction

An excellent example of design for disassembly is Kieren Timberlake's Cellophane House, commissioned by the Museum of Modern Art in New York City for its exhibition "Home Delivery: Fabricating the Modern Dwelling" (2008). The project was a collaborative effort of multiple trades including the architects, fabricators, and suppliers. The five-story house consisted of 1,800 square feet containing two bedrooms and two baths. It was on display from July 20, 2008, to October 20, 2008.

Figure 1.11 Kieran Timberlake, Cellophane House: An example of design for disassembly (DFD)
Photo credit: Peter Aaron

Student Approaches to Sustainable Design

The student projects included in this book illustrate a variety of approaches to sustainable design. By far, the most common approaches are specifying materials from manufacturers making environmental claims about the products and using the appropriate LEED Green Building Rating System, most commonly LEED CI (Corporate Interiors). A deeper understanding of sustainable design can also be expressed in a variety of ways.

Materials Approach: Eco-Medical

Many designers' first experience with sustainable or green design focuses on the surface finishes and furniture and involves selecting "green" flooring, textiles, furniture, and surfaces. Not knowing what else to do, this is a common method of attempting to meet some sustainability goals.

The most common way to select "green" finishes is to read the manufacturer's literature and check for any green endorsement by third-party rating agencies. It is far less common to consult a pathogens list such as the one prepared by MBDC for Cradle to Cradle product certification and Perkins + Will for its own company use, although this list is available to the public.

The designer might do this to confirm the manufacturer's information and ensure no known pathogens have been used in the production of the selected finish. Knowing all of the components included in a finish includes knowing all material content, including any recycled content. For students, the most accessible method of designing for sustainability is often a materials approach.

Rating Systems: Eco-Technic with Some Eco-Medical and Eco-Cultural

The most widely used green building rating system in the U.S. is LEED. The LEED Green Building Rating Systems are easily accessible as Excel spreadsheets on the USGBC website (http://www.usgbc .org/DisplayPage.aspx?CMSPageID=222).

The rating system's check sheets emphasize sustainable material specification as a way toward sustainability. The Materials and Resources section of the rating system assigns credit for the use of regional materials, materials with recycled content, and rapidly renewable resources such as cork, bamboo, and sisal. Some of the other categories allocate points for more sophisticated building modeling, such as the energy and atmosphere, water efficiency, and indoor environmental quality. In response to the complexity of this process, USGBC sells a technical manual specifically geared toward advanced energy

modeling. Slightly more involved than a materials-only approach, use of the LEED checklists provide a more comprehensive list of possible sustainable components in a building.

Conceptual Approach: Eco-Aesthetic, Eco-Cultural, and Eco-Technic

Students apply a variety of conceptual approaches to their design projects. Using the 2005 Cradle to Cradle house design competition—sponsored by William McDonough and the City of Roanoke and devised by Roanoke architect Gregg Lewis—as the basis for a residential studio project provided an opportunity for designers to develop a deeper understanding of cradle-to-cradle.

Using the Cradle to Cradle competition as a context for a residential design, this student's conceptual approach was to make the house part of the site— an extension of the landscape that interacted with the site. The form of the house responds to the site topography and allows for an interaction between inside and outside that is intentionally ambiguous. Integrating nature into the house and orienting the design around a tree reduced the building impact on the site.

Figure 1.12 Stafford Benson: Design for a house using a cradle-to-cradle approach

Biomimicry: Eco-Cultural and Eco-Technic

Students as well as professional designers commonly use nature as a source of inspiration, as have artists, scientists, and other thinkers and creators throughout human history. Biomimetic design (design that imitates nature) is less common. For example, some aspect of nature might be the impetus for the initial design statement, as seen in the previously discussed project. Designing the actual interior based on a natural system takes this approach to a much deeper level and provides a form generator as seen in the hidden house, which derives from the site itself using a partially submerged approach where the green roof appears to be a continuation of the slope of the site.

Ecological Design: Eco-Technic and Eco-Cultural

Designing in response to natural systems such as sunlight availability, to fit a specific site, through the use of regional materials, and other ecological approaches are illustrated by the Geo Living house, where the form of the structure is derived from passive solar and heating strategies in order to create a house that generates as much energy as it uses.

Guest Experience: Eco-Social, Eco-Centric, Eco-Cultural

For the past three years, the NEWH (Network of Executive Women in Hospitality) has sponsored a competition for students to create a sustainable guest experience. The guest experience for

Figure 1.13 Loren Heslep: Design for a house using a biomimicry approach

Figure 1.14 Caroline Bergin: Design for a house using an ecological design approach

which students are designing is how a guest arriving on site might experience the designer's visions of the facility. The resulting projects used the guest experience as a way to narrate the interior experiences. Sustainability has thus expanded beyond a materials approach to also include things such as arrival to the destination and transportation around the site. Further, the projects sought to regulate the guest's use of hand-held electronics, water usage, recycling receptacles, and many other day-to-day experiences to enhance the sustainability of the project.

This approach of narrating sustainability from a user's point of view provides a depth of thinking often omitted when using only a LEED checklist or materials specification approach. By shifting to an experiential design, all aspects of the interior, finishes, furnishings, and equipment are more easily considered.

Site Analysis

The following background research case study demonstrates a student project analysis in preparation for a final project and report. The study included wind, rain, and sun studies as well as an analysis of possible sustainable building systems and photovoltaic (solar panel) arrays that might work well with the actual site.

•Whether guests are exploring the island, riding to the local market, or just getting some exercise, they have sustainable choices to maneuver around the island. Both electric vehicles and bikes are available to rent day or night.

•Unfolding the Strida 5.0 takes ten seconds and immediately reveals its radical triangular frame. Weighing just 10 kg (22 lbs), it is made of tubes of 7000 Series aluminum and wheels, with other components made of glass-reinforced polyamide. The reduction in material use and easy maintenance is pleasing to all audiences.

•The Toyota iQ2 has emerged as one of the pioneers of the electric vehicle era. You can easily use these compact cars to get around the island quickly and efficiently. The Chargepoint systems are located in numerous areas on the island to allow easy charging.

•The Chargepoint Systems are located near the main entrance to the resort. When checking out an electric vehicle, guests receive a digital card that can be swiped to charge the car and will let them know when charging is complete.

•Airbus 380 is a massive 525-passenger aircraft with a 79.8 m (262 ft) wingspan and is an important development in global air travel. The aircraft incorporates as much as 25% lightweight, high-strength composites to reduce overall weight, as well as using light-weighing engines which means that less than 3 liters of aviation fuel are consumed per passenger per 100 km (64 miles). This is lower than the best production cars in Europe for a single occupancy car.

Figure 1.15 Molly Berman: Design for a sustainable guest experience including transportation

la honnête

Sustainability

The goal of the spa's sustainable features is to bring awareness to guests and make it easy for them to contribute. Guests can completely relax while feeling calm and comfort in knowing that they are not harming the environment. These are some of the sustainable features utilized throughout the resort.

One material that is difficult to reuse is glass. This is especially true on Mauritius, where used glass has to be shipped elsewhere to be processed in order to be reusable. La Honnête Resort strives to make use of glass as a functional, structural and decorative element wherever possible to help eliminate this waste.

Glass, even used, is beautiful and sparkles, adding shine to the spa design.

Compact fluorescents are used throughout the resort, saving energy as a more sustainable option than incandescents

In most spaces, fans are used to provide air circulation, limiting the need for air conditioning

Recycling bins are located in each room and clearly labeled to make it easy for guests to recycle

Solar Panels are positioned on the roofs of many buildings, providing solar energy for the resort

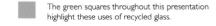

The green squares throughout this presentation highlight these uses of recycled glass.

Figure 1.16 Liz Kulesza: Design for a sustainable guest experience including recycling and energy reduction goals

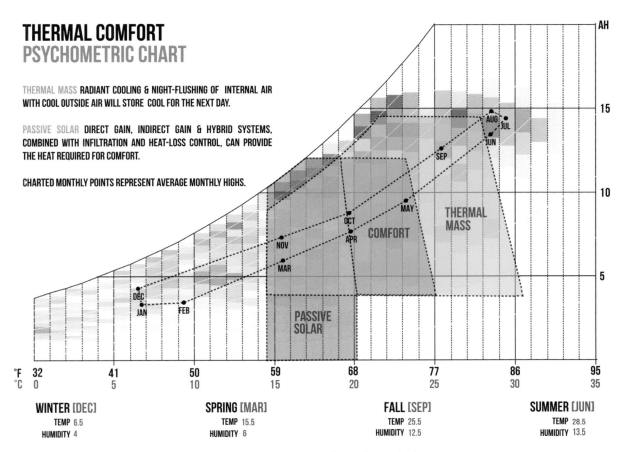

THERMAL COMFORT
PSYCHOMETRIC CHART

THERMAL MASS RADIANT COOLING & NIGHT-FLUSHING OF INTERNAL AIR WITH COOL OUTSIDE AIR WILL STORE COOL FOR THE NEXT DAY.

PASSIVE SOLAR DIRECT GAIN, INDIRECT GAIN & HYBRID SYSTEMS, COMBINED WITH INFILTRATION AND HEAT-LOSS CONTROL, CAN PROVIDE THE HEAT REQUIRED FOR COMFORT.

CHARTED MONTHLY POINTS REPRESENT AVERAGE MONTHLY HIGHS.

°F 32   41   50   59   68   77   86   95
°C 0   5   10   15   20   25   30   35

WINTER [DEC]
TEMP 6.5
HUMIDITY 4

SPRING [MAR]
TEMP 15.5
HUMIDITY 6

FALL [SEP]
TEMP 25.5
HUMIDITY 12.5

SUMMER [JUN]
TEMP 28.5
HUMIDITY 13.5

Figure 1.17 Rebecca Crockett and Lauren Shaw, Thermal Comfort (site analysis)

CLIMATE DATA HEATING & COOLING DEGREES

THE FOLLOWING DATA REFLECTS THAT CONSIDERABLY MORE KILOWATT HOURS ARE USED FOR HEATING THAN ARE USED FOR COOLING.

ALTITUDE 350.0 M
LATITUDE 37.3°
LONGITUDE -80.0°

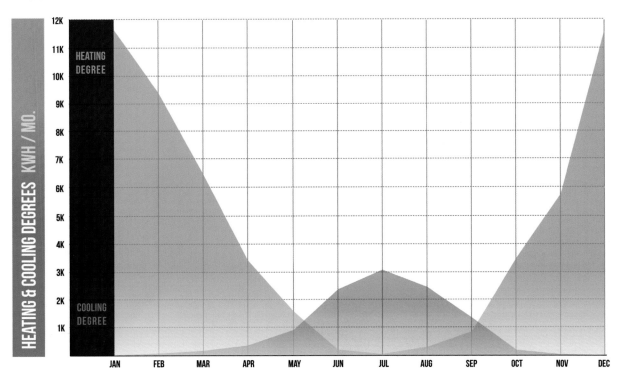

Figure 1.18 Rebecca Crockett and Lauren Shaw, Climate Data (site analysis)

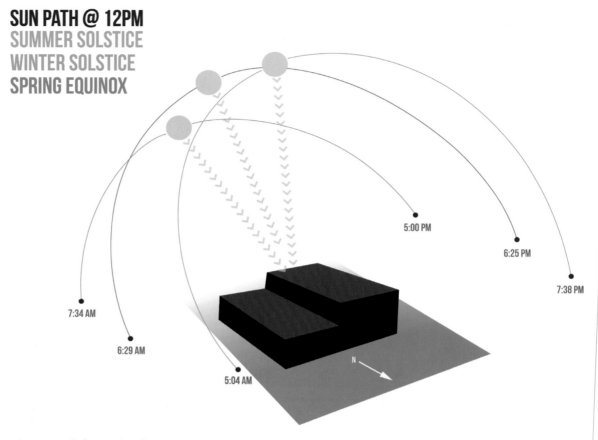

SUN PATH @ 12PM
SUMMER SOLSTICE
WINTER SOLSTICE
SPRING EQUINOX

5:00 PM

6:25 PM

7:38 PM

7:34 AM

6:29 AM

5:04 AM

N

Figure 1.19 Rebecca Crockett and Lauren Shaw, Sun Path (site analysis)

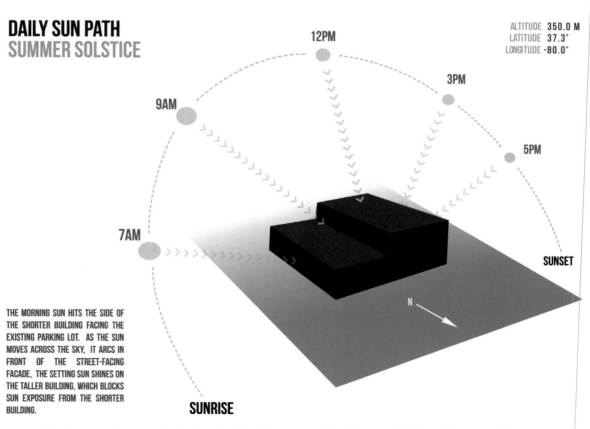

DAILY SUN PATH
SUMMER SOLSTICE

ALTITUDE **350.0 M**
LATITUDE **37.3°**
LONGITUDE **-80.0°**

12PM

3PM

9AM

5PM

7AM

SUNSET

N

THE MORNING SUN HITS THE SIDE OF
THE SHORTER BUILDING FACING THE
EXISTING PARKING LOT. AS THE SUN
MOVES ACROSS THE SKY, IT ARCS IN
FRONT OF THE STREET-FACING
FACADE, THE SETTING SUN SHINES ON
THE TALLER BUILDING, WHICH BLOCKS
SUN EXPOSURE FROM THE SHORTER
BUILDING.

SUNRISE

Figure 1.20 Rebecca Crockett and Lauren Shaw, Daily Sun Path at Summer Solstice (site analysis)

PREVAILING WINDS
ANNUALLY

NORTH

ALTITUDE 350.0 M
LATITUDE 37.3°
LONGITUDE -80.0°

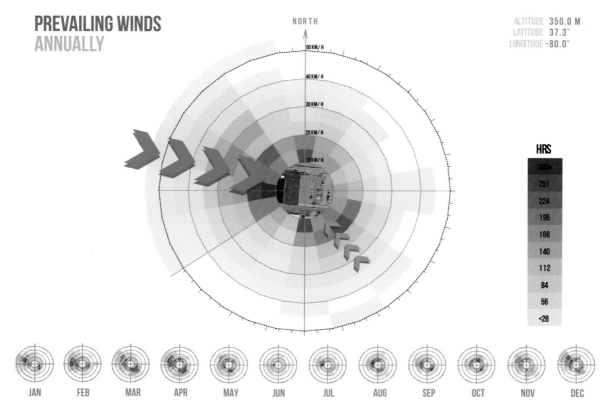

Figure 1.21 Rebecca Crockett and Lauren Shaw, Prevailing Winds: Annually (site analysis)

PREVAILING WINDS
SEASONALLY

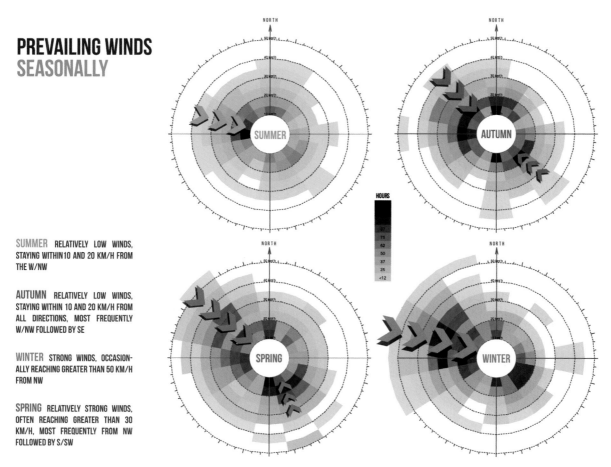

SUMMER RELATIVELY LOW WINDS, STAYING WITHIN 10 AND 20 KM/H FROM THE W/NW

AUTUMN RELATIVELY LOW WINDS, STAYING WITHIN 10 AND 20 KM/H FROM ALL DIRECTIONS, MOST FREQUENTLY W/NW FOLLOWED BY SE

WINTER STRONG WINDS, OCCASIONALLY REACHING GREATER THAN 50 KM/H FROM NW

SPRING RELATIVELY STRONG WINDS, OFTEN REACHING GREATER THAN 30 KM/H, MOST FREQUENTLY FROM NW FOLLOWED BY S/SW

Figure 1.22 Rebecca Crockett and Lauren Shaw, Prevailing Winds: Seasonally (site analysis)

ENERGY DATA WIND & SOLAR POTENTIAL

SOURCE: HTTP://EOSWEB.LARC.NASA.GOV/SSE/
HTTP://LWF.NCDC.NOAA.GOV/

ALTITUDE 350.0 M
LATITUDE 37.3°
LONGITUDE -80.0°

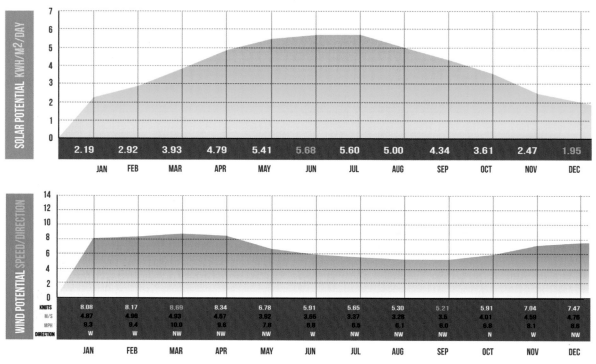

Figure 1.23 Rebecca Crockett and Lauren Shaw, Energy Data: Wind and Solar Potential (site analysis)

THERMAL COMFORT PERCENTAGES
THERMAL MASS EFFECTS & PASSIVE SOLAR HEATING

ALTITUDE 350.0 M
LATITUDE 37.3°
LONGITUDE -80.0°

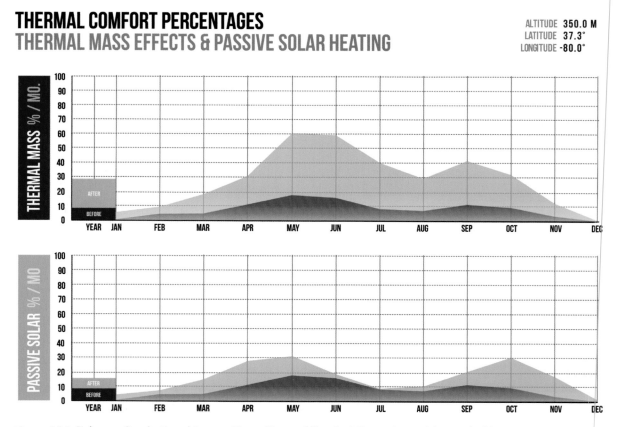

Figure 1.24 Rebecca Crockett and Lauren Shaw, Thermal Comfort Percentages (site analysis)

THERMAL COMFORT
MONTHLY DIURNAL AVERAGES

COMFORT: THERMAL NEUTRALITY RANGE OF COMFORT FOR GIVEN TEMPERATURE AND HUMIDITY. FOR MOST OF THE YEAR, THE RANGE OF COMFORT IS WARMER THAN THE AVERAGE TEMPERATURE.

TEMPERATURE RANGE THE TEMPERATURE FLUCTUATES MUCH MORE IN THE COLDER, WINTER MONTHS (NOVEMBER THROUGH APRIL) THAN DURING THE SUMMER MONTHS

DIRECT SOLAR THE FLUCTUATION OF THE AMOUNT DIRECT SOLAR EXPOSURE AT THIS SITE DID NOT CORRELATE WITH TEMPERATURE. HOWEVER, THE LENGTH OF DIRECT SOLAR EXPOSURE IS AFFECTED, HAVING MORE HOURS OF SOLAR EXPOSURE IN THE SUMMER AND LESS IN THE WINTER

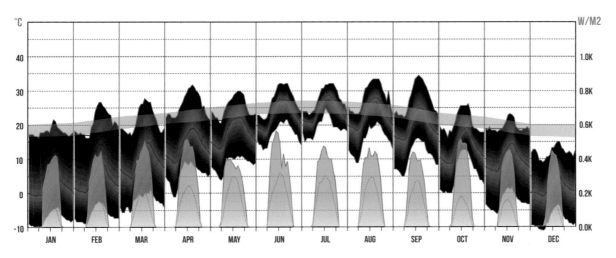

Figure 1.25 Rebecca Crockett and Lauren Shaw, Thermal Comfort Monthly Diurnal Averages (site analysis)

CLIMATE DATA TEMPERATURE & HUMIDITY

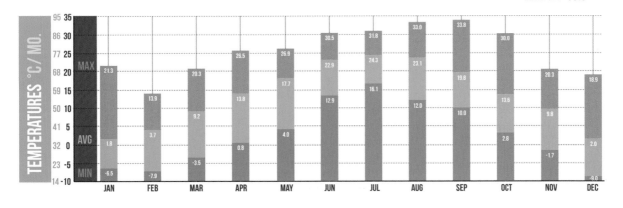

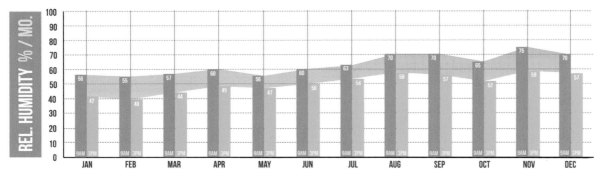

Figure 1.26 Rebecca Crockett and Lauren Shaw, Climate Data: Temperature and Humidity (site analysis)

AVERAGE MONTHLY RAINFALL
MM/MONTH

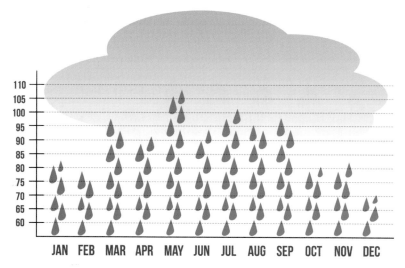

EACH INCH OF RAINFALL GENERATES ABOUT 1,240 INCHES OF RAIN PER 2,000 SQ FT. THE ROOF'S FOOTPRINT IS APPROXIMATELY 8,280 SQ FT, AND THUS HAS THE POTENTIAL TO CAPTURE UP TO 5,133 GALLONS OF WATER PER INCH. (FACTORING IN 85% EFFICIENCY OF WATER CATCHMENT).

THEREFORE, IN THE MONTH WITH THE LOWEST RAINFALL (DECEMBER), ONE COULD EXPECT TO COLLECT AS MUCH AS 14,115 GALLONS.

MAY AVERAGES THE HIGHEST RAINFALL, AND IF A WATER CATCHMENT SYSTEM WAS INSTALLED, ONE COULD COLLECT UP TO 21,623 GALLONS OF WATER.

Figure 1.27 Rebecca Crockett and Lauren Shaw, Average Monthly Rainfall (site analysis)

AIR QUALITY INDEX

"GOOD" AQI IS 0 - 50. AIR QUALITY IS CONSIDERED SATISFACTORY, AND AIR POLLUTION POSES LITTLE OR NO RISK.

"MODERATE" AQI IS 51 - 100. AIR QUALITY IS ACCEPTABLE; HOWEVER, FOR SOME POLLUTANTS THERE MAY BE A MODERATE HEALTH CONCERN FOR A VERY SMALL NUMBER OF PEOPLE. FOR EXAMPLE, PEOPLE WHO ARE UNUSUALLY SENSITIVE TO OZONE MAY EXPERIENCE RESPIRATORY SYMPTOMS.

"UNHEALTHY FOR SENSITIVE GROUPS" AQI IS 101 - 150. ALTHOUGH GENERAL PUBLIC IS NOT LIKELY TO BE AFFECTED AT THIS AQI RANGE, PEOPLE WITH LUNG DISEASE, OLDER ADULTS AND CHILDREN ARE AT A GREATER RISK FROM EXPOSURE TO OZONE, WHEREAS PERSONS WITH HEART AND LUNG DISEASE, OLDER ADULTS AND CHILDREN ARE AT GREATER RISK FROM THE PRESENCE OF PARTICLES IN THE AIR. .

"UNHEALTHY" AQI IS 151 - 200. EVERYONE MAY BEGIN TO EXPERIENCE SOME ADVERSE HEALTH EFFECTS, AND MEMBERS OF THE SENSITIVE GROUPS MAY EXPERIENCE MORE SERIOUS EFFECTS. .

"VERY UNHEALTHY" AQI IS 201 - 300. THIS WOULD TRIGGER A HEALTH ALERT SIGNIFYING THAT EVERYONE MAY EXPERIENCE MORE SERIOUS HEALTH EFFECTS.

"HAZARDOUS" AQI GREATER THAN 300. THIS WOULD TRIGGER A HEALTH WARNINGS OF EMERGENCY CONDITIONS. THE ENTIRE POPULATION IS MORE LIKELY TO BE AFFECTED.

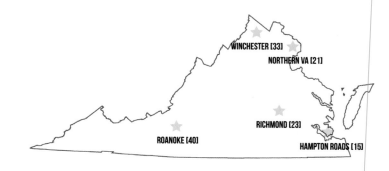

VIRGINIA CITIES [2.1.11]

AS OF FEBRUARY 1, 2011, ROANOKE HAS THE HIGHEST AQI RATING OF ALL MAJOR VIRGINIAN CITIES WITH AN ALMOST "MIDERATE" RATING. BASED ON THE 2010 DATA, APRIL AND AUGUST TYPICALLY HAVE THE POOREST AIR QUALITY. ALTHOUGH THERE WERE FOUR MODERATE AIR QUALITY DAYS IN FEBRUARY, TO ALREADY HAVE A 40 RATING ON THE FIRST DAY OF THE MONTH SUGEGESTS THAT THERE WILL POSSIBLY BE MORE THAN FOUR MODERATE DAYS IN 2011, AND SUBSEQUENTLY, THE NUMBER OF DAYS WITH POOR AIR QUALITY IN THE FOLLOWING MONTHS WILL RISE AS WELL IF ACTION IS NOT TAKEN TO REDUCE THE AMOUNT OF MAN-MADE POLLUTANTS IN THE AIR.

QUALITY INDEX*

0-50	GOOD
51-100	MODERATE
101-150	AFFECTS SENSITIVE
151-200	UNHEALTHY
201-300	VERY UNHEALTHY
301-500	HAZARDOUS

* BASED ON THE AVERAGE OF HOURLY AND 8-HOUR MEASUREMENTS OF OZONE, PARTICULATES, OR NO2 IN PPB (PARTS PER BILLION)

2010 AQI DATA

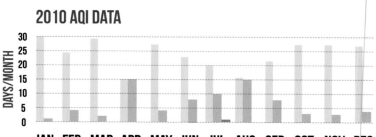

Figure 1.28 Rebecca Crockett and Lauren Shaw, Air Quality Index (site analysis)

Online mapping provides satellite maps of many parts of the world and can be set to show shadows and sunlight transmission across a site to show how sunlight will interact with a design. Many computer programs can integrate actual longitude and latitude to make designing on the site more realistic in the computer model.

A review of specific sustainable design interventions to the site followed the initial research phase. The methods explored included solar retrofits to an existing building, wind power-generated electricity, solar air panels, solar water heating, biogas production and storage, thermal biogas, rainwater collection and greywater reuse, geothermal systems, and the implementation of solar photovoltaics in a variety of configurations and placements.

PASSIVE SOLAR BUILDING DESIGN: WINDOWS, WALLS, AND FLOORS ARE MADE TO COLLECT, STORE, AND DISTRIBUTE SOLAR ENERGY IN THE FORM OF HEAT IN THE WINTER AND REJECT SOLAR HEAT IN THE SUMMER. THIS IS CALLED PASSIVE SOLAR DESIGN OR CLIMATIC DESIGN BECAUSE, UNLIKE ACTIVE SOLAR HEATING SYSTEMS, IT DOESN'T INVOLVE THE USE OF MECHANICAL AND ELECTRICAL DEVICES.

DIRECT / VS INDIRECT SOLAR GAIN [FOR HEATING] DIRECT: ATTEMPTS TO CONCENTRATE THE MAJORITY OF THE BUILDINGS GLAZING ON THE SUN-FACING FACADE, SOLAR RADIATION IS ADMITTED DIRECTLY INTO THE SPACE. TYPICALLY CAN UTILIZE 65-70% OF SOLAR RADIATION.

EXAMPLES OF HOW THIS IS IMPLEMENTED IN DESIGN: APERTURES ON THE SOLAR SIDE OF THE BUILDING USE OF DOUBLE GLAZED AND LOW E GLASS MAIN OCCUPIED SPACES LOCATED ON THE SOLAR SIDE OF THE BUILDING FLOOR SHOULD BE OF HIGH THERMAL MASS TO ABSORB THE HEAT AND PREVENT TEMPERATURE FLUCTUATIONS IN THE BUILDING TO PREVENT OVERHEATING IN THE SUMMER, EAVES OR LOVERS CAN BE INCLUDED LIGHT SHELVES PREVENT OVERHEAT AND DISTRIBUTE DAYLIGHT

INDIRECT: USES A HEAT ABSORBING ELEMENT INSERTED BETWEEN THE SOURCE OF THE SOLAR GAIN AND THE SPACE TO BE HEATED, THUS TRANSFERRING HEAT INDIRECTLY. [THIS IS THE PRINCIPLE BEHIND RADIANT HEATING/COOLING SYSTEMS] USUALLY CONSISTS OF A WALL PLACED BETWEEN THE GLAZING THE INTERIOR [ALSO CALLED A TROMBE WALL] AND CONTROLS THE FLOW OF HEAT INTO THE BUILDING [USUALLY 20-30 CM THICK]. THE AREA OF THE THERMAL STORAGE WALL SHOULD BE 15-20% OF THE FLOOR AREA OF THE SPACE INTO WHICH IT EMITS HEAT. OTHER WAYS TO STORE HEAT IN ORDER TO CONTROL DIURNAL TEMPERATURES INCLUDE: A VENTILATED CONCRETE FLOOR, A CISTERN, WATER WALL OR ROOF POND.

DIRECT/INDIRECT GAIN

1. THE ROOF SHELTERS THE INTERIOR FROM THE HARSH SUMMER SUN, HEATING THE BUILDING INDIRECTLY

2. THE LESS INTENSE WINTER SUN HEATS THE SPACE DIRECTLY OR INDIRECTLY

3. HEAT CAN ENTER THE BUILDING DIRECTLY THROUGH OPEN WINDOWS [APERTURE]

4. SOLAR HEAT IS TRANSFERRED INDIRECTLY AS IT HEATS THE FLOORING [THERMAL MASS], WHICH THEN GRADUALLY RELEASES HEAT.

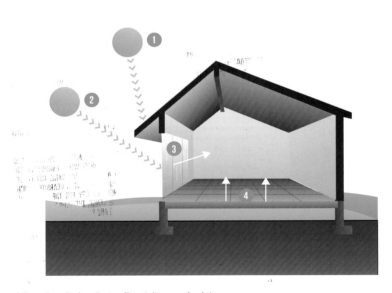

Figure 1.29 Rebecca Crockett and Lauren Shaw, Efficiency and Passive Solar Retrofits (site analysis)

EFFICIENCY PASSIVE SOLAR RETROFITS

OTHER PASSIVE METHODS: AN ATTACHED SUNSPACE/CONSERVATORY: THIS CAN BE ADDED EASILY TO AN EXISTING BUILDING. IT CAN FUNCTION AS AN EXTENSION OF LIVING SPACE, A PREHEATING CENTER FOR VENTILATION AIR, OR AS A GREENHOUSE FOR PLANTS. HOWEVER, THEY ARE CONSIDERED TO BE A CONTRIBUTOR TO GLOBAL WARMING AND THE AIRFLOW BETWEEN THE SUNSPACE AND THE MAIN BUILDING MUST BE CAREFULLY MONITORED. IDEALLY, THE GLAZING SHOULD BE 20-30% OF THE AREA OF THE ROOM TO WHICH IT IS ATTACHED. ALSO, IT SHOULD BE CAPABLE OF BEING COMPLETELY ISOLATED FROM THE MAIN BUILDING TO PREVENT HEAT LOSS IN THE WINTER, AND EXCESSIVE GAIN IN THE SUMMER.

THERMOSIPHON: USES CONVECTION TO CIRCULATE LIQUID WITHOUT THE NECESSITY OF A MECHANICAL PUMP. IT RELIES ON THE HEAT COLLECTED FROM BY A SOLAR COLLECTOR. CAN BE PART OF AN OPEN LOOP OR CLOSED LOOP SYSTEM. [EX: WATER CAN THEN BE CIRCULATED THROUGH CONCRETE FLOORS FOR HEATING]

SOLAR CHIMNEY: IMPROVES THE NATURAL VENTILATION OF BUILDINGS BY USING CONVECTION OF AIR HEATED BY PASSIVE SOLAR ENERGY. DURING THE DAY, SOLAR ENERGY HEATS THE CHIMNEY AND THE AIR WITHIN IT, CREATING AN UPDRAFT OF AIR. THE SUCTION CREATED AT THE CHIMNEY'S BASE CAN BE USED TO VENTILATE

THE BASIC ELEMENTS OF A SOLAR CHIMNEY ARE:

THE SOLAR COLLECTOR AREA: THIS CAN BE LOCATED IN THE TOP PART OF THE CHIMNEY OR CAN INCLUDE THE ENTIRE SHAFT. THE ORIENTATION, TYPE OF GLAZING, INSULATION AND THERMAL PROPERTIES OF THIS ELEMENT ARE CRUCIAL FOR HARNESSING, RETAINING AND UTILIZING SOLAR GAINS

THE MAIN VENTILATION SHAFT: THE LOCATION, HEIGHT, CROSS SECTION AND THE THERMAL PROPERTIES OF THIS STRUCTURE ARE ALSO VERY IMPORTANT.

THE INLET AND OUTLET AIR APERTURES: THE SIZES, LOCATION AS WELL AS AERODYNAMIC ASPECTS OF THESE ELEMENTS MUST BE TAKEN INTO CONSIDERATION. SOLAR CHIMNEYS PRODUCE THE "STACK EFFECT" THAT IS OFTEN USED TO NATURALLY VENTILATE BUILDINGS, DRIVEN BY THE PROPERTY OF BUOYANCY DUE TO THE DIFFERENCE IN INDOOR-TO-OUTDOOR AIR DENSITY RESULTING FROM TEMPERATURE AND MOISTURE DIFFERENCES.

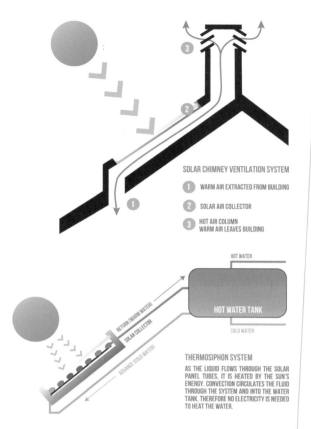

SOLAR CHIMNEY VENTILATION SYSTEM

1 WARM AIR EXTRACTED FROM BUILDING

2 SOLAR AIR COLLECTOR

3 HOT AIR COLUMN
WARM AIR LEAVES BUILDING

HOT WATER

HOT WATER TANK

COLD WATER

RETURN (WARM WATER)
SOLAR COLLECTOR
ADVANCE (COLD WATER)

THERMOSIPHON SYSTEM

AS THE LIQUID FLOWS THROUGH THE SOLAR PANEL TUBES, IT IS HEATED BY THE SUN'S ENERGY. CONVECTION CIRCULATES THE FLUID THROUGH THE SYSTEM AND INTO THE WATER TANK, THEREFORE NO ELECTRICITY IS NEEDED TO HEAT THE WATER.

Figure 1.30 Rebecca Crockett and Lauren Shaw, Efficiency Passive Solar Retrofits (site analysis)

WIND TURBINES: THE MOST COMMON MECHANISM USED TO HARNESS WIND POWER AND CONVERT IT TO ENERGY. BEFORE TURBINES ARE INSTALLED, EXTENSIVE RESEARCH ON THE SITE AND ITS WIND POWER DENSITY [WPD] CONDUCTED. THE WIND POWER DENSITY REFERS TO THE EFFECTIVE POWER OF THE WIND AT A PARTICULAR LOCATION.

THERE ARE TWO TYPES OF WIND TURBINES:

HORIZONTAL SYSTEMS: THIS TYPE OF TURBINE IS USED MOST FREQUENTLY, AND IS THE OLDEST METHOD IN USE.

HORIZONTAL AXIS TURBINE COMPONENTS: THIS SYSTEM CONSISTS OF A MAIN ROTOR SHAFT AND ELECTRICAL GENERATOR PLACED AT THE TOP OF A TOWER. IT MUST BE POINTED INTO THE WIND IN ORDER TO HARVEST ENERGY. SMALL TURBINES CAN BE DIRECTED BY A SIMPLE WIND VANE, BUT LARGE TURBINES USUALLY USE A MOTORIZED WIND SENSOR. MOST TURBINES HAVE A GEARBOX, WHICH QUICKENS THE ROTATION OF THE BLADES, THUS CREATING MORE ENERGY FOR THE ELECTRICAL GENERATOR..DUE TO THE FACT THAT WIND POWER PRODUCT TURBULENCE, THE TURBINE IS USUALLY POSITIONED UPWIND OF ITS SUPPORTING TOWER. TURBINE BLADES ARE STIFF, WHICH PREVENTS THE BLADES FROM BEING PUSHED INTO THE TOWER BY HIGH WINDS. ALSO, THE BLADES ARE PLACED A CONSIDERABLE DISTANCE IN FRONT OF THE TOWER AND ARE SOMETIMES SLIGHTLY TILTED FORWARD INTO THE WIND.

DOWNWIND MACHINES HAVE BEEN BUILT, DESPITE THE PROBLEM OF TURBULENCE (MAST WAKE), BECAUSE THEY DON'T NEED AN ADDITIONAL MECHANISM FOR KEEPING THEM IN LINE WITH THE WIND, AND BECAUSE IN HIGH WINDS THE BLADES CAN ALLOWED TO BEND WHICH REDUCES THEIR SWEPT AREA AND THUS THEIR WIND RESISTANCE. HOWEVER, TURBULENCE MAY LEAD TO FATIGUE FAILURES, SO MOST HORIZONTAL TURBINES ARE OF UPWIND DESIGN.

ADDITIONAL CHARACTERISTICS: AUTOMATIC START-UP, HIGH OUTPUT, NOT AS EFFICIENT IN URBAN AREAS WHERE THERE ARE FREQUENT CHANGES IN ORIENTATION AND SPEED, CAN BE NOISY, AND ARE OFTEN VISUALLY INTRUSIVE. THE TYPICAL DOMESTIC WIND TURBINE HAS A RANGE OF SPEEDS AT WHICH IT IS PRODUCTIVE. THE "CUT IN' SPEED IS THE LOWEST SPEED AT WHICH THE TURBINE WILL WORK, WHICH IS TYPICALLY 7 MPH. THE TURBINE IS MOST PRODUCTIVE AT SPEEDS OF 25 TO 35 MPH, BUT WILL SHUT DOWN TO MAINTAIN MECHANICAL INTEGRITY AT SPEEDS GREATER THAN 45 MPH, ALSO KNOWN AS THE "CUT OUT" SPEED. A TYPICAL WIND TURBINE ONLY CONVERTS 50-60% OF THE WIND THAT PASSES THROUGH IT TO ELECTRICITY, AND UNLIKE PHOTOVOLTAICS, WHICH CREATE ENERGY AT THE SAME RATE NO MATTER THE AMOUNT OF SUN IN THE SKY, A WIND TURBINE CREATES ENERGY EXPONENTIALLY DEPENDING ON THE WIND SPEED.

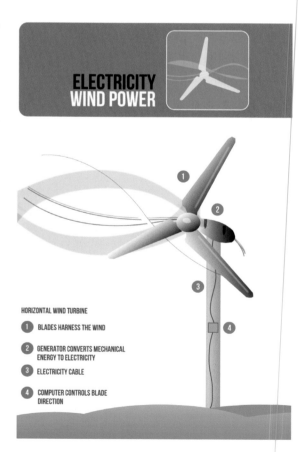

ELECTRICITY
WIND POWER

HORIZONTAL WIND TURBINE

1 BLADES HARNESS THE WIND

2 GENERATOR CONVERTS MECHANICAL ENERGY TO ELECTRICITY

3 ELECTRICITY CABLE

4 COMPUTER CONTROLS BLADE DIRECTION

Figure 1.31 Rebecca Crockett and Lauren Shaw, Electricity: Wind Power (site analysis)

ELECTRICITY WIND 2

VERTICAL SYSTEMS: THE MAIN ROTOR SHAFT IS ARRANGED VERTICALLY. THE TURBINE DOES NOT NEED TO BE POINTED INTO THE WIND TO BE EFFECTIVE, WHICH IS AN ADVANTAGE OVER HORIZONTAL SYSTEMS. THIS IS ESPECIALLY USEFUL ON SITES WHERE THE WIND DIRECTION IS HIGHLY VARIABLE, AND THEY ARE PARTICULARLY SUITED TO URBAN SITUATIONS AND BEING INTEGRATED INTO BUILDINGS. EX: AEOLIAN ROOF SYSTEM

DIFFERENT TYPES OF VERTICAL SYSTEMS:

DARRIEUS WIND TURBINE: "EGGBEATER" TURBINES, OR DARRIEUS TURBINES. THEY HAVE GOOD EFFICIENCY, BUT PRODUCE LARGE TORQUE RIPPLE AND CYCLICAL STRESS ON THE TOWER, WHICH CONTRIBUTES TO POOR RELIABILITY. THEY ALSO GENERALLY REQUIRE SOME EXTERNAL POWER SOURCE, OR AN ADDITIONAL SAVONIUS ROTOR, BECAUSE THE STARTING TORQUE IS VERY LOW. THE TORQUE RIPPLE IS REDUCED BY USING THREE OR MORE BLADES WHICH RESULTS IN GREATER SOLIDITY OF THE ROTOR. SOLIDITY IS MEASURED BY BLADE AREA DIVIDED BY THE ROTOR AREA. NEWER DARRIEUS TYPE TURBINES HAVE AN EXTERNAL SUPERSTRUCTURE TO SUPPORT ITSELF.

GIROMILL: A SUBTYPE OF DARRIEUS TURBINE WITH STRAIGHT BLADES. THE CYCLOTURBINE CAUSES LESS TURBULENCE AND IS SELF-STARTING. THE ADVANTAGES ARE: HIGH STARTING TORQUE, A HIGHER COEFFICIENT OF PERFORMANCE, MORE EFFICIENT OPERATION IN TURBULENT WINDS, AND A LOWER BLADE SPEED RATIO (WHICH LOWERS BLADE BENDING STRESSES).SAVONIUS WIND TURBINE: THESE ARE DRAG-TYPE DEVICES WITH TWO OR MORE SCOOPS (BLADES). THEY ARE SELF-STARTING IF THERE ARE AT LEAST THREE SCOOPS. THEY SOMETIMES HAVE LONG HELICAL SCOOPS TO CREATE A SMOOTHER TORQUE.

OPTIMIZING VERTICAL SYSTEMS PERFORMANCE: THE HEIGHT OF THE ROOFTOP MOUNTED TURBINE TOWER SHOULD BE APPROXIMATELY 50% OF THE BUILDING HEIGHT TO OPTIMIZE FOR MAXIMUM WIND ENERGY AND MINIMUM WIND TURBULENCE. IT SHOULD BE TAKEN INTO CONSIDERATION THAT WIND SPEEDS WITHIN THE BUILT ENVIRONMENT ARE GENERALLY MUCH LOWER THAN AT EXPOSED RURAL SITES.

DISADVANTAGES: TURBULENCE AND PROBLEMS ASSOCIATED WITH VIBRATION (NOISE, & INCREASE OF NEEDED MAINTENCE)LOW ROTATIONAL SPEED LOWER POWER AVAILABLE DIFFICULTY OF MODELLING THE WIND FLOW ACCURATELY TO DESIGN AN EFFICIENT TURBINE.

ADVANTAGES: DISCRETE AND VIRTUALLY SILENT, & THE GENERATOR AND GEARBOX CAN BE PLACED NEAR THE GROUND, ELIMINATING THE NEED OF A TOWER AND IMPROVING ACCESSIBILITY FOR MAINTENANCE

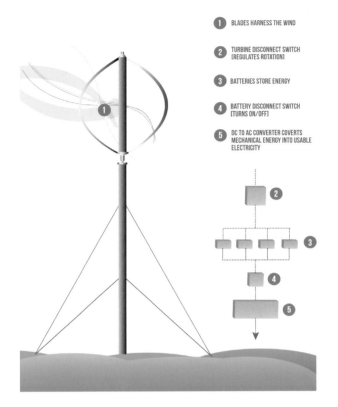

1 BLADES HARNESS THE WIND

2 TURBINE DISCONNECT SWITCH (REGULATES ROTATION)

3 BATTERIES STORE ENERGY

4 BATTERY DISCONNECT SWITCH (TURNS ON/OFF)

5 DC TO AC CONVERTER COVERTS MECHANICAL ENERGY INTO USABLE ELECTRICITY

Figure 1.32 Rebecca Crockett and Lauren Shaw, Electricity: Wind 2 (site analysis)

SOLAR AIR PANELS:

GLAZED SOLAR COLLECTORS: PRIMARILY FOR SPACE HEATING. THEY RECIRCULATE THE BUILDING'S AIR THROUGH A SOLAR AIR PANEL WHERE THE AIR IS HEATED AND THEN RELEASED BACK INTO THE BUILDING. IN ORDER TO BE EFFECTIVE, THE SOLAR PANELS MUST BE WARMER THAN THE ROOM'S TEMPERATURE.

UNGLAZED SOLAR COLLECTORS: USED TO PRE-HEAT VENTILATION AIR IN COMMERCIAL, INDUSTRIAL AND INSTITUTIONAL BUILDINGS WITH A HIGH VENTILATION LOAD. THEY TURN BUILDING WALLS OR SECTIONS OF WALLS INTO LOW COST, HIGH PERFORMANCE SOLAR COLLECTORS. THEY ARE SOMETIMES REFERRED TO AS "TRANSPIRED SOLAR PANELS" AN INTEGRATED PAINTED PERFORATED METAL SOLAR HEAT ABSORBER ALSO SERVES AS THE EXTERIOR WALL. HEAT CONDUCTS FROM THE ABSORBER SURFACE TO THE THERMAL BOUNDARY LAYER OF AIR 1 MM THICK ON THE OUTSIDE OF THE ABSORBER AND TO AIR THAT PASSES BEHIND THE ABSORBER. THE BOUNDARY LAYER OF AIR IS DRAWN INTO A NEARBY PERFORATION BEFORE THE HEAT CAN ESCAPE BY CONVECTION TO THE OUTSIDE AIR. THE HEATED AIR IS THEN DRAWN FROM BEHIND THE ABSORBER PLATE INTO THE BUILDING'S VENTILATION SYSTEM.

THEY CAN RAISE THE AIR TEMPERATURE UP TO 22 °C AND DELIVER AIR TEMPERATURES OF 45-60 °C. THE SHORT PAYBACK PERIOD OF TRANSPIRED COLLECTORS (3 TO 12 YEARS) MAKE THEM A MORE COST-EFFECTIVE ALTERNATIVE TO GLAZED COLLECTION SYSTEMS.

SOLAR THERMAL ENERGY (STE): HARNESSES SOLAR ENERGY FOR THERMAL ENERGY (HEAT).

STE IS DIFFERENT FROM PHOTOVOLTAICS, BECAUSE STE HARNESSES THE SUN'S HEAT WHILE PHOTOVOLTAICS CONVERTS HEAT DIRECTLY INTO ENERGY.

THERE ARE THREE DIFFERENT RATINGS FOR SOLAR THERMAL COLLECTORS:

LOW TEMPERATURE COLLECTORS: FLAT PLATES, COMMONLY USED TO HEAT SWIMMING POOLS.

MEDIUM-TEMPERATURE COLLECTORS: USUALLY FLAT PLATES, BUT CAN BE USED FOR HEATING WATER OR AIR FOR RESIDENTIAL AND COMMERCIAL USE.

HIGH TEMPERATURE COLLECTORS: CONCENTRATE SUNLIGHT USING MIRRORS OR LENSES, AND ARE COMMONLY USED FOR ELECTRIC POWER PRODUCTION.

IN ADDITION TO FLAT PLATE COLLECTORS, EVACUATED TUBE COLLECTORS ARE COMMONLY USED, AND ARE MORE EFFICIENT IN CLOUDY OR COOL CONDITIONS BECAUSE THEY PREVENT HEAT LOSS. THE VACUUM FORMED WITHIN THE TUBES ENSURES THAT HEAT CANNOT ESCAPE THROUGH CONVECTION. THE VACUUM IN BETWEEN THE GLASS TUBES TAKES IN HEAT FROM THE SUN (TO HEAT THE PIPE) AND IS COATED WITH A THERMAL ABSORBENT.

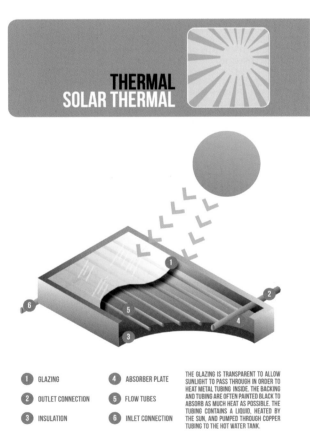

THERMAL
SOLAR THERMAL

1 GLAZING

2 OUTLET CONNECTION

3 INSULATION

4 ABSORBER PLATE

5 FLOW TUBES

6 INLET CONNECTION

THE GLAZING IS TRANSPARENT TO ALLOW SUNLIGHT TO PASS THROUGH IN ORDER TO HEAT METAL TUBING INSIDE. THE BACKING AND TUBING ARE OFTEN PAINTED BLACK TO ABSORB AS MUCH HEAT AS POSSIBLE. THE TUBING CONTAINS A LIQUID, HEATED BY THE SUN, AND PUMPED THROUGH COPPER TUBING TO THE HOT WATER TANK.

Figure 1.33 Rebecca Crockett and Lauren Shaw, Thermal: Solar Thermal (site analysis)

THERMAL SOLAR THERMAL 2

SOLAR ROOF PONDS: USED FOR BOTH HEATING & COOLING. IT CONSISTS OF A ROOF-MOUNTED WATER BLADDER WITH A ADJUSTABLE INSULATING COVER. THIS SYSTEM CAN CONTROL HEAT EXCHANGE BETWEEN INTERIOR AND EXTERIOR ENVIRONMENTS BY COVERING AND UNCOVERING THE BLADDER BETWEEN NIGHT AND DAY. WHEN HEATING IS A CONCERN THE BLADDER IS UNCOVERED DURING THE DAY ALLOWING SUNLIGHT TO WARM THE WATER BLADDER AND STORE HEAT FOR EVENING USE. WHEN COOLING IS A CONCERN THE COVERED BLADDER DRAWS HEAT FROM THE BUILDING'S INTERIOR DURING THE DAY AND IS UNCOVERED AT NIGHT TO RADIATE HEAT TO THE COOLER ATMOSPHERE.

THESE COLLECTORS COULD BE USED TO PRODUCE APPROXIMATELY 50% OF THE HOT WATER NEEDED FOR RESIDENTIAL AND COMMERCIAL USE IN THE UNITED STATES. THE PAYBACK TIME FOR A TYPICAL HOUSEHOLD IS FOUR TO NINE YEARS, DEPENDING ON THE LOCATION AND ITS AVERAGE TEMPERATURE.

SOLAR WATER HEATING CAN REDUCE CO_2 EMISSIONS (FOR A FAMILY OF FOUR): 1 TON/YEAR (IF REPLACING NATURAL GAS) OR 3 TON/YEAR (IF REPLACING ELECTRICITY).

THERMAL MASS MATERIALS: THESE MATERIALS STORE SOLAR ENERGY DURING THE DAY AND RELEASE THIS ENERGY DURING COOLER PERIODS. COMMON THERMAL MASS MATERIALS INCLUDE STONE, CONCRETE, AND WATER. THEY CAN PASSIVELY MAINTAIN COMFORTABLE TEMPERATURES WHILE REDUCING ENERGY CONSUMPTION. [SEE PASSIVE SOLAR RETROFITS FOR DETAILED DESCRIPTION AND MORE PASSIVE SOLAR THERMAL SYSTEMS.]

WAYS TO STORE SOLAR ENERGY FOR HEATING USE:

AQUIFER HEAT STORAGE: NATURALLY OCCURRING AQUIFERS ARE CHARGED WITH HEAT VIA WELLS DURING THE WARMING SEASON. IN THE WINTER, THE SYSTEM GOES INTO REVERSE AND THE WARMTH DISTRIBUTED.

GRAVEL/HOT WATER STORAGE: A PIT WITH A WATERTIGHT PLASTIC LINER IS FILLED WITH A GRAVEL/WATER MIX AS THE STORAGE MEDIUM. THE STORAGE CONTAINER IS INSULATED AT THE SIDES AND TOP.

HOT WATER STORAGE: A STEEL OR CONCRETE INSULATED TANK BUILT PARTLY OR WHOLLY INTO THE GROUND.

DUCT HEAT STORAGE: HEAT IS STORED IN WATER SATURATED SOIL. U-PIPES ARE PLACED IN VERTICAL BOREHOLES, WHICH ARE INSULATED NEAR THE SURFACE. HEAT IS FED INTO AND OUT OF THE GROUND VIA THE U-PIPES.

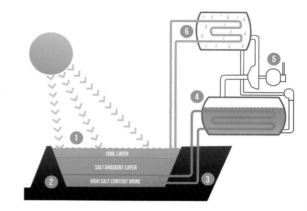

1. THE WATER IS EXPOSED TO DIRECT SOLAR GAIN, WHICH IT ABSORBS AND STORES.

2. THE HEAT DIVIDES THE WATER INTO THREE DIFFERENT LAYERS. THE SALT IN THE WATER PREVENTS THE WARM WATER FROM RISING IN THE POND.

3. A PIPE DRAWS THE WARM WATER OUT OF THE POND WITH A PUMP

4. THE WATER IS CIRCULATED THROUGH A PUMPING SYSTEM WHICH UTILIZES THE HEAT.

5. WHEN USED TO GENERATE ELECTRICITY, THE SYSTEM TRANSFERS THE WATER THROUGH A TURBINE, THEN TO A GENERATOR

6. THE COOLED WATER IS SENT TO THE CONDENSER, THEN RETURNED TO THE POOL TO BE RE-HEATED AND REPEAT THE PROCESS.

Figure 1.34 Rebecca Crockett and Lauren Shaw, Thermal: Solar Thermal 2 (site analysis)

BIOGAS: GAS, WHICH IS USED AS A TYPE OF BIOFUEL, PRODUCED BY THE BIOLOGICAL BREAK-DOWN OF ORGANIC MATTER IN THE ABSENCE OF OXYGEN, KNOWN AS ANAEROBIC DIGESTION. SOME OF THE BIODEGRADABLE MATERIALS USED IN ANAEROBIC DIGESTION TO PRODUCE BIOGAS ARE MANURE, BIOMASS, SEWAGE, MUNICIPAL WASTE, AND PLANT MATERIALS. THE TYPE OF GAS PRODUCED FROM THIS PROCESS IS TYPICALLY METHANE AND CARBON DIOXIDE, WHICH IS THEN COMBUSTED OR OXIDIZED WITH OXYGEN AND USED AS FUEL.

COMPOSITION: THE MOST VALUABLE COMPOUND FOR ENERGY PURPOSES IN THIS SCENARIO IS METHANE, WHICH TYPICALLY MAKES UP 50 TO 75 PERCENT OF BIOGAS. UNFORTUNATELY, THE SECOND MOST PREVALENT COMPOUND IN BIOGAS IS CARBON DIOXIDE, WHICH RANGES FROM 25 TO 50 PERCENT. WATER VAPOR IS ALSO A PRODUCT OF BIOGAS, AND IS CRITICAL IN MAINTAINING ITS TEMPERATURE.

PRODUCTION: BIOGAS IS PRODUCED THROUGH A PROCESS THAT HARNESSES ANAEROBIC DIGEST-ERS, WHICH ARE MICROORGANISMS THAT BREAK DOWN BIODEGRADABLE MATERIAL WITHOUT THE PRESENCE OF OXYGEN. THE ORIGINAL WASTE, TYPICALLY MANURE OR BIOMASS, IS PLACED INTO A MIXING TANK WHERE IT MIXES WITH WATER. IT IS THEN CARRIED BY GRAVITY TRHOUGH AN INLET PIPE TO AN AIR-TIGHT TANK LOCATED BELOW GROUND. IN THIS TANK, THE WATER-WASTE MIXTURE IS EXPOSED TO DIGESTERS AND THE PROCESS OF ANAEROBIC DIGESTIONS BEGINS. AS THE BIOGAS IS CREAED, IT SEPARATES FROM THE WATER-WASTE MIXTURE AND RISES TO THE TOP OF THE TANK WHERE IT IS COLLECTED AND TRANSFERED OUT WITH A GAS LINE. THE WASTE THAT REMAINS AFTER THE ANAEROBIC DIGESTION PROCESS IS OFTEN NUTRIENT-RICH AND KNOWN AS "DIGESTATE". THE DIGESTATE IS THEN REMOVED THROUGH AN OUTLET PIPE WHERE IT CAN BE USED AS FERTILIZER. HOWEVER, DEPENDING ON THE WASTE USED TO CREATE THE BIOGAS, THE DIGESTATE MAY NOT BE SUITABLE FOR FERTILIZER. IF THIS IS THE CASE, DIGESTATE CAN BE INCINERATED TO CREATE ENERGY AS A FORM OF BIOMASS.

THERE ARE TWO ANAEROBIC DIGESTION PROCESSES THAT ARE DETERMINED BY THE TEMPERA-TURE AT WHICH THEY OCCUR:

MESOPHILIC DIGESTION - TAKES PLACE BETWEEN 20 AND 40 DEGREES CELCIUS AND CAN TAKE A MONTH OR TWO TO COMPLETE.

THERMOPHILIC DIGESTION - TAKES PLACE FROM 50 TO 65 DEGREES CELCIUS AND IS FASTER, BUT THE BACTERIA ARE MORE SENSITIVE.

BIOGAS PRODUCTION WITH DIGESTATE SLURRY

1. WASTE OR BIOMASS IS INSERTED INTO INLET TANK.

2. BIODIGESTERS REACT WITH WASTE OR BIOMASS.

3. GAS GENERATED FROM BIODIGESTERS RISES AND SEPARATES INTO GAS CHAMBER.

4. GAS IS COLLECTED FROM CHAMBER WITH A GAS LINE, WHICH WILL TRANSPORT IT TO WHERE IT WILL BE USED.

5. DIGESTATE IS COLLECTED IN OUTLET TANK.

6. DIGESTATE IS RELEASED FROM OUTLET TANK INTO SLURRY WHERE IT IS USED AS FERTILIZER.

Figure 1.35 Rebecca Crockett and Lauren Shaw, Thermal: Biogas (site analysis)

BIOGAS 2

USES OF BIOGAS: ONCE BIOGAS IS COMBINED WITH OXYGEN TO BECOME A FUEL SOURCE, IT CAN BE HARNESSED IN A NUMBER OF WAYS.

BIOGAS CAN BE USED TO CREATE ELECTRICITY THROUGH THE USE OF A COMBINED HEAT AND POWER (CHP) GAS ENGINE. CHP ENGINES PRODUCE ELECTRICITY AND ALSO HARNESS THE HEAT PRODUCED IN THE PROCESS.

THE METHANE PRODUCED IN BIOGAS CAN BE REFINED INTO BIOMETHANE, WHICH IS VERY SIMILAR TO NATURAL GAS. TO ACHIEVE THIS, CARBON DIOXIDE, WATER, HYDROGEN SULFIDE AND PARTICULATES MUST BE COMPLETELY REMOVED THROUGH THE USE OF A BIOGAS UPGRADER. IF BIOMETHANE IS COMPRESSED IT CAN BE USED TO RUN AUTOMOBILES, REPLACING THE NEED FOR GASOLINE.

ADVANTAGES OF BIOGAS: BY HARNESSING MANURE AND HUMAN WASTE, WHICH WITHOUT INTERVENTION BREAKS DOWN TO RELEASE METHANE (WARMS 21 TIMES MORE THAN CO2) AND NITROUS DIOXIDE (WARMS 310 TIMES MORE THAN CO2), ENERGY THAT WOULD NORMALLY BE RELEASED INTO THE ATMOSPHERE AS HARMFUL GLOBAL WARMING AGENTS IS CONVERTED INTO USEFUL ELECTRICITY. METHANE AND NITROUS OXIDE ARE ADDING TO THE GLOBAL WARMING CRISIS, SO BY CONVERTING THIS WASTE INTO BIOGAS THAT CAN BE USED TO FUEL CARS OR RUN ELECTRICAL APPLIANCES WE ARE NOT ONLY REDUCING THEIR NEGATIVE EFFECTS ON THE ENVIRONMENT BUT ALSO REDUCING OUR DEPENDENCE ON OTHER FOSSIL FUELS.

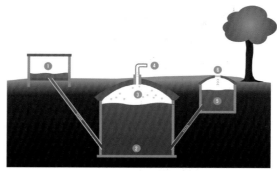

BIOGAS PRODUCTION WITH DIGESTATE CONTAINMENT

1. WASTE OR BIOMASS IS INSERTED INTO INLET TANK.
2. BIODIGESTERS REACT WITH WASTE OR BIOMASS.
3. GAS GENERATED FROM BIODIGESTERS RISES AND SEPARATES INTO GAS CHAMBER.
4. GAS IS COLLECTED FROM CHAMBER WITH A GAS LINE, WHICH WILL TRANSPORT IT TO WHERE IT WILL BE USED.
5. DIGESTATE IS COLLECTED IN OVERFLOW TANK.
6. DIGESTATE IS EVENTUALLY REMOVED AND INCINERATED IN THE FORM OF BIOMASS.

Figure 1.36 Rebecca Crockett and Lauren Shaw, Thermal: Biogas 2 (site analysis)

PHOTOVOLTAICS (PV): GENERATES ELECTRICAL POWER BY CONVERTING SOLAR RADIATION INTO DIRECT CURRENT ELECTRICITY.

PHOTOVOLTAIC POWER GENERATION USES SOLAR PANELS COMPOSED OF CELLS CONTAINING A PHOTOVOLTAIC MATERIAL. MATERIALS COMMONLY USED FOR PHOTOVOLTAICS INCLUDE: SILICON, CADMIUM TELLURIDE, AND COPPER INDIUM SELENIDE/SULFIDE.

PV CELLS ALONE CANNOT PRODUCE ENERGY. THEY MUST BE COUPLED WITH OTHER COMPONENTS. IN ORDER TO BE USED IN BUILDINGS, AN INVERTER IS REQUIRED TO TRANSFORM THE DC CURRENT TO AC CURRENT, WHICH CAUSES AN ENERGY LOSS OF 4–12%.

OFF THE GRID SYSTEMS ARE KNOWN AS A "STANDALONE" SYSTEM. THESE SYSTEMS CONSIST OF A PV CELL, A BLOCKING-DIODE TO PREVENT BATTERY DRAIN DURING LOW-INSOLATION, A BATTERY, AND AN INVERTER. IN ORDER TO BE USED IN BUILDINGS, AN INVERTER IS REQUIRED TO TRANSFORM THE DC CURRENT TO AC CURRENT, WHICH CAUSES AN ENERGY LOSS OF 4–12%.

WHY USE PV CELLS?: THE AMOUNT ENERGY FROM THE SUN THAT REACHES THE EARTH IS ALMOST 6,000 TIMES MORE THAN THE AVERAGE AMOUNT OF POWER CONSUMED BY HUMANS.

ALSO, SOLAR POWER IS POLLUTION-FREE DURING USE. PRODUCTION END-WASTES AND EMISSIONS ARE MANAGEABLE USING EXISTING POLLUTION CONTROLS. END-OF-USE RECYCLING TECHNOLOGIES ARE UNDER DEVELOPMENT, AND PV INSTALLATIONS CAN OPERATE FOR MANY YEARS WITH LITTLE MAINTENANCE OR INTERVENTION AFTER THEIR INITIAL SET-UP.

THERE ARE TWO BASIC TYPES OF COLLECTORS:

FLAT BED COLLECTORS: CONSIST OF METAL PLATES COATED MATTE BLACK BEHIND GLASS OR PLASTIC. THEY ARE TILTED TO MAXIMIZE UPTAKE OF SOLAR RADIATION. BEHIND THE PLATES ARE PIPES CARRYING THE HEAT-ABSORBING MEDIUM – WATER. THEY ARE BEST EMPLOYED TO SUPPLY PRE-HEATED WATER FOR A GAS BOILER OR IMMERSION HEATER. IT IS INCREASINGLY POPULAR THAT THE COLLECTOR SYSTEM INCORPORATES A PHOTOVOLTAIC MODULE TO PROVIDE POWER FOR THE CIRCULATING FAN, MAKING IT A TRUE ZERO FOSSIL ENERGY OPTION.

VACUUM BED COLLECTORS: EVACUATED TUBES ENCLOSED WITHIN AN INSULATED STEEL CASING WORK BY EXPLOITING THE VACUUM AROUND THE COLLECTOR. THIS REDUCES HEAT LOSS, AND MAKES THEM SUITABLE FOR COOLER CLIMATES. THEY HEAT WATER TO 60 DEGREES CELSIUS, SO WATER SYSTEMS MAY NOT REQUIRE ADDITIONAL HEATING. TO REACH THEIR FULL POTENTIAL, BOTH TYPES SHOULD BE LINKED TO A STORAGE FACILITY, WHICH STORES EXCESS WARMTH IN SUMMER TO SUPPLEMENT WINTER HEATING.

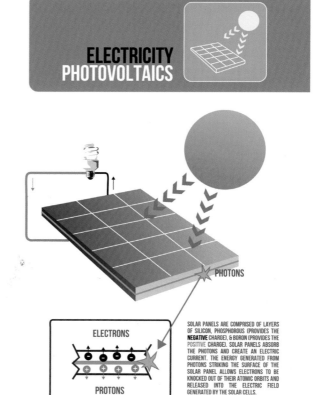

ELECTRICITY PHOTOVOLTAICS

ELECTRONS

PROTONS

PHOTONS

SOLAR PANELS ARE COMPRISED OF LAYERS OF SILICON, PHOSPHOROUS (PROVIDES THE **NEGATIVE** CHARGE), & BORON (PROVIDES THE POSITIVE CHARGE). SOLAR PANELS ABSORB THE PHOTONS AND CREATE AN ELECTRIC CURRENT. THE ENERGY GENERATED FROM PHOTONS STRIKING THE SURFACE OF THE SOLAR PANEL ALLOWS ELECTRONS TO BE KNOCKED OUT OF THEIR ATOMIC ORBITS AND RELEASED INTO THE ELECTRIC FIELD GENERATED BY THE SOLAR CELLS.

Figure 1.37 Rebecca Crockett and Lauren Shaw, Electricity: Photovoltaics (site analysis)

ELECTRICITY PHOTOVOLTAICS 2

BUILDING INTEGRATED PHOTOVOLTAICS (BIPV): **THE FASTEST GROWTH AREA IN THE MANUFACTURING OF PHOTOVOLTAICS IS BIPVS. PVS CAN BE INTEGRATED INTO THE PHYSICAL FACADE OF THE BUILDING. ALTHOUGH MANY BIPVS ARE INTEGRATED DURING NEW CONSTRUCTION, OLDER BUILDINGS CAN ALSO BE RETROFITTED WITH THESE SYSTEMS. OFTEN, THE USE OF BIPVS IS CHEAPER THAN TRADITIONAL MATERIALS AND CAN SAVE MONEY ON LABOR COSTS.**

BUILDING-INTEGRATED PHOTOVOLTAIC MODULES ARE AVAILABLE IN SEVERAL FORMS:

FLAT ROOFS: **PVS CAN BE USED ON FLAT ROOFS BY INSTALLING A THIN SOLAR CELL FILM THAT IS INTEGRATED INTO A FLEXIBLE POLYMER ROOFING MEMBRANE.**

PITCHED ROOFS: **SOLAR CELLS CAN BE DESIGNED TO LOOK AND ACT LIKE REGULAR SHINGLES. THEY EXTEND TYPICAL ROOF LIFE BY PROTECTING INSULATION AND MEMBRANES FROM ULTRAVIOLET RAYS AND WATER DEGRADATION. IT DOES THIS BY ELIMINATING CONDENSATION BECAUSE THE DEW POINT IS KEPT ABOVE THE ROOFING MEMBRANE.**

FACADE: **FACADES CAN BE INSTALLED ON EXISTING BUILDINGS, GIVING OLD BUILDINGS A WHOLE NEW LOOK. THESE MODULES ARE MOUNTED ON THE FACADE OF THE BUILDING, OVER THE EXISTING STRUCTURE, WHICH CAN INCREASE THE APPEAL OF THE BUILDING AND ITS RESALE VALUE. GLAZING: SEMI-TRANSPARENT MODULES CAN BE USED TO REPLACE A NUMBER OF ARCHITECTURAL ELEMENTS COMMONLY MADE WITH GLASS OR SIMILAR MATERIALS, SUCH AS WINDOWS AND SKYLIGHTS.**

ADVANTAGES OF THESE SYSTEMS: **CLEAN GENERATION OF ELECTRICITY GENERATION AT THE POINT OF USE ELIMINATES ADDITIONAL INFRASTRUCTURE COSTS AND LARGER LAND AREA REQUIREMENTS**

OPTIMIZING PV PERFORMANCE: **SOLAR TRACKERS MOVE PV PANELS TO FOLLOW THE PATH OF THE SUN. THIS CAN INCREASE EFFICIENCY BY AS MUCH AS 20% IN WINTER AND 50% IN SUMMER. HOWEVER, IT CAN RAISE COSTS BY REQUIRING MAINTENCE, BUT FOR LARGE BUILDINGS IS OFTEN WORTH THE PRICE INCREASE.**

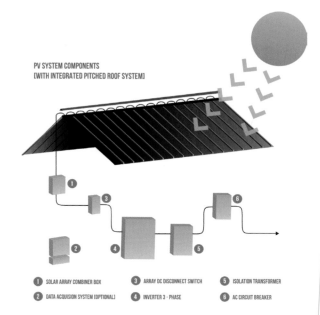

PV SYSTEM COMPONENTS
(WITH INTEGRATED PITCHED ROOF SYSTEM)

1 SOLAR ARRAY COMBINER BOX   3 ARRAY DC DISCONNECT SWITCH   5 ISOLATION TRANSFORMER

2 DATA ACQUISION SYSTEM (OPTIONAL)   4 INVERTER 3 - PHASE   6 AC CIRCUIT BREAKER

Figure 1.38 Rebecca Crockett and Lauren Shaw, Electricity: Photovoltaics 2 (site analysis)

ELECTRICITY PHOTOVOLTAICS 3

MOUNTING SYSTEMS: **THE WAY IN WHICH SOLAR ARRAYS ARE MOUNTED IMPACTS HOW MUCH ENERGY THEY CAN PRODUCE**

DIFFERENT TYPES OF MOUNTING SYSTEMS:

SINGLE-AXIS ADJUSTABLE: **USED FOR FREESTANDING SOLAR ARRAYS, THIS SYSTEM ALLOWS YOU TO ADJUST THE PANEL'S ORIENTATION BASED ON THE SUN'S ORIENTATION THROUGH THE SEASONS.**

DUAL-AXIS ADJUSTABLE: **ALSO USED FOR FREESTANDING SOLAR ARRAYS, THIS SYSTEM HAS A MECHANICAL PIVOT THAT ALLOWS THE PANELS TO FOLLOW THE TRACK OF THE SUN FROM SUNRISE TO SUNSET WITH USE OF PV TRACKING SYSTEM. THE PV TRACKING SYSTEM IS EITHER MECHANICAL OR PASSIVE. THE MECHANICAL TRACKING SYSTEM IS CONTROLLED BY A COMPUTER WITH A SENSOR THAT GAUGES THE POSITION OF THE SUN, WHILE THE PASSIVE SYSTEM USES A DRUM OF OIL THAT IS GRADUALLY HEATED BY THE SUN TO CHANGE THE POSITION OF THE ARRAY.**

FIXED/STATIC: **MOST COMMON/AFFORDABLE. ORIENTED TOWARD THE SUN AT THE ANGLE OF LATITUDE RELEVANT TO THE RESIDENCE. IF YOU LIVE OFF THE GRID IN A LOCATION THAT IS COLD (SHORTER DAYS IN WINTER) FOR THE MAJORITY OF THE MONTHS OF THE YEAR, YOU MAY CHOOSE TO ORIENT YOUR PANELS AT AN ANGLE THAT MORE ADVANTAGEOUSLY TAKES IN WINTER RAYS. BUT IF YOU LIVE ON THE GRID AND GET CREDIT FOR "TURNING BACK THE METER" YOU MAY WANT TO SET YOUR ANGLE TO TAKE IN SUMMER RAYS WHEN THE DAYS ARE LONGER.**

OPTIMIZING SYSTEMS: **STATIC MOUNTED SYSTEMS CAN BE OPTIMIZED BY ANALYZING THE BUILDING'S SUN PATH. PANELS ARE OFTEN SET AT AN ANGLE EQUAL TO THE LATITUDE, AND PERFORMANCE CAN BE IMPROVED BY ADJUSTING THE ANGLE FOR SUMMER OR WINTER. ELECTRICAL OUTPUT IS EXTREMELY SENSITIVE TO SHADING. WHEN EVEN A SMALL PORTION OF A CELL, MODULE, OR ARRAY IS SHADED, WHILE THE REMAINDER IS IN SUNLIGHT, THE OUTPUT FALLS DRAMATICALLY DUE TO INTERNAL 'SHORT-CIRCUITING. THEREFORE IT IS EXTREMELY IMPORTANT THAT A PV INSTALLATION IS NOT SHADED AT ALL BY TREES, ARCHITECTURAL FEATURES, FLAG POLES, OR OTHER OBSTRUCTIONS. SUNLIGHT CAN BE ABSORBED BY DUST, FALLOUT, OR OTHER IMPURITIES AT THE SURFACE OF THE MODULE. THIS CAN CUT DOWN THE AMOUNT OF LIGHT THAT ACTUALLY STRIKES THE CELLS BY AS MUCH AS HALF. MAINTAINING A CLEAN MODULE SURFACE WILL INCREASE OUTPUT PERFORMANCE OVER THE LIFE OF THE MODULE.**

HYBRID SYSTEMS: **DUE TO THE FACT THAT PV SOLAR ARRAYS ALONE DO NOT TYPICALLY PRODUCE ENOUGH ELECTRICITY TO SUSTAIN A BUILDINGS' NEEDS, THE SOLAR ENERGY COLLECTED FROM THE PV CELLS CAN BE COMBINED WITH OTHER SUSTAINABLE ENERGY SYSTEMS. OFTEN, A DIESEL GENERATOR IS USED, WHILE WIND AND BIOGAS ARE OTHER ALTERNATIVES.**

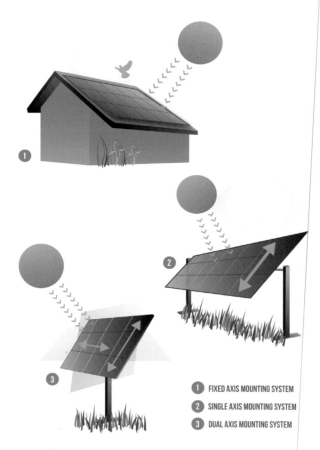

1 FIXED AXIS MOUNTING SYSTEM

2 SINGLE AXIS MOUNTING SYSTEM

3 DUAL AXIS MOUNTING SYSTEM

Figure 1.39 Rebecca Crockett and Lauren Shaw, Electricity: Photovoltaics 3 (site analysis)

BIOMASS: PLANT MATTER GROWN TO GENERATE ELECTRICITY OR PRODUCE HEAT. BIOMASS IS A RENEW-
ABLE ENERGY SOURCE, SINCE IT IS PRODUCED FROM BIOLOGICAL MATERIAL OF A LIVING OR RECENTLY
LIVING ORGANISM. WASTE, HYDROGEN GAS, AND ALCOHOL FUELS ARE ALSO CONSIDERED BIOMASS
BECAUSE THEY ARE BIODEGRADABLE AND HAVE NOT UNDERGONE GEOLOGICAL TRANSFORMATIONS,
UNLIKE FOSSIL FUELS.

THE FOLLOWING PLANTS ARE EXAMPLES OF BIOLOGICAL MATTER THAT CAN BE HARNESSED FOR INDUS-
TRIAL BIOMASS: CORN, HEMP, MISCANTHUS, POPLAR, SORGHUM, SUGARCANE, SWITCHGRASS, WILLOW,
AND A VARIETY OF TREE SPECIES, RANGING FROM EUCALYPTUS TO OIL PALM.

HOW IS BIOMASS CONVERTED INTO ENERGY? THERMAL CONVERSION - THE USE OF HEAT TO CONVERT
BIOMASS INTO ENERGY, TYPICALLY THROUGH INCINERATION, IS THE MOST COMMON METHOD FOR
HARNESSING BIOMASS. OTHER METHODS CAN BE USE (I.E. COMBUSTION), BUT THE EXTENT OF THE
REACTION IS DETERMINED BY THE AMOUNT OF OXYGEN AVAILABLE IN THE BIOMASS. "FOREST RESIDUE"
(I.E. GROUND BRUSH, CLIPPINGS, BRANCHES AND FALLEN TREES) IS MOST OFTEN USED IN THE INCINERA-
TION PROCESS.

CHEMICAL CONVERSION - OCCASIONALLY CHEMICAL PROCESSES ARE USED TO CONVERT BIOMASS INTO
ALTERNATIVE AND MORE COMMON FUELS.

BIOCHEMICAL CONVERSION - THIS METHOD HARNESSES MICRO-ORGANISMS TO BREAK DOWN BIOMASS,
THROUGH THE PROCESSES OF ANAEROBIC DIGESTION, FERMENTATION, OR COMPOSTING. BIOMASS IS
CONVERTED INTO USABLE ENERGY IN THE FORMS OF BIODIESEL, HYDROGEN GAS, AND OTHER FUEL
SOURCES. (REFER TO BIOGAS SECTION FOR MORE INFORMATION)

THE DISADVANTAGES OF BIOMASS: ALTHOUGH BIOMASS IS A HIGHLY RENEWABLE ENERGY SOURCE, IT
EMITS A LARGE AMOUNT OF POLLUTION DUE TO THE WAY ITS ENERNY IS MOST COMMONLY HARNESSED:
INCINERATION. BURNING BIOMASS RELEASES AIR POLLUTANTS SUCH AS CARBON MONOXIDE, NITROGEN
OXIDE, AND VOCS (VOLATILE ORGANIC COMPOUNDS), OFTEN AT LEVELS MUCH HIGHER THAN THAT OF
ALTERNATE FUEL SOURCES SUCH AS COAL OR GAS. THE ONLY DIFFERENCE IN THE PROCESS OF BIOMASS IS
THAT IT BIOMASS REMOVES CO2 FROM THE ATMOSPHERE WHILE IT IS GROWING, BUT THEN CO2 IS
RETURNED TO THE AMOSPHERE AFTER INCINERATION. THIS IS A SERIOUS FLAW IN THE BIOMASS CYCLE
THAT MUST BE ADDRESSED BEFORE IT CAN BE CONSIDERED A TRULY SUSTAINABLE ALTERNATIVE ENERGY
SOURCE.

BIOMASS CYCLE

1. TREES ARE CUT DOWN FOR BIOMASS
2. TREES ARE TRANSPORTED TO INCINERATOR
3. BIOMASS IS INCINERATED
4. INCINERATION RELEASES CO2 INTO ATMOSPHERE
5. CO2 IS ABSORBED BY TREES AND CONVERTED TO OXYGEN
6. SUN ALLOWS FOR PHOTOSYTHESIS, WHICH CONVERTS CO2 INTO OXYGEN
7. NATURAL DECAY AND TIME TURNS BIOMASS INTO FOSSIL FUELS SUCH AS COAL
8. COAL IS ALSO INCINERATED FOR ENERGY, RELEASING CO2 INTO THE ATMOSPHERE

Figure 1.40 Rebecca Crockett and Lauren Shaw, Thermal: Biomass (site analysis)

GREYWATER REUSE: THE PROCESS OF COLLECTING WATER USED FOR DOMESTIC USE THAT WOULD
TYPICALLY BE SENT TO A SEWER OR SEPTIC SYSTEM. GREYWATER DIFFERS FROM BLACKWATER,
WHICH IS WATER COLLECTED FROM TOILETS THAT CONTAINS HUMAN WASTE AND CAN NOT BE REUSED.

HOW SHOULD GREYWATER BE HANDLED?: GREYWATER IS TYPICALLY STORED IN AN UNDERGROUND
CISTERN. IF THE GREYWATER IS BEING USED FOR IRRIGATION PURPOSES, UNDERGROUND PIPES LEAD
FROM THE CISTERN TO THE AREA FOR IRRIGATION WHERE IT IS RELEASED, IN AN EFFORT TO AVOID
EXPOSURE TO HUMANS. GREYWATER CAN ALSO BE RECYCLED BACK INTO THE BUILDING FOR USE IN
TOILETS ONLY. AFTER USE IN A TOILET, IT IS THEN CONSIDERED BLACKWATER AND CAN NOT RETURN
TO THE GREYWATER CYCLE.

LEVELS OF PURIFICATION: DEPENDING ON THE END-USE OF THE GREYWATER, DIFFERENT PURIFICATION
SYSTEMS MAY BE IMPLEMENTED, OR THE GREYWATER MAY BE LEFT UNTREATED. IT IS NOT UNCOM-
MON TO COMBINE MORE THAN ONE OF THESE SYSTEMS IN ORDER TO ENSURE THE WATER HAS
REACHED MAXIMUM LEVEL OF PURIFICATION.

NO PURIFICATION - GREYWATER THAT UNDERGOES NO PURIFICATION PROCESSES HAS MORE LIMITED
REUSE CAPABILITIES. IT CAN BE USED FOR CERTAIN AGRICULTURAL SETTINGS, AND ALSO FOR DOMES-
TIC PURPOSES SUCH AS TOILET FLUSHING, WHERE IT DOES NOT COME INTO DIRECT CONTACT WITH
HUMANS.

MECHANICAL SYSTEMS PURIFICATION - THIS IS A TYPE OF "SOFT PROCESS", WHICH MEANS THAT IT IS
BASED ON PURIFICATION METHODS THAT OCCUR IN NATURE. SOFT MECHANICAL METHODS INCLUDE
SAND FILTRATION, UV RADIATION PURIFICATION, AND LAVA FILTRATION. THE KEY FILTRATION IN EACH
PROCESS IS FOUND IN NATURE, DISTINGUISHING IT FROM HARD PROCESS SYSTEMS.

BIOLOGICAL SYSTEMS PURIFICATION - ANOTHER TYPE OF "SOFT PROCESS" THAT GENERALLY INCORPO-
RATES PLANT LIFE. SOME EXAMPLES OF BIOLOGICAL PURIFICATION SYSTEMS INCLUDE TREATMENT
PONDS AND CONSTRUCTED WETLANDS. IN THIS SYSTEM, GREYWATER PASSES THROUGH A DENSE
COLLECTION OF REEDS AND OTHER DE-NUTRIFYING PLANTS WHICH PROCESS THE WATER AND PURIFY
IT NATURALLY. IN MANY CASES NON-PREDATORY FISH ARE ALSO ADDED TO THESE PONDS AND
RESEVOIRS IN ORDER TO CUT DOWN ON PESTS AND CREATE A COMPLETE ECOSYSTEM. THE DOWNSIDE
TO THIS SYSTEM IS THAT IT GENERALLY REQUIRES A LARGE AREA FOR IMPLETEMENTATION.

"HARD PROCESS" SYSTEMS PURIFICATION - THESE ARE SYSTEMS DESIGNED FOR PURIFICATION OF
LARGE QUANTITIES OF GREYWATER AND ARE NOT PRACTICAL FOR ON-SITE, SINGLE-FACILITY USE
EXAMPLES OF "HARD PROCESS" METHODS INCLUDE DISTILLATION AND MEMBRANE FILTRATION.

GREYWATER RECLAMATION WITH SAND FILTRATION SYSTEM

1. GUTTERS DELIVER RAIN WATER TO TANK
2. WATER COLLECTED FROM DOMESTIC USE: SINKS, SHOWERS, DISHWASHERS (NOT TOILETS)
3. WATER FLOWS THROUGH SAND AND GRAVEL FILTER
4. FILTERED WATER COLLECTS IN BELOW-GROUND CISTERN
5. WATER PUMPED TO HOUSE FOR USE IN TOILETS
6. BLACKWATER SENT TO SEPTIC SYSTEM
7. WATER USED FOR IRRIGATION

Figure 1.41 Rebecca Crockett and Lauren Shaw, Water: Greywater Reuse (site analysis)

RAINWATER COLLECTION: THE PROCESS OF COLLECTING AND HARNESSING RAINWATER FOR IRRIGATION AND/OR DOMESTIC REUSE PURPOSES. THE FUNCTIONALITY AND PURPOSE OF WATER COLLECTION IS COMPLETELY DEPENDENT UPON THE TYPE OF ENVIRONMENT WHERE THE WATER IS COLLECTED.

RAINWATER FOR IRRIGATION: THE LOCATION OF THE RAINWATER CATHCMENT SYSTEM DIRECTLY RELATES TO ITS USE FOR IRRIGATION. IF IT IS LOCATED IN A DRY, ARID ENVIRONMENT THAT RECEIVES LITTLE RAINFALL, IT IS NOT LIKELY THAT ENOUGH RAINWATER WILL BE HARNESSED TO MEET THE IRRIGATION DEMANDS TO MAINTAIN A GREEN YARD. A LESS RESOURCE-DEPENDANT AREA THAT RECIEVES RELATIVELY FREQUENT RAINFALL WOULD BE THE APPROPRIATE LOCATION FOR

CATCHMENT TYPES: BARRELS (ABOVE GROUND) AND CISTERNS (BELOW GROUND) ARE THE TWO METH-ODS BY WHICH RAINWATER IS CAUGHT AND STORED. THE SIZE OF YOUR BARREL OR CISTERM IS DEPEN-DENT ON HOW MUCH RAIN THE PARTICULAR LOCATION RECIEVES AND WHAT THE DESIRED USE OF THE RAINWATER. IF YOU LIVE IN AN AREA THAT RECEIVES PERIODIC OR FREQUENT RAIN AND ONLY WANT TO USE THE WATER TO IRRIGATE A SMALL SECTION OF GARDEN, RAIN BARRELS THAT FEED A HOSE WITH GRAVITY WOULD SUFFICE. RAIN WATER WOULD NEED TO BE COLLECTED IN A CISTERN (UNDERGROUND) IF YOU WANT TO USE IT FOR IRRIGATION AND FUNCTIONS IN THE HOUSE (FLUSHING TOILETS, ETC).

BELOW-GROUND IRRIGATION & DOMESTIC REUSE CISTERN

① GUTTERS DELIVER RAIN WATER TO TANK

② WATER FLOWS THROUGH SAND AND GRAVEL FILTER

③ FILTERED WATER COLLECTS IN BELOW-GROUND CISTERN

④ WATER USED FOR IRRIGATION

⑤ WATER PUMPED TO HOUSE FOR DOMESTIC USE

ABOVE-GROUND IRRIGATION BARREL

① GUTTERS DELIVER RAIN WATER TO TANK

② WATER COLLECTED IN ABOVE-GROUND RAIN BARREL

③ WATER IS PASSIVELY DELIVERED TO DESIRED LOCATION BY GRAVITY

Figure 1.42 Rebecca Crockett and Lauren Shaw, Water: Rainwater Collection (site analysis)

GROUND SOURCE HEAT PUMP: ALSO KNOWN AS A GEOTHERMAL HEAT PUMP, IS A CENTRAL HEATING AND/OR COOLING SYSTEM THAT DERIVES HEAT FROM THE EARTH. BECAUSE THE SUBTERRANIAN TEMPERATURE OF THE EARTH REMAINS AT A RELATIVELY CONSTANT TEMPERA-TURE OF 55 DEGREES FAHRENHEIT, IT IS A NATURAL HEAT SOURCE. THE EARTH IS USED AS A HEAT SOURCE IN THE WINTER, PULLING HEAT UP FROM THE GROUND, AND AS A HEAT SINK IN THE SUMMER.

WHY USE A GROUND SOURCE HEAT PUMP? THE DAY-TO-DAY COSTS OF HEATING AND COOLING A HOUSE ARE GREATLY REDUCED WITH THE USE OF A GROUND SOURCE HEAT PUMP BECAUSE OF THE REDUCTION IN THE AMOUNT OF ENERGY REQUIRED TO RUN MECHANICAL SYSTEMS. WHETHER A BUILDING IS ON OR OFF THE GRID, GROUND SOURCE HEAT PUMPS CAN SIGNIFICANTLY REDUCE THE NEED FOR ADDITIONAL COSTLY RESOURCES NEEDED TO HEAT OR COOL A BUILDING.

HOW DOES A GROUND SOURCE HEAT PUMP WORK? PIPES ARE PLACED AT LEAST 6 FEET BENEATH THE EARTH'S SURFACE WHERE THE TEMPERATURE REMAINS CONSTANT (~55 DEGREES F). BY RUNNING WATER OR REFRIGERANT THROUGH THEM (USUALLY GLYCOL), THE VERTICAL OR HORIZONTAL UNDERGROUND PIPES ARE HEATED BY THE AMBIENT TEMPERATURE OF THE EARTH. THE WATER OR GLYCOL CARRIES THE HEAT UP TO THE SURFACE WHERE IT IS RELEASED INTO THE BUILDING AS HEAT. IN THE SUMMER, THIS PROCESS CAN BE REVERSED, REMOVING HEAT FROM THE BUILDING AND TRANSFERRING IT BACK INTO THE GROUND.

VERTICAL VS HORIZONAL IMPLEMENATION: THE AMOUNT OF LAND AVAILABLE DETERMINES HOW THE GROUND SOURCE HEAT PUMP IS INSTALLED.

VERTICAL - WELLS ARE DRILLED DEEP INTO THE GROUND, AND PIPES ARE RUN PERPENDICULAR TO THE EARTH'S SURFACE. THIS IS THE METHOD TYPICALLY EMPLOYED FOR BUILDINGS IN MORE DENSELY POPULATED AREAS THAT MAY NOT HAVE ACCESS TO OPEN LAND.

HORIZONTAL - TRENCHES ARE DUG HORIZONTALLY, AND PIPES ARE RUN PARALLEL TO THE EARTH'S SURFACE. THIS METHOD REQUIRES MUCH MORE SURFACE AREA AND IS BETTER FOR REMOTE BUILDINGS ON LARGE PLOTS OF LAND. THIS PROCESS IS TYPICALLY LESS EPENSIVE THAN THE VERTICAL WELL METHOD.

HORIZONTAL CLOSED LOOP GROUND SOURCE HEAT PUMP

① CIRCULATION PUMP

② HEAT EXCHANGE ABSORBS/DISCHARGES HEAT

③ OPTIONAL HOT WATER HEATER

④ COLD WATER TRANSFER TO BUILDING

⑤ HOT WATER TRANSFER TO BUILDING

⑥ BURIED LOOP ABSORBS/DISCHARGES HEAT

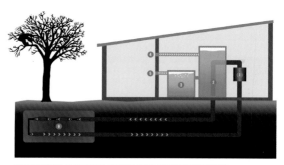

Figure 1.43 Rebecca Crockett and Lauren Shaw, Thermal: Ground Source Heat Pumps (site analysis)

GROUND SOURCE HEAT PUMPS 2

OPEN LOOP VS CLOSED LOOP: THE TYPE OF SOIL AND ACCESS TO A GROUNDWATER SOURCE DETERMINE WHETHER A CLOSED OR OPEN LOOP SYSTEM IS USED.

OPEN LOOP - THIS IS THE IDEAL SYSTEM, BEING THE MOST COST EFFECTIVE, BUT RELIES ON PARTICULAR SOIL CONDITIONS AND ACCESS TO A WELL OR GROUND WATER. IN THIS STSYTEM, WELL WATER, HEATED BY THE AMBIENT TEMPERATURE OF THE EARTH, IS DRAWN UP AND INTO A MECHANICAL SYSTEM WITHIN THE BUILDING. THIS MECHANICAL SYSTEM CONTAINS AN ANTIFREEZE AGENT (SUCH AS GLYCOL OR METHANOL), AND A HEAT EXCHANGE TAKES PLACE WITHOUT THE ANTIFREEZE AGENT AND WELL WATER BEING IN DIRECT CONTACT WITH ONE ANOTHER - THEY REMAIN SEPARATED BY THE PIPING THAT DREW UP THE WELL WATER. THIS ALLOWS THE WELL WATER TO BE RETURNED TO THE GROUND IN THE SAME CONDITION THAT IT WAS EXTRACTED.

CLOSED LOOP - WHEN SOIL CONDITIONS AND/OR ACCESS TO GROUND WATER ARE NOT AVAILABLE, A CLOSED LOOP SYSTEM MUST BE EMPLOYED. THIS SYSTEM RELIES ON THE HEAT EXCHANGE OF GROUND HEAT TO TUBES FILLED WITH ANTIFREEZE LIQUIDS THAT CARRY THE HEAT BACK TO THE BUILDING. THE ANTIFREEZE AGENT USED IS USUALLY EITHER GLYCOL OR METHANOL, SINCE BOTH ARE BIODEGRADABLE SUBSTANCES. IT IS ONLY CLOSED LOOP SYSTEMS THAT REQUIRE A VERTICAL OR HORIZONTAL PIPE SYSTEM.

GROUND SOURCE HEAT PUMP COMPONENTS

1. CIRCULATION PUMP
2. HEAT EXCHANGE ABSORBS/DISCHARGES HEAT
3. OPTIONAL HOT WATER HEATER
4. COLD WATER TRANSFER TO BUILDING
5. HOT WATER TRANSFER TO BUILDING
6. BURIED LOOP ABSORBS/DISCHARGES HEAT
7. WELL WATER RETURN
8. WELL WATER SUPPLY

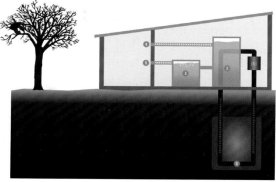

HORIZONTAL CLOSED LOOP GROUND SOURCE HEAT PUMP

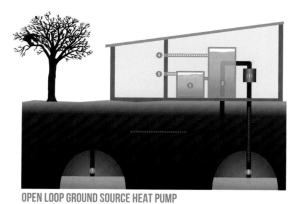

OPEN LOOP GROUND SOURCE HEAT PUMP

Figure 1.44 Rebecca Crockett and Lauren Shaw, Thermal: Ground Source Heat Pumps 2 (site analysis)

BASELINE BUILDING DATA REDUCED HEAT ISLAND POTENTIAL

ALTITUDE 350.0 M
LATITUDE 37.3°
LONGITUDE -80.0°

ANALYSIS: THE BUILDING'S DARK ROOF AND PAVED SURROUNDINGS CONTRIBUTE TO THE HEAT ISLAND EFFECT IN ROANOKE. THIS EFFECT CAN RAISE TEMPERATURES SEVERAL DEGREES, CAUSING INCREASED COOLING LOADS AND HIGHER ENERGY DEMANDS.

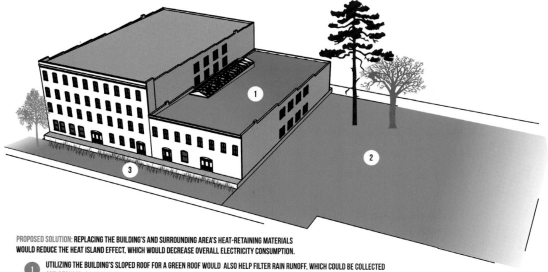

PROPOSED SOLUTION: REPLACING THE BUILDING'S AND SURROUNDING AREA'S HEAT-RETAINING MATERIALS WOULD REDUCE THE HEAT ISLAND EFFECT, WHICH WOULD DECREASE OVERALL ELECTRICITY CONSUMPTION.

1. UTILIZING THE BUILDING'S SLOPED ROOF FOR A GREEN ROOF WOULD ALSO HELP FILTER RAIN RUNOFF, WHICH COULD BE COLLECTED AND RESUSED AS GREYWATER.

2. TRANSFORM THE BUILDING'S LARGE PARKING LOT INTO GREEN SPACE, POSSIBLY EVEN FOR AGRICULTURAL USE.

3. REMOVE UNNECESSARY PAVED AREA BETWEEN THE SIDEWALK AND THE BUILDING'S ENTRANCE AND REPLACE WITH PLANTS TO COUNTER CO2 EMISSIONS.

Figure 1.45 Rebecca Crockett and Lauren Shaw, Baseline Building Data: Reduced Heat Island Potential (site analysis)

All of these considerations could then be applied to the actual building site.

One of the most daunting questions is how to go beyond the mere specification of sustainable (or what is hoped to be sustainable) materials. A useful framework to consider might be one of the previously mentioned approaches. Further, the research of the site itself lends a layer of understanding for the design that exceeds basic materiality and makes the design regionally appropriate.

A Proposed Framework

In his book *Earth in Mind*, David Orr, Paul Sears Distinguished Professor of Environmental Studies and Politics at Oberlin College, claimed, "no student should graduate from any educational institution without a basic comprehension of things like the following:

- The laws of thermodynamics
- The basic principles of ecology
- Carrying capacity
- Energetics
- Least-cost; end-use analysis
- Limits of technology
- Appropriate scale
- Sustainable agriculture and forestry
- Steady state economics
- Environmental ethics" (2004)

An understanding of these 10 over-reaching concepts can also inform any design. For example, environmental ethics stresses the rights of all species.

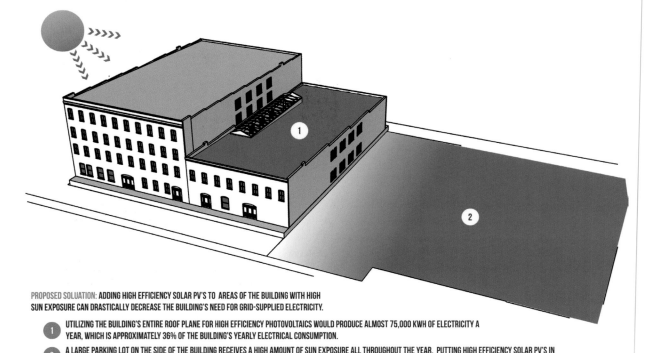

BASELINE BUILDING DATA PHOTOVOLTAIC POTENTIAL

ALTITUDE **350.0 M**
LATITUDE **37.3°**
LONGITUDE **-80.0°**

ANALYSIS: ELECTRICITY MAKES UP 75% OF THE BUILDING'S TOTAL ENERGY CONSUMPTION. THE BUILDING'S TOTAL ELECTRICAL CONSUMPTION IS APPROXIMATELY 205,000 KWH PER YEAR, AND IS USED TO POWER MISCELLANOUS EQUIPMENT, LIGHTING, AND HVAC SYSTEMS.

PROPOSED SOLUATION: ADDING HIGH EFFICIENCY SOLAR PV'S TO AREAS OF THE BUILDING WITH HIGH SUN EXPOSURE CAN DRASTICALLY DECREASE THE BUILDING'S NEED FOR GRID-SUPPLIED ELECTRICITY.

1 UTILIZING THE BUILDING'S ENTIRE ROOF PLANE FOR HIGH EFFICIENCY PHOTOVOLTAICS WOULD PRODUCE ALMOST 75,000 KWH OF ELECTRICITY A YEAR, WHICH IS APPROXIMATELY 36% OF THE BUILDING'S YEARLY ELECTRICAL CONSUMPTION.

2 A LARGE PARKING LOT ON THE SIDE OF THE BUILDING RECEIVES A HIGH AMOUNT OF SUN EXPOSURE ALL THROUGHOUT THE YEAR. PUTTING HIGH EFFICIENCY SOLAR PV'S IN THIS AREA COULD HAVE THE POTENTIAL TO PRODUCE ENOUGH ELECTRICITY TO COVER ALL OF THE BUILDING'S ELECTRICAL NEEDS.

Figure 1.46 Rebecca Crockett and Lauren Shaw, Baseline Building Data: Photovoltaic Potential (site analysis)

ENERGY USE: FUEL

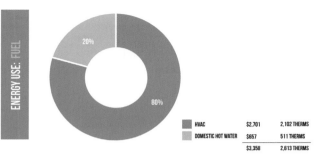

ANALYSIS: MOST FUEL IS USED TO HEAT THE BUILDING DURING THE WINTER. VERY LITTLE FUEL IS NEEDED TO HEAT WATER.

PROPOSED SOLUTION: UTILIZING PASSIVE SOLAR TECHNIQUES WILL HELP RETAIN THE SUN'S NATURAL ENERGY DURING COLDER WEATHER AND LESSEN THE NEED FOR ARTIFICIAL HEAT.

SOLAR ENERGY CAN ALSO BE USED TO PASSIVELY HEAT WATER, AND POSSIBLY ELIMINATE THE NEED FOR FUEL ENTIRELY.

HVAC	$2,701	2,102 THERMS
DOMESTIC HOT WATER	$657	511 THERMS
	$3,358	2,613 THERMS

ENERGY USE: ELECTRICITY

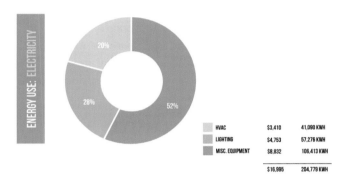

ANALYSIS: MOST ELECTRICITY IS USED TO POWER MISC. EQUIPMENT. THIS INCLUDES BUT IS NOT LIMITED TO: COMPUTERS, COPIERS, BREAK ROOM APPLIANCES, AND OTHER VARIOUS ELECTRONIC DEVICES. LIGHTING AND HVAC SYSTEMS CONSUME THE OTHER REMAINING HALF OF ELECTRICITY.

PROPOSED SOLUTION: THE ELECTRICAL LOAD FOR MISC. EQUIPMENT CAN BE MINIMIZED BY SPECIFYING ENERGY EFFICIENT DEVICES [SUCH AS THOSE WITH ENERGY STAR CERTIFICATION], AND ALSO BY POWERING DOWN ELECTRONICS WHEN THEY ARE NOT IN USE AFTER WORK HOURS.

USING ENERGY EFFICIENT LIGHTING SUCH AS LEDS OR COMPACT FLUORESCENTS CAN REDUCE THE AMOUNT OF ENERGY USED TO ILLUMINATE THE SPACE. LIGHTING FIXTURES CAN ALSO BE PLACED ON A TIMER TO ENSURE THE LIGHTS ARE ACTUALLY NEEDED. MAXIMIZING THE AMOUNT OF DAYLIGHT THAT PENETRATES THE SPACE ALSO ELIMINATES THE NEED FOR SUPPLEMENTAL ARTIFICIAL LIGHT.

HVAC SYSTEMS DEMAND THE MOST ELECTRICITY DURING SUMMER MONTHS WHEN AIR CONDITIONING IS USED. BY EMPLOYING NATURAL VENTILATION TECHNIQUES AND USING PROPER SHADING DEVICES, UNWANTED SOLAR HEAT GAIN CAN BE AVOIDED.

HVAC	$3,410	41,090 KWH
LIGHTING	$4,753	57,276 KWH
MISC. EQUIPMENT	$8,832	106,413 KWH
	$16,995	204,779 KWH

Figure 1.47 Rebecca Crockett and Lauren Shaw, Energy Use: Fuel and Electricity (site analysis)

ANNUAL CARBON EMISSIONS

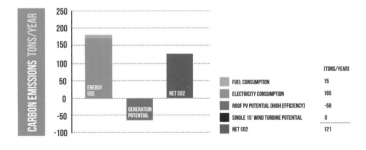

	[TONS/YEAR]
FUEL CONSUMPTION	15
ELECTRICITY CONSUMPTION	165
ROOF PV POTENTIAL [HIGH EFFICIENCY]	-59
SINGLE 15' WIND TURBINE POTENTIAL	0
NET CO2	121

ANALYSIS: MOST OF THE BUILDING'S CARBON EMISSIONS CAN BE ATTRIBUTED TO ENERGY CONSUMPTION. NET CO2 EMISSIONS COULD BE LESSENED BY ALMOST ONE THIRD [59 TONS/YEAR] BY GENERATING SUSTAINABLE ENERGY.

PROPOSED SOLUTION: HIGH EFFICIENCY PV PANELS CAN BE INSTALLED ON BOTH THE ROOF AND SURROUNDING LAND TO GENERATE SUSTAINABLE ENERGY AND DIMINISH THE BUILDINGS' NEGATIVE IMPACT ON THE ENVIRONMENT.

ANNUAL ENERGY USE: COST

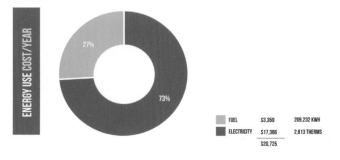

ANALYSIS: ELECTRICITY COMPRISES MOST OF THE TENANTS' BUILDING EXPENSES. FUEL ONLY ACCOUNTS FOR APPROXIMATELY ONE FOURTH OF THE TOTAL ENERGY EXPENSES AND IS CONSIDERABLY HIGHER DURING THE WINTER.

PROPOSED SOLUTION: BY UTILIZING HIGH EFFICIENCY PV PANELS, THE TENANT COULD SAVE UP TO $6,000 EACH YEAR. IF PV PANELS WERE PLACED IN AREAS OTHER THAN THE ROOF, EVEN MORE SAVINGS COULD BE ATTAINED.

ALTHOUGH FUEL USE IS SMALL IN COMPARISON, IT COULD STILL BE LESSENED BY INSTALLING A BIO-DIGESTER TO GENERATE SUSTAINABLE FUEL.

FUEL	$3,359	209,232 KWH
ELECTRICITY	$17,366	2,613 THERMS
	$20,725	

Figure 1.48 Rebecca Crockett and Lauren Shaw, Annual Carbon Emissions and Annual Energy Use: Cost (site analysis)

RENEWABLE ENERGY POTENTIAL

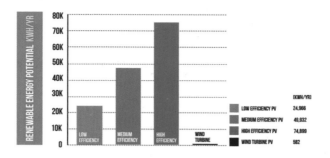

ANALYSIS: ALTHOUGH THERE IS NO POTENTIAL FOR WIND GENERATED ENERGY, HIGH EFFICIENCY PVS COULD GENERATE UP TO 49,932 KWH EACH YEAR. THIS ONLY ACCOUNTS FOR PVS INSTALLED ON THE ROOF - PVS INSTALLED ON SURROUNDING LAND COULD POTENTIALLY PROVIDE ENOUGH ENERGY TO MEET THE ENTIRE BUILDINGS' ENERGY NEEDS.

PROPOSED SOLUTION: HIGH EFFECIENCY PVS SHOULD BE INSTALLED ON BOTH THE ROOF AND SURROUNDING LAND TO ELIMINATE THE BUILDING'S NEED FOR GRID SUPPLIED ENERGY. FOR MAXIMUM EFFECIENCY, THE PV PANELS SHOULD BE PLACED AT A 30 DEGREE ANGLE IN DECEMBER AND 76 DEGREE ANGLE IN JULY. PIVOTING PV PANELS WILL ALLOW FOR ROTATION TO VARYING DEGREES THROUGHOUT THE YEAR TO ENSURE PROPER PLACEMENT IN RELATION TO THE SUN.

	[KWH/YR]
LOW EFFICIENCY PV	24,966
MEDIUM EFFICIENCY PV	49,932
HIGH EFFICIENCY PV	74,898
WIND TURBINE PV	582

LIFE CYCLE ENERGY USE & COST

LIFE CYCLE ELECTRICITY USE	6,337,516 KWH
LIFE CYCLE FUEL USE	71,329 THERMS
LIFE CYCLE ENERGY COST	$280, 423

* CALCULATIONS FOR 30 YEAR LIFE AND 6.1% DISCOUNT RATE

ANALYSIS: MOST ELECTRICITY IS USED TO POWER MISC. EQUIPMENT. THIS INCLUDES BUT IS NOT LIMITED TO: COMPUTERS, COPIERS, BREAK ROOM APPLIANCES, AND OTHER VARIOUS ELECTRONIC DEVICES. LIGHTING AND HVAC SYSTEMS CONSUME THE OTHER REMAINING HALF OF ELECTRICITY.

PROPOSED SOLUTION: THE ELECTRICAL LOAD FOR MISC. EQUIPMENT CAN BE MINIMIZED BY SPECIFYING ENERGY EFFICIENT DEVICES (SUCH AS THOSE WITH ENERGY STAR CERTIFICATION), AND ALSO BY POWERING DOWN ELECTRONICS WHEN THEY ARE NOT IN USE AFTER WORK HOURS.

USING ENERGY EFFICIENT LIGHTING SUCH AS LEDS OR COMPACT FLUORESCENTS CAN REDUCE THE AMOUNT OF ENERGY USED TO ILLUMINATE THE SPACE. LIGHTING FIXTURES CAN ALSO BE PLACED ON A TIMER TO ENSURE THE LIGHTS ARE ACTUALLY NEEDED. MAXIMIZING THE AMOUNT OF DAYLIGHT THAT PENETRATES THE SPACE ALSO ELIMINATES THE NEED FOR SUPPLEMENTAL ARTIFICIAL LIGHT.

HVAC SYSTEMS DEMAND THE MOST ELECTRICITY DURING SUMMER MONTHS WHEN AIR CONDITIONING IS USED. BY EMPLOYING NATURAL VENTILATION TECHNIQUES AND USING PROPER SHADING DEVICES, UNWANTED SOLAR HEAT GAIN CAN BE AVOIDED.

Figure 1.49 Rebecca Crockett and Lauren Shaw, Renewable Energy Potential and Life-Cycle Energy Use and Cost (site analysis)

BASELINE BUILDING DATA FUEL & ELECTRICITY CONSUMPTION

ALTITUDE **350.0 M**
LATITUDE **37.3°**
LONGITUDE **-80.0°**

ANALYSIS: ELECTRICITY AND FUEL MAKES UP 75% AND 25% OF ENERGY CONSUMPTION, RESPECTIVELY. ELECTRICITY CONSUMPTIONS REMAINS HIGHER THAN 15,000 KWH ALL YEAR, PEAKING IN THE SUMMER MONTHS DUE TO INCREASED COOLING LOADS. FUEL CONSUMPTION IS USED PRIMARILY IN THE WINTER MONTHS FOR HEATING LOADS, DROPPING BELOW 50 THERMS FOR THE SUMMER MONTHS.

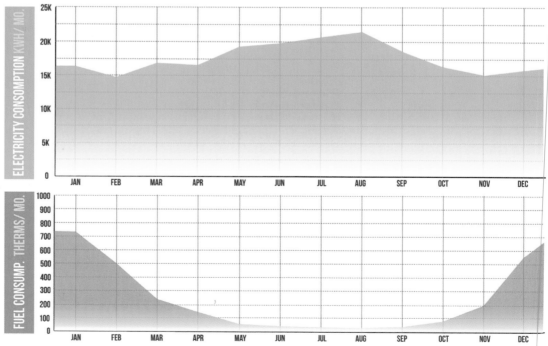

Figure 1.50 Rebecca Crockett and Lauren Shaw, Baseline Building Data: Fuel and Electricity Consumption (site analysis)

Taking this sort of approach to a new site requires a designer to consider all local flora and fauna on a site with an eye toward protecting native habitats. Further, a consideration of the carrying capacity of the place might suggest that new construction is not the right solution if insufficient water is found, for example.

Outline for a Typical Process

1. *Pre-Design*
   - Inspiration and conceptual approach (based on ecology, carrying capacity, appropriate scale, and environmental ethics)
   - Program
   - Precedent studies
   - Evidence-Based Design/information gathering/research

2. *Schematic Design*
   - Plan
     - Adjacency matrix
     - Bubbles/blocks
     - Circulation studies
     - Preliminary scenarios that respond to concept and program
   - 3D Thumbnail sketching and preliminary SketchUp modeling
   - Develop in elevation and section

3. *Design Development*
   - Enter in computer
   - Select materials, finishes, furniture, and equipment (least cost-end use and economics)
   - Develop in elevation and section (in detail)
   - Detailing of custom work

4. *Final Presentation*
   - Production drawings
   - Possible partial construction documents/specifications

Discussion Questions and Exercises

1. Engage in a group discussion about the approaches to sustainability mentioned in this chapter. Where do you find yourself unable to move forward with your design? What level are you comfortable taking a project to? What else do you need to know to complete a 100 percent sustainably designed project? What does this mean to you?
2. Create a useful or beautiful (ideally both) object or installation from 100 percent found and used everyday objects.
3. Using the frameworks outlines by Guy and Farmer, how would you characterize biomimicry? Cradle-to-cradle? Can you give an example for each approach from this chapter?

Key Terms

Architecture 2030

carbon neutral

carbon offset

eco-cultural

eco-medical

eco-technic

integrated project delivery

ISO 14024:1999

life-cycle costing

net zero

salicornia

transmaterial

zero carbon

zero-energy building

Sources

Architecture 2030. 2010. Accessed June 25, 2013. http://architecture2030.org/2030_challenge/the_2030_challenge.

Bayley, Roger. 2012. The Challenge Series. http://www.thechallengeseries.ca/chapter-07/net-zero/.

Carbon Neutral Building. 2012. Accessed June 25, 2013. http://carbonneutralbuilding.net/.

Cradle to Cradle Certified Program. 2013. Accessed June 25. http://c2ccertified.org/.

———. 2013. Accessed June 25. http://c2c.mbdc.com/c2c/.

Department for Communities and Local Government. 2008. *Definition of Zero Carbon Homes and Non-Domestic Buildings*. Eland House, Bressenden Place, London: Crown Copyright.

Department of Energy, EnergyStar. http://www.energystar.gov/index.cfm?c=about.ab_index.

Forest Stewardship Council. http://www.fsc.org/about-fsc.html.

Gensler. 2010. "Global Leadership for Changing Times: Redefine What is Possible through the Power of Design." Presented at the 2010 Design Futures Council 9th Annual Leadership Summit on Sustainable Design, Atlanta, GA, October 2010.

Good Environmental Choice Australia. "About." http://www.geca.org.au/about/

Green, Michael. 2010. "Recycled Interiors." Accessed April 17, 2012. http://www.michaelbgreen.com.au/recycled-interiors.

GreenGuard Certification from UL Environment. 2013. Home page. Accessed June 25. http://www.greenguard.org/en/index.aspx

Guy, Brad, and Nicholas Ciarimboli. 2006. *Design for Disassembly Guide*. Hamer Center for Community Design, Pennsylvania State University for King County, Washington. Accessed June 25, 2013. http://your.kingcounty.gov/solidwaste/greenbuilding/documents/Design_for_Disassembly-guide.pdf

Guy, S. and Farmer, G. 2001. "Reinterpreting Sustainable Architecture: The Place of Technology," *Journal of Architectural Education*, Vol. 54, No. 3. 140–8.

HOK. 2012. Homepage. Accessed June 25, 2013. http://www.hok.com/.

Kats, G. 2009. *Greening Our Built World: Costs, Benefits and Strategies*. Washington DC: Island Press.

Mattheissen, L.F., and Morris, P. 2004. "Costing Green: A Comprehensive Cost Database and Budgeting Methodology" Davis Langdon Corporation. Accessed June 26, 2013. http://www.davislangdon.com/upload/images/publications/USA/2004%20Costing%20Green%20Comprehensive%20Cost%20Database.pdf

MBDC. 2013. Homepage. Accessed June 26. http://mbdc.com/detail.aspx?linkid=2&sublink=8. (Now found at http://www.c2ccertified.org/).

National Resources Defense Council. 2012. Accessed April 17. http://www.nrdc.org/buildinggreen/links/default.asp#lifecycle.

Perkins + Will. 2012. Accessed June 23. http://transparency.perkinswill.com/Main.

Pleass, Shantk, and Paul Torcellini. 2010. "Net Zero Energy Buildings: A Classification System Based on Renewable Energy Supply Options." Technical Report NREL/TP-550-44586. Oak Ridge, TN: U.S. Department of Energy. Accessed June 25, 2013. http://www.nrel.gov/sustainable_nrel/pdfs/44586.pdf.

Public Architecture. 2013. Homepage. Accessed June 23 http://www.publicarchitecture.org.

SCS Global Services. 2013. Scientific Certification Systems. Accessed June 25. http://www.scsglobalservices.com/bifma-level?scscertified=1.

SOM. 2010. "Recognizing the Challenge: The Need for a 100-Year Vision for the Great Lakes and St. Lawrence River Region." Presented at the 2010 Design Futures Council 9th Annual Leadership Summit on Sustainable Design, Atlanta, GA, October.

Stewart, Lea. 2009. "100% Recycled Cardboard Interior Is Totally Tubular." *Inhabit.com,* December 10. Accessed June 23, 2013. http://inhabitat.com/100-recycled-cardboard-interior-is-totally-tubular/

The Challenge Series. 2012. "Millennium Water." Accessed February 16. http://www.thechallengeseries.ca/chapter-07/net-zero/

Thomas, James. 2012. "Net Zero Buildings." Green Resources on Glumac. Accessed February 16. http://www.glumac.com/articles/Net_Zero_Buildings.html.

Timberlake, J., and S. Kieran. 2004. *Refabricating Architecture: How to Manufacturing Methodologies are Poised to Transform Building Construction.* New York: McGraw-Hill.

U.S. Department of Energy. 2012. "Zero Energy Buildings." http://zeb.buildinggreen.com/.

USGBC. 2013. "About." http://www.usgbc.org/DisplayPage.aspx?CMSPageID=124.

Online Tools for Life-Cycle Costing

International Design Center for the Environment

http://www-1.idce.org/

Whole Building Design Guide—Life Cycle Tools

http://www.wbdg.org/index.php

Federal Energy Management Program

http://www1.eere.energy.gov/femp/program/lifecycle.html

2

RETAIL
PROJECTS

....

Objectives

- Students will understand the current issues and trends in sustainable retail design.

- Students will be familiar with the organizations and resources for retail design trends and guidelines.

- Students will be able to describe the unique features of sustainable retail design.

Overview

"Sustainable retail" may sound like an oxymoron but in fact, many retail design clients and retailers seek sustainable facilities. So, too, do consumers; many people want to feel they are doing the right thing for the environment, even when shopping. Subsequently, this mindset has impacted the design of retail spaces.

Current Issues in Retail Design

The retail industry must contend with several issues, some of which it has not faced previously. These include online retail, world economic conditions, and reduced consumption patterns. Trends within the marketplace have a profound effect on design, and the need to respond to the economy, an ever-increasing use of Internet shopping by consumers, and the need to provide immediate service have led to several new phenomena in retail design.

Trends

The Retail Industry Leaders Association (RILA) launched the **Retail Sustainability Initiative (RSI)** in 2007 to address regulatory compliance and sustainability challenges in retail through a coordinated effort. RILA is comprised of retail industry leaders and advocates for the retail industry in Washington, D.C., informing lawmakers about the impacts of governmental decisions on the retail sector. A 2012 report produced by RILA combines the efforts of its 20 retail partners:

Belk
Best Buy
The Gap Stores, Inc.
H-E-B
The Home Depot
IKEA
JCPenney
Lowe's
Meijer
Petco
PetSmart
Publix
Safeway
Sears
Staples
Target
VF Corporation
Walgreen's
Walmart
Whole Foods Markets

The organization's *2012 Retail Sustainability Report: Successes, Challenges, and a Vision for the Future* focuses on three principal areas: the operational footprint of retail, the product journey, and the integration of stores into the community. Additionally, five domains comprise RILA's sustainability initiative: energy and greenhouse gas emissions; waste and recycling; product and supply chains; environmental compliance; and communicating, reporting, and engaging. Examples of what retailers can do to comply with these five domains includes installing building automation systems (monitors, alarms, and controls), retrofitting old heating systems, and installing low-energy lighting systems that use LEDs or fluorescent lamps to replace higher-use halogen and incandescent lamps.

These initiatives serve to help RILA share best practices with its members, develop future practices, and communicate and advocate for increased sustainability efforts in the retail industry. The organization works with several stakeholders including landlords, suppliers, employees, the Environmental Protection Agency, and retail and product manufacturers. By providing tangible advice to stakeholders the goal is that they can then create sustainable buildings. For example, retailers might minimize waste by recycling plastic, cardboard, and construction waste, thus diverting it from the landfill. The RSI Report of 2012 provides such guidance to all of its constituent groups.

According to the most recent RILA report, the top four trends in sustainable retail are:

1. Working across sectors to achieve sustainability goals
2. Turning from sustainability as a cost- and risk-reduction measure to an opportunity for business growth
3. Developing systems for continuous improvement
4. Fostering transparency in operations within the supply chain (8)

Future Directions

In addition to enumerating the four trends mentioned, RILA also projects trends in the retail industry it sees taking place within the next five to ten years. These include:

- Sustainability will become integrated into the retail industry.
- The drive to manage supply chain impacts will transform retail-supplier relationships.
- Industry collaboration will become the standard.
- Business models will evolve as consumption habits change (9).

The benefits of a more sustainable approach include a more efficient business, less risk, new innovation, retention and recruitment of top talent, new geographies, new products, and improved reputations (9–10). Retailers have recognized the push by consumers to be more sustainable and have begun to recognize that sustainable practices equate to good business. As such, retailers are exploring several ways to change the industry.

The Pop-Up Store Phenomenon

One such option, a **pop-up store**, is a temporary retail venue located in an empty building, a small storefront, or sometimes along a street. The pop-up store provides one way in which retailers seek to bridge the economy and the need to be instantly responsive while also taking low-risk actions. Composed of pre-assembled parts and constructed on-site, the pop-up store often resides within an abandoned retail space or open, outdoor site. The temporary nature of the pop-up store allows for it to be more responsive than traditional retail venues. One of the first retailers to use the pop-up concept was Target, in 2002. Since then, it has created 20 other pop-up experiences.

The pop-up phenomenon has been dubbed "Nowism" by some trend watchers and is defined as "consumer ingrained lust for instant gratification [that] is being satisfied by a host of novel, important (offline and online) real-time products, services, and experiences." This trend is driven by abundance and a focus on the need for experiences that are in this case temporary and quick (Trendwatching 2009).

The very temporary nature of the pop-up store led writer Kylie Wroblaski to argue in an August 2012 article for *Interiors and Sources Magazine,* "Here Today Gone Tomorrow," that the inherent nature of pop-up stores is unsustainable in that they are temporary constructions that often end up in the landfill. This can be overcome, however, through the use of recycled and recyclable panels and parts that are constructed to be easily moved and deconstructed—like those used for trade show booths. Furthermore, component parts might be sold off as a part of the pop-up experience or reused in a future pop-up (18–19).

Online Retail versus the Retail Store

Many shoppers now use brick-and-mortar stores as a way to view products they will subsequently purchase for less money from someone else, in many cases online. One company that has tried to intervene in this process is bookseller Barnes and Noble. The company's e-reader, the Nook, allows customers to walk the store and download books they see and others they might be interested in. Free Wi-Fi and the introduction of coffee lounges either inside or next to the store create an environment where reader-customers are encouraged to stay in the store and download more books. Not all retailers have successfully embraced such a model, however.

The Abandoned Big Box Store

One phenomenon of late-20th-century retailing has been the abandonment of big box stores for even larger stores in nearby locations. Walmart is the prime example of this activity. Despite a corporate commitment to sustainability, since 1988 Walmart has been upsizing its stores once they have established a market share. When this happens, a Walmart Supercenter with enhanced services such as vision care, hair and nail salons, and groceries replaces a standard Walmart. Each Supercenter contains about 182,000 square feet versus a standard store that contains only about 106,000 square feet. These abandoned concrete boxes pepper the landscape of most towns and cities, as do abandoned strip malls and Main-Street storefronts. These empty buildings present an interesting challenge to designers: How do you reuse such real estate to contribute to the life and vitality of a community?

Additional Global Issues in the Retail Industry

Although retailers in all countries are not dealing with exactly the same issues, there are several that seem to overlap between the United Kingdom, the United States, and Australia. For example, according to its website, the key issues international professional services firm Price Waterhouse Cooper has described facing the retail industry in the UK are price deflation versus rising costs; overseas sourcing (especially China); consumer demographics (who is buying what), including the increased use of Internet buying; accounting and reporting requirements; and tax issues (www.pwc.co.uk). The U.S. retail industry faces these same concerns. According to the website of industry consulting firm Taylor Woodings, Australia is just beginning to see the entry of overseas brands into the marketplace on a large scale and faces rising interest rates, tighter markets (more competition and less profit), the high costs of doing business (paying for real estate and personnel), and online shopping (Taylorwoodings.com).

Research in Retail Design

Research in retail design has traditionally focused more on the psychology of buying and marketing than on the design of space for retail activities. Further, scientific study about retail design is a relatively new phenomenon (Quartier 2008). Recent areas of academic research in retail include lighting as an atmospheric tool (Quartier et al 2008), staging an authentic experience in retail (Plevoets, et al, 2010), and research on how to conduct research for retail design

(Petermens and Van Cleempoel, et al, 2010). Researchers Petermans and Van Cleempoel focus on three concepts in their research on retail design: holism (perception of entire in-store atmosphere), research in design (exploring design-related phenomenon), and tacit knowledge (the experiences of all stakeholders—customers, salespeople, merchandisers and others) (2010). The authors point out that retail design is still an emerging area of interior design. Most research that has been completed has been done from either a marketing or psychology point of view; information from both disciplines is required for good design (Quartier 2008).

Retail design is defined as encompassing "an understanding of what will work aesthetically in a retail environment, including tangible (i.e., fixed material) as well as intangible (i.e., immaterial or atmospheric) design elements" (Petermans and Van Cleempoel, 2010). Branding and differentiation from the competition are key components to the retailer. Defining the experience as distinct from other retailers is used to attract and retain customers. A need to know and understand the customers and actual shopping behavior is critical to the good design of retail spaces.

Quarteir, et al (2008) distill the retail experience into three separate areas of research—retailer/brand, consumer, and the translation into design or 3D. Within the realm of translation to 3D, there is exterior design, interior design (layout, routing, design language), in-store communication (signs and tone of voice), and visual merchandising. The study of the interior experiences has been termed **atmospherics.** The atmosphere is composed of both micro- and macro-level characteristics. Micro characteristics describe the physical characteristics of the retail space, such as color, light, music, and sound. Macro (also called "molar" by the authors) characteristics consist of emergent properties resulting from the micro characteristics—they are a sum of all the characteristics combined.

Of these characteristics in the interior retail environment (color, light, sound), the one that has received the most scientific research is lighting. Lighting research for retail environments concludes that people are drawn to light; therefore, lighting a particular place or item draws attention. Two studies (Boyce et al 1996; Cuttle and Brandston, 1995) show the link between lighting and profit through the use of energy-efficient light fixtures in a grocery store and a furniture store. Energy costs were increased by 25 percent and sales increased by 35 percent. Thus, well-designed sustainable light sources (fluorescent and LED) can increase sales.

Retail Design Considerations

During the past decade-plus, successful retailers have gone beyond bricks and mortar to include an Internet and social media presence. Many stores have integrated the use of the World Wide Web within their physical facilities. Additionally, store fixtures must be flexible for rapid and frequent change. Once constructed of permanent wood shelving, today's store fixture is movable, reconfigurable, and changeable. A variety of types of display help to create visual interest. Budgets are smaller, so attention to detail and creative reuse are paramount.

Research indicates that women are responsible for most purchases. According to Claire Behar, Senior Partner and Director of New Business Development at Fleishman-Hillard New York,

Over the next decade, women will control two-thirds of consumer wealth in the United States and be the beneficiaries of the largest transference of wealth in our country's history. Estimates range from $12 to $40 trillion. Many Boomer women will experience a double inheritance windfall, from both parents and husband. The Boomer woman is a consumer that luxury brands want to resonate with.

In light of this, providing gender-driven areas (separate areas for men and women) is important. Further, legibility (clear signage and navigation), and resting zones are increasingly important as the population ages. The largest segment of the population—roughly 76 million people—is composed of baby boomers, those born between 1946 and 1964, and this group is nearing retirement.

In order to design retail spaces, it is important to understand some basic environmental conditions that impact human behavior. Kim Johnson, professor in the Department of Design, Housing, and Apparel at the University of Minnesota, shares the concepts of environmental psychologist Paco Underhill as presented in his book *Why We Buy*. Underhill describes several techniques that can be used to either enhance or deter sales. For example, a **transition zone** can be used to slow the shopper's pace by placing product in the middle of a wide aisle. **Chevroning** involves angling the shelves to increase buying by placing the product toward the shopper. In contrast, the **Butt Brush Effect** deters shoppers from lingering in an area; crowded shoppers will leave when they bump into things. According to Underhill, providing a seating area indicates care for the customer and promotes a longer visit. One of the most important features of the design for a clothing retailer is the design of the dressing rooms. This is where most buying decisions are made, so it is important to make these areas as user friendly as possible. Flattering lighting, such as incandescent halogen or warm white fluorescent, sufficient space, strategic mirrors, and accessories such as benches and hooks all contribute to a positive experience for the customer. (Johnson 2004, 1).

Resources for Sustainable Design Information

There are several online resources for information on sustainable retail. As previously mentioned, many groups have been formed to assist retailers with making better green choices.

Green Retail Design
http://www.greenretaildecisions.com/
The Green Retail Decisions website covers current headlines in the retail industry and what various companies are currently doing to engage sustainability. For example, Kohl's department store's addition of more electric car charging stations was mentioned recently. The site provides research resources and news feeds about sustainable design efforts in the retail industry. Each year, a Green Retail Decisions Innovation Summit is held. The advisory board of the organization includes senior executives from Kroger, Walmart, Macy's, Staples, Walgreens, and other well-known retail chains. The mission of the organization is to help improve the profitability of retailers by providing best practices for sustainable retail including practices for the supply chain, marketing, and implementation of sustainability goals.

The Sustainability Consortium
http://www.sustainabilityconsortium.org
The Sustainability Consortium (TSC) is committed to reducing the environmental and social impacts of consumption. The website offers information on adopting a life-cycle approach as well as the science and tools needed to be more sustainable. TSC has global participation and works to improve consumer product sustainability. The group was formed in response to the extraordinary sustainability challenges the world will face when the population reaches 9 billion by 2050. The consortium members learn how to apply a life-cycle approach to their products.

IDEO: A Design and Innovation Consulting Firm
http://www.ideo.com/
According to Steven Bishop and Dana Cho of **IDEO**, understanding a shopper's context is the way to make green products and services that meet expectations. Bishop

and Cho claims 87 percent of people are seriously concerned about the environment, yet additional research shows this has little impact on buying decisions. Thus, designers wanting their work to have a positive effect on the environment must understand and address buyer motivation and methods of purchasing to provide a more sustainable experience. Without this understanding, designers could discourage sustainable behavior without intending to.

Bishop and Cho describe five different shopping modes observed in consumers: **mission mode** (get in and get out), **restock mode** (replenishing the basics), **background mode** (with friends as a more social experience), **celebration mode** (treating oneself), and **beyond the store mode** (shopping for a vacation or event), (2008). In each of these experiences, the shopper's orientation requires different physical designs. For example, a fitting room can provide the immersive experience for the beyond-the-store-mode shoppers, while in-store coffee lounges serve the background-mode shopper. A second way to capture the mode of the shopper is to create "design moments." A **design moment** is a special experience created through the use of lighting, atmosphere, and opportunity.

In order to get a shopper to pay more for a green product, a variety of methods might be used, according to Bishop and Cho. Although the price of green products is coming down, most still cost a bit more. Organic foods that are locally sourced tend to cost more than mass-produced food distributed by multinational corporations. But shopper recommendations might provide confidence for a shopper trying to decide whether to spend the extra money on local or organic food. Third-party validation or top-shelf picks validate a green product. A designer could work with a retailer to implement strategies that involve product placement along with basic space planning. Aisles arranged by environmental impact tell the shopper where to stay for a particular type of product. Providing an editing space for

shoppers to switch items in the cart for better green alternatives as well as environmental impact information on the back of receipts might encourage green purchasing. Some shoppers will respond to check-out lines for "green champions" or having their environmental impact displayed above the check-out line. Other ideas Bishop and Cho propose to enhance a retail store's sustainability, include:

- Microclimates—controlling temperature with local plants, ventilation, etc., and not mechanical HVAC
- Parking privileges for carpoolers
- Village mode, where the produce section of a grocery store is also a greenhouse or community garden
- Delivery of weekly staples to the customer's door to encourage reduced trips for necessities

A designer who understands human behavior and motivation while shopping as well as the different ways in which people shop will be better able to design for a more sustainable experience. Creating a green experience for customers provides something many people want and encourages them to do the right thing.

Firm Approaches to Sustainable Retail Design

Some firms have responded to the new demands of the retail industry in some very creative ways. One example is the Green Room Retail Design Agency in the United Kingdom. With office in Birmingham and London, the Green Room has completed projects across Europe and in the Middle East as well as in the rest of the United Kingdom (Greenroomretail.co.uk). The Green Room advertises several market driven experiential solutions, such as concessions, experiential events, pop-ups, digital concepts, and **POS** (point of sale) **+ POP** (point of purchase; seasonal displays) with **GWP** (Gifts with Purchase). By allowing for retail experiences that do not always require a physical brick-and-mortar facility, the Green Room is on the leading edge of sustainable retail.

Case Studies

The following case studies include a firm design completed using LEED CI (Corporate Interiors) for Retail and a series of student projects demonstrating varying levels of sustainable design. Approaches to sustainable retails design are diverse. The following case studies show a range of solutions spanning brick-and-mortar stores to pop-up venues.

INTEC Group: Charles Luck Showroom (eco-technic, materials approach)

INTEC's Charles Luck Showroom design met LEED Gold certification. To meet LEED Gold, the project included several LEED criteria, including the use of sustainable finishes (locally sourced), access to daylight and outdoor views, and the reuse of an existing building and its windows. Charles Luck is a retailer of stone products, with locations throughout Virginia, North Carolina, Maryland, and Washington, DC. This showroom is located in historic Georgetown, Va., and features Luck Stone products including both sandstone and marble. The interior design decisions contributed to many of the LEED credit categories including Materials and Resources Credit 4: Recycled Content (10 percent of the total building's materials, by value, were made using recycled materials), Materials and Resources Credit 5: Regional Materials (66.65 percent of the total building materials, by cost, were manufactured within 500 miles of the project and another 32.5 percent were extracted from within 500 miles), and Indoor Environmental Quality Credit 4.5: Low-Emitting Materials—(furniture).

Additional sustainability measures included reduced energy use for lighting, natural ventilation, and environmentally preferable cleaning products, to name a few. (Charles Luck, 2012)

Student Project Examples

Several of the student project examples described here are entries for the **Planning and Visual Education** (PAVE) Annual Student Design Competitions. **PAVE** was first founded in 1992, and its objective is to support students in the field of retail design and merchandising. Three years of projects from students in the interior design program at Virginia Tech include designs for Macy's Shoes, Godiva Chocolates, and a Sephora Cosmetics pop-up store. The solutions vary from predominantly material solutions to more holistic, sustainable approaches, such as design for disassembly.

Figure 2.1 Charles Luck Showroom, Georgetown, Va., INTEC: Exterior

Figure 2.2 Charles
Luck Showroom:
Entry door

Figure 2.3 Charles Luck Showroom: Detail of
tile, brick, and stone shelves

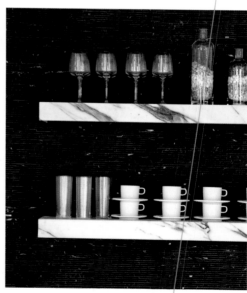

Figure 2.4 Charles Luck Showroom: Detail of
tile and stone shelves

Figure 2.5 Charles Luck Showroom: Interior view showing a variety of sustainable interior materials

Figure 2.6 Charles Luck Showroom: Interior of stone selection area

Lindsey Richards Kite— Macy's (eco-technic, eco-aesthetic)

This project takes a predominantly materials approach to sustainability. Sustainable eco-resin product 3Form is used to achieve the concept of "interlinking" within the shoe department itself and to the rest of the Macy's store. A single plane turns and bends to link one space with another and one plane with another. Recessed fluorescent, LEDs, and color-corrected metal halide lamps are used to provide both energy-efficient and pleasing lighting throughout. Design Tex sustainable fabric choices for seating and low-VOC paint complement the 3Form interiors.

Figure 2.7 Lindsey Kite, Macy's Shoe Store: PAVE Design Competition entry, Honorable Mention recipient

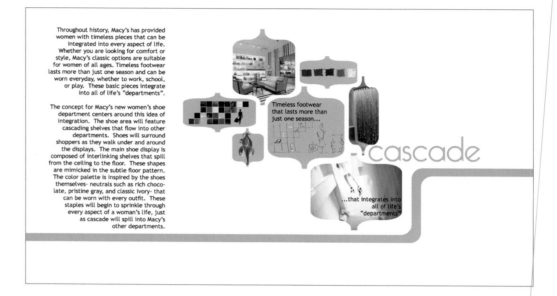

Figure 2.8 Lindsey Kite, Macy's Shoe Store: Floor plan and details

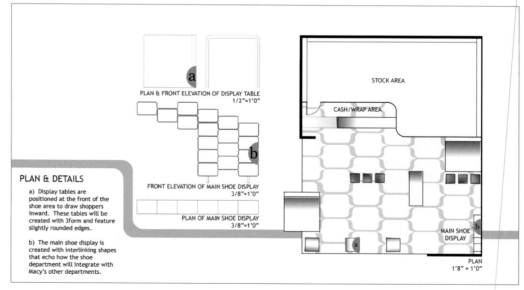

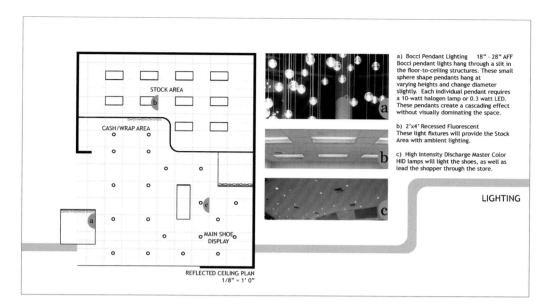

a) Bocci Pendant Lighting   18" - 28" AFF
Bocci pendant lights hang through a slit in the floor-to-ceiling structures. These small sphere shape pendants hang at varying heights and change diameter slightly. Each individual pendant requires a 10-watt halogen lamp or 0.3 watt LED. These pendants create a cascading effect without visually dominating the space.

b) 2'x4' Recessed Fluorescent
These light fixtures will provide the Stock Area with ambient lighting.

c) High Intensity Discharge Master Color
HID lamps will light the shoes, as well as lead the shopper through the store.

LIGHTING

STOCK AREA

CASH/WRAP AREA

MAIN SHOE DISPLAY

REFLECTED CEILING PLAN
1/8" = 1' 0"

Figure 2.9 Lindsey Kite, Macy's Shoe Store: Lighting plan

cascade

FRONT SECTION
1/4" = 1'0"

ELEVATIONS & SECTIONS

REAR SECTION
1/8" = 1'0"

Figure 2.10 Lindsey Kite, Macy's Shoe Store: Interior elevations and sections

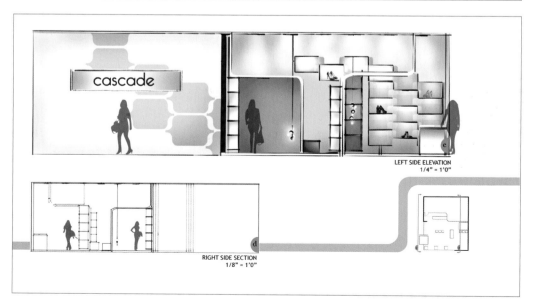

cascade

LEFT SIDE ELEVATION
1/4" = 1'0"

RIGHT SIDE SECTION
1/8" = 1'0"

Figure 2.11 Lindsey Kite, Macy's Shoe Store: Interior elevations and sections

Figure 2.12 Lindsey Kite, Macy's Shoe Store: 3D rendered view

Figure 2.13 Lindsey Kite, Macy's Shoe Store: 3D rendered view and materials

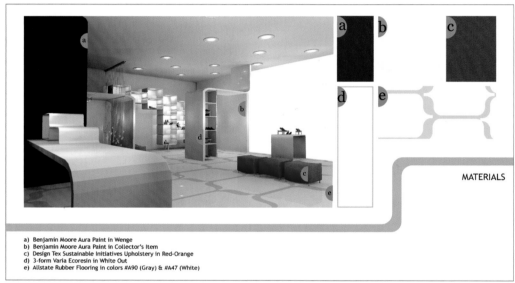

MATERIALS

a) Benjamin Moore Aura Paint in Wenge
b) Benjamin Moore Aura Paint in Collector's Item
c) Design Tex Sustainable Initiatives Upholstery in Red-Orange
d) 3-form Varia Ecoresin in White Out
e) Allstate Rubber Flooring in colors #A90 (Gray) & #A47 (White)

Figure 2.14 Lindsey Kite, Macy's Shoe Store: Fixture detail

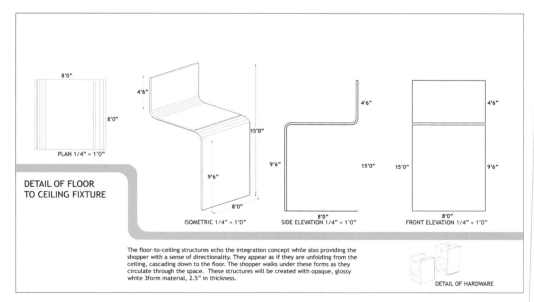

8'0"

8'0"

PLAN 1/4" = 1'0"

DETAIL OF FLOOR TO CEILING FIXTURE

4'6"

15'0"

9'6"

8'0"

ISOMETRIC 1/4" = 1'0"

4'6"

9'6"

15'0"

8'0"

SIDE ELEVATION 1/4" = 1'0"

4'6"

15'0"

9'6"

8'0"

FRONT ELEVATION 1/4" = 1'0"

The floor-to-ceiling structures echo the integration concept while also providing the shopper with a sense of directionality. They appear as if they are unfolding from the ceiling, cascading down to the floor. The shopper walks under these forms as they circulate through the space. These structures will be created with opaque, glossy white 3form material, 2.5" in thickness.

DETAIL OF HARDWARE

PLAN OF CASH WRAP
1/4"=1'0"

FRONT ELEVATION OF CASH WRAP
1/4"=1'0"

PERSPECTIVE & DETAILS
The floor-to-ceiling structures' flowing gesture is repeated horizontally in the cash wrap surface. Extra storage is provided with the interlocking shapes that mimic the main shoe display. The cash wrap pours down flush with the floor, creating a visual barrier between the shoppers and the employees.

Figure 2.15 Lindsey Kite, Macy's Shoe Store: 3D rendered view and details

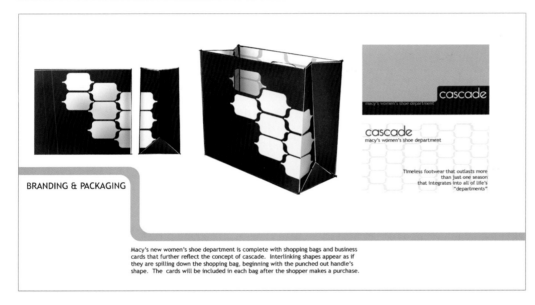

BRANDING & PACKAGING

cascade
macy's women's shoe department

Timeless footwear that outlasts more than just one season that integrates into all of life's "departments"

Macy's new women's shoe department is complete with shopping bags and business cards that further reflect the concept of cascade. Interlinking shapes appear as if they are spilling down the shopping bag, beginning with the punched out handle's shape. The cards will be included in each bag after the shopper makes a purchase.

Figure 2.16 Lindsey Kite, Macy's Shoe Store: Branding and packaging

Jamie Matthews Ivey— Macy's (eco-medical, eco-technic)

The concept statement for this project begins with "Green never looked so good." The project includes low-VOC paint (Benjamin Moore), FSC-certified hardwoods, eco-resin (a sustainable plastic) shoe displays, and sustainable wallcoverings (Xorel) and carpets (InterfaceFLOR) throughout. MasterColor HID lamps combined with recessed fluorescents and the minimal use of multi-faceted reflector halogen lamps (MR16s) provide an energy-efficient lighting solution for the project.

Figure 2.17 Jamie
Ivey, Macy's Shoe
Store

Figure 2.18 Jamie
Ivey, Macy's Shoe
Store: Concept and
3D view

concept statement for *shine*

Modern, yet inviting. Macy's is a department store known for quality goods, a wide selection of name brands, great sales and promotions, and large open stores that feel comfortable yet luxurious. The "shine" shoe department incorporates these key aspects with its open layout and use of upscale materials. The feel of the space is modern and soft, with a fresh but subtle color palette, reflective mirrors, soft upholstery and carpet, and warm hardwood. The star logo is the defining symbol of the Macy's brand. To highlight this, the geometry of a star and its corresponding pentagon are incorporated into the shoe displays, cash wrap, and overall layout. The logo "shine" is a play on words: stars shine, shoes are shined, mirrors shine, and the overall feeling is bright and shiny. Women will come, shop, buy, and "shine with Macy's".

"Green" never looked so good. To incorporate Macy's environmental philosophy, sustainable materials are included in the design throughout the space. Low VOC paint on the ceiling, FSC-certified hardwood, eco-resin shoe displays, and sustainable wallcovering and carpet are used throughout the space. Finally, Energy Star touchscreen monitors are utilized to find information about Macy's, the shoes and their brands, and shoe/size/color availability. These monitors will also give the customer the ability to purchase items on screen.

Figure 2.19 Jamie
Ivey, Macy's Shoe
Store: 3D view

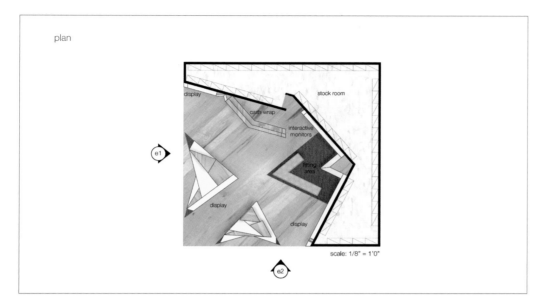

plan

scale: 1/8" = 1'0"

Figure 2.20 Jamie Ivey, Macy's Shoe Store: Plan

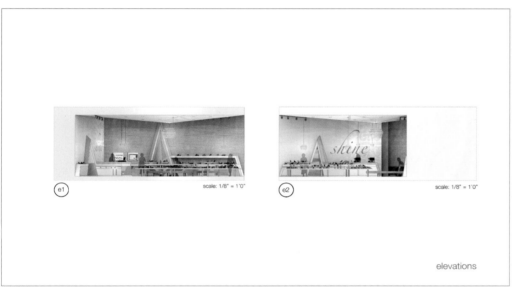

e1 scale: 1/8" = 1'0"

e2 scale: 1/8" = 1'0"

elevations

Figure 2.21 Jamie Ivey, Macy's Shoe Store: Interior elevations

branding

Figure 2.22 Jamie Ivey, Macy's Shoe Store: Branding and 3D view

Figure 2.23 Jamie Ivey, Macy's Shoe Store: 3D view

Figure 2.24 Jamie Ivey, Macy's Shoe Store: Materials

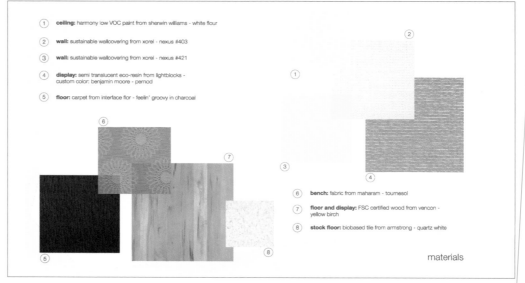

1. **ceiling:** harmony low VOC paint from sherwin williams - white flour

2. **wall:** sustainable wallcovering from xorel - nexus #403

3. **wall:** sustainable wallcovering from xorel - nexus #421

4. **display:** semi translucent eco-resin from lightblocks - custom color: benjamin moore - pernod

5. **floor:** carpet from interface flor - feelin' groovy in charcoal

6. **bench:** fabric from maharam - tournesol

7. **floor and display:** FSC certified wood from vencon - yellow birch

8. **stock floor:** biobased tile from armstrong - quartz white

materials

Figure 2.25 Jamie Ivey, Macy's Shoe Store: Reflected ceiling plan

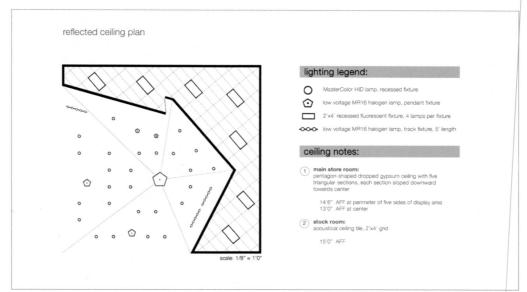

reflected ceiling plan

lighting legend:

○ MasterColor HID lamp, recessed fixture

⬠ low voltage MR16 halogen lamp, pendant fixture

▭ 2'x4' recessed fluorescent fixture, 4 lamps per fixture

◇◇◇ low voltage MR16 halogen lamp, track fixture, 5' length

ceiling notes:

1. **main store room:**
   pentagon-shaped dropped gypsum ceiling with five triangular sections, each section sloped downward towards center

   14'6" AFF at perimeter of five sides of display area
   13'0" AFF at center

2. **stock room:**
   acoustical ceiling tile, 2'x4' grid

   15'0" AFF

scale: 1/8" = 1'0"

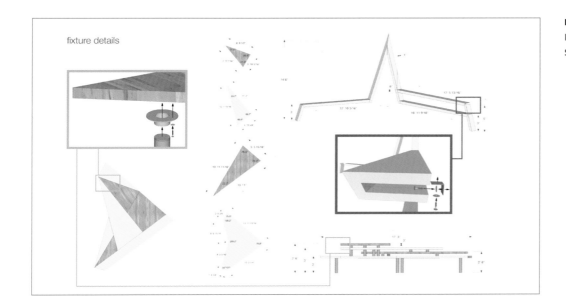

fixture details

Figure 2.26 Jamie Ivey, Macy's Shoe Store: Fixture details

Rachel Erickson—Godiva Chocolatier (eco-aesthetic)

This project relied on the use of sustainable materials, such as DesignTex fabrics and Sherwin William no-VOC paints, and energy-efficient recessed compact fluorescent lighting to achieve an interior flowing space inspired by melted chocolate. This was accomplished through the use of surfaces that appeared to melt into one another and through choosing a rich brown color palette. Organic forms morph through the shop to reinforce the design concept.

Figure 2.27 Rachel Erickson, Godiva Chocolatier

Figure 2.28 Rachel Erickson, Godiva Chocolatier: Elevation

Figure 2.29 Rachel Erickson, Godiva Chocolatier: Plan

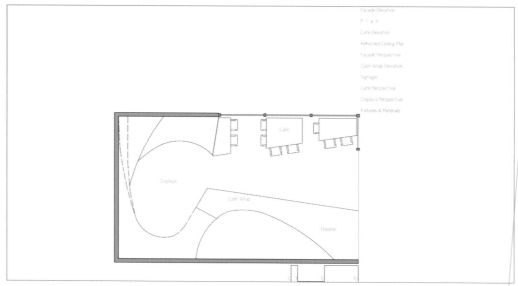

Figure 2.30 Rachel Erickson, Godiva Chocolatier: Interior elevation and lighting plan

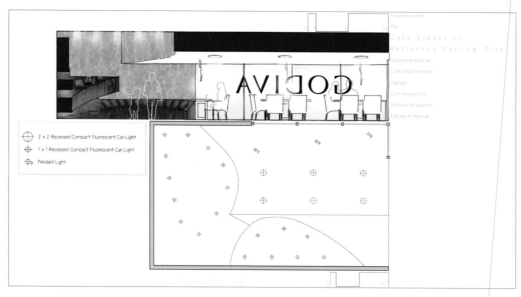

Figure 2.31 Rachel Erickson, Godiva Chocolatier: Interior perspective

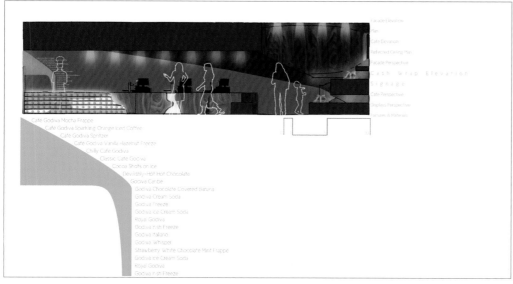

Figure 2.32 Rachel Erickson, Godiva Chocolatier: Interior elevation

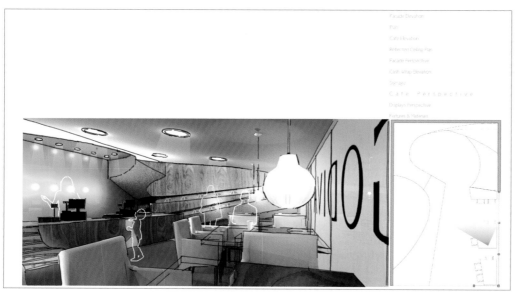

Figure 2.33 Rachel Erickson, Godiva Chocolatier: Interior perspective

Figure 2.34 Rachel Erickson, Godiva Chocolatier: Interior perspective

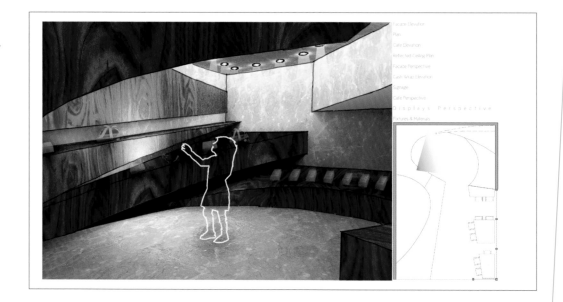

Figure 2.35 Rachel Erickson, Godiva Chocolatier: Materials

Cathleen Campbell— Sephora Pop-Up Store (biomimicry, eco-technic)

The metamorphosis of a butterfly inspires the folded-plate roof design for this pop-up store solution. A ribbed structural system mimics the veins of a butterfly's wings and provides a way for the pop-up store to expand and be easily moved and re-assembled. The individual units of the store consist of semi-truck trailer units set on a rail system. Thus, the entire idea is sustainable and relies on the use and reuse of shipping containers. The sustainability approach couples shipping container reuse with design for disassembly.

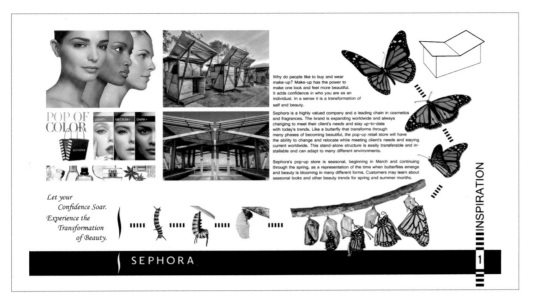

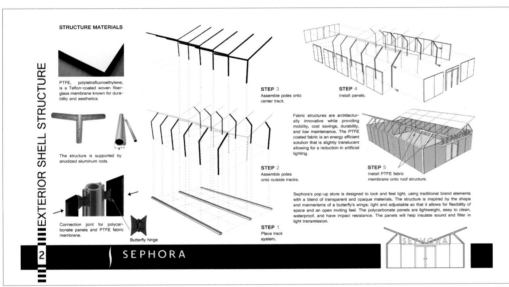

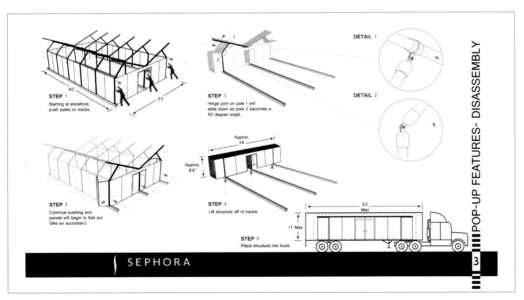

Figure 2.39 Cathleen Campbell, Sephora Pop-Up Store: Floor plan

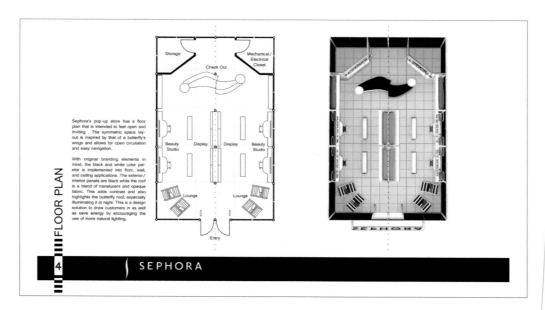

Sephora's pop-up store has a floor plan that is intended to feel open and inviting . The symmetric space layout is inspired by that of a butterfly's wings and allows for open circulation and easy navigation.

With original branding elements in mind, the black and white color palette is implemented into floor, wall, and ceiling applications. The exterior/interior panels are black while the roof is a blend of translucent and opaque fabric. This adds contrast and also highlights the butterfly roof, especially illuminating it at night. This is a design solution to draw customers in as well as save energy by encouraging the use of more natural lighting.

Figure 2.40 Cathleen Campbell, Sephora Pop-Up Store: Fixture assembly details

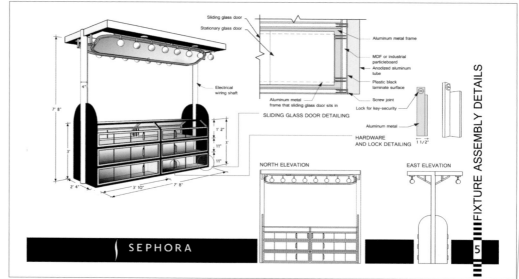

Figure 2.41 Cathleen Campbell, Sephora Pop-Up Store: Interior 3D rendering

Figure 2.42
Cathleen Campbell,
Sephora Pop-Up
Store: Interior 3D
rendering

Figure 2.43
Cathleen Campbell,
Sephora Pop-Up
Store: Interior 3D
rendering

Figure 2.44
Cathleen Campbell,
Sephora Pop-Up
Store: Interior 3D
rendering

FLLW Gift Store

A second retail project completed by students was an adaptive reuse project for the A.D. German Warehouse. The warehouse was designed by Frank Lloyd Wright in 1917 in Richland Center, Wisc. It was rehabilitated into a multi-use facility project including a museum, condominiums, and a Frank Lloyd Wright gift store. The gift store sells Frank Lloyd Wright memorabilia, including everything from notecards and books to furniture and light fixtures.

Jessica Calloway (adaptive reuse, eco-technic)

The first sustainability measure used for this project was to reuse a historically significant building. The solution maintains the brick walls and concrete floor and ceilings throughout. This effort not only reuses an historic building but also relies on the minimal use of new materials. The gift store includes custom-designed displays made of locally grown and sustainably managed maple. LED lighting allows for energy-use reduction, and Calloway uses the LEED CI rating system to guide her design decisions throughout the project.

Figure 2.45 Jessica Calloway, A.D. German Warehouse Museum Shop: Concept page

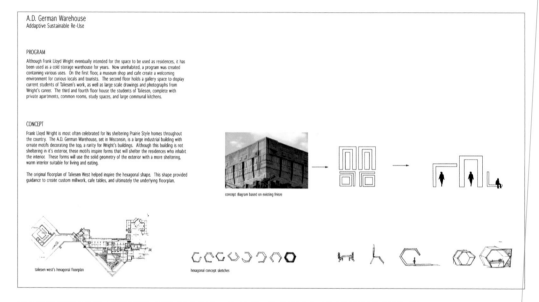

Figure 2.46 Jessica Calloway, A.D. German Warehouse Museum Shop: Interior 3D rendering

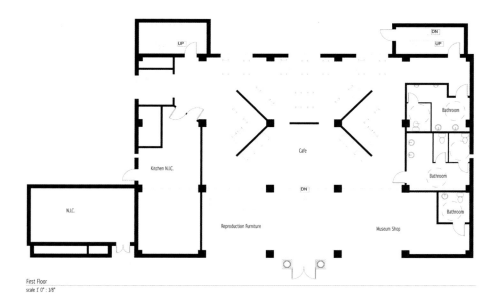

Figure 2.47
Jessica Calloway,
A.D. German
Warehouse Museum
Shop: Plan

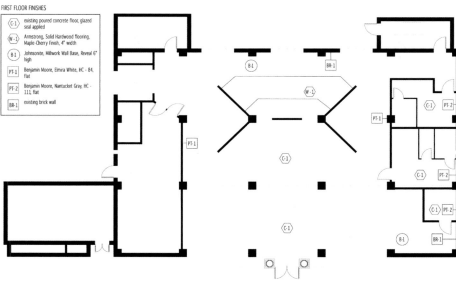

Figure 2.48
Jessica Calloway,
A.D. German
Warehouse Museum
Shop: Finishes plan

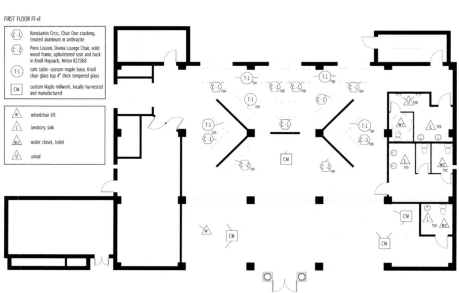

Figure 2.49
Jessica Calloway,
A.D. German
Warehouse Museum
Shop: Furniture,
fixtures, and
equipment plan

Figure 2.50
Jessica Calloway,
A.D. German
Warehouse Museum
Shop: Finishes
selections

Figure 2.51
Jessica Calloway,
A.D. German
Warehouse Museum
Shop: Reflected
ceiling plan

Figure 2.52
Jessica Calloway,
A.D. German
Warehouse Museum
Shop: Behavioral
analysis plan

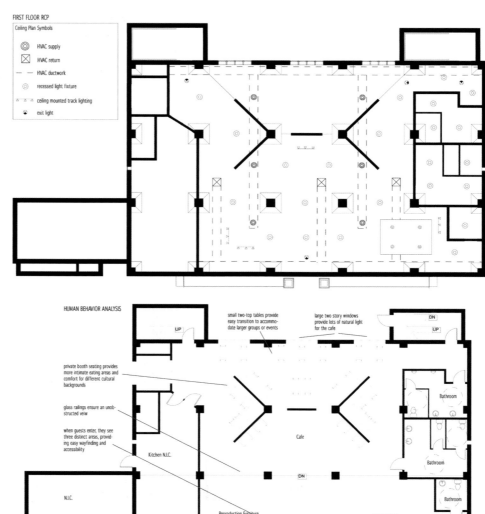

LEED 2009 for Commercial Interiors
Project Checklist

				Sustainable Sites	Possible Points:	21
Y	?	N				
		N	Credit 1	Site Selection	1 to 5	
		N	Credit 2	Development Density and Community Connectivity	6	
		N	Credit 3.1	Alternative Transportation—Public Transportation Access	6	
		N	Credit 3.2	Alternative Transportation—Bicycle Storage and Changing Rooms	2	
		N	Credit 3.3	Alternative Transportation—Parking Availability	2	

Y	6			Water Efficiency	Possible Points:	11
Y			Prereq 1	Water Use Reduction—20% Reduction		
Y	6		Credit 1	Water Use Reduction	6 to 11	

	13			Energy and Atmosphere	Possible Points:	37
Y			Prereq 1	Fundamental Commissioning of Building Energy Systems		
Y			Prereq 2	Minimum Energy Performance		
Y			Prereq 3	Fundamental Refrigerant Management		
Y	2		Credit 1.1	Optimize Energy Performance—Lighting Power	1 to 5	
Y	2		Credit 1.2	Optimize Energy Performance—Lighting Controls	1 to 3	
Y	7		Credit 1.3	Optimize Energy Performance—HVAC	5 to 10	
Y	2		Credit 1.4	Optimize Energy Performance—Equipment and Appliances	1 to 4	
		N	Credit 2	Enhanced Commissioning	5	
		N	Credit 3	Measurement and Verification	2 to 5	
		N	Credit 4	Green Power	5	

	10			Materials and Resources	Possible Points:	14
Y			Prereq 1	Storage and Collection of Recyclables		
Y	1		Credit 1.1	Tenant Space—Long-Term Commitment	1	
Y	1		Credit 1.2	Building Reuse	1 to 2	
Y	1		Credit 2	Construction Waste Management	1 to 2	
Y	2		Credit 3.1	Materials Reuse	1 to 2	
		N	Credit 3.2	Materials Reuse—Furniture and Furnishings	1	
Y	2		Credit 4	Recycled Content	1 to 2	
Y	2		Credit 5	Regional Materials	1 to 2	
		N	Credit 6	Rapidly Renewable Materials	1	
Y	1		Credit 7	Certified Wood	1	

	12			Indoor Environmental Quality	Possible Points:	17
Y			Prereq 1	Minimum IAQ Performance		
Y			Prereq 2	Environmental Tobacco Smoke (ETS) Control		
		N	Credit 1	Outdoor Air Delivery Monitoring	1	
		N	Credit 2	Increased Ventilation	1	
		N	Credit 3.1	Construction IAQ Management Plan—During Construction	1	
		N	Credit 3.2	Construction IAQ Management Plan—Before Occupancy	1	
Y	1		Credit 4.1	Low-Emitting Materials—Adhesives and Sealants	1	
Y	1		Credit 4.2	Low-Emitting Materials—Paints and Coatings	1	
Y	1		Credit 4.3	Low-Emitting Materials—Flooring Systems	1	
Y	1		Credit 4.4	Low-Emitting Materials—Composite Wood and Agrifiber Products	1	
Y	1		Credit 4.5	Low-Emitting Materials—Systems Furniture and Seating	1	
Y	1		Credit 5	Indoor Chemical & Pollutant Source Control	1	
Y	1		Credit 6.1	Controllability of Systems—Lighting	1	
Y	1		Credit 6.2	Controllability of Systems—Thermal Comfort	1	
Y	1		Credit 7.1	Thermal Comfort—Design	1	
Y	1		Credit 7.2	Thermal Comfort—Verification	1	
Y	1		Credit 8.1	Daylight and Views—Daylight	1 to 2	
Y	1		Credit 8.2	Daylight and Views—Views for Seated Spaces	1	

	1			Innovation and Design Process	Possible Points:	6
Y	1		Credit 1.1	Innovation in Design: Specific Title	1	
		N	Credit 1.2	Innovation in Design: Specific Title	1	
		N	Credit 1.3	Innovation in Design: Specific Title	1	
		N	Credit 1.4	Innovation in Design: Specific Title	1	
		N	Credit 1.5	Innovation in Design: Specific Title	1	
		N	Credit 2	LEED Accredited Professional	1	

				Regional Priority Credits	Possible Points:	4
		N	Credit 1.1	Regional Priority: Specific Credit	1	
		N	Credit 1.2	Regional Priority: Specific Credit	1	
		N	Credit 1.3	Regional Priority: Specific Credit	1	
		N	Credit 1.4	Regional Priority: Specific Credit	1	

	42			Total	Possible Points:	110

Certified 40 to 49 points   Silver 50 to 59 points   Gold 60 to 79 points   Platinum 80 to 110 points

Figure 2.53 Jessica Calloway, A.D. German Warehouse Museum Shop: LEED CI checklist

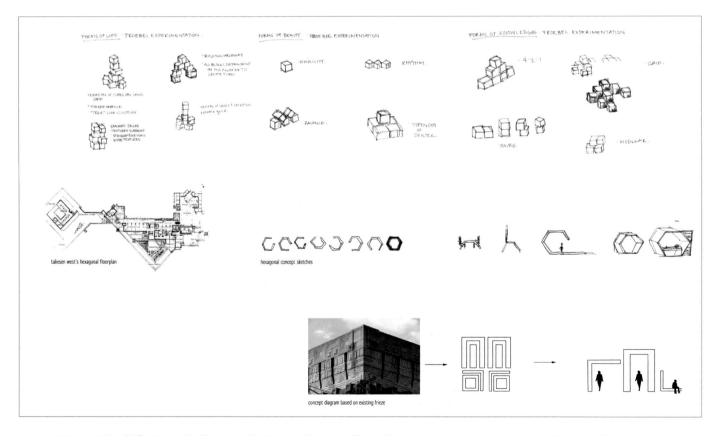

Figure 2.54 Jessica Calloway, A.D. German Warehouse Museum Shop: Conceptual sketches inspired by Froebel Blocks

Jamie Matthews Ivey (adaptive reuse, eco-technic)

Like the previously described project, this one also reuses an historic building for new purposes. Guided by the LEED CI rating systems, the project focuses on energy reduction and the use of sustainable, recycled, and reclaimed materials. Reclaimed lumber (wood that was salvaged from a demolished building such as a barn) is used extensively throughout the project to create new wood flooring and display units. Additional sustainable finishes include ceramic tile, a quartz countertop, concrete, and glass. Energy-efficient fluorescent lamps and LED strip lighting light the retail space. The LEED CI checksheet allows Ivey to take a more holistic approach to the sustainable aspects of the project.

Figure 2.55 Jamie Ivey, A.D. German Warehouse Museum Shop: Concept

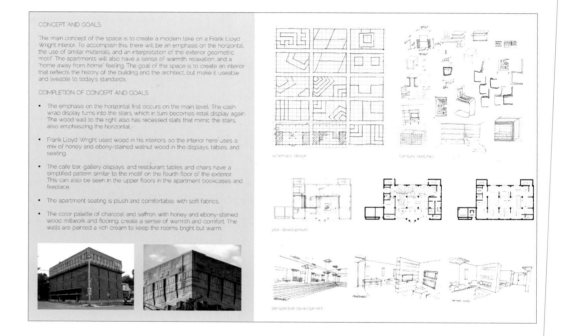

Figure 2.56 Jamie Ivey, A.D. German Warehouse Museum Shop: Museum store 3D rendered view

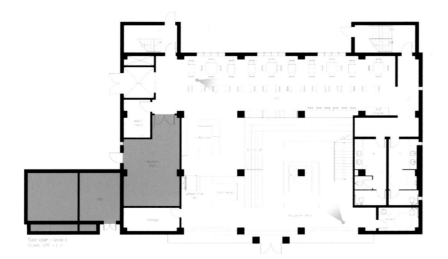

Figure 2.57 Jamie Ivey, A.D. German Warehouse Museum Shop: Plan

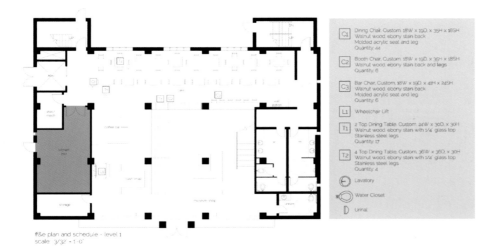

Figure 2.58 Jamie Ivey, A.D. German Warehouse Museum Shop: Furniture, fixtures, and equipment plan

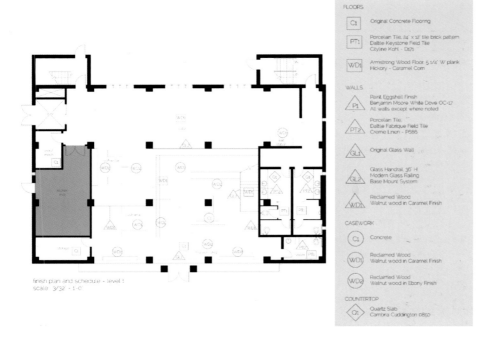

Figure 2.59 Jamie Ivey, A.D. German Warehouse Museum Shop: Finishes plan

Figure 2.60 Jamie
Ivey, A.D. German
Warehouse Museum
Shop: Reflected
ceiling plan

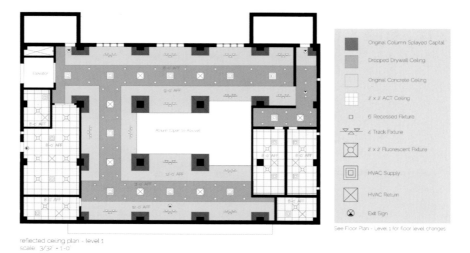

Figure 2.61 Jamie
Ivey, A.D. German
Warehouse Museum
Shop: Built-in details

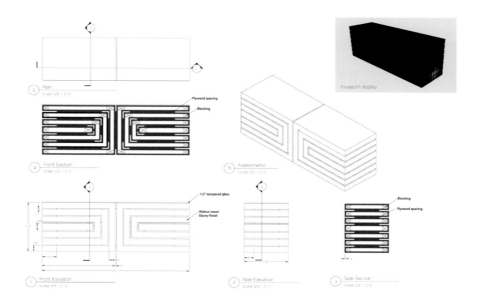

Figure 2.62 Jamie
Ivey, A.D. German
Warehouse Museum
Shop: LEED CI
checklist

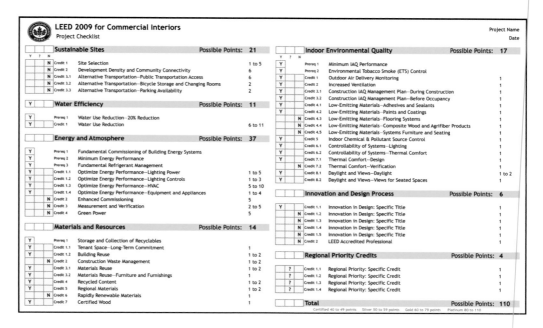

Applicable LEED Checklists

For designers wishing to obtain LEED certification for their projects, two possible checklists can be used for a retail project: LEED CI or LEED NC. Specific retail guidelines were developed in recognition of the special requirements of a retail environment, particularly in the area of lighting.

LEED for Retail

The LEED for Retail guidelines are found in two unique rating systems—LEED for New Construction: Retail and LEED for Corporate Interiors: Retail. The guidelines were developed to encourage and promote sustainable interiors for retail spaces. As with all other LEED Rating Systems, the ones for retail are based on LEED NC and LEED CI.

The LEED NC: Retail checklist includes several specific modifications for retail facilities. For example, under Materials and Resources: Credits 3 through 7, a definition of retail furniture is provided to assist designers with acquiring points for this key component in a retail design. As a fixture unique to the retail environment, specific guidance is provided to the designer as to how to obtain points in this area. A similar series of modifications have been made for LEED CI for Retail. (e.g., the inclusion of information on retail furniture and fixtures).

The specific modifications for both LEED NC and LEED CI Retail can be found on the USGBC website at http://www.usgbc.org/leed#rating. The checklist is provided in the Appendices.

Planning Guidelines

Retail layouts can use a variety of approaches. The most common include a straight layout, a diagonal layout, a curved layout, a geometric layout, or a mixed layout using two or more of these approaches. The plan views included provide overall guidance on passage widths as well as a typical accessible fitting room layout. To enhance the sustainability of the layout, the most efficient arrangement of the fixtures for a given building needs to be determined. Different shapes lend themselves to different arrangements.

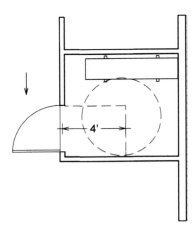

Figure 2.63 Plan prototype: Accessible fitting room

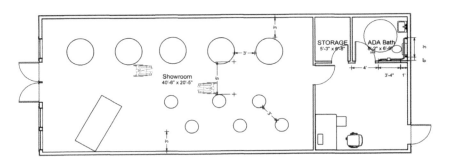

Figure 2.64 Typical curved fixture retail layout

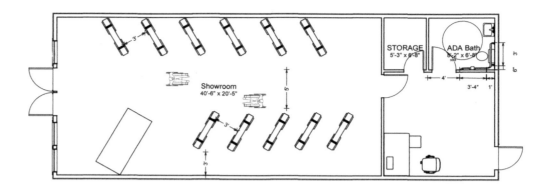

Figure 2.65 Typical diagonal fixture retail layout

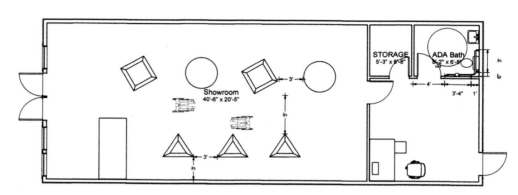

Figure 2.66 Typical geometric fixture retail layout

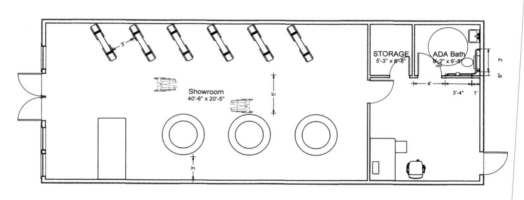

Figure 2.67 Typical mixed-type fixture retail layout

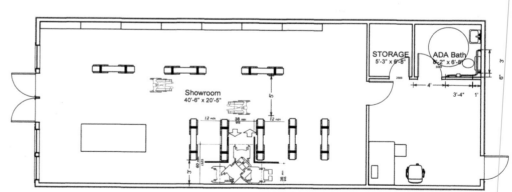

Figure 2.68 Typical straight fixture retail layout

Discussion Questions and Exercises

1. Make a list of every store you have visited in the past week. Research at least two of these companies to determine if they have a sustainable retail policy. If so, describe it. Does this impact your desire to shop at this location in the future? If so, how?
2. Group discussion: What are the ethical issues related to retail design and consumption? What can each person do to impact our own consumption patterns? List at least five specific actions you can personally take to reduce your use of purchased items and commit to doing these five things.

Key Terms

atmospherics

background mode

beyond the store mode

Butt Brush Effect

celebration mode

chevroning

design moment

GWP (gift with purchase)

IDEO

mission mode

pop-up store

POS + POP

Planning and Visual Education (PAVE)

restock mode

The Retail Industry Leaders Association

Retail Sustainability Initiative (RSI)

transition zone

Sources

Association for Retail Environments. *Retail Environments.* www.retailenvironments.org

Bishop, Steve, and David Cho. 2008. "From Plague to Paradigm: Designing Sustainable Retail Environments" *Rotman Magazine* Spring 2008: 56-61.

Boyce, P.R., C.J. Lloyd, N.H. Eklund, and H.M Brandston. 1996. "Quantifying the Effects of Good Lighting: The Green Hills Farms Project," in *Proceedings of the Illuminating Engineering Society,* 1–37. New York: Rendselear Polytechnic, Lighting Research Center.

Cuttle, C. and H.M. Brandston. 1995. "Evaluation of retail lighting." *Journal of the Illuminating Engineering Society* 24(2): 33–57.

Gupta, E. 2013. "Shopper Research Is Making Retail Design Scientific." *Business Standard Magazine.* Accessed June 27. http://www.business-standard.com/article/management/shopper-research-is-making-retail-design-scientific-113031000252_1.html

Johnson, K. 2004. "Shopping Behaviors: Implications for the Design of Retail Spaces." *Implications* I(5): 1–5.

Pegler, M. 2010. *Green Retail Design.* Cincinnati: Media Group International.

Charles Luck. 2012. *LEED Certification Project Review Report,* June 25.

http://www.envirosell.com/downloads/TheEvolutionOfRetailDesign.pdf Accessed March 26, 2014.

Petermans, Ann, and Koenraad Van Cleempoel. 2010. "Research in Retail Design: Methodological Consideration for an Emerging Discipline." Presented at the Design and Emotions Conference, Chicago, IL. October. Accessed June 27, 2013. http://uhasselt.academia.edu/AnnPetermans/Papers/259895/Research_in_Retail_Design_methodological_considerations_for_an_emerging_discipline.

Massara, Francesco. 2010. "Retail Environments: Design Places to Sell." *Research and Design Connections* 4. Accessed Aug. 30.

Trendwatching, 2009. "Nowism: Why Currency is the New Currency." Accessed June 27, 2013. http://www.trendwatching.com/trends/nowism/.

Wroblaski, K. 2012. "Here Today Gone Tomorrow." *Interiors and Sources* (August): 18–19.

Quartier, Katelijn, Christiaans, Henri and Van Cleempoel, Koenraad. (2008). "Retail design: Lighting as an Atmospheric Tool, Creating Experiences which Influence Consumers Mood and Behavior in Commercial Spaces." http://shura.shu.ac.uk/496/ Retrieved 4/25/14

Pleveots, Bie, Petermans, Ain, Van Cleempoel, Koenraad. (2010) "Developing a Theoretical Framew..rk for Understanding (Staged) Authentic Retail Settings in Relation to the Current Experience Economy. www.drs2010.umontreal.ca/data/pdf/097.pdf Retrieved 4/25/14

www.neilsen.com/us/en/newswire/2013/U-S-women-control-the-purse-strings.html

3

HEALTHCARE
PROJECTS

....

Objectives

- Students will understand and be able to discuss the most relevant issues in sustainable healthcare design.

- Students will know where to find resources for Evidence-Based Design decisions in healthcare design.

- Students will see how other students and firms have created sustainable interiors for healthcare settings.

- Students will understand the impact of sustainable interiors and nature on health.

Overview

Healthcare has been a central issue to many in the United States during the past decade. Rising insurance costs and the increase in the number of uninsured led to significant changes in the U.S. healthcare system in the recent past with the enactment of President Obama's healthcare plan, the Affordable Care Act. Despite the political debates over the need for such a plan and whether this is the best approach, the rise in healthcare costs in the United States impacts nearly everyone. Further, people are living longer than ever before and have come to expect excellent healthcare. As people age and develop health issues, the need for facilities and practitioners also increases.

Brief History of Healthcare Facilities in the United States

Healthcare facilities in the United States originally followed a monastery model with open wards. As late at the mid-20th century, the open ward was still widely in use—multiple patients were housed in a large area overseen by a group of nurses. The advent of private rooms is a relatively new phenomenon. In fact, many facilities still rely on dual-occupant rooms for most healthcare needs.

Prior to the 1920s, most people in the United States were uninsured. The rise of the American Medical Association in the 1900s led to a more organized U.S. healthcare system. It was during this time that railroad companies first developed medical programs for their employees. The early-20th-century understanding of germs and disease led to the first modern hospitals around 1910. (Penicillin was discovered in the 1920s, although it did not go into use for 20 years.) In the 1930s, Blue Cross first started insuring private individuals for healthcare. President Roosevelt established the "Economic Bill of Rights" in the 1940s that included healthcare (PBS, 2013). By the 1950s, healthcare for the poor was an accepted federal responsibility, and many childhood diseases were being successfully eradicated or controlled. By the 1970s, more than 700 private insurance companies provided healthcare. As healthcare costs escalated, President Nixon centralized cancer research at the National Institute of Health (NIH) and worked to establish national health insurance, although that effort failed. The 1980s saw corporations consolidating hospitals under private ownership and *capitation*—payments to doctors— became common. The Human Genome project was started in the 1990s with goal of identifying the 100,000 genes in human DNA.

Healthcare Around the World

According to the World Health Organization (WHO), the United States is the only industrialized country without government-run healthcare. Great Britain's system is entirely government administered, while France and Canada have a private system funded mostly by the government. Switzerland's system stands alone as a privately run institution with governmental regulation. The WHO also indicates the 80 percent of people around the world ascribe to traditional medicine—primarily herbal and locally practiced traditions including acupuncture and other alternative medications. Ironically, roughly 70 to 80 percent of people in industrialized countries have also tried some form of "alternative" medical intervention (herbal supplements, homeopathic remedies, acupuncture, Reiki, and the like).

Current Issues in Healthcare Design

The concern for sustainable healthcare has been a prominent issue for the past decade. With the rise of **Evidence-Based Design (EBD)**, healthcare design has benefited more than any other design specialty from a focus on design research. An EBD approach asks designers to base their decisions on research findings instead of designing the way they always have. The demand for healthy interior environments has overlapped with sustainability initiatives such as improved indoor air quality, reduction on environmental toxins, and increased access to daylight. The use of evidence-based medicine by doctors has led to a natural understanding and openness to the use of EBD in the healthcare industry.

The Center for Health Design (CHD)

First formed by a group of healthcare and design professionals in 1993, the **Center for Health Design (CHD)** works to "transform healthcare environments for a healthier, safer world through design research, education, and advocacy" (http://www.healthdesign.org/chd/about). The center's website contains a variety of helpful tools and resources for design practitioners and healthcare individuals. Included on the website is information

about the Pebble Project (sample case studies to represent different evidence-based strategies) as well as **Evidence-Based Design accreditation and certification (EDAC)**—the certification test and credential for a healthcare design professional. The Ripple Database, also located on the website, provides a free and open source of information on healthcare design and includes more than 150 design strategies used by Kaiser Permanente in its own projects.

Kaiser Permanente is a leading healthcare provider that has been providing services for more than 60 years. A single doctor originally founded the company during the Great Depression. Sidney Garfield, MD, borrowed money to build a hospital for employees of the Colorado River Aqueduct Project and built Contractors General Hospital in Desert Center for the injured workers. An engineer/insurance agent then suggested that workers pre-pay a certain amount per day to be able to have access to the hospital and to cover cost. Since that time, Kaiser Permanente has been a leading healthcare provider and has been focused on improving healthcare services in the United States.

The CHD website also includes a Clinic Design area with design solutions, a free magazine (*Health Design News*), project examples, and on online store where research studies can be purchased along with podcasts, white papers, videos, and books. The center website provides a convenient repository for the latest information on EBD for healthcare.

Evidence-Based Design (EBD)

As previously mentioned, evidence-based design is now commonly used in healthcare design. The concept originated with evidence-based medicine and the notion that evidence should inform the decision-making process. **Evidence-based medicine (EBM)** had been around since the mid-19th century. The concept is to use mathematical and statistical information about medical interventions to address a patient's condition. Although the Center for Health Design and Evidence-Based Design accreditation and certification focus on Evidence-Based Design for healthcare, this approach is used in corporate office design, hospitality design, and other types of design as well. EDAC provides a three-part study guide for those planning to seek certification. The Evidence-Based Design accreditation and certification designates that a designer has a thorough comprehension of Evidence-Based Design in healthcare and is prepared to apply this to a healthcare project. The process outlined by EDAC for Evidence-Based Design and research includes eight steps toward evidence-based design solutions:

1. Define evidence-based goals and objectives.
2. Find sources for relevant evidence.
3. Critically interpret relevant evidence.
4. Create and innovate Evidence-Based Design concepts.
5. Develop a hypothesis.
6. Collect baseline performance measures.
7. Monitor implementation of design and construction.
8. Measure post-occupancy performance results.

(http://www.healthdesign.org/edac/about)

The EDAC exam is administered through Castle testing sites across the United States and Canada and is open to anyone wanting to take it. Results are given to the candidate at the testing center upon successful completion of the exam.

EDAC and the State of Healthcare Today

In its EBD study guide, CHD identifies seven current trends in healthcare:

1. Public focus on quality and safety
2. Reimbursement challenges
3. Aging population and caregiver shortages
4. Health information technology
5. Genomics and technology
6. Emergency room saturation and disaster preparedness
7. Sustainable healthcare (CHD, 7)

Each of these trends signals specific design decisions. For example, the plethora of online health information suggests a need for Internet access for visitors and patients within the healthcare setting. In response to recent **HA-MRSA (hospital acquired methicillin-resistant *Staphylococcus aureus*)** outbreaks, a public focus on safety has resulted in the installation of additional hand-washing facilities. Healthcare professionals who have failed to wash their hands between patients most commonly spread HA-MRSA from an infected individual to others.

In addition to the Center for Healthcare Design and its resources, there are several other useful sources for healthcare design and ongoing maintenance as well. Examples include *Facilities Care Magazine,* individual designers and researchers writing about healthcare design, and LEED for Healthcare.

Facilities Care Magazine

Facilities Care Magazine, published by Columbia Books LLC, provides another source of information for interior designers working with healthcare venues. Dedicated to the ongoing maintenance of healthcare facilities (as opposed to their new construction), this magazine provides useful insights into issues such as durability of various finishes and furnishings. The magazine—available in hard copy and online at www.facilitycare.com—covers topics from the role of furniture manufacturers in Evidence-Based Design to the retail experience in healthcare facilities. Many of these topics have a direct influence on the design of healthcare facilities.

Biophilic Design and Health

Noting the beneficial relationship between nature and design, architect Stephen Kellert wrote and edited a book on biophilic design (Kellert, Heerwagen, and Mador, 2008). It describes many benefits of designing with nature on human health. "**Biophilic**" describes the inherent human desire to be part of nature. E.O. Wilson's early work on biophilia, *The Biophilia Hypothesis* (1993), described Wilson's theory about the affinity between man and nature. **Biophilia** is defined as an innate love of the natural world (Collins English Dictionary). Thus, biophilic design seeks to envelope the theory of biophilia into the design process.

In his chapter for Kellert's *Biophilic Design*, Ulrich writes about the evidence-based biophilic design research that shows improved emotional well-being, stress reduction, pain alleviation, and other positive health outcomes for people as a result of a biophilic design approach. A **positive health outcome** is described as one that can be measured or otherwise observed. Measurements might include survey responses or financial benefits.

When a situation exceeds an individual's ability to cope, the person is considered to be under **stress**. Since stress compromises well-being, its reduction is a key goal of successful healthcare design. Ulrich expounds on the restorative effect of nature, views, and daylighting (Kellert, Heerwagen, and Mador, 2008, 90). According to the research presented, patient stays and pain medication can both be reduced through exposure to views of nature. Further, daylight is associated with the reduction of both pain and depression, and a well-designed garden can provide restorative effects to patients (See studies by Roger Ulrich in Kellert et al). Thus, it is in everyone's interest—provider, patient, and designer—to engage biophilic design principles in healthcare design, and arguably, other types of design as well.

Principles of Biophilic Design

According to Kellert, biophilic design has six primary dimensions: environmental features, natural shapes and forms, natural patterns and processes, light and space, place-based relationships, and evolved human-nature relationships. Together, these six contributing factors can provide a map for creating biophilic designs.

Environmental Features

Environmental features describe the various characteristics of what is found in nature. These include 12 key attributes:

1. color
2. water
3. air
4. sunlight
5. plants
6. animals
7. natural materials
8. views and vistas
9. façade greening
10. geology and landscape
11. habitats and ecosystems
12. fire

Natural Shapes and Forms

A finite number of shapes found in nature can be used to describe the natural world. Eleven elements inform the principle of natural shapes and forms:

1. botanical motifs
2. tree and columnar supports
3. animal motifs
4. shells and spirals
5. egg, oval, and tubular forms
6. arches, vaults, and domes
7. shapes resisting straight lines and right angles
8. simulations of natural features
9. biomorphy (resembles a living organism's shape or appearance)
10. geomorphy (resembles the earth in shape or appearance)
11. biomimicry (mimicking life systems)

Natural Patterns and Processes

The way in which nature operates can be distilled into some basic patterns. Fourteen attributes describe these natural patterns and processes:

1. sensory variability
2. information richness
3. age, change, and the patina of time
4. growth and efflorescence (gradual unfolding)
5. central focal point
6. patterned wholes
7. bounded spaces
8. transitional spaces
9. linked series and chains
10. integration of parts to wholes
11. complementary contrasts
12. dynamic balance and tension
13. fractals (geometric pattern that repeats at many different scales)
14. hierarchically organized ratios and scales

Light and Space

The way in which light appears in nature can easily be used as a design element. The various configurations and appearances of light and space contain the following 12 attributes:

1. natural light
2. filters and diffused light
3. light and shadow
4. reflected light
5. light pools
6. warm light
7. light as shape and form
8. spaciousness
9. spatial variability
10. spaces as shape and dorm
11. spatial harmony
12. inside-outside spaces

Place-Based Relationships

The manner in which people connect to a place provides the genesis for place-based relationships. This element is composed of these 10 attributes:

1. geographic connections to place
2. historic connection to place
3. ecological connection to place
4. cultural connection to place
5. indigenous materials
6. landscape orientation
7. landscape features that define building form

8. integration of culture and ecology
9. spirit of place
10. avoiding placelessness

Evolved Human–Nature Relationships

The evolved human–nature relationship references the early work of Kaplan and Kaplan and include 12 attributes, which are:

1. prospect and refuge
2. order and complexity
3. curiosity and enticement
4. change and metamorphosis
5. security and protection
6. mastery and control
7. affection and attachment
8. attraction and beauty
9. exploration and discovery
10. information and cognition
11. fear and awe
12. reverence and spirituality

(All lists are from Kellert Table 1.1, 15)

LEED and Health

Based on an older set of guidelines called the "Green Guidelines for Healthcare," the USGBC has developed the LEED Green Building Rating System for Healthcare. As with all LEED Guidelines, the LEED for Healthcare guide can be found on the council's website at http://www.usgbc.org/DisplayPage.aspx?CMSPageID=1765.

All LEED guidelines for specific typologies are based on the LEED for New Construction Guidelines, with some changes made for the specific use. For example, the specific LEED for Healthcare Guidelines credits include the following additional credits beyond the basic LEED rating system requirements:

- Environmental assessment prerequisite (Sustainable Sites)
- Connection to the natural world, places of respite and connection to the natural world, direct access for patients (Sustainable Sites)

- Minimized use of potable water for medical equipment (Water Efficiency)
- Additional water use reduction credits for measurement and verification, building equipment, cooling towers, and food waste systems (Water Efficiency)
- Community containment of airborne contaminant releases (Energy and Atmosphere)
- Prerequisite for mercury reduction (Materials and Resources), PBT (polybutylene terephthalate) source reductions for mercury, lead, cadmium, and copper, added credits for furniture and medical furnishings and design flexibility (Materials and Resources)
- Prerequisite for hazardous material removal in renovation projects (Indoor Environmental Quality)
- Acoustic control, low-emitting materials credit (Indoor Environmental Quality)
- Additional prerequisite and points for integrated project planning (Innovation in Design). (www.usgbc.org/resources/leed-2009-healthcare-vs-leed-2009-new-construction-credit-comparision)

Thus, the LEED Rating Systems was customized for healthcare design specifically.

Ergonomics in Healthcare

Ergonomics is the design of interior environments and objects to reduce operator fatigue and discomfort and to maximize productivity. Good ergonomic design is important in all environments and particularly in healthcare, where the entire focus is on patient well-being. One company that has engaged in ongoing research and product development for proper ergonomics is Humanscale. In its white paper, Humanscale noted that the average computer station in a hospital environment might have more than 30 different users in a single day. Thus, the designers at Humanscale have developed four standards for designers to use when selecting these types of in-room stations

from their research over the past 25 years.

An in-room station is a medical records station located within the exam room. As medical records have been converted to digital record keeping, computer stations have been added to nursing stations, exam rooms, and other areas of the healthcare environment. A single computer might by used by all nurses and doctors during multiple shifts. These stations should:

1. be intuitive, with independent keyboard and monitor adjustability.
2. have support for sitting and standing positions.
3. be flexible to accommodate all users comfortably.
4. be easy to use and maneuverable in compact spaces.

A few examples of these types of ergonomic work tools include adjustable sit-stand workstations on wheels, sit-stand wall-mounted systems, nursing station tools that offer easy and intuitive adjustments, and ergonomic seating with antimicrobial fabric.

Bariatric Concerns

According to *Healthcare Design Magazine*, about one-third of all medical patients are considered bariatric and can no longer be stigmatized and separated from other patients as the number of obese patients continues to rise. A bariatric patient weighs 350 pounds or more. With more than 65 percent of all people in the U.S. population considered either overweight or obese, designing for the overweight is a reality of design for all environments. In response to these changes, roughly one-third of all furniture should accommodate bariatric patients and be mixed in with the other seating. Some key concerns for bariatric patients include adequate numbers of bariatric chairs, skin health (need for ventilation due to increased sweat production), infection control (from the additional moisture), comfort, and dignity. In writing for the Obesity Action Coalition, psychologist Sean Connolly, PhD, describes the relationship between obesity and low self-esteem. According to "Seating With Dignity," written by the furniture designers at KI, designers must remember that not all people—including bariatric patients—are made the same way. According to the KI Design and Development Team and Metaphase Design Group, key design considerations should include not only the dimensions of furnishings but also the way in which people interact with furniture and providing all of this in an environment of respect. One of the challenges often faced by bariatric patients is getting up from a chair. Using the arms is a common way to do this, thus the arms of the chair must be strong enough to hold the weight in addition to the chair itself. And according to Helen Kerr, product designer and developer, it is important to remember that obesity is a "medical condition, not a failure of personality" (Kerr, 2008).

Healthcare acquired infections (HAI) affect approximately 2 million people per year in the United Sates. Of these cases, 90,000 result in death. This is more deaths per year than from breast cancer, AIDS, and prostate cancer combined. (Harris, 2011) Common pathogens (bacteria or virus that can cause disease) in the healthcare environment include *C. diff* (*Clostridium difficile*), VRE (Vancomycin-resistant *enterocci*), and MRSA (methicillin-resistant *Staphylococcus aureus*). Antibiotic-resistant "super bugs" such as these are on the rise and present a huge challenge for healthcare providers (Harris, 2011).

Founded in 1946 and operationally located within the Department for Health and Human services, the Centers for Disease Control (CDC) established the following infection prevention checklist in July of 2011 for creating healthier healthcare facilities for outpatient care (http://www.cdc.gov/hai/settings/outpatient/checklist/outpatient-care-checklist.html):

I. Administrative Policies and Facility Practices
  A. Facility Policies
    1. Written policies
    2. Infection prevention policies that are reviewed annually at least
    3. Trained infection control person
    4. Adherence supplies available
  B. General Infection Prevention Education and Training
    1. Healthcare personnel receive regular training on infection prevention policies
    2. Competency and compliance with specific prevention policies
  C. Occupational Health
    1. Healthcare personnel are trained on OSHA blood-borne pathogen standard upon hire and annually.
    2. The facility maintains a log of needle sticks, sharps injuries, and other employee exposure events.
    3. Following an exposure event, post-exposure evaluation and follow-up.
    4. Hepatitis B vaccination at no cost.
    5. Post-vaccination screening.
    6. All personnel are offered annual influenza vaccine at no cost.
    7. All personnel with potential TB exposure are screened for TB upon hire and annually.
    8. Facility has respiratory protection program.
    9. Respiratory fit testing is provided.
    10. Facility has written protocols for managing/preventing job-related and community acquired infections of healthcare personnel.
  D. Surveillance and Disease Reporting
    1. Updated list of diseases reportable to public health authority is readily available to personnel.
    2. Facility can demonstrate compliance with mandatory reporting requirements.
  E. Hand Hygiene
    1. Facility provides readily accessible supplies necessary for adherence to hand hygiene protocols.

2. Healthcare personnel are educated regarding hand washing protocols.
3. The facility periodically monitors and records adherence to hand hygiene protocols and provides feedback to personnel.

F. Personal Protective Equipment (PPE)
   1. The facility has sufficient and appropriate PPE.
   2. Healthcare personnel receive training on proper selection and use of PPE.

G. Injection Safety
   1. Medication purchasing decisions at the facility reflect selection of vial sizes that most appropriately fit the procedure needs of the facility.
   2. Injections are required to be prepared using aseptic technique in a clean area free from contamination or contact with blood, bloody fluids, or contaminated equipment.
   3. Facility has policies and procedures to track healthcare provider access to controlled substances to prevent theft.

H. Respirator Hygiene/Cough Etiquette
   1. The facility has policies and procedures to contain respiratory secretions in persons who have signs and symptoms of respiratory infections, beginning at point of entry to the facility and continuing through visit duration.
   2. The facility educates healthcare professionals on the importance of infection prevention measures with specific regard to respiratory pathogens and examining patients with signs/symptoms of respiratory infection.

I. Environmental Cleaning
   1. Facility has written policies and procedures for routine cleaning and disinfection of environmental services, including identification of responsible personnel.

2. Environmental services staff receive job training and competency validation at hire and when policies change.
3. Training and equipment are available to ensure that healthcare providers wear appropriate PPE to preclude exposure to infectious agents or chemicals.
4. Cleaning procedures are periodically monitored and assessed to ensure they are consistently and correctly performed.
5. The facility has a policy/procedure for decontamination of spills of blood or other bodily fluids.

J. Reprocessing of Reusable Medical Devices
   1. Facility has policies and procedures to ensure that reusable medical devices are cleaned and reprocessed appropriately prior to use on another patient.
   2. Policies, procedures, and manufacturer reprocessing instructions for reusable metical devices used in the facility are available in the preprocessing area(s).
   3. Healthcare personnel responsible for reprocessing reusable medical devices are appropriately trained, and competencies are regularly documented.
   4. Training and equipment are available to ensure that healthcare personnel wear appropriate PPE to prevent exposure to infectious agents or chemicals.

K. Sterilization of Reusable Instruments and Devices
   1. All reusable critical instrument and devices are sterilized prior to reuse.
   2. Routine maintenance for sterilization equipment is performed according to manufacturer instructions.

3. Policies and procedures are in place outlining facility response in the event of reprocessing error/failure.

L. High-Level Disinfection of Reusable Instruments and Devices

1. All reusable semi-critical items receive at least high-level disinfection prior to use.

2. The facility has a system in place to identify which instrument was used on a patient via a log for each procedure.

3. Routine maintenance for high-level disinfection equipment is performed according to manufacturer instructions; maintenance records are available.

II. Personnel and Patient-Care Observations

A. Hand Hygiene Performed Correctly

1. Before contact with the patient or their immediate care environment

2. Before exiting the patient's care area after touching the patient or the patient's immediate care environment

3. Before performing an aseptic task

4. After contact with blood, body fluids, or contaminated surfaces

5. When hands move from a contaminated body site to a clean body site during patient care

B. Personal Protective Equipment (PPE) is correctly used

1. PPE is removed and discarded prior to leaving the patient's room or care area.

2. Hand hygiene is performed immediately after removal of PPE.

3. Gloves are provided and properly utilized.

4. Gowns are provided and properly utilized.

5. Facial protection is provided and properly utilized.

C. Injection Safety

1. Needles and syringes are used for only one patient.

2. The rubber septum on a medication vial is disinfected with alcohol prior to piercing.

3. Medication vials are entered with a new needle and a new syringe even when obtaining additional doses for the same patient.

4. Single dose medication vials, ampules, and bags or bottles or intravenous solution are used for only one patient.

5. Medication administration tubing and connectors are used for only one patient.

6. Multi-dose vials are dated by healthcare provider when they are first opened and discarded within 28 days unless the manufacturer specifies a different date for the opened vial.

7. Multi-dose vials are dedicated to individual patients whenever possible.

8. Multi-dose vials to be used for more than one patient are kept in a centralized medication area and do not enter the immediate patient treatment area.

9. All sharps are disposed of in a puncture-resistant sharps container.

10. All controlled substances are kept locked within a secure area.

D. Point-of-Care Testing

1. New single-use, auto-disabling lancing device is used for each patient.

2. If used for more than one patient, the point-of-care testing meter is cleaned and disinfected after every use according to manufacturer instructions.

E. Environmental Cleaning

1. Environmental surfaces, with an emphasis on surfaces in proximity to the patient and those that are frequently touched, are cleaned and then disinfected with an EPA-registered disinfectant.

2. Cleaners and disinfectants are used in accordance with manufacturer instructions.

F. Reprocessing of Reusable Instruments and Devices

1. Reusable medical devices are cleaned, reprocessed, and maintained according to the manufacturer instructions.
2. Single-use devices are discarded after use and not used for more than one patient.
3. Reprocessing area has a workflow pattern such that devices clearly flow from high contamination areas to clean/sterile areas.
4. Medical devices are stored in a manner to protect from damage and contamination.

G. Sterilization of Reusable Instruments and Devices
   1. Items are thoroughly pre-cleaned according to manufacturer instructions and visually inspected for residual soil prior to sterilization.
   2. Enzymatic cleaner or detergent is used for pre-cleaning and discarded according to manufacturer instructions.
   3. Cleaning brushes are disposable or cleaned and high-level disinfected or sterilized after each use.
   4. After pre-cleaning, instruments are appropriately wrapped/packaged for sterilization.
   5. A chemical indicator is placed correctly in the instrument packs in every load.
   6. A biological indicator is used at least weekly for each sterilizer and with every load containing implantable items.
   7. For dynamic removal-type sterilizers, a Bowie-Dick test is performed each day the sterilizer is used to verify efficacy of air removal.
   8. Sterile packs are labeled with the sterilizer used, the cycle or load number, and the date of sterilization.
   9. Logs for each sterilizer cycle are current and include results from each load.
   10. After sterilization, medical devices and instruments are stored so that sterility is not compromised.
   11. Sterile packages are inspected for integrity and compromised packages are reprocessed prior to use.
   12. Immediate-use steam sterilization, if performed, is only done in circumstances in which routine sterilization procedures cannot be performed.
   13. Instruments that are flash-sterilized are used immediately and not stored.

H. High-Level Disinfection of Reusable Instruments and Devices
   1. Flexible endoscopes are inspected for damage and leak tested as part of each reprocessing cycle.
   2. Items are thoroughly pre-cleaned according to manufacturer instruction and visually inspected for residual soil prior to high-level disinfection.
   3. Enzymatic cleaner or detergent is used and discarded according to manufacturer instructions.
   4. Cleaning brushes are disposable or cleaned and high-level disinfected or sterilized after each use.
   5. For chemicals used in high-level disinfection, manufacturer instructions are followed for preparation, testing, and replacement.
   6. If automated reprocessing equipment is used, proper connectors are used to assure that channels and lumens are appropriately disinfected.
   7. Devices are disinfected for the appropriate length of time as specified by manufacturer instructions.
   8. Devices are disinfected at the appropriate temperature as specified by manufacturer instructions.
   9. After high-level disinfection, devices are rinsed with sterile water, filtered water, or tap water followed by a rinsed with 70 to

90 percent ethyl or isopropyl alcohol.

10. Devices are dried thoroughly prior to reuse.

11. After high-level disinfection, devices are stored in a manner to protect from damage or contamination.

Health of the Planet and Health of People

According to Pierce and Jameton, environmental ethics and philosophy can provide significant guidance to the healthcare industry. Many of the issues currently facing medical professionals also raise ethical questions. Examples include assisted suicide, the use of breathing machines for those who are brain dead, and the notion of using someone's genetic makeup to pre-treat and diagnose disease. The very notion of prolonging life is an ethical notion for some people. The specific ethical dilemmas that Pierce and Jameton address relate to the environmental impact that the healthcare industry has on the planet.

Biocentrism

The main principle of **biocentrism** or "biocentric egalitarianism" is that all living creatures have an equal right to life and health. In his book *Respect for Nature* (1986), author Paul Taylor, argues for biocentrism. He describes two interconnected concepts that capture this approach: every organism has its own good that can either be supported or prevented by humans, and all organisms have inherent worth. The notion that all life forms have an inherent worth suggests an egalitarian notion of healthcare. A reliance on nature as an example for design solutions coupled with a healthy respect of the natural world provides a way to design with environmental ethics in mind.

Eco-Centrism/Holism

An **eco-centric** approach sees the interconnectedness of all living things.

Nature and man can be viewed holistically as interconnected beings with a world system. This is captured by author Aldo Leopold's land ethic in *A Sand County Almanac*. Leopold's central thesis is, "We will only protect what we love." Again, a respect for nature and humanity's role as a part of nature can help to guide a designer toward the creation of healthy interior environments that respond positively to nature. Examples of this approach could include taking advantage of views, natural daylighting, and situating buildings to have minimal impact on the natural systems around them.

Environmental Impact of Healthcare

According to Pierce and Jameton, "The healthcare system significantly damages the environment—by the overall materials scale of its activities and by the variety, toxicity, and volume of its waste stream" (43). In the United States, one in nine employees works within the healthcare system. Representing 13 percent of the Gross Domestic Product (GDP), healthcare encompasses more than 7,000 hospitals, 20,000 long-term care facilities, 300,000 medical and dental offices and clinics, and 10,000 home healthcare companies. (45)

According to healthcare design expert Sara Marberry (2013), the Affordable Care Act (ACA) will have a significant impact on healthcare facilities. She says that the big box model for hospitals is on its way out and that about 80 percent of existing buildings are more than 15 years old, with some dating back to the 1800s. Consolidation will most likely impact the size and scope of healthcare design projects over the next five to ten years, according to Marberry. The emphasis will likely shift from inpatient facilities to more ambulatory care centers. Hospitals will be forced to be more cost effective and efficient. Designers must be able to understand the business of healthcare and will need to be able to design to respond to the changing needs. Not only will EBD be important, but the value of design as a way of being economical and efficient will also be highlighted.

The need for 24-hour access coupled with the large size of many of these facilities, the energy use, water consumption, and waste production are key components of healthcare environments. Medical waste and its potential toxicity have long presented environmental risks. Each state has its own medical waste policies and procedures. The primary ways in which it is handled include incineration, autoclaves, mechanical and chemical disinfection, microwaving, and irradiation. According to the EPA, about 90 percent of medical waste is incinerated (Basura). Infection or **red bag waste** accounts for roughly 15 percent of the total medical waste stream. Plastics contribute another 20 percent of the total, which also includes heavy metals, cytotoxic (toxic cells) agents from chemotherapy, and radioactive wastes as the by-products of x-rays and other procedures. Known toxins include **polyvinyl chlorides (PVCs)** used in intravenous (IV) bags, di-ethylexyl-phthalate (DEHP) used as a softening agent in PVCs, and the many pharmaceuticals and medicinal preparations from living organisms (biologicals) that can end up in the local water supply (Pierce and Jameton, Chapter 4). Serious consideration of the waste and environmental impact must be included from the very beginning of a healthcare project in order to lessen the overall environmental impact. Designers need to provide for this type of waste stream and include disposal and storage areas consistent with the local laws and requirements.

The Healthcare Plastics Recycling Council (HPRC)

As mentioned previously, plastics are used extensively throughout the healthcare environment. In recent decades, plastics have become widely used in the medical industry for many reasons. Shorter hospital stays coupled with the rise of infectious diseases has resulted in the use of more disposable medical devices—many of which are plastic (Sastri, 2010).

In response to the growing use of plastics, the **Healthcare Plastics Recycling Council (HPRC)** was founded in 2009 by a group of medical professionals, including people from Stanford Hospital and Clinics and Kaiser Permanente, to address the recycling of the many plastics used in healthcare. Plastics are the primary disposable material used throughout the healthcare environment. The work of this group includes design guidelines for recycling plastics (instead of incineration), value chain mapping (looking at the entire life cycle of a plastic), and pilot study resources to show how this method can and has worked. (http://www.hprc. org/#!work)

Plastic is an environmental concern for many reasons. According to Knoblauch with *Scientific American*, the mass production of plastics began in the 1940s. Today, roughly 4 percent of world oil is used to make plastics. Phthalates (a component of plasticizers) can be found in the bodies of nearly every adult and eight out of ten babies. Plastics buried in landfills eventually find their way into the local groundwater supply. The U.S. Center for Disease Control has noted that 93 percent of people in the United States have detectable levels of BPA (biphenol A, found in the plastic bottles and the lining of food packaging) in their urine.

The American Association of Healthcare Interior Designers (AAHID)

The **AAHID** is a non-profit organization founded in 2004 with the mission to provide interior design services to the healthcare industry via qualified individuals who meet education, examination, and training requirements. Certification offered by this specialized group of interior designers provides an additional level of credential to those who demonstrate the knowledge and skills to practice healthcare design. To become certified, a designer must meet the work experience and education guidelines as well as pass the AAHID exam. The exam is offered twice a year, in April and October, and consists of 150 questions covering planning, pre-design, and design. Applicants must submit a portfolio to sit for the exam, and once assessed, must complete one hour of continuing education every two years. Exam results are delivered within 60 days of completing the test. The *AAHID 2013 Candidate Handbook* can be found online (www.aahid.org). The organization's website also includes a variety of resources to assist designers. Online articles address topics ranging from carpet use to bariatric design guidelines.

Healthcare Council IFMA

Another organization that might be of interest to those considering a career in healthcare design is the **International Facility Management Association (IFMA)**. IFMA was founded in 1980 and today has 130 chapters and 17 affiliated industry councils with over 23,000 members worldwide. This group also offers the Healthcare Institute (an IFMA Alliance Partner) that meets twice annually and provides a resource for those working with healthcare facilities. The institute provides the latest findings about the ongoing maintenance and care of the healthcare interior environment, and provides conferences, seminars, and current news to healthcare facility managers and design professionals.

Research in Healthcare Design

Research in Healthcare Design is centralized in a few universities around the world and a few repositories of information. As mentioned previously, the Center for Health Design is one of

these resources. The *HERD Journal* (Health Environments Research and Design) is the only journal dedicated solely to presenting the latest academic research in healthcare design. Short Abstracts are available on the HERD website (www.herdjournal.com). The journal is published quarterly. Recent research efforts include a study of the impacts of bedside technology, pre- and post-occupancy evaluations of a children's hospital, a case study of two waiting rooms and the influence of positive distractions on children, and study about the use of daylighting in an ICU.

In addition, professional case studies and other reports are posted on the Center for Health Design's website and are also published in *Healthcare Design* magazine.

Characteristics and Classification of Healthcare Facilities

According to EDAC, there are several ways in which healthcare settings are classified. When categorized according to size, a small hospital is considered as fewer than 100 beds, a medium is 100 to 500, and a large hospital exceeds 500 beds. Typically, healthcare communities are either community-based or non-community based. An example of a non-community-based healthcare facility would include a student health center at a university or a prison hospital. In other words, they are not open to the community at large. Healthcare settings are also divided into inpatient, outpatient, or a combination of the two. Ownership models of healthcare facilities include public and federal, such as the VA (Veterans Administration), voluntary and not-for-profit, proprietary, and doctor-owned. Finally, the length of patient stay can also create separate categories such as short-stay (less than 30 days), long-term (exceeds 30 days), and acute specialty (CHD, 49).

Although some commonalities exist to all facilities, each one has its own design requirements.

Student Project Examples

Student approaches to sustainable healthcare design range from the use of sustainable materials and finishes to the inclusion of a biophilic healing approach to the interior environment using nature and other elements of EBD research findings. Each of the projects was completed as a part of a design studio, and the duration ranges from a one-week competition project to a four-week semester project. Some are team projects and others were completed individually. The projects show the diverse range of facility types in healthcare design, the variety of medical conditions, and the various populations being treated. The final project won an Honorable Mention in the 2009 ASID National Student Design Competition.

Jessie Oliver—Pediatric Oncology (eco-technic, biophilic)

The Pediatric Oncology Facility emphasizes healing through a connection to nature. Located in Washington, D.C., the design relies on a child's new relationship to nature for those who have grown up in a "concrete jungle." The design seeks to engage each child in play through dropped ceilings, intersecting planes, enlarged joinery details, and patterned upholstery and textures. Through the emphasis on play and views of nature, children are encouraged to heal and thrive.

Figure 3.1 Jessie Oliver, Pediatric Oncology Center: Concept page

waiting room

The first floor waiting room of Washington, D.C.'s Pediatric Oncology Center offers the perfect atmosphere for children to use their imagination and leave all their worries about cancer behind. The space not only provides a variety of seating, both for adults and children, but it also features computer workstations and an adjacent playroom in order to satisfy every user's needs.

furniture

A   Pop Stick Chairs & Table, Paul Frank   B   Spark Side Chair, Knoll   C   Circa Modular Seating & Table, Steelcase

Figure 3.2 Jessie Oliver, Pediatric Oncology Center: Waiting room

Sonata Casegood by Steelcase Nurture

The infusion center introduces the idea of using interior courtyards to bring natural light centrally into the building while also giving children and their families an opportunity to connect to the outdoors. The geometric patterns on the glass are used to direct a child's eye through the courtyard, which is necessary due to their unfamiliarity with nature .

Each infusion space includes a junior-sized treatment chair, and 2-3 extra seating options. Privacy curtains also allow families to have time to themselves, but easy accessibility from the nurse's station in case of an emergency.

Infusion Center

Figure 3.3 Jessie Oliver, Pediatric Oncology Center: Infusion room

level one

As patients and their families first step foot into this pediatric oncology center, they are immediately greeted with a large, airy atrium featuring a nicely landscaped interior courtyard-- a pleasant breath of fresh air after escaping the busy streets of Washington, D.C.

The three corridors stemming from the atrium lead patients to their area of need. New cancer patients would be directed toward the central corridor, which houses the infusion waiting area and provides easy access to exam rooms (back) and the infusion center (left). The cafeteria and public restrooms are also located in the central region of the building for most convenient access to patients, visitors, and staff.

The right corridor is reserved for patients who are receiving radiation therapy. Due to the lack of windows on this side of the building, a small interior courtyard is utilized to provide natural light in addition to the healing qualities of nature.

The staff quarters are located centrally in the back of the building for easy accessibility to all medical areas. Doctors and nurses are also provided a sense of privacy from patients and their families with the addition of their own exit/entry and staff elevators.

Each medical area is clearly marked by hanging wooden signs with colored letters for easy wayfinding. (pictured right)

scale: 1/32" = 1'-0"

interior courtyard

fire-rated stairwell

patient/visitor elevator

staff elevator

room key

1	atrium	19	consulting room	28	radiation check-in/out	10	charting
2	reception	20	mechanical	29	radiation gowned waiting + dressing	11	soiled utility + biohazard
3	storage	21	data room	30	infusion check-in/out	12	exam nursing station
4	staff kitchen	22	electrical room	31	infusion waiting	13	clean utility
5	staff restroom	23	janitor's closet	32	cafeteria	14	exam room
6	vending	24	entry to adjacent hospital	33	public restrooms	15	staff lounge + restroom
7	infusion nursing station	25	staff restroom	34	linear accelerator	16	storage
8	infusion room	26	lab	35	control room	17	staff office
9	patient restroom	27	blood draw	36	storage closet	18	pharmacy

Figure 3.4 Jessie Oliver, Pediatric Oncology Center: Plan and infusion waiting room

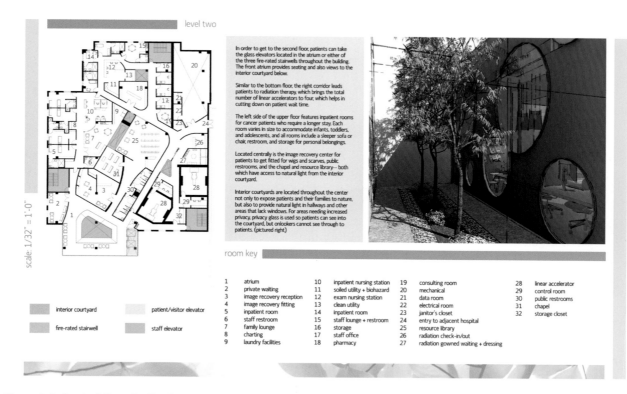

level two

In order to get to the second floor, patients can take the glass elevators located in the atrium or either of the three fire-rated stairwells throughout the building. The front atrium provides seating and also views to the interior courtyard below.

Similar to the bottom floor, the right corridor leads patients to radiation therapy, which brings the total number of linear accelerators to four, which helps in cutting down on patient wait time.

The left side of the upper floor features inpatient rooms for cancer patients who require a longer stay. Each room varies in size to accommodate infants, toddlers, and adolescents, and all rooms include a sleeper sofa or chair, restroom, and storage for personal belongings.

Located centrally is the image recovery center for patients to get fitted for wigs and scarves, public restrooms, and the chapel and resource library-- both which have access to natural light from the interior courtyard.

Interior courtyards are located throughout the center not only to expose patients and their families to nature, but also to provide natural light in hallways and other areas that lack windows. For areas needing increased privacy, privacy glass is used so patients can see into the courtyard, but onlookers cannot see through to patients. (pictured right)

scale: 1/32" = 1'-0"

interior courtyard

fire-rated stairwell

patient/visitor elevator

staff elevator

room key

1	atrium	10	inpatient nursing station	19	consulting room	28	linear accelerator
2	private waiting	11	soiled utility + biohazard	20	mechanical	29	control room
3	image recovery reception	12	exam nursing station	21	data room	30	public restrooms
4	image recovery fitting	13	clean utility	22	electrical room	31	chapel
5	inpatient room	14	inpatient room	23	janitor's closet	32	storage closet
6	staff restroom	15	staff lounge + restroom	24	entry to adjacent hospital		
7	family lounge	16	storage	25	resource library		
8	charting	17	staff office	26	radiation check-in/out		
9	laundry facilities	18	pharmacy	27	radiation gowned waiting + dressing		

Figure 3.5 Jessie Oliver, Pediatric Oncology Center: Plan and exterior garden view

Michelle Grant, Katie Herber, and Cara Holmes— Rural Healthcare Clinic (eco-technic, eco-social)

The 180 Degrees After-School Facility for Teenage Mental Health responds to the increasing need for substance abuse treatment among teenagers in rural communities, such as southwestern Virginia. The facility provides counseling to youths at risk. The entire project uses sustainable materials, finishes, and furnishings. The product-focused approach includes Green Label Plus certified carpet, pre-consumer recycled content tile, and Greenguard-certified eco-resin panels. Low-emitting Designtex fabrics are used on the lounge seating. The design takes advantage of natural daylighting and LED low-energy use solutions.

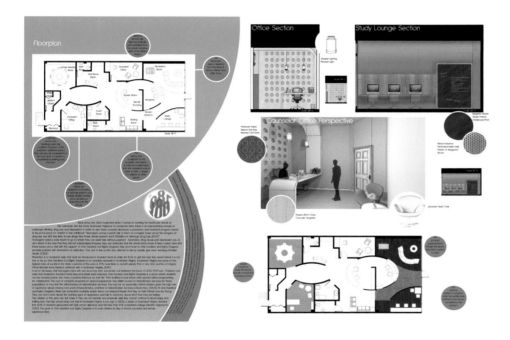

Figure 3.6 Michelle Grant, Katie Herber, and Cara Holmes, 180 Degrees After-School Facility for Teenage Mental Health: Board 1

Figure 3.7 Michelle Grant, Katie Herber, and Cara Holmes, 180 Degrees, After-School Facility for Teenage Mental Health: Board 2

Jennifer Boyd—Assisted Living Rehabilitation Center (biomimicry, eco-technic)

Branch Out is a rehabilitation center for teenagers that is designed to assist them through addiction to healing. The inspiration for the center is a tree house. A main central hall connects all parts of the facility, much as the trunk of a tree holds all the branches. Sustainability is achieved through connections to nature, the use of DIRTT wall panels (DIRTT is a wall panel manufacturer and the acronym stands for Do it Right This Time), a central skylight providing internal natural lighting, and sustainable materials, finishes, and furniture.

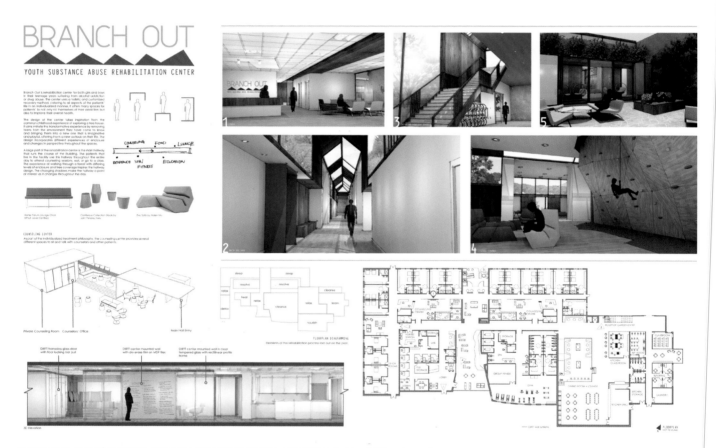

Figure 3.8 Jennifer Boyd, Branch Out Rehabilitation Facility: Presentation board

Figure 3.9 Jennifer Boyd, Branch Out Rehabilitation Facility: Sectional elevation

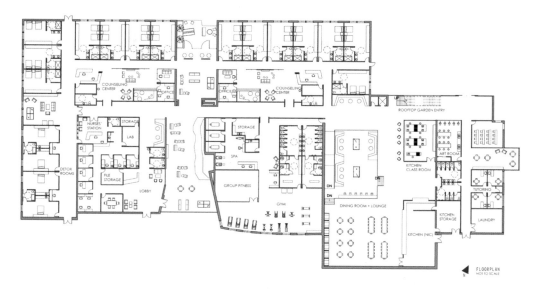

Figure 3.10
Jennifer Boyd,
Branch Out
Rehabilitation
Facility: Plan

Figure 3.11
Jennifer Boyd,
Branch Out
Rehabilitation
Facility: Interior
rendering of
climbing wall

Figure 3.12
Jennifer Boyd,
Branch Out
Rehabilitation
Facility: Interior
rendering of light-
filled corridor

Figure 3.13
Jennifer Boyd,
Branch Out
Rehabilitation
Facility: 3D
rendering of outdoor
garden space

Figure 3.14
Jennifer Boyd,
Branch Out
Rehabilitation
Facility: Interior
rendering of check-
in area

Figure 3.15
Jennifer Boyd,
Branch Out
Rehabilitation
Facility: Interior
rendering of stair
and bike storage
area

Kala Letts—INOVA Dementia Care Facility (biophilic, eco-medical)

The INOVA Dementia Care Facility embraces a biophilic approach to design. The concept was to create an ambiance centered on the hearth to enhance the sense of being at home in the environment. An open, breezy meadow motif was used to pull in nature throughout the facility. Sustainable materials used throughout the spaces include linoleum flooring and low-VOC paints, adhesives, and coatings.

Firm Approaches to Sustainable Healthcare Design

Healthcare design requires a specialized knowledge set. As a result, firms will often specialize in healthcare design, such as Wilmot Sanz, or have a healthcare design division, such as Perkins + Will.

Perkins + Will has detailed one model of the design process. Beginning in pre-design, a client might choose from a variety of typical patient room layouts using some generic plan prototypes developed by the firm. The optimal size for each exam room is also determined during this phase. Relying on the most current research conducted in-house, published in the *HERD Journal* and other healthcare journals, and located at the Center for Health Design online repository, the firm then moves into schematic design for the project. Perkins + Will has several research mechanisms in place including AREA (Advance Research Expand Apply), their Center for Excellence conferences and newsletter, and regular contributions, "Designing for Health," to *Contract Magazine*. The company also partners with several universities around the United States to advance its research.

INOVA Regional Department for Alzheimer's & Dementia
Alexandria, Virginia

Set in a tucked away site in Alexandria, Virginia, the Inova Regional Department for Alzheimer's and Dementia has assigned an exclusive long-term care wing attached to its new facility. The interior is directionally facing north in order to promote daylighting and the overall reduction of artificial lighting, which is known to help the circadian rhythm of Alzheimer's and dementia patients. The new wing will also be taking advantage of the expansive roof by having planters and greenery available to the patients as a secure and stress eliminating environment. This facility is designed to feature the hearth as the center of the home, a well-known concept for comfort. In order to give release to the compressed, enveloping spaces, the motif of an open breezy meadow is used to pull in biophilic elements of nature without compromising sanitation and allergy issues common to elderly long-term care. The natural landscaping

Reception Atrium

Figure 3.16 Kala Letts, INOVA Alzheimer's/ Dementia Facility: Interior rendering reception area and concept

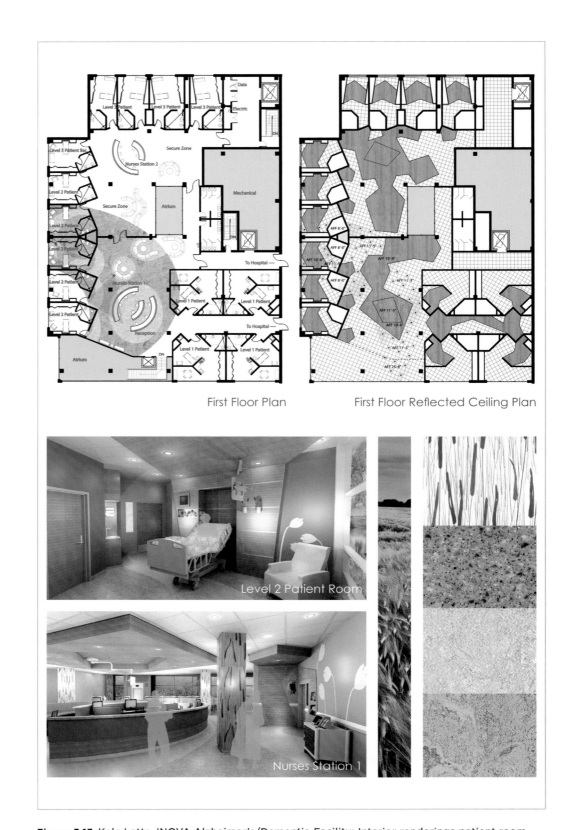

First Floor Plan

First Floor Reflected Ceiling Plan

Level 2 Patient Room

Nurses Station 1

Figure 3.17 Kala Letts, INOVA Alzheimer's/Dementia Facility: Interior renderings patient room and nurse's station, first floor plan, and RCP

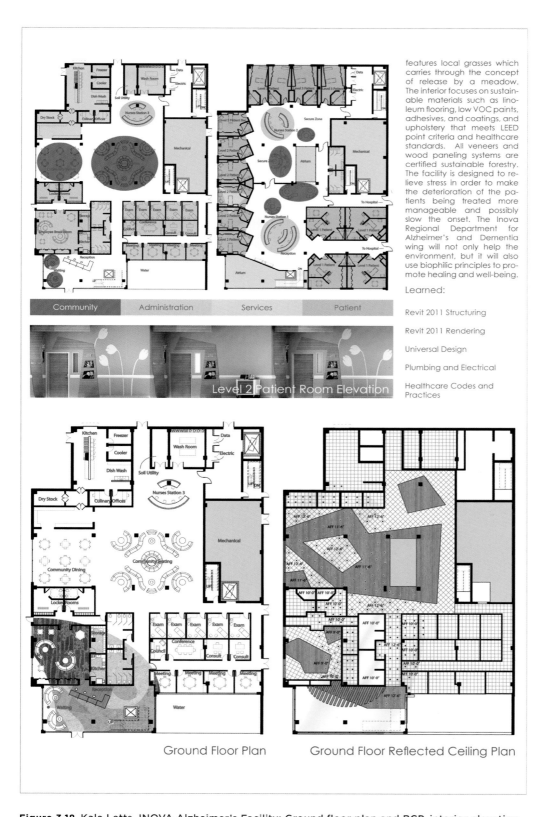

features local grasses which carries through the concept of release by a meadow. The interior focuses on sustainable materials such as linoleum flooring, low VOC paints, adhesives, and coatings, and upholstery that meets LEED point criteria and healthcare standards. All veneers and wood paneling systems are certified sustainable forestry. The facility is designed to relieve stress in order to make the deterioration of the patients being treated more manageable and possibly slow the onset. The Inova Regional Department for Alzheimer's and Dementia wing will not only help the environment, but it will also use biophilic principles to promote healing and well-being.

Learned:

Revit 2011 Structuring

Revit 2011 Rendering

Universal Design

Plumbing and Electrical

Healthcare Codes and Practices

| Community | Administration | Services | Patient |

Level 2 Patient Room Elevation

Ground Floor Plan

Ground Floor Reflected Ceiling Plan

Figure 3.18 Kala Letts, INOVA Alzheimer's Facility: Ground floor plan and RCP, interior elevation and space allocation diagrams

Some of the research the firm's designers incorporate into projects includes use of:

- its own precautionary materials database
- nature for healing environments and relaxation as well as pain reduction
- light for natural healing and reduced length of stay.
- patient lift installation to decrease staff injuries.
- form and color for wayfinding
- decentralized nurse stations for shorter walking distances.
- positive distractions, such as art, to improve mood and overall physiological state.
- seamless floors, coved skirting, no ledges, sanitizing hand gel stations, antimicrobial finishes, and non-permeable surfaces to facilitate infection control (Day 2012).

Wilmot Sanz—INOVA Fairfax Hospital South Patient Tower (eco-technic, eco-medical)

The new INOVA tower, encompassing 216,000 square feet. includes 120 medical/surgical beds and 54 ICU beds. The Fairfax Hospital Expansion project was designed to meet LEED certification. Green features of the building include a living roof, native plantings outside, low- or no-VOC materials for improved indoor air quality, local and regional materials, and low-emissivity windows. The design illustrates the hospital's commitment to sustainability and health.

Figure 3.19 Wilmot Sanz Architects, INOVA Fairfax South Patient Tower and Women's Hospital: Exterior rendering

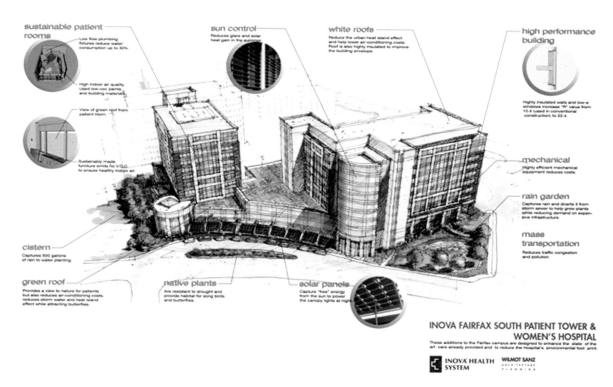

Figure 3.20 Wilmot Sanz Architects, INOVA Fairfax South Patient Tower and Women's Hospital: Diagram of sustainable features

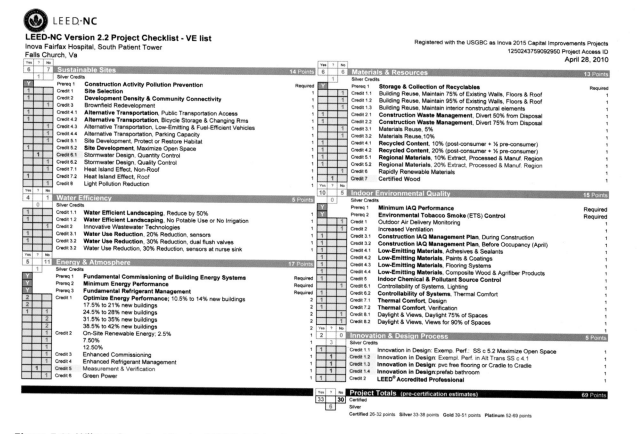

Figure 3.21 Wilmot Sanz Architects, INOVA Fairfax South Patient Tower and Women's Hospital: LEED checklist

Wilmot Sanz—Sibley Memorial Hospital Cancer Center (eco-technic)

Designed to meet LEED criteria for healthcare, the Sibley Memorial Radiation Oncology Facility included a 10-stop educational tour to demonstrate all the "green" features of the building. The intention of the tour was to satisfy a LEED Innovation in Design Green Education credit. Since the District of Columbia, where the facility is located, is one where all new buildings over 50,000 square feet had to meet LEED certification, the new facility was designed to this standard. The ways in which this was accomplished include using regional materials (sourced within a 500-mile radius) and including materials with recycled content and materials that were Forest Stewardship Council (FSC) certified. More than half of the building's materials came from regional sources. The interior design includes access to daylight and views for most spaces that use a roof monitor to enhance access to daylight, thus reducing the reliance on electric lighting in some spaces. A green roof lowers the ambient temperature of the surrounding area, and a cistern collects rainwater for landscape irrigation. Low-flow toilets and faucets also contribute to the potable water efficiency of the building.

Several certifications for interior materials contribute to the sustainable features of the building and to the good indoor air quality. Linoleum flooring integrates rapidly renewable contents such as cork, linseed oil, and jute (used on the backing). Further, this flooring is a naturally bio-static material that inhibits the growth of germs—a critical feature in a healthcare environment. All carpeting meets the Carpet and Rug Institute's gold standard for low emissions, and the backing contains 20 percent recycled content. Interior wood finishes are SFC certified with low-VOC finishes and stains. The designers created PVC-free interiors using rubber wall base, and PVC-free wall covering and wall protection rails.

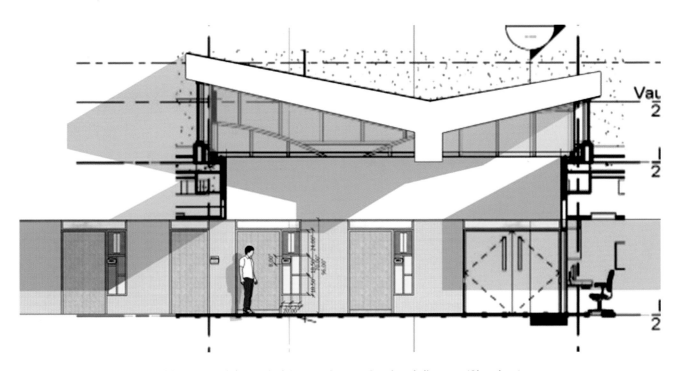

Figure 3.22 Wilmot Sanz, Sibley Memorial Hospital Cancer Center: Sectional diagram (Sketchup)

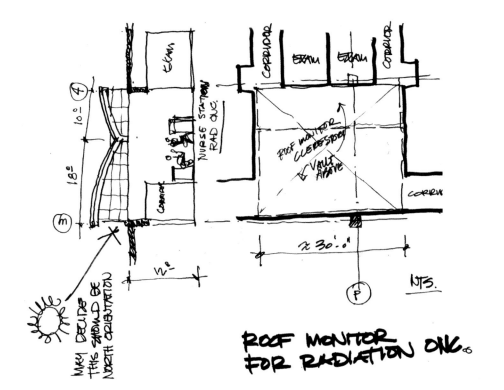

Figure 3.23
Wilmot Sanz, Sibley
Memorial Hospital
Cancer Center:
Sketch of proposed
roof monitor

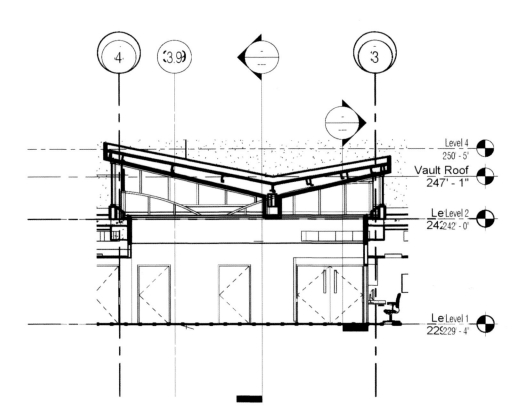

Figure 3.24
Wilmot Sanz,
Sibley Memorial
Hospital Cancer
Center: Construction
drawing of roof
monitor

Figure 3.25 Wilmot Sanz, Sibley Memorial Hospital Cancer Center: Interior view of space with roof monitor

Perkins + Will—Arlington Free Clinic (biophilic, eco-medical, eco-technic)

While small, the under-10,000-square-foot Arlington Free Clinic has all aspects of a sustainable project: economy, social equity in that it is a free clinic, and ecology. The purpose of the clinic is to show that everyone deserves healthcare

and that this service can be delivered by way of a clean and well-designed environment. In 2008, Perkins + Will was retained to create a design for the facility. Nationally known designer Tama Duffy Day used a flower motif as inspiration to produce a design with a strong central core. The rectilinear pattern of the previous design was replaced with an organic design centered on an oval-shaped core.

As the first LEED Gold free clinic in the United States, the Arlington Clinic includes several sustainable features. An innovative educational program uses a series of 25 signs to educate visitors and users of the space about sustainability. All of the furniture and 47 percent of the finishes were regionally obtained, and more than 85 percent of the construction waste was recycled, including all demolished materials such as ceiling tiles, wallboard, wood, and flooring. Other important characteristics of the design resulted in 30 percent water-use reduction and an energy-use reduction of 40 percent.

In addition to striving for LEED Gold, Day also used an EBD approach for the design of the clinic, according

Figure 3.26 Perkins + Will, Arlington Free Clinic: Conceptual diagram

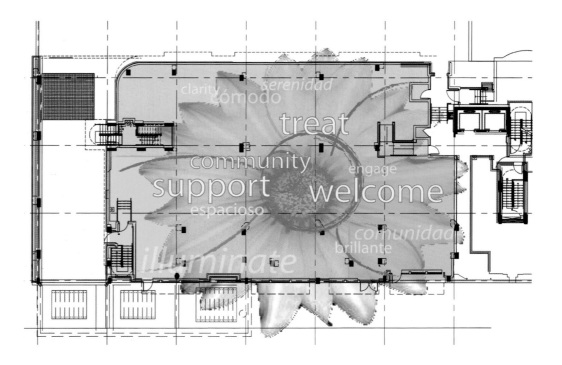

to an article posted on the Interiors and Sources website (2011). As a result of research studies, more natural light was integrated to create a light-filled environment, and sinks were placed in each exam room, since research shows that this promotes regular hand washing to reduce the spread of infection. In addition, a straightforward layout reduces stress and contributes to easy wayfinding.

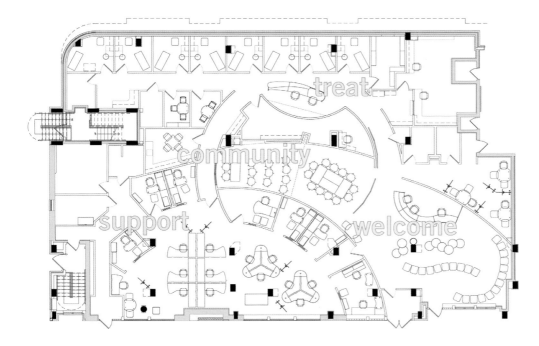

Figure 3.27 Perkins + Will, Arlington Free Clinic: New floor plan

Figure 3.28 Perkins + Will, Arlington Free Clinic: Reception area (Ken Hayden Photography)

Figure 3.29 Perkins + Will, Arlington Free Clinic: Exam room corridor (Ken Hayden Photography)

Figure 3.30 Perkins + Will, Arlington Free Clinic: Column detail (Ken Hayden Photography)

Figure 3.31 Perkins + Will, Arlington Free Clinic: Entrance to conference room (Ken Hayden Photography)

KSA Interiors with Earl Swensson Associates—Rockingham Memorial Hospital (RMH) (eco-technic)

As the first hospital in Virginia to achieve LEED Gold certification, the RMH is also one of only seven hospitals in the United States over 100,000 square feet to achieve this LEED designation. Interior designers at KSA Interiors were charged with the furniture specification and installation for the entire 620,000-square-foot facility. Existing furnishings were reused in the new facility and had to be carefully integrated with new selections.

Sustainable features of the new hospital include the integration of natural light throughout occupied spaces, water efficiency, energy-efficient lighting, recycling during construction, no VOC material and finish selections, and the use of green cleaning products, according to the hospital's website.

Figure 3.32 KSA Interiors with ESA, Rockingham Memorial Hospital: Café
Photo credit: Eric Taylor

Figure 3.33 KSA Interiors with ESA, Rockingham Memorial Hospital: Café
Photo credit: Eric Taylor

Figure 3.34 KSA
Interiors with
ESA, Rockingham
Memorial Hospital:
Waiting Room
Photo credit:
Eric Taylor

Figure 3.35 KSA
Interiors with
ESA, Rockingham
Memorial Hospital:
Waiting room
Photo credit:
Eric Taylor

Figure 3.36 KSA
Interiors with
ESA, Rockingham
Memorial Hospital:
Infusion area
Photo credit:
Eric Taylor

A Possible Design Process and Resources for Students

The typical design process includes a staged approach beginning with programming, schematic design, and then moving into design development and ultimately contract documents. The bulk of the information gathering takes place during the initial stage. This process normally includes collecting background research, code information, case studies, and space requirements. In the case of healthcare environments, the specific equipment contained within each space should be noted during this process.

Plan Prototypes

The following plan prototypes outline some of the critical elements to consider before beginning the actual design. These include planning for bariatric concerns, applying a universal design approach to the entire project, and providing space for critical elements such as crash carts. A **crash cart** (also called a code cart) is a movable cart with life-saving equipment in the event a patient experiences a life-threatening event. These prototypes are based on accessibility requirements, universal design recommendations, and research conducted by Perkins + Will and Ellerbee Beckett. Both firms emphasize the need for standardization that also allows for flexibility. Jim Bynum of Perkins + Will emphasizes, however, that one size does not fit all (2006).

One of the most interesting findings in Bynum's work was that single-handed rooms (rooms oriented the same way) worked best for acute care, while mirror-image rooms (rooms that mirror each other along a shared wall) seemed to work best in critical care environments—a finding that is different from industry trends. The plan prototypes developed for the Acute Care room, Adaptable Acuity room, and ICU room are based on those developed by Perkins + Will at their 2006 Center of Excellence design charrette. The rooms were designed to accommodate a variety of activities including daily living, consulting, patient assessment, procedures, therapy, transfers, and treatments.

The case for single-handed rooms includes consistency, the elimination of a shared headwall (which minimizes sound transmission), minimized travel distance from patient bed to toilet, and improved patient safety because the number of nurses' errors is reduced. On the other hand, mirror-image rooms allow for staff to see into more than one room at a time, shared staff work areas, a common headwall to share medical utilities, mid-board toilets, and reduced first costs (over single-handed rooms). There might also be a case made for improved patient visualization (the ability of healthcare personnel to see patients) through mirror-image rooms. (Bynum, 2006).

Applicable LEED Checklist

The LEED for Healthcare Checklist can be found in the Appendix (16) along with an EBD furniture (9) checklist and several other useful guidelines and checklists. As mentioned previously, the LEED checklist for healthcare design includes several additional requirements above and beyond the normal LEED checklist to ensure patient health and well-being.

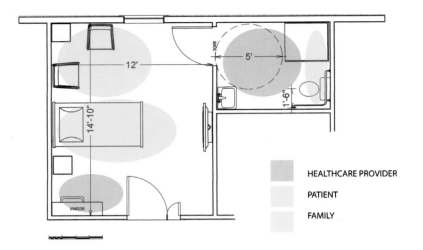

Figure 3.37 Typical patient room zones

HEALTHCARE PROVIDER

PATIENT

FAMILY

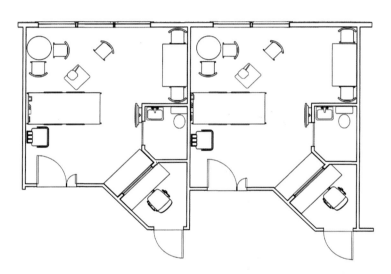

Figure 3.38 Acute care room based on Perkins + Will Conference for Excellence charrette, 2006

Figure 3.39 Acute care room rendering

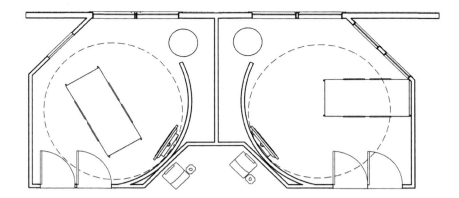

Figure 3.40
Adaptable acuity
care room based
on Perkins + Will
Conference for
Excellence charrette,
2006

Figure 3.41 Acuity
care room rendering

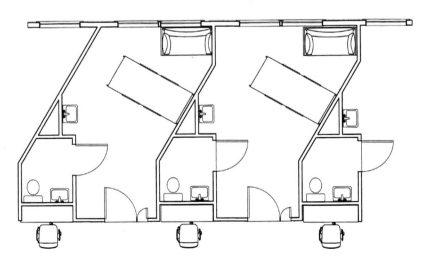

Figure 3.42
Adaptable acuity
care room based
on Perkins + Will
Conference for
Excellence charrette,
2006

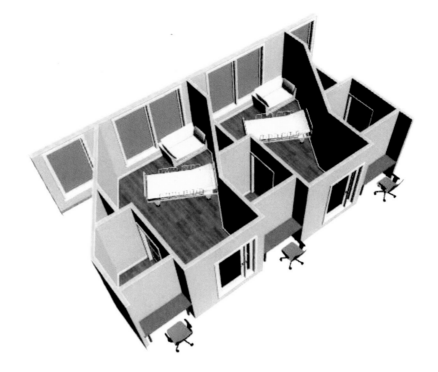

Figure 3.43
Adaptable acuity
care room rendering

Figure 3.44 ICU
room based on
Perkins + Will
Conference for
Excellence charrette,
2006

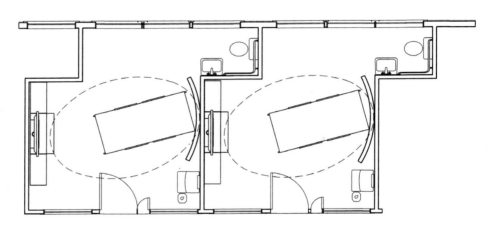

Figure 3.45 ICU
room rendering

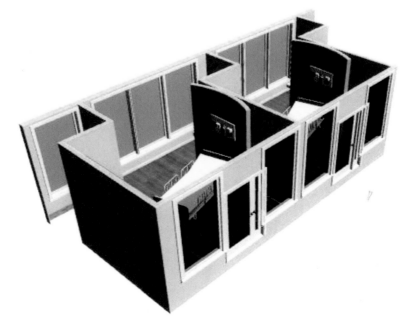

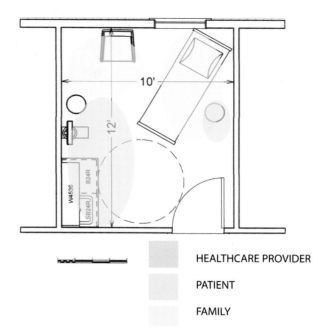

Figure 3.46 Typical exam room, 120 square feet, showing zones

HEALTHCARE PROVIDER

PATIENT

FAMILY

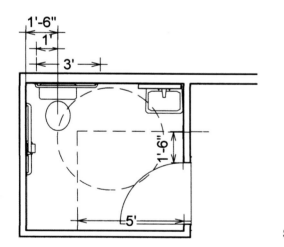

Figure 3.47 ADA toilet room: Plan

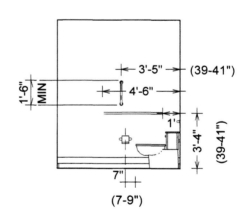

SEE ANSI AND ADA FOR ADDITIONAL INFORMATION

Figure 3.48 ADA toilet room: Elevation 1

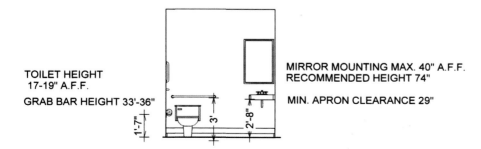

TOILET HEIGHT
17-19" A.F.F.

GRAB BAR HEIGHT 33'-36"

MIRROR MOUNTING MAX. 40" A.F.F.
RECOMMENDED HEIGHT 74"

MIN. APRON CLEARANCE 29"

Figure 3.49 ADA toilet room: Elevation 2

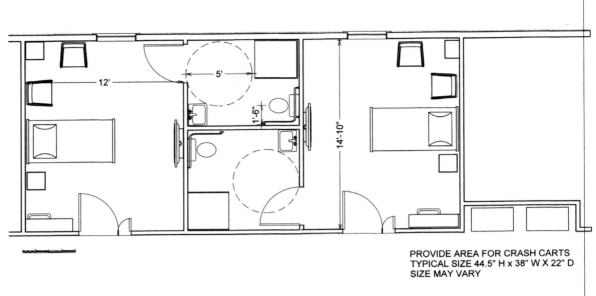

PROVIDE AREA FOR CRASH CARTS
TYPICAL SIZE 44.5" H x 38" W X 22" D
SIZE MAY VARY

Figure 3.50 Patient room corridor showing crash cart alcove

Figure 3.51
Medical reception

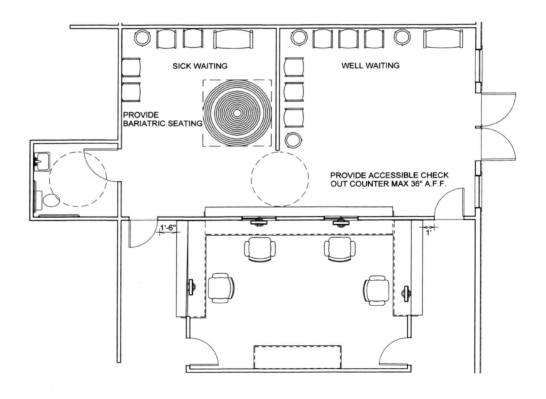

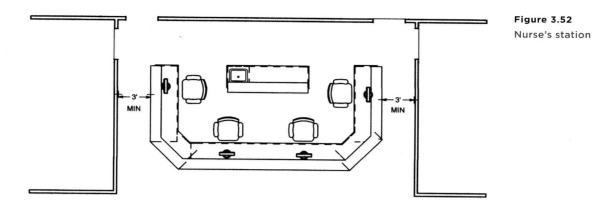

Figure 3.52
Nurse's station

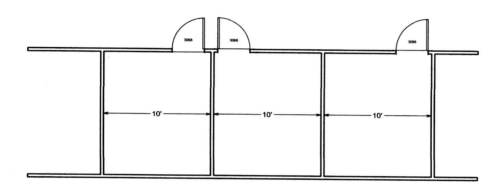

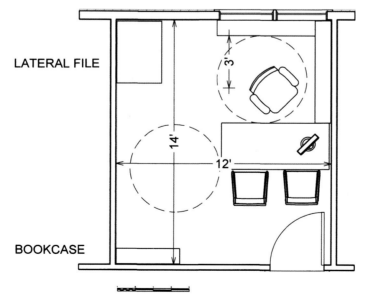

Figure 3.53
Accessible doctor's office

LATERAL FILE

BOOKCASE

Discussion Questions and Exercises

1. Discuss the impact of medical ethics on healthcare design.
2. Discuss the impact of environmental ethics and theories such as biocentrism on healthcare design and delivery.
3. Find three articles that discuss the impact of nature on health and well-being and be prepared to discuss how you might integrate this into a design project.
4. In your opinion, what is the biggest issue facing healthcare today? Why?

Key Terms

American Association of Healthcare Interior Designers (AAHID)

biocentrism

biophilia

biophilic

Center for Health Design (CHD)

crash cart

evidence-based design (EBD)

evidence-based design accreditation and certification (EDAC)

evidence-based medicine (EBM)

eco-centric/eco-centrism

International Facility Management Association (IFMA)

HAI (Health Associated Infections)

HERD Journal (Health Environments Research and Design)

HA-MRSA (hospital acquired methicillin-resistant *Staphylococcus aureus*)

Healthcare Practice Recycling Council (HPRC)

positive distraction

positive health outcome

polyvinyl chloride (PVC)

red bag waste

stress

Additional Key Terms

In 2011, the Center for Health Design published a glossary of terms with agreed-upon definitions for Evidence-Based Design. This 71-page document can be located at www.healthdesign.org under the "Research" tab.

These terms include:

medical errors

patient falls

patient satisfaction

patient waiting

staff efficiency

staff satisfaction

Sources

Augustin, S. 2009. *Place Advantage: Applied Psychology for Interior Architecture.* New Jersey: John Wiley and Sons.

Basura Medical Waste Resources. 2013. "Treatment of Medical Waste." Accessed June 26. http://www.wastemed.com/treatment.htm.

Bynum, J. 2006. "Healthcare: Inpatient Room Design," Center for Excellence Conference, published in-house by Perkins + Will.

Cama, R. 2009. *Evidence-Based Healthcare Design.* New Jersey: John Wiley and Sons.

Center for Health Design. 2008. *1:An Introduction to Evidence-Based Design.* Concord, CA: The Center for Health Design.

Connolly, S. 2013. "Self Esteem, Insecurity and Obesity," for the Obesity Action Coalition. Accessed June 25. www.Obesityaction.org.

Cornell University Ergonomics. http://ergo.human.cornell.edu/cutools.html

Duffy Day, Tama. 2012. "Healthcare Interiors," presentation to IDEAS Student Group at Virginia Tech, October 19.

Harris, D. 2011. "Environmental Design for Infection Prevention: Healthcare Facility Design." (KI and Furnishing Knowledge).

Humanscale. (n.d.). "Whitepaper: Ergonomics Supporting Healthcare-Specific Technology."

Interiors and Sources. 2011. "Arlington Free Clinic." Sept. 28. http://www.interiorsandsources.com/tabid/3339/ArticleID/13017/Default.aspx.

Kellert, Stephen, Judith Heerwagen, and Martin Mador. 2008. *Biophilic Design.* Hoboken, NJ: Wiley and Sons.

Kerr, Helen. 2008. "Today's Bariatric Trends." *Healthcare Design Magazine,* April 20. Accessed Sept. 12, 2012. www.healthcaredesignmagazine.com

Marberry, Sara O. 2013. "Industry Consolidations Shape Future of Healthcare Design," *Healthcare Design Magazine,* March 6. Accessed June 26. http://www.healthcaredesignmagazine.com/article/industry-consolidations-shape-future-healthcare-design?page=2.

"Seating with Dignity: Success Factors for Bariatric Furniture." (2008). (:KI Design and Development and Metaphase Design Group).

PBS. 2013. Accessed June 25. http://www.pbs.org/healthcarecrisis/history.htm

Pierce, Jessica, and Andrew Jameton. 2004. *The Ethics of Environmentally Responsible Health Care.* New York: Oxford University Press.

Sastri, Vinny. 2010. *Plastics in Medical Devices: Properties, Requirements and Applications.* Burlington, MA: Elsevier, Inc.

Thompson, Debra. 2010. "RHM Gets Gold Certification." RMH Medical Center, Oct. 28. Accessed September 12, 2012. http://www.rmhonline.com/Main/News/RMH_Gets_Gold_Certification_for_Building_Green_253.aspx.

4

CORPORATE PROJECTS

....

Objectives

- Students will understand the issues related to sustainable workplace design.

- Students will be able to describe how offices have evolved and changed.

- Students will be able to respond to different cultural needs in office design.

- Students will know where to look for information on new trends in sustainable office design.

- Students will be able to use LEED CI to guide them in their own office designs.

Overview and History

Office design represents the biggest sector for interior design. Since the mid-20th century, designers have helped businesses plan their office spaces. Beginning with Taylorism through today, office design has undergone many changes in response to the needs of the workplace.

Taylorism

Named for American inventor and engineer Frederick Taylor, **Taylorism** refers to a method of scientific management designed to increase office efficiency through a standardized approach. By providing the proper work set-up, worker production and efficiency would increase. Combining the efficiency work of Frederick W. Taylor with the motion study work of Frank and Lillian Gilbreth led to time-and-motion studies. Such studies impacted many areas of design including kitchen layouts and office design. The impact of this work on office design can be seen in the works of Frank Lloyd Wright at both the Larkin Building and the Johnson Wax facility.

Bürolandschaft "Office Landscape"

Bürolandschaft, or **office landscaping**, was a concept developed in Germany in the 1950s and 60s. Inspired by the open office from the 1940s in America, Germans Eberhard and Wolfgang Schnelle developed the office landscape concept. Informal layouts were enhanced by good lighting and the placement of plants. The desks themselves looked much like a landscape (Curl, 2000).

Action Office

The **Action Office** idea originated with Herman Miller in the 1960s. Under the direction of president of research, Robert Propst, the system's modular furniture and action office was designed and launched.

Cube Clusters

The unfortunate outcome of modular systems furniture was the cube farm phenomenon. **Cube clusters** consist of an open office space filled with repetitive cubicles. Identical office cubical spaces are created throughout the space.

Virtual Office

Today's office is characterized by more flexibility and has been driven—as has most office innovation—by technological advances. It is now possible to have employees who telecommute from home and who only occasionally even need to come into the physical office. The **virtual office** allows people to have all the services of a traditional office without needing a physical office space.

Current Issues in Corporate Design

One of the biggest issues facing corporations today is a challenging economy. The need to maximize usable space while also retaining the best employees has had an impact of the types of spaces within the typical workplace. John Czarnecki, editor in chief of *Contract Magazine*, notes in the May 2012 issue that there are three factors are affecting the current workplace: how people work today compared to 20 years ago, how companies accommodate changes in how people work, and the question about whether designers are leading or following. It is clear that Czarnecki sees the designer's role as one who should be out in front of the trend in office design as opposed to following what is already taking place (26).

Hospitality Influence

Lauren Rottet wrote an article for the May 2012 issue of *Contract* that explored hospitality design's influence on workplace design. Specifically hotel and restaurant design offer several amenities not previously seen in office design. According to Rottet, the primary way in which this takes place is by using the visitor's experience as a tool guiding design, beginning with the entry sequence and ending with departure. The use of branding, commonly found in hotels, informs the approach to office design.

Branding has become a significant issue in corporate design. Companies want to sell their own brand and have it be distinctive from that of others. Excellent recent examples of this include Apple and Google. Both companies have sought to brand their environments and separate themselves, through the use of design, from their competitors. Not only does this appeal to potential customers, it also attracts employees who see the brand as a personal expression of their own values.

Flexibility

In addition to branding, flexibility has also become a key driver in office design. Architecture firm NBBJ focused on flexibility in its recent design of the Bill and Melinda Gates Foundation campus located in Seattle, Washington. Combining five leased spaces into a single LEED Platinum facility allowed the Gates Foundation to focus more effectively on its mission: "We have big goals: eradicating polio, cutting in half childhood deaths and the number of hungry people in Africa, and overhauling the U.S. education system. We now have a location that will help us reach those goals with our partners, while keeping us connected" (Martha Choe, Chief Administrative Officer). During a seven-year collaboration, project goals and an aesthetic approach led to a space that reflected the corporation's culture.

Using a series of workshops and prototypes combined with some design research, the design team developed a 40/60 closed/open workplace design. This combination of open and closed offices led to the flexibility the company required to achieve its goals. The resulting design has produced an employee satisfaction rating of 90 percent (NBBJ, 2013).

LEED CI

Another big driver in office design is the LEED CI rating system. Like all LEED Green Building Rating Systems, LEED CI awards points for daylight and views. The higher the percentage of people with daylight and views, the more points received. The impact this has had on office design is significant. Perimeter private offices have been moved into the core and open office spaces with lower partitions have been allocated to the exterior walls in order to achieve these points. This has basically reversed the way office design was traditionally done.

Telecommuting/ Telepresence

One response to the need for efficiently used space combined with technological innovation in the past decade has been the rise of telemeetings and telecommuting. Through the use of online vehicles such as Skype, GoToMeeting, Facetime, and other applications, meeting attendees from around the world can meet face-to-face using the Internet. This results in less expense through reduced travel. Further, employees can work from home offices and still meet with colleagues as if they were physically present. This can result in a reduced need for office space as well as provide a better work-life balance for employees.

Real Estate Trends

According to Norm Miller, PhD, from the Center for Real Estate at the University of San Diego (March 2013), the evolving workplace is characterized by four trends:

1. Move to more standardized work spaces
2. Non-dedicated office space for sharing with more on-site amenities
3. A growing acceptance and encouragement of telecommuting and third place use
4. More collaboration work spaces and functional project teams

Space Type	Size in Sq. Ft.
Assigned/unassigned office	132
Reserveable office hoteling	121
Prayer/meditation	112
Mothers room	88
Phone/focus, heads down	77
Assigned/unassigned workstation	56
Reservable workstation	
Hoteling	54
Touchdown space	38
Outdoor meeting, patio	1,480
Café	725
Open/enclosed multi-purpose room (13+ people)	460
Enclosed video conference	442
Enclosed game room	298
Open game room	207
Open/enclosed small meeting room (6–8 people)	178
Open 1 on 1 (2–4 people)	122
Open/enclosed 1-on-1	120

Table 4.1 Typical Distributed Work Spaces
Source: Knoll, http://www.knoll.com/media/466/356/WP_DistributedWork.pdf, p. 9

Manufacturers' Research

Several office systems furniture manufacturers conduct their own research and development into workplace trends and needs. A recent study by Knoll outlined what they call "the Emerging Work Model." According to Mike O'Neill, senior director of workplace research at Knoll, and Tracy Wymer, vice president of workplace strategy, several trends emerge from this new model: less square footage required per worker; greater variety in space types; a lot of smaller, individual work spaces; lots of collaborative spaces; flexibility and choice; and an understanding that cost and satisfaction are the top measures of success. The complete study can be found on the firm's website, http://www.knoll.com/media/466/356/WP_DistributedWork.pdf.

In the study, the "distributed work environment" contains several design features: It has smaller and denser individual spaces, more types of group spaces, more seats for collaboration in spaces, and a reduction in large, formal meeting spaces. Distributing the work across this variety of spaces results in a 33 percent cost savings during the first year. The study included 40 organizations from 11 different industries and multiple countries. Of the people involved in the study, 90 percent were using this model in some way.

The amount of square footage per employee has declined from 227 square foot per person in 2002 to 135 square foot per person in 2012. The need for corporations to be leaner in response to increased global competition and tight economic conditions has led to the need to accommodate workers in less real estate while also making sure their needs are met.

In addition to costing less, reduced square footage also has the added benefit of being more sustainable. Smaller, better-designed, and more efficient workplaces use fewer resources and are more sustainable.

A recent CoreNet Global Survey noted in the May 2012 issue of *Contract*

Organization Characteristics	Conventional Workspace	Distributed Workspace
Number of employees	512	512
Square feet per person	195	130
Rentable square footage	100,000	67,000
Annual lease cost of space per square foot	$36	$36
Annual operating cost per square foot	$20	$21.40
Construction cost per square foot	$175	$175
Construction cost, total*	$17,500,000	$11,725,000
Annual facilities operating and lease cost	$5,600,000	$3,845,800
Total annual year 1 cost	$23,100,000	$15,570,800

Table 4.2
Distributed work programs provide greater efficiency of dollar investment

*includes buildout and furniture

Source: Knoll, http://www.knoll.com/media/466/356/WP_DistributedWork.pdf, p. 9

indicated that 40 percent of global corporate real estate managers surveyed said that by 2017, individual space utilization will be 100 square feet or less. CoreNet Global is an association of corporate real estate and workplace professionals with 7,000 members, including 70 percent of the Fortune 100 companies. (78). The primary reason given for this increased reduction in square footage is the increased emphasis on collaborative space and work approaches. Furniture manufacturers are responding to the trend with new products that nest, build up and not out, and allow for both mobility and centralized storage solutions.

Five Trends: Knoll

Like many commercial furniture companies, Knoll constantly monitors the marketplace and has seen the development of a handful of trends in design for corporations. Knoll says that organizations will continue to be distributed across a variety of locations, and the need for enabling technologies and social collaboration tools such as FaceTime, GoToMeeting, and Skype will become more pronounced. In addition, the company predicts a coming shortage of knowledge workers and an increased demand for more flexibility in the workplace. The shortage of knowledge workers—although primarily in the STEM areas (science, technology, engineering, and math)—also extends into other occupations where a four-year college degree is required. In the next decade, 78 million baby-boomers will retire. Combined with this, fewer college students are pursuing STEM areas. This has led to the decrease in knowledge workers. Those graduating from college seek a better work-life balance than workers have in the past, resulting in an increased need for flexibility. Finally, Knoll says, there will be continued pressure for more sustainable organizations and work styles.

Herman Miller and Globalization Trends

Globalization is a reality of life in the 21st century. Most people have access to people and companies around the world through the World Wide Web. Many companies have global offices and interests.

Herman Miller has recognized the need for understanding design in a world marketplace and has delineated the different cultural demands of the corporate environment in the BRIC countries: Brazil, Russia, India, and

China. As the fastest growing economies in the industrialized world, this is where the greatest increase in the workforce is being seen. Working globally means designing for a balance of open vistas and protective spaces. The proportion and type of these spaces varies among the different cultures. Cultural attitudes impact the design of offices and must be taken into account to create any truly sustainable office.

Brazil In an open and friendly culture such as Brazil's, relationships are key to a successful design. Lively conversations and heated debate are socially accepted norms of communication and must be accommodated in the design of the space. A typical open office environment would include a tendency toward benching, with a typical workstation size of 5 feet x 5 feet up to 6 feet x 6 feet. The typical table/desk would be 5 to 6 feet long and 2.5 feet wide. Low panels (4 feet high) both encourage and account for frequent interaction between employees. Middle and senior managers work in private offices. There is an increased emphasis on proper ergonomics in Brazilian design since the offices are very standardized. Employers want to attract and retain good workers and provide multiple services for them including a gym, medical facilities, a bookstore, movie rental, and a bank.

Russia By contrast, the inner-office culture in Russia is largely hierarchical. Senior management often makes decisions without staff involvement. As such, managers prefer to have higher quality furniture in their private office and be separated from the general workforce. The people are accustomed to both living and working together in small places. Most companies prefer a desk system. While office design is being driven largely by European and American work styles, hierarchy is very important in Russia. The need to retain paper documents and large archival facilities is still a dominant force in Russian office design. Although there is

some technology, a lack of political and economic liberalization has resulted in slower technological growth.

India The caste system once dominated Indian culture and still exists today. The caste system in India dates back 3,000 years and consists of four distinct groups or casts: Brahmans (priests, the highest caste), Kshatriyas (warriors), Vaishyas (merchants), and Sudras (laborers). Traditionally, contact between the castes, particularly around food and water, was to be avoided. One of the most notable differences to Western society is that 95 percent of the people are still in arranged marriages. Traditional offices are managed from the top down, while larger companies are more flexible in the management style. As India does more business internationally, the impact on office design has been impacted.

While office design is evolving toward a more open spatial configuration, there is a blend of benching and panel-based systems. The inclusion of some private offices is important, although a decrease in hierarchy is evolving. A typical workstation is 5 feet x 5 feet to 6 feet x 6 feet, with a 5 feet x 2.5 feet desk, with one pedestal per person.

China In China, a designer should be aware of the importance of extended family and the use of feng shui (an ancient art of placement literally translated as "wind and water") for arrangement. Feng shui, in particular, can have a significant impact on office design. For example, having one's back to the door violates basic principles of feng shui. Being seated with regard to the cardinal directions (N,S, E, or W) can also be viewed as either positive or negative. This custom is integrated into contemporary design in places such as Hong Kong and Singapore and is a significant factor to consider for many Chinese people.

The group is more important than the individual in China. The office often runs like a patriarchic family. Accustomed to little privacy, office partitions are generally low, and people can communicate from a seated position. Most office environments are open, with either a panel-based system or benching. As in India, a typical workstation is 5 feet x 5 feet to 6 feet x 6 feet, with a 5 feet x 2.5 feet desk, with one pedestal per person The customary panel height is 4 feet. Some private offices should be provided for senior-level managers.

Globalization Studies: Steelcase

Steelcase has also conducted extensive research on culture and design for the workplace. A recent issue of *360 Research* (2012) addresses mapping the work patterns in different countries. Researchers included the United States, Great Britain, France, Germany, India, China, Morocco, Italy, Spain, and the Netherlands. Work styles were evaluated in a variety of ways. How occupants felt about space and optimizing for density varied from those with a low tolerance (the United States, Great Britain, France, Italy, the Netherlands, and Germany) versus those for whom there was a high tolerance for density (Russia, Morocco, India, and China). These groups were then subdivided further between those who accepted working away from the office versus those who do not.

Additional divisions were identified between trust and control environments (how open workers were regarding sharing information with one another) and compartmentalized work and life separations versus blurred boundaries between life and work. All of these categorizations of cultural preferences help to shape the design of an office environment.

Office Culture

Haworth's research on office culture has centered on the culture within an organization and how this can vary. Corporate cultures are diagnosed along a continuum from flexible to focused (incremental change) and along a second continuum of internal to external.

Developed by the University of Michigan School of Business, this Competing Values Framework can guide designers toward the appropriate office solutions for a particular organization. One writer posits that corporate cultures have predominant features distinguished by collaboration, creation, control, or competition (Cameron, 2011).

Steelcase and Office Third Places

Steelcase has offered recent research about the need for so-called **third places** in office design. These include comfortable seating areas, little cafés, and other extra spaces where people can both congregate and work alone away from their desks.

Flexibility and Casework

One area greatly affected by the need for flexibility has been casework. **Casework** refers to commercial grade cabinets. According to New York architect Andrew Franz, flexible workspaces increase productivity within the corporate office environment. Nonfixed, modular casework is easy to move around and can be used differently by different people, allowing for flexibility and efficiency. Five precepts have been identified to accomplish this: Make it portable and movable, use local and reclaimed, apply integral beats (for example, the use of a recessed finger pull on a drawer instead of adding a knob or external pull), go modular and standardized, and consider end-of-life scenarios. (Franz, 2012).

Stand–Sit Workstations

One of the recent findings of ergonomics experts and furniture manufacturers is that sitting for prolonged periods of time is harmful to human health. According to Dr. James Levine, an endocrinologist with the Mayo Clinic, the risks associated with too much sitting include obesity, high blood sugar, excess body fat around the midsection, and metabolic syndrome (Levine, 2013). Furniture manufacturer Humanscale has recently introduced a standing workstation (called Float) for office workers. Likewise, Steelcase has introduced a treadmill computer workstation (Walkstation by Details). The notion behind both of these is to get people standing up and moving throughout the day for better health.

The science of having office furniture that supports human health and well-being and maximizes productivity and safety is known as **ergonomics**. Sustainability seeks to create healthy interiors that are good for both people and the environment. Thus, a good ergonomic environment is also sustainable. The Humanscale website contains a host of whitepapers related to ergonomic research and sustainability under the Resources tab.

Office Ergonomics

In his 2007 report written for KI Furniture, Drew Bossen, a physical therapist with Atlas Ergonomics, describes the benefits of good ergonomics for performance and productivity. According to the report, 70 percent of people in the United States have sedentary jobs. Further simple observation reveals that people are not sitting upright and using good posture all day. Movement is a critical consideration when designing. Swedish orthopedic doctor Alf Nachemson's landmark study in 1976 revealed the different pressures put upon the back in different positions. While a recumbent position provides only 24 pounds per square inch of pressure on the back, sitting in a slouched position can be as high as 190 pounds per square inch. In fact, research does not even confirm that sitting with upright, "good" posture alleviates strain on the back over time. Active breaks (moving around) provide more support for back health than sitting still in an upright position. Thus, the latest thinking in the field of ergonomics relates to adjustability. Employee health and satisfaction increases are related

to being able to move and make quick adjustments to personal equipment such as chairs, desktops, keyboards, and other peripherals.

Research completed by Humanscale for its whitepaper on ergonomics (http://www.humanscale.com/userfiles/file/WhitePaper-Ergo.pdf) indicates that the average workstation height of 29.5 inches is actually appropriate for a 6-foot-4-inch-tall male (representing 5 percent of the population or less). Other areas of concern include monitor placement, light level, control over hand and wrist position, and other environmental features. The proper hand and wrist position is known as **hands-in-lap posture**. Hands-in-lap posture allows the wrists to be curved down as if holding a tennis ball while typing. Task chairs should be easily adjustable to accommodate movement and personal preferences. Monitors should be placed to correspond with the natural tendency to gaze downward at a 15-degree angle. Thus the top of the monitor should not be higher than eye level or further than an arm's length away. Multiple monitors can also create ergonomic issues. Repeated neck and head movement—rotation, flexing, and extending—can lead to neck injury.

E-Coupling

E-coupling consists of a coil built into a device such as a low-power cell phone, iPod, or MP3 player that is then placed on a matching power supply coil built into the surface (desktop or tabletop); this creates an electromagnetic field. An example of a medium-power device is a laptop.

For more information, see http://www.alticor.com/ACE/FultonInnovations.aspx.

Hoteling

Hoteling refers to desks that are left unassigned and can be used by various office workers who are coming into the office only occasionally. The desks are reserved as needed. The concept of hoteling dates to the 1990s. The idea responds to changes in the global marketplace wherein some corporations have employees who must travel between locations. Visiting a specific locale only a couple times a year obviously does not require a personal office for that employee, but it does require some office space to work in. High real estate costs and the need for employees to travel between offices have driven the evolution of hoteling during the past 20 years. One example of this system includes a "free-desking" area where a traveler locates an empty desk via an online reservation system within a designated hoteling area of the office. Due to the negative response to this concept, designers and corporations are working to provide more amenities, such as enabling technologies (for example, wireless Internet), centralized file storage, and available white boards, that will appeal to the traveler within the hoteling area. (Wroblaski, 2012)

Conferencing

With the emphasis on digital communication using Skype, GoToMeeting, and other online-based communication tools, the need for conferencing facilities has surged. As such, the conference room has been undergoing some changes. Lowered tables, more comfortable chairs, tablet pulls, and powerpods provide a new degree of flexibility to the conference room. A powerpod permits multiple devices to be plugged in a one time in several areas of the table. The tablet pulls allow users to sit back from the table and use their tablet computers and other devices (Wiens, 2011).

Sustainable Corporate Design

In an article for the September 2012 *Contract*, architect Sandy Mendler outlines what is next for sustainable design. In addition to the standard approaches of reducing energy use, using healthy materials, and integrating daylighting, designers must now create a holistic approach that includes a focus on experience, connection with cultural history, an engagement with the natural world, diversity, interconnectedness, resilience, and local materials in order to produce an authentic experience that is enduring (66–67). According to Mendler, the bar for sustainable design continues to be raised through both rating systems and codes. For example, the first International Code Council *Green Construction Code* was issued in 2012. Ultimately, designers need to create good buildings in harmony with natural systems.

And in addition to creating good buildings, designers need to specify interior materials and products that also reflect a degree of respect for the planet. According to Humanscale's whitepaper on sustainable office design, "Honest sustainability infuses every step of product design—it cannot be effectively 'retrofitted' once a beautiful visual aesthetic has been achieved" (3). To this end, the factors listed below make for a truly sustainable product (according to Humanscale):

1. Product weight
2. Number of parts
3. Recycled and recyclable content
4. Aluminum components
5. Ease of disassembly and upgradeability
6. Distribution practices
7. Quality and durability

When choosing a product to meet sustainable design objectives, several factors must be considered. The list above refers to information that should be available from any company from which you choose your product selections.

Research in Corporate Design

Leigh Stringer, vice president of the international design firm HOK, recently published a book detailing the "green workplace." Topics discussed include driving forces, challenges, new ways of working, and a multitude of other issues involved in creating the workplace environment that encourages sustainable behavior. While the book is intended to induce culture shift within an organization wanting to remake itself in a more sustainable footprint, there are several implications for design. Stringer outlines some of the first challenges, which include new modes of working (30 million people in America spend significant time working in alternative venues outside the office such as coffee houses), commuting (which obviously has implications for both energy consumption and time), as well as the value that people seek in their lives and work pursuits (della Cava, 2006). Consumers are driving green design, management strategies, and the market; ultimately these changes can be honestly reflected in a company's public relations efforts and can save that organization money. Together, these forces led Stringer to conclude that the future green economy is already here.

Alternative work strategies to accomplish increased efficiency and reduced square footage goals include shared addresses (a desk shared by two or more employees), group addresses (for a team space), activity settings (such as third-space venues), free addresses (not assigned to any specific individual), hoteling, satellite offices (full-service office alternatives that can be shared with others seeking the same type of venue), **remote telecenters** (drop-in offices away from the main office and closer to the client), home offices, and virtual offices. All of these dramatically change the footprint of the typical corporate office setting. Three ways in which this is visible include fewer assigned offices, fewer overall desks, and more teaming areas. These options do not work for all types of employees and tend to be most successful among those who are highly autonomous and self-motivated. Working at home or in an alternate location would

not work well for someone who required a great deal of supervision (Stringer, 2009).

Student Approaches to Sustainable Corporate Design

For the following examples, each student project depicts a corporate headquarters for a nonprofit organization of the student's choice. For the project, students were provided with three possible floor plates (in various sizes) and a list of 10 nonprofits from which to choose. The first part of the project included a branding an identity exercise to determine what the headquarters should look and feel like based on the organizational culture and day-to-day activities. The second step of the process was test fitting to see which of the three buildings best suited the needs of the client.

Molly Flora—Livestrong (biomimcry, eco-social)

Inspired by the function of the human heart, the Livestrong plan is designed around paths of circulation that pulse— movement during activity and when at rest—and collaboration of the parts. The plan demonstrates these concepts with varying-width hallways leading to collaboration spaces throughout the floor plate. Sustainable materials used throughout the space contribute to the health of the environment and the people within it. Manufacturers with a sustainable social agenda (including Haworth, Shaw, and Armstrong Flooring) were chosen to further reflect the concept. For example, Armstrong Flooring makes donations to Homes for our Troops, a nonprofit community organization that helps provide homes for veterans. They also support sustainable forest management projects as a part of their commitment to sustainability.

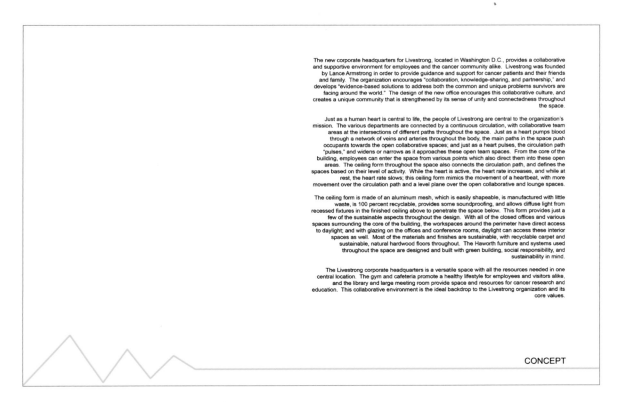

The new corporate headquarters for Livestrong, located in Washington D.C., provides a collaborative and supportive environment for employees and the cancer community alike. Livestrong was founded by Lance Armstrong in order to provide guidance and support for cancer patients and their friends and family. The organization encourages "collaboration, knowledge-sharing, and partnership," and develops "evidence-based solutions to address both the common and unique problems survivors are facing around the world." The design of the new office encourages this collaborative culture, and creates a unique community that is strengthened by its sense of unity and connectedness throughout the space.

Just as a human heart is central to life, the people of Livestrong are central to the organization's mission. The various departments are connected by a continuous circulation, with collaborative team areas at the intersections of different paths throughout the space. Just as a heart pumps blood through a network of veins and arteries throughout the body, the main paths in the space push occupants towards the open collaborative spaces; and just as a heart pulses, the circulation path "pulses," and widens or narrows as it approaches these open team spaces. From the core of the building, employees can enter the space from various points which also direct them into these open areas. The ceiling form throughout the space also connects the circulation path, and defines the spaces based on their level of activity. While the heart is active, the heart rate increases, and while at rest, the heart rate slows; this ceiling form mimics the movement of a heartbeat, with more movement over the circulation path and a level plane over the open collaborative and lounge spaces.

The ceiling form is made of an aluminum mesh, which is easily shapeable, is manufactured with little waste, is 100 percent recyclable, provides some soundproofing, and allows diffuse light from recessed fixtures in the finished ceiling above to penetrate the space below. This form provides just a few of the sustainable aspects throughout the design. With all of the closed offices and various spaces surrounding the core of the building, the workspaces around the perimeter have direct access to daylight; and with glazing on the offices and conference rooms, daylight can access these interior spaces as well. Most of the materials and finishes are sustainable, with recyclable carpet and sustainable, natural hardwood floors throughout. The Haworth furniture and systems used throughout the space are designed and built with green building, social responsibility, and sustainability in mind.

The Livestrong corporate headquarters is a versatile space with all the resources needed in one central location. The gym and cafeteria promote a healthy lifestyle for employees and visitors alike, and the library and large meeting room provide space and resources for cancer research and education. This collaborative environment is the ideal backdrop to the Livestrong organization and its core values.

CONCEPT

Figure 4.1 Molly Flora, Livestrong Headquarters: Concept page

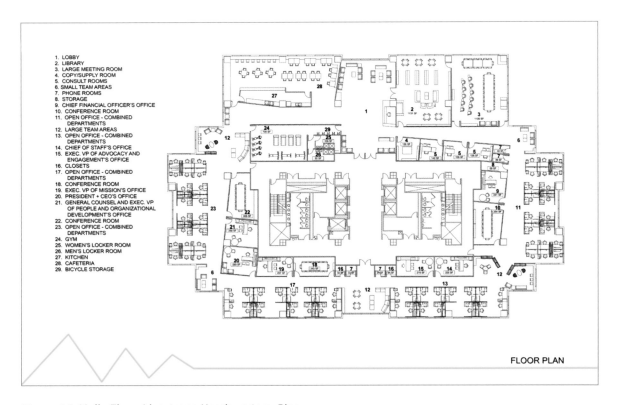

1. LOBBY
2. LIBRARY
3. LARGE MEETING ROOM
4. COPY/SUPPLY ROOM
5. CONSULT ROOMS
6. SMALL TEAM AREAS
7. PHONE ROOMS
8. STORAGE
9. CHIEF FINANCIAL OFFICER'S OFFICE
10. CONFERENCE ROOM
11. OPEN OFFICE - COMBINED DEPARTMENTS
12. LARGE TEAM AREAS
13. OPEN OFFICE - COMBINED DEPARTMENTS
14. CHIEF OF STAFF'S OFFICE
15. EXEC. VP OF ADVOCACY AND ENGAGEMENT'S OFFICE
16. CLOSETS
17. OPEN OFFICE - COMBINED DEPARTMENTS
18. CONFERENCE ROOM
19. EXEC. VP OF MISSION'S OFFICE
20. PRESIDENT + CEO'S OFFICE
21. GENERAL COUNSEL AND EXEC. VP OF PEOPLE AND ORGANIZATIONAL DEVELOPMENT'S OFFICE
22. CONFERENCE ROOM
23. OPEN OFFICE - COMBINED DEPARTMENTS
24. GYM
25. WOMEN'S LOCKER ROOM
26. MEN'S LOCKER ROOM
27. KITCHEN
28. CAFETERIA
29. BICYCLE STORAGE

FLOOR PLAN

Figure 4.2 Molly Flora, Livestrong Headquarters: Plan

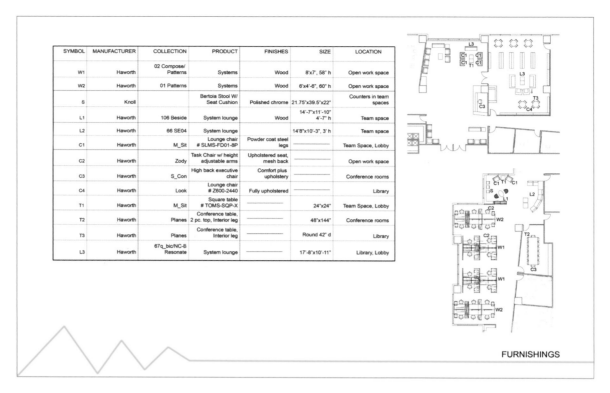

SYMBOL	MANUFACTURER	COLLECTION	PRODUCT	FINISHES	SIZE	LOCATION
W1	Haworth	02 Compose/ Patterns	Systems	Wood	8'x7', 58" h	Open work space
W2	Haworth	01 Patterns	Systems	Wood	6'x4'-6", 60" h	Open work space
S	Knoll		Bertoia Stool W/ Seat Cushion	Polished chrome	21.75"x39.5"x22"	Counters in team spaces
L1	Haworth	106 Beside	System lounge	Wood	14'-7"x11'-10" 4'-7" h	Team space
L2	Haworth	66 SE04	System lounge		14'8"x10'-3", 3' h	Team space
C1	Haworth	M_Sit	Lounge chair # SLMS-FD01-8P	Powder coat steel legs		Team Space, Lobby
C2	Haworth	Zody	Task Chair w/ height adjustable arms	Upholstered seat, mesh back		Open work space
C3	Haworth	S_Con	High back executive chair	Comfort plus upholstery		Conference rooms
C4	Haworth	Look	Lounge chair # Z600-2440	Fully upholstered		Library
T1	Haworth	M_Sit	Square table # TOMS-SQP-X		24"x24"	Team Space, Lobby
T2	Haworth	Planes	Conference table, 2 pc. top, Interior leg		48"x144"	Conference rooms
T3	Haworth	Planes	Conference table, Interior leg		Round 42" d	Library
L3	Haworth	67q_bic/NC-B Resonate	System lounge		17'-8"x10'-11"	Library, Lobby

FURNISHINGS

Figure 4.3 Molly Flora, Livestrong Headquarters: Partial furniture plan

PERSPECTIVE - LOBBY

Figure 4.4 Molly Flora, Livestrong Headquarters: 3D view, lobby

Figure 4.5 Molly Flora, Livestrong Headquarters: 3D view, library

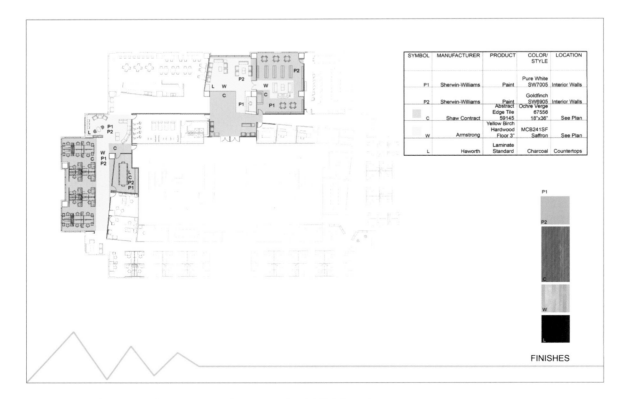

SYMBOL	MANUFACTURER	PRODUCT	COLOR/ STYLE	LOCATION
P1	Sherwin-Williams	Paint	Pure White SW7005	Interior Walls
P2	Sherwin-Williams	Paint	Goldfinch SW6905	Interior Walls
C	Shaw Contract	Abstract Edge Tile 59145	Ochre Verge 67556 18"x36"	See Plan
W	Armstrong	Yellow Birch Hardwood Floor 3"	MCB241SF Saffron	See Plan
L	Haworth	Laminate Standard	Charcoal	Countertops

FINISHES

Figure 4.6 Molly Flora, Livestrong Headquarters: Partial finishes plan

Figure 4.7 Molly Flora, Livestrong Headquarters: 3D view, conference room

Figure 4.8 Molly Flora, Livestrong Headquarters: 3D view, team/open office space

Rachel Brennan—Charity Water (biomimcry)

Because the client company focuses on providing clean drinking water, this design used water as a source of inspiration. The floor plan illustrates a fluidity of spatial configurations where people can flow from one space into the next. This fluidity is captured in the ceiling planes and furnishings as well.

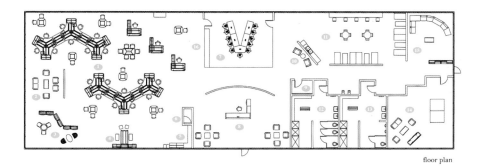

floor plan

Figure 4.9 Rachel Brennan, Charity Water Headquarters: Plan

①	open office space	3758.23 sq. ft.	⑨ coat closet	63.24 sq. ft.
②	lounge	210.42 sq. ft.	⑩ touchdown	83.7 sq. ft.
③	private area	330.91 sq. ft.	⑪ cafe	969.54 sq. ft.
④	team zone	109.32 sq. ft.	⑫ womens locker	460 sq. ft.
⑤	printing & coffee	120 sq. ft.	⑬ mens locker	460 sq. ft.
⑥	storage	28.40 sq. ft.	⑭ play area	861.47 sq. ft.
⑦	presentation	696 sq. ft.	⑮ touchdown 2	405.72 sq. ft.
⑧	reception	1078.96 sq. ft.	⑯ bike rack zone	90 sq. ft.

2

Figure 4.10 Rachel Brennan, Charity Water Headquarters: 3D view, collaboration space

5

floor plan

the curvilinear shape of the collaboration desks helps reiterate the idea of fluidity. there are small tables within each curve to support team work or quick meetings. the curves in the carpet are reflected on the ceiling to provide depth and better visual appeal. the acoustical ceiling tile and carpet help to reduce noise.

Figure 4.11 Rachel
Brennan, Charity
Water Headquarters:
3D view, lounge

the lounge is located next to the collaboration zones in order to
encourage employees to take a break or collaborate further in a
more relaxed environment. the screen creates a sense of privacy
while still allowing light to flow through to the collaboration
areas. there is also a private area for employees to make personal
phone calls located behind the lounge.

floor plan

6

Figure 4.12 Rachel
Brennan, Charity
Water Headquarters:
3D view,
presentation space/
conference room

the presentation room is located next to the cafe in order to serve lunch easily during
meetings. the v-shaped desk gives everyone sitting at the table the ability to see the
presentation.

7

floor plan

Figure 4.13 Rachel
Brennan, Charity
Water Headquarters:
Reception area

a large part of their buisness involves fundraising and bringing clients in,
meaning they need larger welcoming and meeting areas. therefore, the reception area serves
not only as a greeting place but also gives the client or visitor an opportunity to
learn more about charity : water by having corning glass behind the receptionist
desk. This glass is a new technology that when touched, acts as a computer screen.
Information about the company will be displayed here as well as a map to show
current projects taking place or where areas have already had wells installed.

floor plan

8

Jamie Ivey—Doctors Without Borders (eco-aesthetic, eco-technic)

The primary design approach used in this project was to break through borders between rooms and surfaces within the space. Surfaces that extend from the floor onto the wall then transform into three-dimensional elements within the space. Sustainable materials and finishes used throughout contribute to a LEED-compliant interior design. Warm surfaces of maple are contrasted with the bright red wrapping element that extends throughout the design.

Figure 4.14 Jamie Ivey, Doctors Without Borders Headquarters: Concept page

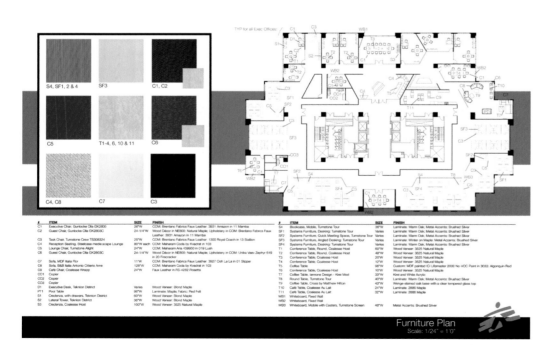

Figure 4.15 Jamie Ivey, Doctors Without Borders Headquarters: Furniture plan

Figure 4.16 Jamie Ivey, Doctors Without Borders Headquarters: Floor finishes plan

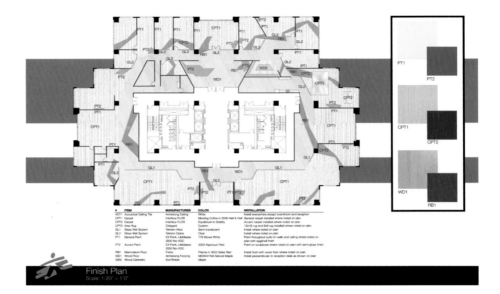

Figure 4.17 Jamie Ivey, Doctors Without Borders Headquarters: Floor plan

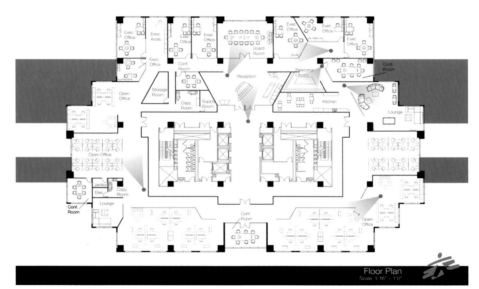

Figure 4.18 Jamie Ivey, Doctors Without Borders Headquarters: 3D view, reception area

Figure 4.19 Jamie Ivey, Doctors Without Borders Headquarters: 3D view, board room

Figure 4.20 Jamie Ivey, Doctors Without Borders Headquarters: 3D view, open office area

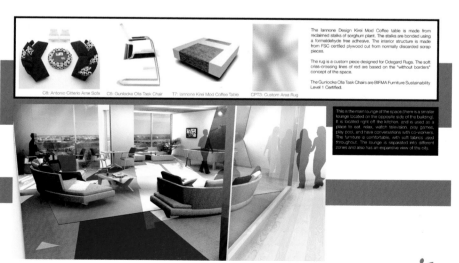

Figure 4.21 Jamie Ivey, Doctors Without Borders Headquarters: 3D view, lounge

Figure 4.22 Jamie
Ivey, Doctors
Without Borders
Headquarters: 3D
view, executive
offices and resource
library

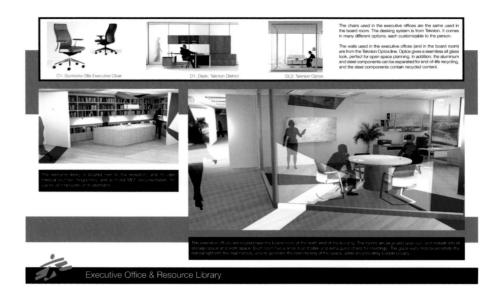

Executive Office & Resource Library

Ashley Broderick— Charity Water (eco-social, eco-medical)

This Charity Water design uses the actual yellow jerry can watering vessels as a source of design inspiration. Recycled water containers create partitions for spatial separation, and a large replica of the jerry can is used in the raised conference space. All products meet

BIFMA (Business and Institutional Furniture Manufacturers Association) certification level one sustainability criteria indicating that they have met a third-party sustainability standard. Reclaimed lumber is used to create a wood ceiling, and the interior paints contain no VOCs. The design created a fun-loving and familial environment that captured the culture of the organization.

Figure 4.23 Ashley Broderick, Charity Water Headquarters: Concept page

The culture of Charity: Water is active, fun-loving, and familial. The office community takes great pride in trying to make a personal connection with the public and their donors. Due to this, it was very important for me to dispel the typical notions for a corporate office, and to approach Charity's office environment to mimic the company and employees' personality. The concept for this corporate office is to have a casual open office environment that supports the active energy of its employees. The goal in the planning of the space was to eliminate barriers, encourage transparency, and allow for maximum collaboration.

The floor plan was designed to support the office departments with cluster formations. Each department contains a private office for the department head with open work-stations for the employees. In support of each area are two meeting spaces, one open and one closed, to provide privacy when needed. The office core consists of the main conference room, the play space (for generating ideas and office activities), and the lobby. These three areas are the core and the hierarchy of the office, which support Charity: Water's ideals of collaboration and public outreach.

One of the most enjoyable entities of this project was intertwining sustainable features into the design concept. Due to the casual, simple nature of the concept, it was easier to generate a direction for a sustainable approach. A lot of reclaimed and reused materials were used throughout the office design. The ceiling was left open to expose its industrial features. All ceiling were lowered on closed spaces to allow daylight to sweep throughout the space. Charity: Water jerry cans are displayed in and on top of crates through the space, and the private offices are also made crate-like with a reclaimed wood structure.

The challenges I encountered while designing the space had to do with special layout, balance, and adapting to the existing structure. This was my first corporate space design, so I had a very hard time understanding how to fill the space. When working with a lot of square footage, it become very easy to misjudge how much unused space would be left over. I learned how to really break down the potential needs for the company, and revert back to assessing the needs of the employees when making program decisions. In terms of balance, I had the task of expressing an energetic, open space without going overboard with eccentric elements. At the end of the day, I was designing an office environment, so in order to achieve an environment that was casual balanced with professionalism, I had to be very particular about decisions such as when to use color, when to have playful elements, and how much of these two things to use. The existing structure was especially a challenge because three out of the four exterior walls were floor to ceiling windows all the way around with no solid walls. Having such a complicated condition affected my pre-existing ideas for plumbing locations, as well as how I would have any walls meet the exterior. Fortunately, with the open and casual culture of Charity water, I did not have to work with too many walls, and found ways to manipulate the space plan in a way that created a solution to an all-glass exterior.

[charity: water]

corporate office

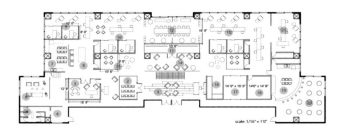

Figure 4.24 Ashley Broderick, Charity Water Headquarters: Floor plan

1. Lobby	8. Recreation/Lounge	15. Creative
2. Press Room	9. Financial	16. Mail Room/Copies
3. CEO Office	10. Water Programs	17. Studio
4. Bike Racks	11. Meeting Spaces	18. Storage
5. Changing Room	12. Conference Room	19. Kitchen
6. CEO Meeting Room	13. Library	20. Event Space
7. Kitchen	14. Playspace	21. Technology

The open floor plan is arranged in clusters. Spaces are organized into departments, all of which are supported by meeting areas- open and private. Private offices are pulled inward with workstations on the ouskirts to maximize use of daylight and break down hierarchy.

[charity: water floor plan]

Figure 4.25 Ashley Broderick, Charity Water Headquarters: Furniture plan

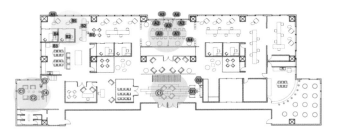

Mark	Quant.	Description	Fabric/Finish	Remarks	Mark	Quant.	Description	Fabric/Finish
A1	2	HAWORTH Patterns ; Studio Table 29"h , 120"w, 63"d	Linen Laminate	BIFMA Level 1 Certified Product	D1	1	HAWORTH Mumbai	Zebrano Veneer
A2	2	HAWORTH Patterns; Bench 17.5"h, 72"w, 22"d	Melba Wood; Tellure Spring Fabric	BIFMA Level 1 Certified Product	D2	1	HAWORTH Mumbai	Zebrano Veneer
A3	16	HAWORTH Very; Task Chair	Fog Trim, Metallic Gunmetal Base Metric Scuba Fabric	BIFMA Level 2 Certified Product	B5	11	FRITZ HANSEN pk22; Lounge Chair	Wicker, Satin Brush Stainless Steel
B1	31	HAWORTH Zody; Task Chair	Smoke Trim, Metallic Gunmetal Base Grade C Twilight Fabric		C3	2	VITRA; Eames Elephant 16.5"h, 16.25"w, 31"d	Classic Red, Plywood
B2	19	HAWORTH X Series; Desk w/ LIM Light	Melba Laminate		C4	3	VITRA; Cork Family 13"h, 12.25"d	Turned Natural Cork
B3	8	HAWORTH Penelope Chair	Black Mesh		A4	6	HERMAN MILLER ; Tatone 14.25"h, 30.75"w, 30.75"d	Blue Stretch Fabric
B4	4	HAWORTH Compose; Storage	Retro Walnut	BIFMA Level 1 Certified Product	A5	1	HERMAN MILLER ; Tato 16.25"h, 25.75"w, 17.25"d	Yellow Stretch Fabric
C1	7	HAWORTH q_bic Chair	Scuba	BIFMA Level 1 Certified Product	A6	1	HERMAN MILLER ; Tatino 17.125"h, 19.125"w, 19.125"d	Red Stretch Fabric
C2	1	HAWORTH q_bic Bench	Tellure Sunflower	BIFMA Level 1 Certified Product				

furniture plan

Figure 4.26 Ashley Broderick, Charity Water Headquarters: Finishes plan

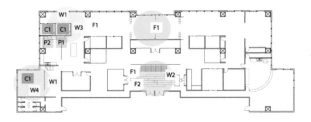

Type	Tag	Finish	Remarks
wall	W1	HAWORTH Enclose; Moveable Walls, Frameless Glass	BIFMA Level 1 Certified Product
wall	W2	Gypsum Wall Board, White	
wall	W3	COMMUNITY FORKLIFT, Reclaimed Lumber	
wall	W4	PLYBOO Tambour green, TP-RG48	
paint	P1	BENJAMIN MOORE Natura van courtland blue, HC-145	Zero VOC, ordorless
paint	P2	BENJAMIN MOORE Natura sounds of nature ,556	Zero VOC, ordorless
floor	F1	L.M. SCOFIELD COMPANY polished concrete	
floor	F2	COMMUNITY FORKLIFT, Reclaimed Lumber	
carpet	C1	InterfaceFLOR Style # 14256	

finish plan

Figure 4.27 Ashley Broderick, Charity Water Headquarters: 3D view, lobby

Figure 4.28 Ashley Broderick, Charity Water Headquarters: 3D view, conference area

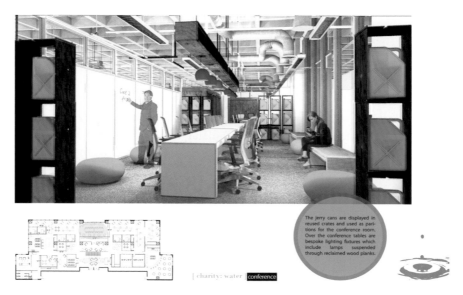

Figure 4.29 Ashley Broderick, Charity Water Headquarters: 3D view, offices and workstations

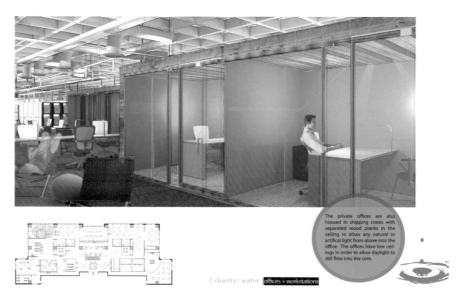

Figure 4.30 Ashley Broderick, Charity Water Headquarters: 3D view, CEO conference area

The mezzanine is inspired by charity: water's jerry can. The CEO can either entertain donors below or above in the mezzanine. The adjacent wall is made of bamboo slats that open up on the end to reveal the bike storage on the opposite side.

| charity: water | ceo conference

Morgan Thorne— Livestrong (eco-technic)

The founder of Livestrong, Lance Armstrong, won the Tour de France multiple times. Thus, the path/route of the race provided the concept for this project. The interior circulation of the space undulates and turns much as the path the riders must take when on the tour. Sustainable features include green wall (a wall that has living plants growing on it) installations, sustainable furniture, fixtures, equipment, and finishes, as well as low-flow faucets and double-flush toilets.

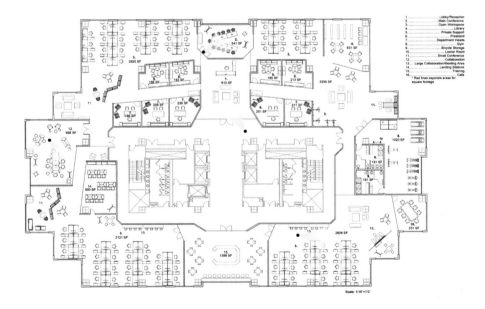

Figure 4.31 Morgan Thorne, Livestrong Headquarters: Plan

Figure 4.32 Morgan Thorne, Livestrong Headquarters: Finishes plan

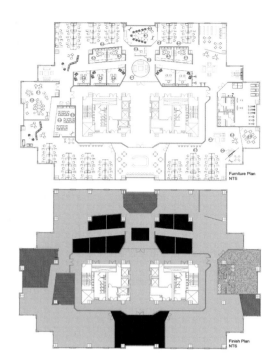

Mark	Description	Manufacturer
A-1	67 q_bic/NC-B Resonate	Haworth
A-2	Patterns Reception Desk	Haworth
A-3	X99 Task	Haworth
A-4	12 Compose/X Series	Haworth
A-5	Zody	Haworth
A-6	35 York	Haworth
A-7	83 Enclose/Compose/Planes	Haworth
B-1	46 Planes/Enclosed	Haworth
B-2	EZ 65	Haworth
C-1	74 Planes/Enclosed	Haworth
C-2	Improv SE	Haworth
C-3	53 Planes	Haworth
C-4	Very Wire Stacking	Haworth
D-1	K700 Stool	Haworth
D-2	84 Enclose/Compose/SE04	Haworth
D-3	Premise Table and b_sit Chair	Haworth
D-4	45 Executive Conference	Haworth

Armstrong Linoleum
Marmorette with NATURCote
LP091 Mushroom

Tandus Carpet
Sculpted Flannel 06117

Armstrong
Maple - Midnight
3 1/4 in. Solid Hardwood Plank

ECOsurfaces
Rubber Flooring
ECOsand 1000 Beach Bum

Figure 4.33 Morgan Thorne, Livestrong Headquarters: 3D view, reception area

Figure 4.34 Morgan Thorne, Livestrong Headquarters: 3D view, conference area

Figure 4.35 Morgan Thorne, Livestrong Headquarters: 3D view, teaming area

Figure 4.36 Morgan Thorne, Livestrong Headquarters: 3D view, of open office

Firm Approaches to Sustainable Corporate Design

Many design and architecture firms specialize in corporate design. Some of these are full-service companies that engage in all aspects of the building; others might contract for a specific set of services related to a multi-firm project.

KSA—Union Bankshares (eco-tehcnic)

Union Bankshares provides an example of the latter type of approach. Located in Ruther Glen, Virginia, the corporate headquarters for Union Bankshares Corporation was completed in September 2007. This project has earned LEED certification through innovative features such as a raised floor with under-floor air distribution to improve the indoor air quality, a green roof to reduce heat island effect and improve water efficiency, daylighting, and the use of low-emitting materials. (Heat island effect is when the local temperature rises as a result of hard surfaces, particularly asphalt paving and sidewalks.)

KSA Interiors was hired by Union Bankshares Corporation to partner with the project architects in seeking LEED certification and to take the lead role in planning and performing an adjacency and space needs study for relocating the corporate headquarters from Bowling Green, Virginia. KSA conducted a needs assessment of employees, ranging from the initial staff to a status estimate of 10 years in the future and a departmental adjacency matrix for the workplace.

Through the development of schematic drawings, the design team was able to provide various workspace options that offered an open and collaborative work environment as well as the flexibility of hoteling options for employees who required only limited use of the office due to frequent travel and telecommuting technologies.

Figure 4.37 KSA Interiors, Union Bankshares: Lounge

Figure 4.38 KSA Interiors, Union Bankshares: Kitchenette

Figure 4.39 LEED
Checklist for Union
BankShares

LEED-NC Version 2.2 Project Checklist

Union Bankshares Corporation
Caroline County, Virginia

Yes	?	No				
1		**13**	**Sustainable Sites**			**14** Points
Y			Prereq 1	**Construction Activity Pollution Prevention**		Required
		1	Credit 1	**Site Selection**		1
		1	Credit 2	**Development Density & Community Connectivity**		1
		1	Credit 3	**Brownfield Redevelopment**		1
		1	Credit 4.1	**Alternative Transportation**, Public Transportation Access		1
		1	Credit 4.2	**Alternative Transportation**, Bicycle Storage & Changing Rooms		1
		1	Credit 4.3	**Alternative Transportation**, Low Emitting & Fuel Efficient Vehicles		1
		1	Credit 4.4	**Alternative Transportation**, Parking Capacity		1
		1	Credit 5.1	**Site Development**, Protect or Restore Habitat		1
		1	Credit 5.2	**Site Development**, Maximize Open Space		1
		1	Credit 6.1	**Stormwater Design**, Quantity Control		1
		1	Credit 6.2	**Stormwater Design**, Quality Control		1
		1	Credit 7.1	**Heat Island Effect**, Non-Roof		1
1			Credit 7.2	**Heat Island Effect**, Roof		1
		1	Credit 8	**Light Pollution Reduction**		1

Yes	?	No				
4		**1**	**Water Efficiency**			**5** Points
1			Credit 1.1	**Water Efficient Landscaping**, Reduce by 50%		1
1			Credit 1.2	**Water Efficient Landscaping**, No Potable Use or No Irrigation		1
		1	Credit 2	**Innovative Wastewater Technologies**		1
1			Credit 3.1	**Water Use Reduction**, 20% Reduction		1
1			Credit 3.2	**Water Use Reduction**, 30% Reduction		1

Yes	?	No				
1		**16**	**Energy & Atmosphere**			**17** Points
Y			Prereq 1	**Fundamental Commissioning of the Building Energy Systems**		Required
Y			Prereq 2	**Minimum Energy Performance**		Required
Y			Prereq 3	**Fundamental Refrigerant Management**		Required
		10	Credit 1	**Optimize Energy Performance**		1 to 10
		1	Credit 2.1	**On-Site Renewable Energy**, 5%		1
		1	Credit 2.2	**On-Site Renewable Energy**, 10%		1
		1	Credit 2.3	**On-Site Renewable Energy**, 20%		1
		1	Credit 3	**Enhanced Commissioning**		1
1			Credit 4	**Enhanced Refrigerant Management**		1
		1	Credit 5	**Measurement & Verification**		1
		1	Credit 6	**Green Power**		1

continued...

Gensler—Fried Frank LLC (eco-technic)

The Washington, D.C. office of the international corporate and financial law firm Fried Frank won an IIDA Gold Award in 2012. The office, designed by Gensler's D.C. office, meets LEED criteria. The arrangement of the spaces allows for maximum daylight and views. Interior glass partitions and a glass stair railing permit daylight to extend into interior rooms. A combination of LED and fluorescent lamps contribute to reduced energy use and improved lighting efficiency. Interior finishes include low VOC paint, sustainable carpeting, and FSC-certified wood.

Figure 4.40 Gensler, Fried Frank Law Office, Washington, D.C.: Reception desk

Figure 4.41 Gensler, Fried Frank Law Office, Washington, D.C.: Conference room

Figure 4.42 Gensler, Fried Frank Law Office, Washington, D.C.: Interior stair and screen wall

Figure 4.43 Gensler, Fried Frank Law Office, Washington, D.C.: Elevator lobby

Figure 4.44 Gensler, Fried Frank Law Office, Washington, D.C.: Lounge area

Figure 4.45 Gensler, Fried Frank Law Office, Washington, D.C.: Sitting area outside conference room

Figure 4.46 Gensler, Fried Frank Law Office, Washington, D.C.: Large conference room

Figure 4.47 Gensler, Fried Frank Law Office, Washington, D.C.: Corridor in open office

Plan Prototypes

The following plan prototypes outline a few of the common spaces used in a corporate setting. Layouts for systems furniture are readily available at manufacturer websites such as steelcase.com, Haworth.com, HermanMiller.com, Teknion.com, Knoll.com, and others. The final prototype shows the general difference in designs for the BRIC countries (Brazil, Russia, India, and China).

Figure 4.48 Small conference room

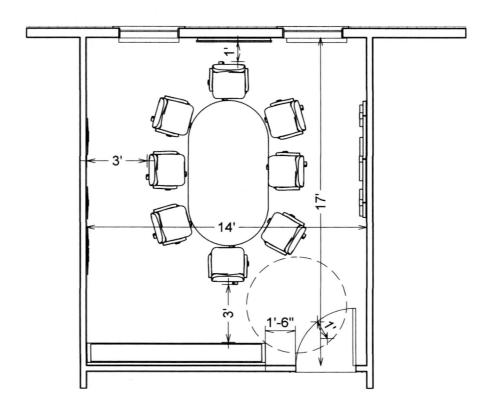

Figure 4.49 Open office with perimeter benching and private office at the middle

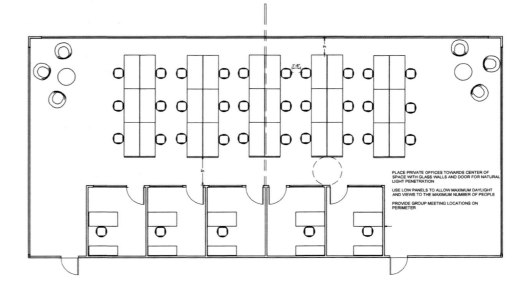

PLACE PRIVATE OFFICES TOWARDS CENTER OF SPACE WITH GLASS WALLS AND DOOR FOR NATURAL LIGHT PENETRATION

USE LOW PANELS TO ALLOW MAXIMUM DAYLIGHT AND VIEWS TO THE MAXIMUM NUMBER OF PEOPLE

PROVIDE GROUP MEETING LOCATIONS ON PERIMETER

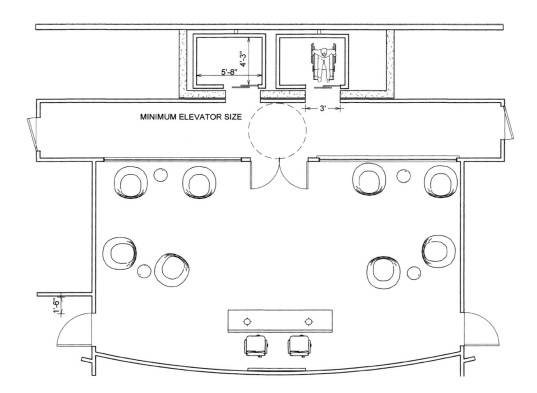

Figure 4.50
Corporate lobby and elevators

5'-8"

4'-3"

MINIMUM ELEVATOR SIZE

3'

1'-6"

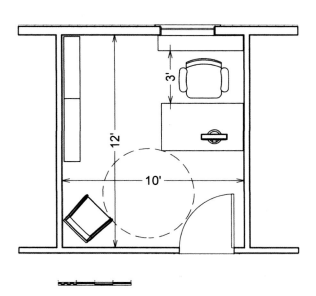

3'

12'

10'

Figure 4.51 Small private office

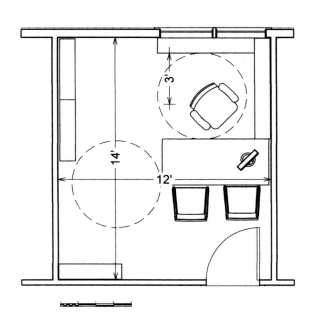

3'

14'

12'

Figure 4.52 Medium private office

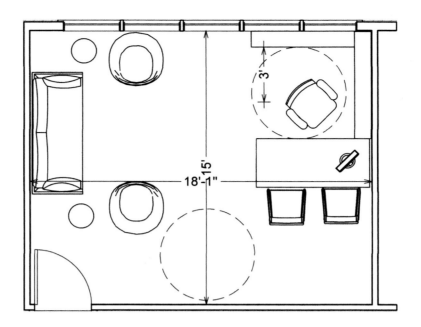

Figure 4.53 Large private office

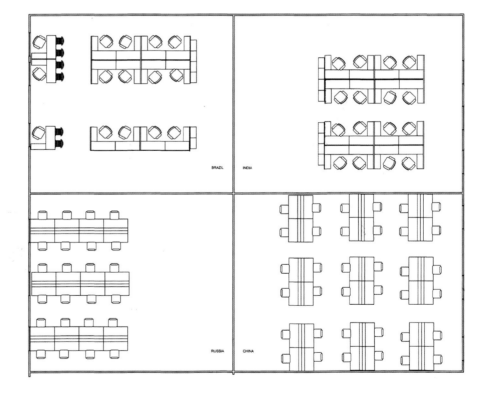

Figure 4.54 Typical layouts for BRIC countries based on research by Herman Mille

LEED Checklist

Depending on whether the office being designed is located within an existing building or a new one will determine which LEED checklist to use. The most appropriate choice to govern commercial interiors is LEED CI. If an entirely building is being designed, the team might select LEED for New Construction, LEED NC. Both are included in the Appendices.

Discussion Question

What are some implications of the changing workplace to design?

Key Terms

Action Office

BIFMA

Bürolandschaft, "office landscape"

casework

cube clusters

e-coupling

ergonomics

hands-in-lap posture

hoteling

remote telecenters

Taylorism

third place

virtual office

Sources

Bossen, D. 2007. "Improved Workplace Performance and Productivity through Movement: The Emerging Role of Adjustability." KI, June 2007. Accessed June 27, 2013. www.ki.com.

Cameron, K. 2011. "An Introduction to the Competing Values Framework." Haworth.com, Nov. Accessed June 27, 2013.

http://www.haworth.com/en-us/Knowledge/Workplace-Library/Pages/WorkspaceLibrary.aspx. *Contract Magazine*, May 2012.

HermanMiller.com. 2010. "Culture and Work Styles in BRIC Countries." Research summary. http://www.hermanmiller.com/research/research-summaries/culture-and-work-styles-in-the-bric-countries.html.

Curl, James Stevens. 2000, "Bürolandschaft." *A Dictionary of Architecture and Landscape Architecture*. 2000. Retrieved June 27, 2013. Encyclopedia.com: http://www.encyclopedia.com/doc/1O1-Brolandschaft.html

della Cava, Marco. 2006. "Working out of a Third Place." USA Today, October 4. Accessed June 26, 2013. http://usatoday.com/tech/2006-10-04-third-space_x.htm.

Franz, Andrew. 2012. "Casework's New Look," *Interiors and Sources*, May: 72–6.

Heschmeyer, Mark. (March 13, 2013) "Changing Office Trends Hold Major Implications for Future Office Demand." www.costar.com Accessed 4/25/2014 interview with Norm Miller

Humanscale. 2010. "Whitepaper: Specifying Green: 8 Considerations for Maximum Sustainability." Online Whitepaper. Accessed June 25, 2013. http://www.humanscale.com/resources/resources.cfm?assettypeid=11.

Johnson, L. 2011. "Charging Ahead: Intelligent Wireless Power for Real World Environment." KI Furniture Manufacturing. Accessed June 25, 3013. http://www.ki.com/uploadedFiles/Docs/literature-samples/white-papers/ChargingAhead_WhitePaper.pdf

Levine, James. 2012. "What Are the Risks of Sitting Too Much?" *Adult Health, Mayo Clinic*, June 16. Accessed June 26, 2013. http://www.mayoclinic.com/health/sitting/AN02082.

Mendler, S. 2012. "What Is Next for Sustainable Design?" *Contract Magazine*, September: 67–8.

Sah, V., Miller, N., Ghosh, B. (2013). Are Green REITs Valued More?. *Journal of Real Estate Portfolio Management*, 19 (2), 169-177, 9.

NBBJ. 2013. Homepage. Accessed June 27. http://www.nbbj.com/work/bill-melinda-gates-foundation/

O'Neill, Michael and Wymer, (2011) Tracey. The Metrics of Distributed Work. http://www.knoll.com/media/466/356/WP_DistributedWork.pdf

Puleio, J. n.d. "Whitepaper: Spotlight on Ergonomics: Designing Healthy Work Environments." Humanscale.com

Stringer, Leigh. 2009. *The Green Workplace*. New York: Palgrave Macmillan.

"The Same But Different." 2012. 360 Research, 65. Accessed June 27, 2013. http://360.steelcase.com/articles/the-same-but-different-mapping-the-patterns-of-work-cultures/.

Wiens, J. 2011. "Conferencing in Comfort," *Interiors and Sources*, April: 16–17.

Wroblaski, K. 2012. "Design for Day," *Interiors and Sources*, May: 30–3.

Websites

Haworth
http://www.haworth.com/en-us/Knowledge/Workplace-Library/Pages/WorkspaceLibrary.aspx

Herman Miller
http://www.hermanmiller.com/research/topics/all-topics.html

HumanScale
http://www.humanscale.com/resources/resources.cfm?assettypeid=11

Knoll
http://www.knoll.com/

Steelcase
http://360.steelcase.com/

5

HOSPITALITY PROJECTS

Objectives

- Students will be able to locate sustainable resources for hospitality projects.

- Students will be able to describe the trends in hospitality design, including sustainability.

- Students will be able to describe a variety of sustainable project approaches used in hospitality design.

Overview

Hospitality design includes hotels, spas, and restaurants. Some also consider assisted living design as a form of hospitality design. Hotel design is often divided into mid-range economy hotels and luxury hotels with public spaces and private rooms. Restaurant design includes nightclubs, bars, lounges, casual dining, quick service, and fine dining. As an industry reliant primarily on disposable income and business clientele, hospitality designs must attract people.

Current Issues in Hospitality Design

Top concerns of the hospitality industry during the past decade include sustainability and the reduced cost of "going green," a renewed emphasis on nutrition, health and fitness, and the need for unique experiences that differentiate a hospitality venue from its competitors. The tension between luxury and sustainability has challenged designers to create unique environments with many amenities while also making them sustainable.

There are many commentators discussing the top trends in hospitality design—*Hospitality Design Magazine*, material suppliers such as Interface Flor, and hospitality designers. The common trends cited include sustainability, regional influences, luxury, technology and connectivity, and wellness.

Although the apparently contradictory issues of sustainability and luxury appear in many lists, the industry is trying to reach a happy medium with regard to the sustainable luxury experience—recognizing that hospitality itself is a luxury but that decisions and experiences can also be more sustainable.

Part of the new design focus has been on creating an exotic experience. The global marketplace has opened designers to entirely new cultures and places—Marrakech, Istanbul, Cambodia, Dubai, and Mauritius, to name a few. Each place provides new and rich cultural scenery and a depth of culture that creates both the opportunity to learn and the challenge of introducing a brand without overshadowing the place and people.

Boutique Hotels

Mandy Aggett, lecturer in Hospitality Management at the Plymouth University in the United Kingdom (2007) defines a **boutique hotel** as one with fewer than 100 rooms that provides personalized services. The services most valued by guests, according to Aggett, included cleanliness, room service, and friendly staff. The room amenities most impacting a positive experience were location, quality, personalized service, and design and hominess. Unique interior architecture, furniture, and building comprised the specific design features that appealed to guests.

The boutique hotel has continued to increase in popularity over the past decade. Several of the larger hotel chains—Marriott, Renaissance, and others—count boutique hotels among their assets. Unique locations and luxurious touches accompanied by stylish décor and award-winning gourmet restaurants characterize the boutique hotel. Most importantly, design features prominently in the boutique hotel. Design features would include local furniture, furnishings, and artwork that demonstrate the historical and unique characteristics of the place. Unique lighting, trim work, room size and shape, and other unusual features would further contribute to the experience.

In a report compiled by the **Boutique and Lifestyle Lodging Association (BILA)** and prepared by academics from Purdue University, New York University, and Hong Kong Polytechnic, a panel of 40 industry professionals determined that boutique hotels are characterized by five attributes: cultural/historical/authentic, individual hotel (not a chain), interesting and unique, many high quality rooms, and social spaces such as living rooms and libraries (Day et al, 2011). According to the same report, the boutique hotel type traces its origins to the 1978 Blake's Hotel in London. As people seek to have authentic and unique experiences, the boutique hotel provides a venue for this activity.

Lifestyle Hotels

Although similar to a boutique hotel in terms of providing a unique experience, the **lifestyle hotel** tends to have a contemporary aesthetic, high levels of technology, and a focus on wellness. A lifestyle hotel tends to be larger than a boutique hotel. Both types—lifestyle and boutique—are designed to elicit an emotional response. As such, the goal is to make people happy, energized, joyful, and amused. By recognizing the individual, the guest will be creatively inspired and stimulated (Day et al., 2011).

Sustainable Hospitality Design

As one of the key concerns facing professionals in the hospitality industry, several organizations are now dedicated to sustainable hospitality, including the Network of Executive Women in Hospitality, the Hospitality Sustainable Purchasing Consortium, the Sustainable Hospitality Group, and Hospitality Sustainability Resources, LLC. These groups represent various constituencies and concerns owners, operators, and designers face when creating a sustainable facility.

Network of Executive Women in Hospitality (NEWH)

The Network of Executive Women in Hospitality (NEWH), a member organization of trade professionals, was founded in 1984 to promote a high standard of achievement for women in hospitality. The NEWH sponsors its own *NEWH Magazine* and an annual student design competition focused on the "sustainable guest experience." One area featured on the website is a sustainability section that includes links to several sustainable design resources. Included in these resources are manufacturers' links, information on LEED, a Sustainable Hospitality Forum link, and information on events highlighting sustainable hospitality. NEWH participates in the annual Hospitality Show in Las Vegas and sponsors its own events such as the student competition and webinars on sustainable hospitality.

Hospitality Sustainable Purchasing Consortium

Launched by leaders of the hospitality industry in 2011, the Hospitality Sustainable Purchasing Consortium pools members for building, furnishing, and supplying hotels with materials and products that are better for the guests, the local community, and the planet. The consortium includes design firms (such a RTKL), manufacturers for the hotel industry (such as Sealy and Simmons), and hotel chains (for example, Marriot). Examples of the products that are indexed include everything from room finishes such as carpet, paint, and casegoods to bedding and cleaning products. The organization's **Hospitality Sustainable Purchasing Index (HSPI)** is a database available to hospitality partners that can be used to inform the purchase of products, to check environmental performance reports, and to review the overall performance of a supplier with regard to corporate social responsibility and environmental and product sustainability. A partial list of current members includes American Standard, Delta Faucet, Interface FLOR, Kimball International, Sealy, and Simmons.

Research in Hospitality Design— Hotels

One academic program focused on hospitality design research, the Cornell School of Hotel Administration through the Center for Hospitality Research, hosts a bi-annual Hospitality Design Roundtable. The Fifth Roundtable took place in October 2011 and focused on boutique hotels. While the 2011 report summary from the event featured a short summary of the 2009 Roundtable during which LEED was discussed, the report also concluded that a LEED-certified building costs a 3- to 5-percent premium above standard construction. Shortcomings with the LEED rating systems included a bias toward urban location (does not work well for resorts), a lack of appropriateness for hotels that have special operating conditions, and that the LEED checklist does not work on a global scale (for example, outside the United States, it can be hard to recycle construction waste). Roundtable participants also suggested that not all LEED buildings use less energy. The participants felt other green standards

such as Energy Star and Green Globe might work better for the hotel industry. The report referenced a general consensus among architects and designers that green design was important to hospitality design—not only because it is the right thing to do but also because it is what customers want—despite some of their concerns about LEED.

Additional sustainability roundtables took place in 2010 and 2011. Topics of discussion included the supply chain, green operations, and customers' perceptions of "green." They concluded that customers are interested in green accommodations and, when given the choice, will choose a green hotel over one that is not. Numerous hotels and their sustainability reports can be found on the Cornell website at http://www.hotelschool.cornell.edu/research/chr/as a part of the Student Sustainability Reporting Competition. The Student Sustainability Reporting Competition challenges hotel administration students to create a "mock sustainability report for an imaginary hotel."

The primary academic journal for research on the hospitality industry is *The International Journal of Hospitality and Tourism Administration*. The journal focuses on the current issues in the industry. Taking an applied research approach (testing research ideas in actual facilities), recent topics in the journal have included sustainable tourism, guest expectations and experiences, cultural diversity, and travel safety.

Recent studies in the journal have concluded that green certifications are important to hotel guests; these research efforts have also articulated the benefits of sustainable hotels. Millar and Baloglu (2011) identified some sustainable features to which guests respond positively including refillable soap and shampoo dispensers, recycling center and bins, linen and towel policies (washing by request only), and energy-efficient lighting.

Butler (2008) conducted a literature review about sustainable hotel operations and identified some key components for adoption. As green building construction costs decrease, sustainable building and design is preferable for many reasons, including reduced energy costs, reduced water use, lower greenhouse gas emissions, and reduced maintenance costs. The author identified several specific measures to retrofit an existing facility as well as for new construction: install compact fluorescent lighting and low-flow showers, limit the use of individual shampoos and soaps, consider updating hotel construction standards to take site and orientation into account for passive solar gains, consider tax incentives for green construction, and understand that low or no volatile organic compounds emitted will enhance the indoor air quality leading to healthier guests and employees.

Research in Hospitality Design— Restaurants

There is overlap between the research about hotels (which include restaurants) and restaurant design. Research with a direct application to space planning a restaurant resulted from a study by Robson and Kimes (2011). These researchers concluded that banquette (padded bench style seats) seats were not preferred over tables and that placing tables closer than 12 inches to one another was also not preferred. While banquette seating works well for a business lunch, many restaurant guests prefer other types of seating. The report indicated that while spacing preferences varied by gender and ethnicity, most people experienced 6-inch spacing between tables negatively and preferred 12-inch spacing at a minimum.

According to Stephani Robson of Cornell University, as much as 95 percent of the reason people choose to purchase is based on an emotional response. Many things contribute to this emotional reaction, including the attitude of the host, the atmosphere of the restaurant, and where the guest is seated. The seating selection can be done by a host/hostess or by the diner. When given the choice, people like to sit next to some type of permanent feature such as a wall or low partition. The purpose of the meal can also impact seating choice. For example, a window seat might be chosen for a romantic meal, while a job interview might suggest a more "anchored" setting such as a corner table. Those dining alone prefer anchored seats (next to permanent features). Empty tables will always be selected first, and rarely will strangers share tables even when the layout might suggest this approach through the use of long tables with many chairs. Restaurateurs are in the business to make money. While many people prefer booth seating, this is also the type of seating with the lowest turnover in a restaurant— people tend to sit longer in booths. Thus, owners might prefer table seating.

In addition to space planning, other areas of sustainability research in restaurant design concern consumer behavior, food type and sourcing, and waste disposal. The sustainability of a restaurant is ultimately tied to its success. Customers prefer to have a sustainable experience, thus the use of locally sourced and organic food appeals to potential diners. Further, the use of locally made or sourced furniture and accessories can also contribute to a sustainable interior. Other concerns about restaurant sustainability relate to ongoing operation. Many restaurants now compost their food scraps, recycle kitchen oils and other waste, and use green cleaning products. Designers must create areas for these tasks to take place.

Student Approaches to Hospitality Design

Student approaches to hospitality are illustrated through series of projects: Three years of the NEWH Sustainable Hospitality Competition using three different sites: Mauritius; Old Sweet

Springs, West Virginia; and Yellow Sulphur Springs in Christiansburg, Virginia. The projects include hotels and resorts as well as restaurant designs; they also showcase different approaches to sustainable design for hospitality.

Restaurant Projects

The restaurant projects exhibit three different conceptual genres. The first approach uses the cuisine as inspiration for the design; the second approach derives the design concept from the site; and the third method focuses on guest experiences.

Cuisine (eco-social, eco-cultural)

Using a "slow food" concept demonstrates a cuisine approach to the restaurant. The slow food movement, founded in 1986 by Italian Carlo Petrini, encourages people to slow down and enjoy the dining experience. The movement encourages the use of locally sourced food that is cooked and eaten slowly. Following initial site analysis, the designer focused on obtaining all foods from local sources (defined as within a 100-mile radius). The adjacency to a local farmer's market enhanced this approach. The basic concept for the restaurant was inspired by the notion of understanding where

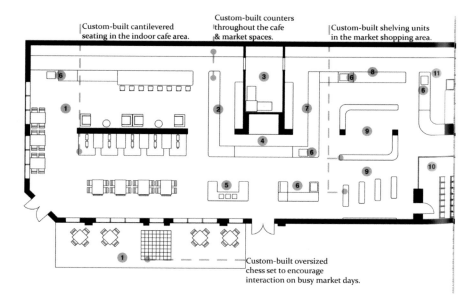

Custom-built cantilevered seating in the indoor cafe area.

Custom-built counters throughout the cafe & market spaces.

Custom-built shelving units in the market shopping area.

Custom-built oversized chess set to encourage interaction on busy market days.

Figure 5.1 Candice Davis, Slow Food Restaurant: Plan

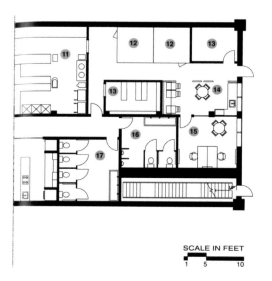

Figure 5.2 Candice Davis, Slow Food Restaurant: Plan

SCALE IN FEET
1   5   10

1. CAFE
2. GRILL
3. DISHWASHING & STORAGE
4. FRESH SELECTIONS BAR & BRICK OVEN PIZZA
5. INFORMATION DESK
6. CHECKOUT COUNTER
7. SIDE DISHES
8. ARTISANAL MEATS & CHEESES
9. MARKET SHELVING
10. CANNING CENTER & COMMUNITY CLASSROOM
11. BAKERY DISPLAY & KITCHEN
12. REFRIGERATED STORAGE
13. DRY STORAGE
14. EMPLOYEE LOUNGE
15. OFFICE
16. MEN'S RESTROOM
17. WOMEN'S RESTROOM

Figure 5.3 Candice Davis, Slow Food Restaurant: 3D view of dining

Figure 5.4 Candice Davis, Slow Food Restaurant: Food preparation area

Figure 5.5 Candice Davis, Slow Food Restaurant: Market store area

one's food comes from. The resulting design showcases local foods using a fresh selections bar and brick-oven pizza shop. Local farmers can sell their artisanal meats and locally made cheeses, canned products, and baked goods in the market at the rear of the restaurant. Guests are encouraged to relax and sit for a while in order to have a slow-food experience.

A second example using sustainable cuisine as the inspiration is the 357 Salem Avenue Organic Restaurant, located in Roanoke, Virginia. In this instance, the seasonal availability of various crops determines the menu and helps to shape the design. Like the food, the interior of the restaurant changes with each season. For example, the colored lights change seasonally, as do the signage and cuisine.

Technology is then used to provide interaction with the food being grown on-site adjacent to the restaurant. The restaurant places iPads with cameras on site, and then all gardens can be viewed in real-time in the restaurant.

Figure 5.6 Lauren Shaw, Organic Seasonal Restaurant: Plan

Figure 5.7 Lauren Shaw, Organic Seasonal Restaurant: Bar and lounge

Figure 5.8 Lauren Shaw, Organic Seasonal Restaurant: Lounge in winter

Figure 5.9 Lauren Shaw, Organic Seasonal Restaurant: Bar and lounge in spring

Figure 5.10 Lauren Shaw, Organic Seasonal Restaurant: Dining area in summer

Figure 5.11 Lauren Shaw, Organic Seasonal Restaurant: Dining area in summer

Figure 5.12 Lauren Shaw, Organic Seasonal Restaurant: Integrated technology

INTEGRATED TECHNOLOGY: the touchscreen technology located in the restaurant and on the farmland bridges the gap between the interior and exterior.

1. visitors are invited to explore the adjacent site and the touchscreen system serves as a means of wayfinding.

2. education is essential to understanding the importance of eating local and organic food. patrons can engage in an interactive learning program.

3. the restaurant's menu and nutritional information can be accessed from anywhere.

4. while inside the restaurant, the visitor can view the food they are eating as it is being harvested. an on-screen map of the site indicates where the video feed is being broadcasted from.

Site/Nature as Inspiration (biophilic)

The Umi project illustrates the use of the site (beachfront) as the inspiration for the design. The primary orientation of the restaurant seating is to the ocean. The concept for the project—a wave—is evident in the undulating walls, floor patterns, and ceiling planes.

Experience as Inspiration (eco-social, eco-cultural)

For the restaurants designed as a part of the NEWH Sustainable Hospitality competition, the guest experience served as the conceptual approach. Depending on the interpretation of "sustainable experience," each solution provides a slightly different scenario.

Figure 5.13
Steve Chang, Umi
Restaurant: Process
Work

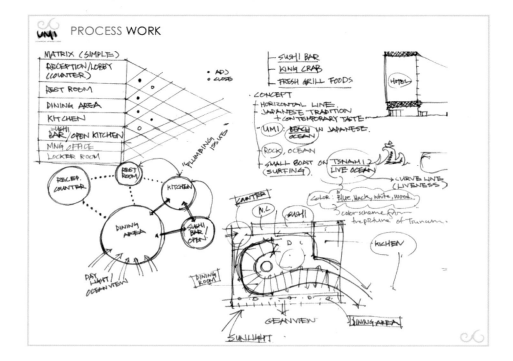

Figure 5.14
Steve Chang, Umi
Restaurant: Plan

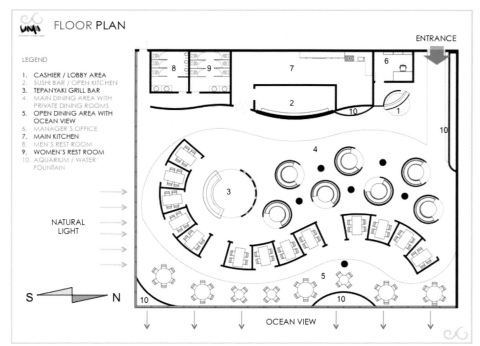

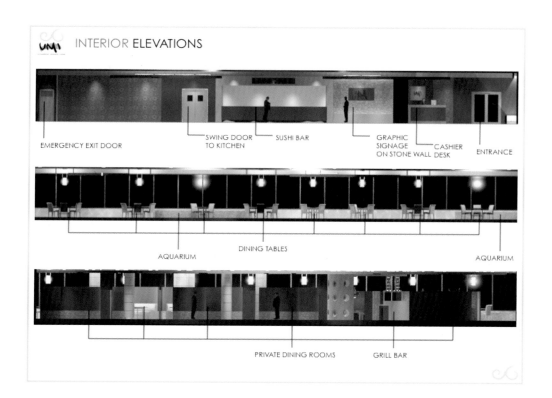

INTERIOR ELEVATIONS

EMERGENCY EXIT DOOR

SWING DOOR TO KITCHEN — SUSHI BAR

GRAPHIC SIGNAGE ON STONE WALL — CASHIER DESK — ENTRANCE

AQUARIUM

DINING TABLES

AQUARIUM

PRIVATE DINING ROOMS — GRILL BAR

Figure 5.15
Steve Chang,
Umi Restaurant:
Sectional elevations

3D PERSPECTIVE VIEWS / Dining Hall

Figure 5.16
Steve Chang, Umi
Restaurant: 3D view
at entry

Figure 5.17
Steve Chang, Umi
Restaurant: 3D view
of Japanese grill

3D PERSPECTIVE **VIEWS** / Grill Bar

Japanese Grill (Tepanyaki) is also a very famous recipe. Usual Tepanyaki restaurants have many grill tables, but UMI has a big round grill bar on the center so people are able to order their foods and pick them up like a buffet.

Figure 5.18 Steve
Chang, Umi
Restaurant: 3D view
of window seats

3D PERSPECTIVE **VIEWS** / Dining Hall with Ocean View

UMI is designed under the consideration of sustainable issue. Firstly, the location of the restaurant is south east. So the restaurant has curtain windows to both south and east side and it makes the restaurant be able to have both sunlight from the south side and ocean view to the east.

Bamboo flooring is chosen for the sustainable reason and use of Benjamin Moore paint and Knoll environmental wall covering makes the space be more sustainable. Many natural materials like woods and stones are used to obtain both sustainability and traditional Japanese taste.

An example of this approach is found in the "Antebellum" project, which uses an experiential approach, with the intention of taking a step back in time. The complex provides guests with the opportunity to harvest their own food in the morning that they will eat later in the day, thus providing guests with a direct experience of their food's source.

+ DESIGN CONCEPT

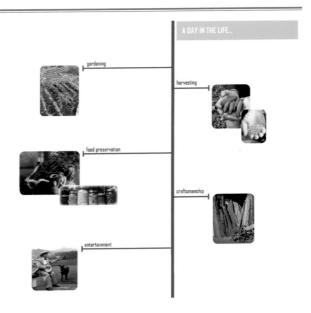

A DAY IN THE LIFE...

gardening

harvesting

food preservation

craftsmanship

entertainment

Taking the idea of "Back to Antebellum" and reviving the fundamental qualities of the past, Old Sweet Springs receives new life with a warm, sleek aesthetic contrasting the original neoclassical exterior. The new Antebellum idea incorporates modern amenities into a historical experience of the simpler lifestyle the 1800s offered.

Buildings today are designed with the intent to be sustainable. However, if we look to our past, we can clearly see that our ancestors were taking the right approach all along. At the resort, sustainability can be observed as an experience and not just an intent. Reverting back to the concept of a self-sufficient community provides maximum opportunities to work in sync with nature rather than against it. Ample land supports the growth of enough crops and farm animals to fully support the resort. Natural spring sources are not only used for healing qualities but also aid in supporting the resort's self sufficiency.

Guests are given the opportunity to experience some of the things that was a part such a natural cycle of daily living in the 1800s. Education is an important factor when trying to establish a strong sustainable language. Hands on experience can sometimes be the best way to learn, which is why guests are encouraged to be involved as much as they desire.

Guests can begin their day by walking through the community garden to harvest food later used to prepare meals and food preservation. Additional activities include cooking/canning workshops, woodworking workshops, and dance lessons of the local dance. The resort also caters to the modern era through a luxurious spa, wine tasting bar, and upscale restaurant.

While the resort can accommodate visits of any length of time, events and activities can be enjoyed more thoroughly during an extended stay. Whether it be escaping from city life, returning to one's roots, or simply looking for a get-away, "Back to Antebellum" guests will not only be relaxed and refreshed, but educated on a simpler, self-sustaining way of life that Old Sweet Springs once offered.

Figure 5.19 Denise Pendleton, Back to Antebellum Restaurant: Concept

+ LIGHT DINING PERSPECTIVE

While not operational year-round, the outdoor Highland Dining provides the opportunity to relax and enjoy the cleansing mountain air.

HIGHLAND DINING-
Outdoor dining experience serving breakfast/brunch and evening tea. While the meal is being prepared, guests are encouraged to take a dip in the refreshing mineral pool or welcome the sun on the yoga plaza.

ARRIVAL

SETTLE-IN

SUNRISE

7:00 AM
Literally waking up with the chickens to harvest fruits, vegetables, and herbs to be used in breakfast preparation.

8:00 AM
While chefs prepare unique cuisine from fresh produce, guests are encouraged to experience the healing waters of the mineral spring or find inner relaxation on the yoga plaza.

9:30 AM
After collecting fruits and herbs from the permaculture gardens, guests can dine on breakfast or brunch that they helped hand-pick.

SUNSET

Figure 5.20 Denise Pendleton, Back to Antebellum Restaurant: 3D view of Highland Dining

A double fireplace separates the private dining area from the chef's kitchen. The chef's kitchen is open to guests to take lessons on canning, preserving, and preparing the food harvested on the resort grounds. A mobile cook top can be brought into the dining area for a more personal dining experience if desired.

The upper level (not featured) is used to store preserved food and herb drying.

MONROE RETREAT
Guests can experience a private dining experience in a traditional, southern kitchen separate from the main quarters. A window through to the kitchen allows guests to view the chefs preparing the meal.

ARRIVAL
SETTLE-IN

SUNRISE

7:00 AM
Literally waking up with the chickens to harvest fruits, vegetables, and herbs to be used in breakfast preparation.

8:00 AM
While chefs prepare unique cuisine from fresh produce, guests are encouraged to experience the healing waters of the mineral spring or find inner relaxation on the yoga plaza.

9:30 AM
After collecting fruits and herbs from the permaculture gardens, guests can dine on breakfast or brunch that they helped hand-pick.

2:00 PM
With morning activities complete, a relaxing trip to the spa provides the modern conveniences guests are accustomed to while getting in tune with nature.

8:00 PM
Guests can enjoy a sunset dinner prepared in front of them by the chefs. Guests are encouraged to become involved in the dining experience.

SUNSET

Sustainable Hotels and Spas

Designers of hotels and spas take inspiration from a variety of arenas. These include the guest experience, the site, and the clientele profile.

Sustainable Guest Experience (eco-technic)

Using an old postcard as inspiration resulted in a guest experience that seeks to remind the visitor of times passed. The main lobby reinforces this concept through the use of traditional furnishings, area rugs, and chandeliers. Strategically placed recycling bins and reusable maps support the environmentally responsible guest. Although the interiors appear quite traditional, the building features a state-of-the-art geothermal heating system and grey water reuse throughout.

A very different guest experience is provided by Sweet Springs, the golf

Figure 5.22 Morgan Thorne, A Warm Welcome: 3D view of check-in

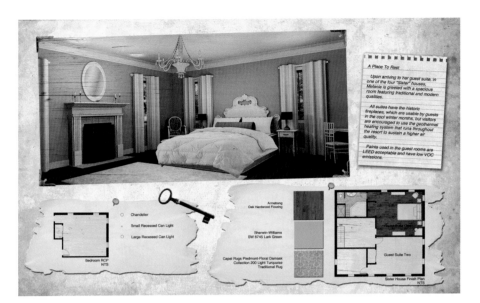

Figure 5.23 Morgan Thorne, A Warm Welcome: 3D view of guest room

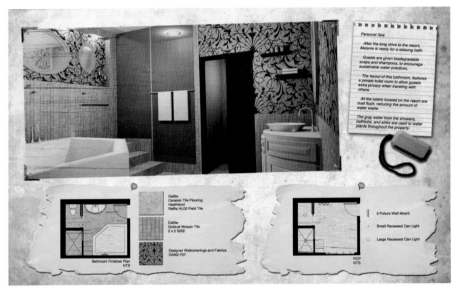

Figure 5.24 Morgan Thorne, A Warm Welcome: 3D view of personal spa

Figure 5.25 Morgan Thorne, A Warm Welcome: 3D view of outdoor springs

Figure 5.26 Morgan Thorne, A Warm Welcome: 3D view of spa

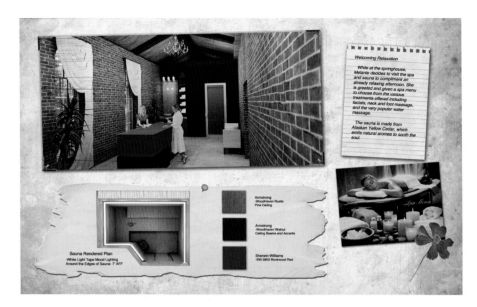

Figure 5.27 Morgan Thorne, A Warm Welcome: 3D view of spa

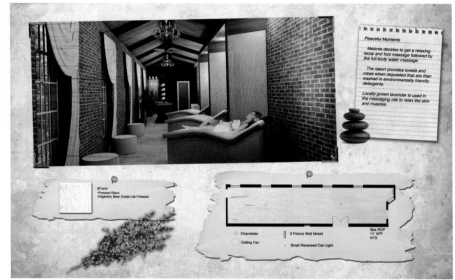

Figure 5.28 Morgan Thorne, A Warm Welcome: 3D view of massage area

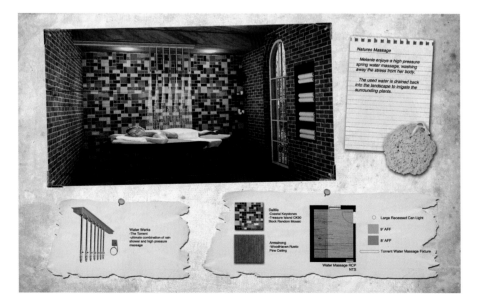

retreat for returning military veterans. The resort encourages newly returned soldiers to convalesce in the beautiful and peaceful surroundings of rural West Virginia. An organic vegetable garden and 18-hole golf course complement the historic buildings on the site. The experiential aspect of the project focuses on golf and recreational healing.

Figure 5.29 Rosie Santo Domingo, Sweet Springs: Concept

Figure 5.30 Rosie Santo Domingo, Sweet Springs: 3D view of reception

Figure 5.31 Rosie Santo Domingo, Sweet Springs: Organic vegetable garden

Figure 5.32 Rosie Santo Domingo, Sweet Springs: Golf course shop

Inspiration from Site/Buildings (eco-cultural, eco-technic)

The Jeffersonian-styled building on the site provided a strong inspiration for several projects. Arched windows, traditional staircases, hardwood floors, and the retention of historic detail support the sustainable guest experience, which is augmented by photovoltaic water heating and paperless guest services (guests are encouraged to use hand dryers instead of paper towels in washrooms and to order services using a touch screen in the guest room). Thus, the traditional-appearing hotel features up-to-date "smart building" features and beautiful views of the outdoors. Smart building features include the placement of controls and panels in each room. Guests can control the lights, temperature, sound, and other features of the room from a touch screen.

Figure 5.33 Kelly Preston, Sweet Springs: 3D view of dining room

Figure 5.34 Kelly Preston, Sweet Springs: 3D view of guest room

Figure 5.35 Kelly
Preston, Sweet
Springs: 3D view of
reception

Figure 5.36 Kelly
Preston, Sweet
Springs: 3D view of
bathhouse lounge

Sample Completed Project

The following example presents a single
project from initial conception through
the final project presentation.

Kristi Nowak—Blend

Kristi Nowak started this project by
creating a concept based on a desired
guest experience through a sequence of
spaces. The first figure illustrates the
concept and images the student used to
direct the design, while the second image
shows the spaces where the experiences
were to take place on a master plan.

Nowak then explored the initial concept
using three-dimensional sketching and
notations to capture the experience of
"Blending the Barrier." Plan views were
also created as a part of this stage.

Once the basic imagery and finishes
had been chosen, the experiences were
then entered into Sketchup and modeled
to begin the refinement of the design.

For the final presentation, the student
compiled all design decisions—including the
process sketches—into a final page layout
that described the sustainable finishes and
concepts used throughout the project to
create a sustainable guest experience.

blend..

CONTRASTS

The small island of Mauritius is described as "a jewel in the Indian Ocean that has evolved into a harmonious mosaic of cultures and religions." This blend of contrasting ideas and beliefs has inspired the design of the Mauritius One and Only Resort and Spa. Contrasting elements are paired together to create a harmonious blend and give guests a luxurious yet eco friendly escape.

▶ **"BLENDING THE BARRIER"**
green incentive program

Luxury and sustainability are two large ideas that strongly contrast each other. Many believe you can only have one, and not the other. However, this is not the case. At the Mauritius One and Only Resort and Spa, opposing elements are merged together in effort to obtain a larger goal: blending the barrier between luxury and sustainability. The goal is to exemplify these two ideas can be very cohesive. In order to do so, guests are given the choice to participate in the green incentive program. While they are staying at a resort that incorporates green practices, such as solar panels and use of gray water, it is important to demonstrate they too have a role in breaking this barrier. Points are given to guests who exemplify green practices, such as attending a yoga class or even eating at the restaurant on site that carries locally harvested foods. At the end of the trip, the points are tallied up and can either be used at some place on the resort or put towards their next visit.

Figure 5.37 Kristi Nowak, Blend Resort: Concept

GUEST EXPERIENCE:
01. Check in
02. Spa: *yoga*
03. Guest room
04. Restaurant: live entertainment
05. Spa: *check in*
06. Spa: *treatment room*
07. Departure

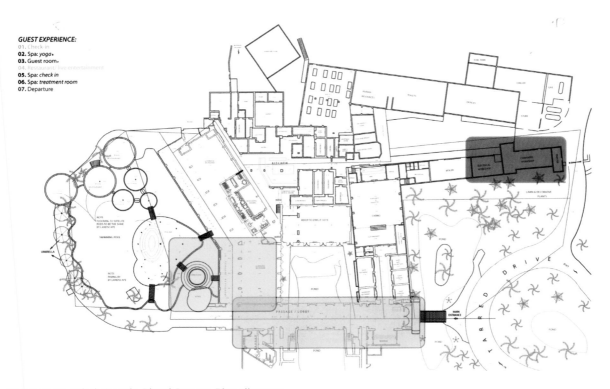

Figure 5.38 Kristi Nowak, Blend Resort: Plan diagram

Figure 5.39
Kristi Nowak,
Blend Resort:
Concept sketches

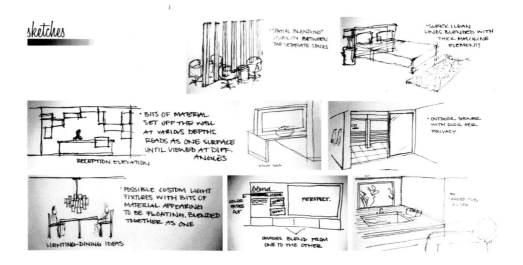

Figure 5.40
Kristi Nowak,
Blend Resort:
Plan sketches

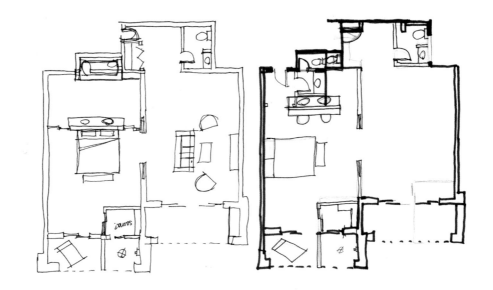

Figure 5.41
Kristi Nowak, Blend
Resort: Process 3D
view of reception

•REMOVE EXTRA LINES

MATERIAL

↑

||in.

↑

Figure 5.42 Kristi Nowak, Blend Resort: Process 3D view of bathroom

ROTATE? *MATERIAL, CHANGED TO FAUX BOIS – BISQUE/REED*

blend..

EXPERIENCES

The outdoor lounge serves as a space for guests to hang out, meet others, and discuss past experiences. Vertical wooden slats spatially blend different nooks and give a sense of privacy.

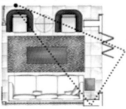

OUTDOOR LOUNGE

Resort Restaurant

Eating at the resort's restaurant, which offers a full menu of locally grown and harvested foods, earns guests 2 points per visit.

Use of Stucco

Stucco is used throughout the entire resort for not only its great thermal properties but also to make use of the excess amount of glass on the island.

RCP LEGEND
- ○ 6" Recessed Compact Fluorescent
- ● Pendant

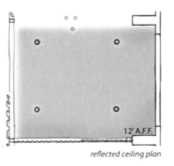

12' A.F.F.

reflected ceiling plan

Figure 5.43 Kristi Nowak, Blend Resort: Outdoor lounge

 YOUR MIND

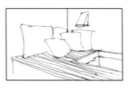

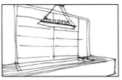

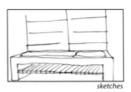

sketches

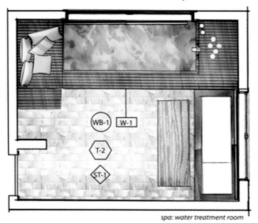

spa: water treatment room

FINISH SCHEDULE

FLOORS

TILE	MANUFACTURER	STYLE	COLOR
T-2	United Tile	Moda	Siena

BASE

WOOD BASE	MANUFACTURER	STYLE	COLOR
WB-1	Teragren	Studio	Base Natural

WALLS

STUCCO	MANUFACTURER	STYLE	COLOR
ST-1	Produced on site		Cream

MILLWORK

WOOD	MANUFACTURER	STYLE	COLOR
W-1	Teragren	Studio	Cara-melized

Figure 5.44 Kristi Nowak, Blend Resort: Water spa treatment room

blend.. YOUR BODY

The yoga studio incorporates a glass nana wall that can fully open up to the views and sounds of the surroundings. Transparent 3form blends the waiting room and studio to create a relaxing environment overall.

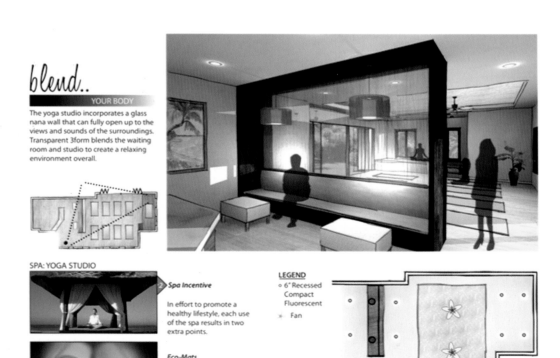

SPA: YOGA STUDIO

Spa Incentive

In effort to promote a healthy lifestyle, each use of the spa results in two extra points.

Eco-Mats

The yoga studio makes use of Eco Yoga Mats which are composed of all-natural rubber and jute fiber.

LEGEND
○ 6" Recessed Compact Fluorescent
✳ Fan

10' A.F.F.
10'6" A.F.F.

reflected ceiling plan

Figure 5.45 Kristi Nowak, Blend Resort, Spa: Yoga studio

Firm Approaches to Hospitality Design

As is the case with many design specializations, certain firms focus on the hospitality design sector exclusively.

WATG

WATG's mission is "to design destinations that lift the spirit." As a leading hospitality design firm, WATG has designed projects in 160 countries and territories around the world. Services offered by the firm include architecture, interiors, landscape architecture, and planning. The firm's approach to sustainable design includes the use of local materials, natural ventilation, habitat protection and sensitive siting, community benefits (providing a place for the community to enjoy nature and offering a winery that the community can access) and culture preservation, as well as energy conservation and alternative cooling strategies. The firm was founded in 1945 in Hawaii as Wimberly and Cook.

Two examples of WATG's approach are the Bardessono project, located in Napa Valley, and the Haptik project.

Bardessono (eco-cultural, eco-technic)

Located on a 4.9-acre site, the Bardessono Resort features 62 guest rooms, a spa, a restaurant, and meeting space. Each room has its own courtyard. Conceptually, the project design sought to blend in with the agrarian setting of the Napa Valley region. In addition to the use of sustainable materials, both solar power and geothermal energy were integrated into the building. The hotel and spa have received a LEED Platinum rating.

Figure 5.46 WATG, Bardessono: Guest room garden

Figure 5.47
WATG, Bardessono:
Solar panels on roof

Figure 5.48
WATG, Bardessono:
Main entry showing
green wall

Figure 5.49
WATG, Bardessono:
Courtyard

Figure 5.50
WATG, Bardessono:
Private dining area

Figure 5.51
WATG, Bardessono:
Pool deck

Figure 5.52
WATG, Bardessono:
Interior sculpture
with skylight above

Figure 5.53
WATG, Bardessono:
Guest room bath
and outdoor shower

Figure 5.54
WATG, Bardessono:
Guest room fireplace

Figure 5.55
WATG, Bardessono:
Guest room

Figure 5.56
WATG, Bardessono:
Faucet detail

Figure 5.57
WATG, Bardessono:
Stonehenge feature

Haptik (eco-technic, eco-medical)

The Haptik suite won the USGBC Competition for a Sustainable Suite in 2010. The name of the suite comes from the Greek word meaning "to experience interactions using the sense of touch." The suite includes a variety of sustainable materials including eucalyptus sheets and a reclaimed lumber headboard. The finishes consist of no-VOC paint, FSC-certified wood, LED lights, and a NanaWall glass wall system. The shower is located in a private outdoor courtyard. The technological aspects of the design include features such as controls that allow a guest to customize his or her own temperature and lighting using the phone. A smart key provides access to the room and doubles as a train and bus pass.

Figure 5.58
WATG, Haptik: Guest
room plan

Figure 5.59 WATG,
Haptik: Guest room
view from balcony
looking in "Sleep"

Figure 5.60
WATG, Haptik: Guest
room view from bed
looking out "Entry"

Figure 5.61 WATG, Haptik: Guest room bath with balcony shower "Bath"

Figure 5.62 WATG, Haptik: Guest room view of balcony "Entertainment"

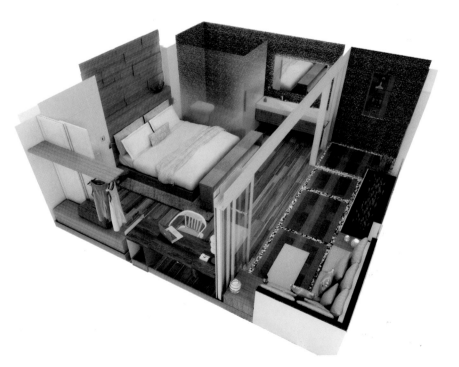

Figure 5.63 WATG, Haptik: Guest room 3D overview of room

Resources for Students

There are many resources available to students to assist them with hospitality design. The project examples are provided to demonstrate a variety of approaches. In addition, *Hospitality Design Magazine* provides excellent case studies for students to use as do books such as *Hotel Design: Planning and Development*, by W. Rutes, R. Penner, and L. Adams.

Project Checklist: Typical Design Process

Each project follows a similar design process. Ideally, sustainability is infused throughout this process and is not a later addition.

Pre-Design

During the pre-design phase 3 activities take place:

1. Inspiration and Conceptual Approach
According to some of the trends identified by experts in the field, the locale and local culture can provide a source of inspiration for a project. By identifying with a specific location, sustainable practices such as the use of indigenous resources and local traditions can easily be integrated into the design process.

2. Program
Several sources provide generic programming guidelines for restaurants, hotels, and other hospitality facilities. When combined with the specific client needs and local constraints, the beginning program emerges. Standard prototypes and clearances as well as building code and accessibility requirements should also be identified in the program.

3. Precedent Studies
Case studies of similar projects and others within the region provide a starting place for new designs.

Evidence-Based Design/ Information Gathering/Research

Research studies provided on many of the above-mentioned websites as well as those found in *Hospitality Design, Interior Design*, and other resources provide current research and issues in hospitality design. Centers such as the one located at Cornell University are continuously studying many aspects of the hospitality industry including the guest experience, specific types of faculties, and new, sustainability-related findings and innovations in the industry.

Schematic Design

The formation of a schematic design follows a traditional path including the use of the plan, adjacency matrix, bubbles/blocks, and circulation studies. A focus on reduced square footage (overall size), water-use reduction, and passive solar and ventilation start the integration of locally responsive strategies. Preliminary scenarios will respond to concept and program and may include 3D thumbnail sketching and preliminary Sketchup modeling, as well as some developments in elevation and section.

Design Development

As a project moves into design development, the actual material choices, lighting fixtures and lamp selections, and furnishing selections will either contribute to or detract from the project's overall environmental footprint.

Materials Evaluation Protocol

It is important when choosing finishes to examine their content. If a material is unfamiliar, consulting either the MBDC website (http://www.mbdc.com/detail.aspx?linkid=2&sublink=9) or the Perkins + Will Transparency site (http://transparency.perkinswill.com/) provides information about common toxins in materials. The MBDC website includes a list of restricted chemicals and banned chemicals. The chemicals listed are divided into known carcinogens and suspected carcinogens. (See Appendix 5 Checklist for Materials.)

Codes and Regulations/Industry—Specific Standards

Once the material in question has passed these two preliminary lists of toxic chemicals, then the rating systems for sustainability should be assessed. For example, according to Elaine Aye, principal of Green Building Services, and Alicia Snyder-Carlson, senior consultant with Green Building Services, in "Taking Control" for *Interiors and Sources* magazine (May 2012, 118–22), part of the due diligence of product selections and specification includes checking certifications such as Underwriters Laboratories (UL) and American Society for the Testing of Materials (ASTM)—both are recognized leaders in the testing of materials and products for safety. They recommend Building for Environmental and Economic Sustainability (BEES) software and the Environmental Protection Agency's Comprehensive Procurement Guidelines as well. A final suggestion reminds designers to consider the entire life cycle of the product, not just the initial cost. An additional measure includes the use of a new chemical green screening process, The Clean Production Action (CPA) GreenScreen for Safer Chemicals, that provides a comparative chemical screening approach and encourages the use of safer chemicals (http://www.cleanproduction.org/ Accessed March 26, 2014).

The Eco Library Matrix regularly included in *Interiors and Sources* profiles the "Scope of Certifications," "Life-Cycle Considerations," and "Transparency" of many of the best-known product certifications including C2C, Energy Star, FSC Certified, Green Label, and Green Seal.

Applicable LEED Checklist

The two LEED checklists that can be used for hospitality projects are LEED for Commercial Interiors and LEED for New Construction, depending on the project type (See Appendixes 12 and 18).

Planning Guidelines

The following plan prototypes provide basic clearance information for seating in restaurants as well as a typical accessible guest room design.

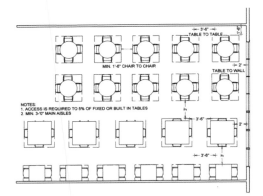

Figure 5.64 Typical table clearances

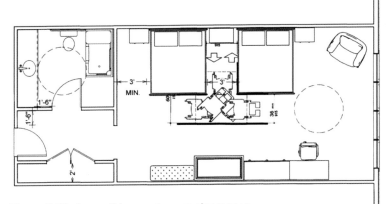

Figure 5.65 Accessible guest room clearances

Discussion Question and Exercise

Borrow five materials you might want to use for a current design project from your resource library and assess them against the banned chemicals list and the transparency list. Then identify any green certifications the materials have. What did you find? How will this alter your design? Or will it?

Key Terms

Boutique and Lifestyle Lodging Association (BILA)

boutique hotel

Hospitality Sustainable Purchasing Index (HSPI)

lifestyle hotel

Sources

Aggett, M. 2007. "What Has Influenced Growth in the UK's Boutique Hotel Sector?" *International Journal of Contemporary Hospitality Management*, 19(2): 169–77.

Busch, Jennifer. 2011. "Three Trends in Hospitality Design." *Interface*, May 11. Accessed June 28, 2013. http://interfaceflorblog.com/three-trends-in-hospitality-design.

Butler, J. 2008. "The Compelling 'Hard Case' for 'Green' Hotel Development." *Cornell Hospitality Quarterly*, 49(3): 234–44.

Day, J., D. Quadri, and D. Jones. (2011). *Boutique and Lifestyle Hotels: Emerging Definitions*. Prepared for Frances Kiradjian, Founder of Boutique and Lifestyle Lodging Association, California.

Gutsche, Jeremy. 2007. "Michael Adams, Editor In Chief of *Hospitality Design Magazine* (Interview). *Trendhunter*, May 14. http://www.trendhunter.com/trends/michael-adams-editor-in-chief-of-hospitality-design-magazine-interview

Millar, M., and S. Baloglu. 2011. "Hotel Guests' Preferences for Green Guest Room Attributes" *Cornell Hospitality Journal* 52(3): 302–11.

Robson, S. K. A., and S. E. Kimes. 2011. "Consumers' Responses to Table Spacing in Restaurants." *Cornell Hospitality Quarterly*, 52(3): 253–64.

www.hotelschool.cornell.edu/research/chr/events/roundtables/recent/sustainability/

6

CULTURAL, CIVIC, AND INSTITUTIONAL PROJECTS

....

Objectives

● Students will be aware of various types of cultural, civil, and institutional projects.

● Students will understand a variety of sustainability issues governing these types of projects.

● Students will be able to describe how designers have created sustainable solutions for cultural, civic, and institutional spaces.

Overview

The category cultural, civic, and institutional design is quite broad and covers most of the types of design projects not discussed in other chapters. For example, pro-bono projects (such as those done for Architecture for Humanity or Habitat for Humanity), museums and other cultural centers (such as performing arts theaters), airports and jails, as well as many more are all under this umbrella term. Governmental projects including both federal and state as well as all branches of the armed forces are also presented in this chapter. Because of the broad scope of these project types, some common principles and concerns will provide the basis for the chapter discussion.

Within the domain of **government design**, nearly every other type of design might be included—residential housing, retail, healthcare, hospitality, and office design. The **Government Services Administration (GSA)** is the single biggest landlord in the country. The Public Buildings Service division of the GSA oversees 9,624 assets including over 370.2 million square feet of workspace (http://www.gsa.gov/portal/category/100000we). Since these topics are addressed elsewhere in this book, the focus for this chapter will be on some of the many building types not otherwise covered. These include jails and prisons, airports, museums and large cultural centers, convention centers, libraries, fire and police stations, post offices, and pro bono works such as disaster relief, international outreach projects, and others.

Government Agencies: Requiring LEED

As people learn more about climate change and the need for sustainability, discussions of sustainable design have become more public. The predominant green building rating system in the United States is LEED. With the recent popularity of LEED, many governmental bodies and agencies have started requiring LEED certification levels for all new buildings. In some cases, the requirement is to meet the benchmark provided by a LEED system; in others it is to actually obtain certification through the USGBC. The United States Green Building Council (USGBC) is a not-for-profit organization formed in 1993 to promote sustainability in the building and construction industry through the certification of green buildings. Industry professionals and experts in sustainable design develop all of the LEED rating systems as administered by the USGBC. According to the USGBC website, "Various LEED initiatives including legislation, executive orders, resolutions, ordinances, policies, and incentives are found in 442 localities (384 cities/towns and 58 counties and across 45 states), in 34 state governments (including the Commonwealth of Puerto Rico), in 14 federal agencies or departments, and numerous public school jurisdictions and institutions of higher education across the United States." Federal initiatives and adoptions include the use of LEED by the Department of

Agriculture, the Department of Energy, the Department of Health and Human Services, Department of the Interior, Department of State, Department of Veterans Affairs, the Environmental Protection Agency, the Government Services Administration (GSA), and others. Three branches of the armed services—the air force, army, and navy—all require that their new buildings meet LEED certification. Added to this are numerous state and local governments.

GSA on Sustainability

In 2006, 19 federal agencies signed a memorandum of agreement to design, construct, and operate high performance sustainable buildings. In 2007, by executive order, properties of the GSA have to meet the following criteria: reduce metered energy use by 3 percent per year and reduce metered energy use by 30 percent and water use by 16 percent by 2015 (GSA website). The GSA uses LEED criteria and all newly constructed and significantly renovated facilities within its portfolio must meet LEED Gold criteria.

Safety

Following the events of September 11, 2001, and other terrorist-related attacks, some key concerns facing new building construction of government, institutional, and public facilities relate to the need for safety. Placement of the building, points of entry, the mailroom, and many other variables now influence the interior spaces around creating a safe environment.

Waste Management

A significant challenge for public buildings relates to waste. The management of trash, recycling, and wastewater all present significant challenges. Allowing for recycling behavior necessitates specialized waste and recycling containers as well as processing and storage areas.

Design Domains

The design for government agencies, institutional, civic, and cultural design sectors all have their own specific concerns, some of which are outlined here.

Schools

While different types of learning institutions can be categorized under varying use group types in the building codes (higher education is under business, for example), the design of learning environments at all levels features some similarities. Several groups and industry specialists focus specifically on learning environments. The **Collaborative for High Performance Schools (CHPS)** promotes improved student performance through better buildings. The collaborative has outlined National Core Criteria for the high performance school environment. A six-part manual outlines best practices for schools, districts, and designers to create and ultimately build and operate high performance schools. The manual criteria address site, materials, energy and water efficiency, indoor environmental criteria, innovation and performance, and integrated project delivery.

Classifications of Educational Facilities

According to the Whole Building Design Group (WBDG) website made available through the National Institute of Building Sciences (wbdg.org), educational spaces are classified into seven basic types: child development centers; elementary education; K–8th grade; secondary education; high school and junior college; university; and training and computer centers.

Current Research about Schools

A study by the Partnership for 21st-Century Skills (P21) provided research showing that the interior environment of the school dramatically impacts student performance. P21 was founded in 2002 with stakeholders from the U.S. Department of Education, AOL Time Warner, Apple Computers, Cisco Systems, Dell, Microsoft Corporation, and the National Education Association among others. The organization is focused on K–12 education and readiness for higher education. According to its research, test scores improved by 11 percent when a dilapidated interior was rehabilitated.

The researchers also described the state of schools today, most of which were constructed to meet Industrial-Age educational needs. Started in the late 1800s, the first schools were designed to produce skilled workers for the factory. This system taught reading, writing, history, and math and focused on the memorization of facts. A one-size-fits-all approach segregated students by age into various classes. Secondary education was to provide professional and managerial training. The standard classroom environment no longer meets the needs of 21st-century education and learning styles. The new educational environment needs to focus on how people learn, thus providing flexible learning studios that are friendly, open, and accessible and that promote collaboration, cooperation, and interaction.

The study indicates that, while sustainable construction can cost 2 to 3 percent more, the benefits are 20 times that over the lifetime of the building. The need to integrate technology seamlessly into the education environment is also recommended, as this helps increase student engagement, promote greater achievement, facilitate communication, and build 21st-century skills required in today's world.

The final finding of the study: the standard 50-minute duration for a class period needs to be reconsidered. According to recent research, while students in the United States spend 1,100 hours in school (K–12 education), those in other countries who are outperforming U.S. students on standardized tests spend an average of 701 hours in school, or only 63 percent of the time that American students spend in school.

Learning Style Research

Howard Gardner is currently the Hobbs Professor of Cognition and Education in the Harvard Graduate School of Education. His multiple intelligence theory outlines eight different **learning styles** (ways in which people learn): linguistic, logical-mathematical, spatial, musical, naturalist, body-kinesthetic, interpersonal, and intrapersonal. (Gardner 2011). All individuals possess some level of all intelligence types, and no two people have exactly the same learning makeup. Other researchers have created other names for (and numbers of) these styles. The idea behind multiple intelligence theory is that two people might be able to master the same skill but might reach that level of mastery in very different ways. This development has some basis in heredity and some basis in environment and experience. Thus, the design of the classroom would have a significant impact on learning.

The ways in which design might positively might impact learning include some of the following:

1. High ceilings and good ventilation to support kinesthetic, fitness-smart activities
2. Reading spaces (spaces for quiet)
3. Spaces for interaction
4. Music spaces
5. Real-time monitoring of kilowatt gains from solar panels (mathematical)
6. Vistas to the outside (naturalist and spatial)
7. Natural daylighting
8. Words on the walls or other surfaces
9. Areas in which to move around

Table 6.1

Intelligences	Description
Linguistic	An ability to analyze information and create products involving oral and written language such as speeches, books, and memos
Logical-Mathematical	An ability to develop equations and proofs, make calculations, and solve abstract problems
Spatial	An ability to recognize and manipulate large-scale and fine-grained spatial images
Musical	An ability to produce, remember, and make meaning of different patterns of sound
Naturalist	An ability to identify and distinguish among different types of plants, animals, and weather formations that are found in the world
Bodily-Kinesthetic	An ability to use one's own body to create products or solve problems
Interpersonal	An ability to recognize and understand other people's moods, desires, motivations, and intentions
Intrapersonal	An ability to recognize and understand one's own moods, desires, motivations, and intentions

Based on Table 2: Garner's Eight Intelligences
Davis, K., J. Christodoulou, S. Seider, and H. Gardner. *The Theory of Multiple Intelligences.*

Manufacturers' Research

In response to the reported need for new types of learning environments, several manufacturers have undertaken their own research studies. For many companies, this would be the way to develop new products in conjunction with academic institutions. Through shared research, new products are developed and ultimately marketed and sold.

The Steelcase LearnLab Environment

As part of its research agenda, Steelcase worked with various groups to develop a learning lab. A learning lab is a learning facility where new ways of organizing teaching and learning can take place. Often the furniture is movable. According to the company's research, benefits of the learning lab are as follows:

- Fully supports the learning process: information access, understanding, transfer, and assessment

- Facilitates collaboration and teamwork for large and small groups
- Easily supports multiple teaching and learning styles
- Allows the instructor to teach from any location in the classroom
- Dramatically improves student engagement
- Triangulation of content, which means it is easily visible from anywhere in the classroom
- Removal of information-sharing barriers, which further democratizes how people access and share information by allowing students to contribute their ideas quickly and seamlessly (Steelcase.com)

KI

Like Steelcase, systems furniture manufacturer KI has also conducted its own research on learning environments. The findings are presented in the booklet "Creating the New Learning Environment: Enhancing Student Success through Principles of Space Planning and Design," by William Dittoe, a founding member of Educational Facilities Consultants. According to the author, the primary shift occurring is from the traditional classroom with a teacher at the front lecturing to rows of seated students, to a more interactive and less hierarchical studio model environment. Further, the studio environment is characterized by flexible space that supports interaction. Hands-on learning activities replace passive learning and lecturing. The studio environment also allows for behavioral changes. Students might begin to interact more with both the teacher and other students. According to Dittoe, the teacher becomes a facilitator, and the students feel freer to participate. Learning communities allow for collaborative learning and for people to be interconnected. The spaces that combine to create the optimal learning environment are linked studios, faculty offices within the heart of the studio space, a commons area for gathering, and usable pathways connecting all the spaces.

A second KI report, "Learning Per Square Foot: Shifting the Education Paradigm," cites a study that says the United States has the highest college drop-out rate of any industrialized country. Further, many companies complain that those who do graduate are ill prepared for the workforce. Combined with this, 24-hour-a-day technology access has revolutionized the way homework is being done. Recent research suggests that 71 percent of children aged 12 to 17 have a cell phone and 80 percent of these say they sleep with their cell phones: 38 percent send text messages every day and 93 percent go online. The need to provide integrated technology and use it as a part of the classroom is obvious to engage this group of young adults. The art of teaching has been replaced with the need for engaging. Amy Keifer, KI vice-president for the Education Market, outlines the design goals as follows: Plan and design holistically integrated informal learning spaces, enable 24/7 technology and support, advance environmental objectives (sustainable materials and improved indoor air quality), deliver flexibility, and redefine success. Learning can be measured in several ways—not only how students perform on exams, but also how they function in groups, for example. (Keifer n.d, 15.)

Public Library Design

As with educational environments, libraries are also undergoing radical changes. Instead of simple repositories of information, they are now serving as places to enable learners to analyze, synthesize, and evaluate resources as well as create new knowledge. The library now includes multiple spaces for learning, presentation, team collaboration, and individual learning. The American Association of School Libraries (AASL) has called the new library "an intellectual gymnasium."

While many of the spatial requirements have remained the same, new additional space types respond to new needs.

Types of Spaces

The library typically includes the following space types:

- Collection space
- Public electronic workstation space
- User seating space
- Staff work space
- Meeting space
- Special use space
- Non-assignable space (mechanical, etc.)

Although the library is no longer simply a place to store books, there are some general calculation guidelines for how to account for the books in the library.

Calculating space for books:

- 36-inch wide aisles
- Total number of volumes divided by 10

Calculating space for periodicals:

- Divide current number of periodicals by 1.5 (also assuming 36-inch wide aisles

In addition to printed books and periodicals, access to electronic information is also a key component of the library environment. Several types of electronic workstations might be found:

- Public access computer stations (PACs)
  - Seated: 40 square feet
  - Standing: 20 square feet
- Computer stations: 75 square feet
- Microfiche station: 35 square feet

Typically, a library is designed to include 5 seats for every 1,000 users in the service population. Within this, each type of seating area has specific requirements:

- Table seating: 25 square feet per seat
- Study carrel: 30 square feet
- Lounge area sea: 35 square feet per seat

The staff areas provide workspace for librarians and other staff needed to assist library patrons. Typically, staff work areas require about 150 square feet each.

In addition to the primary library functions, the library as a **learning commons** (a central area where students can go to study and learn) will also include community meeting rooms. When using theater-style seating, multiply the number of seats by 10 square feet per person; when designing for conference room seating, the number of seats is multiplied by 25 square feet per person.

A variety of other special-use spaces might also be included as outlined in Table 6.2.

In addition to all the individual space needs, circulation and entry areas generally account for 20 to 30 percent of the gross square footage, according to the Whole Building Design Guidelines for Libraries on the WBDG website.

Emerging Issues in Library Design

The Whole Building Design Guidelines (found at www.wbdg.org) state that the two major emerging issues in public library design include the integration of technology and sustainable design. In a library several things contribute to a sustainable design. The integration of natural daylight can reduce energy consumption by reducing the time that overhead lights are needed. Lower shelving units can allow daylight to penetrate deeper into the library space as can glass interior partitions. Sustainable finishes and furniture will also help meet sustainable design goals. For example, the use of FSC certified wood for shelving would contribute to this goal. Since many use the library for computer searches and printing, having readily available paper recycling on site would help reduce waste. Finally, using EnergyStar rated computers, printers, and other equipment would make the entire design more sustainable.

Museum Design

The need to store, archive, and exhibit objects of cultural heritage and the past presents specialized design challenges. For example, while sustainability often suggests the need for more natural daylighting, in the context of a museum, natural lighting often needs to be avoided

Items in Special-Use Areas	Square Footage Required per Item
Atlas Stand	35
Bulletin Board	9
Display Case	50
Index Table	140
Map File	35
Microfilm Cabinet	10
Newspaper Rack	25
Paperback Rack	35
Photocopier	50
Staff Locker	4
Vertical Files	10

TABLE 6.2 Library Space Allocations

Source: http://www.wbdg.org/design/libraries.php

in order to protect the museum collection. Artifacts often need to be stored in temperature- and humidity-controlled environments with specialized interior lighting to prevent their deterioration. The heating, ventilation, and air-conditioning units required for this might require more energy than a typical system. Thus, there are often some sustainability challenges in these environments.

Design Guidelines

According to "Design Guidelines for Museums, Archives and Art Storage Facilities," some basic design guidelines for museums environments include:

1. Avoid severe swings in temperature and humidity.
2. Pay careful attention to fenestration and wall systems to avoid condensation.
3. Specify an airtight enclosure to maintain humidity levels.
4. Avoid interior shading devices at windows (this is to avoid condensation from building up on the windows).
5. Skylights should be high performance with integrated condensate gutters and a heat source near the skylight (O'Brien 2011).

Principles of Exhibit Design

Exhibit design is an additional specialization within the design of the museum. According to exhibit specialists Davis and Edquist of e.d|x (an exhibit design firm in Seattle), a good exhibit will tell a story, promote interactivity, allow for discovery, be accessible to all, provide for an individual experience, and be sustainable.

Bitgood and Patterson add to this some key architectural considerations for successful museum design:

1. Visibility (lighting, visual obstacles; visual screens)
2. Proximity
3. Position of the exhibit object (relationship to other objects, eye level)

4. Realism (the more real, the more positive the experience)
5. Sensory competition (takes away from the experience)
6. Other design factors
(1987)

Prison Design

Like many of the other design specialties discussed in this chapter, designing for incarceration facilities is a niche market. In a 2012 interview, Peter Severin focused on prisons in the United Kingdom and Australia. According to Severin (chief executive for SA Corrective Services in Australia), 65 to 77 percent of prisoners re-offend. Severin has proposed updating prison design standards to the 21st century in order to help address the problem of recidivism and to make prisons work better for staff. One way in which this is accomplished is through increased control of those coming into the prison, using X-ray machines and medical detectors. Having full visibility into a cell also assists in quicker searches when needed. The cell design proposed provides several electronic surveillance mechanisms as well as a carefully designed cell that provides for both prisoner and staff needs over time, according to industrial designer Nathan Murphy.

Types of Prison Environments

Prisons are generally divided into two basic categories. **High-security** environments require a high level of supervision and control, while **low-security** environments usually consist of small living units without direct supervision. In both cases, efficiency is important, as the rates and costs of incarceration continue to rise. Technology is very important as a way to monitor prisoners. For the best impact, a system that is not immediately visible is recommended. The monitoring is more effective if the prisoner does not see it, according to Severin.

Civic Design

Many firms engage in design for the public good. This type of design ranges from design for those who cannot afford it to the design of public buildings. Several organizations have been created to support related social concerns, including Architecture for Humanity. Vast ranges of projects have been completed in service of the overall good. One example of this is "The 1%" pro bono program offered through Public Architecture. The 1% program asks architects and designers to donate 1 percent of their time to designing for the public good. Frequently, this means designing for people and causes that could not otherwise afford these services. Endorsed by the American Institute of Architects (AIA), this program seeks to strengthen nonprofits through good design (theonepercent.org).

Transportation Hubs

This category includes airports, bus stations, train stations, and intermodal hubs (those containing multiple forms of transportation in one place). Although each type is different, all face similar issues. Security, clear wayfinding and signage, comfort, convenience, and positive distractions all contribute to the successful design of a transportation facility.

Railway Station Design

Although passenger train travel is not a standard mode of transportation for many people in the United States, it is the norm in many European and Asian countries. As such, several high-style train stations have been designed throughout history and into the present day. Examples include Zaha Hadid's series of rail stations in Innsbruck, Austria, the Central Railway Station in Luxembourg, and several new stations in China. Historically, Great Britain and countries across Europe highlighted train travel through station design, including such masterpieces as the St. Pancras Station in London, the Gare de Lyon in Paris, Santa Maria Novella in Florence, Santa Lucia in Venice, and many others.

Bus Stops and Stations

Many designers have created novel designs for individual bus stops and stations. Some notable examples include the new Hoofdorp bus station in the Netherlands and Dennis Oppenheim's new bus station in Ventura California. (For additional images, see weburbanist.com)

Airport Design

Airports are unique design environments in that they tend to be open 24 hours a day (in large international airports), have extreme security requirements, and must accommodate an ever-increasing number of travelers. As with most other sectors, technological improvements in aircraft require better technology in airports. Some examples of these new technologies include more automation in airplane flying, onboard wireless technology, and improved deicing strategies.

Despite the current rise in fuel prices and struggling United States and European economies, the rate of international air travel is increasing (with most of this increase in international travel taking place in Asia). In March 2012, the U.S. Federal Aviation Administration (FAA) predicted that passenger travel will double by 2032. Airlines carried 739.3 million passengers in 2013, and are expected to increase to 1.2 billion by 2032. (http://www.faa.gov/about/office_org/headquarters_offices/apl/aviation_forecasts/aerospace_forecasts/2014-2034/media/2014_FAA_Aerospace_Forecast.pdf. Accessed March 26, 2014)

In the United States, the FAA has very detailed guidelines regulating airport design, including everything from signage to employee clothing. The FAA website includes a section on the environment that addresses the topics of air quality, noise, compatible land use, sustainability, and wildlife hazard mitigation. Sustainable actions are designed to reduce environmental impact, maintain sustainable economic growth, and social progress for the local community.

Student Approaches to Cultural, Civic, and Institutional Design

There are a wide variety of projects used to engage students in civic, cultural, and institutional design. The following examples include student designs for all three: museum designs (cultural), a home for runaways (institutional), a learning commons (educational), and a pro bono project.

Student Museum Design— A. D. German, Richland Center, WI

The program for the museum project for the A. D. German Warehouse included displays for architectural works by Taliesin School of Architecture students and large-format photographs of legendary architect Frank Lloyd Wright's work.

Stafford Bensen (eco-technic)

The inspiration for this project came from the color pencil drawings by Wright. Both the color palette and design presentation derived from this drawing style. Diagramming from Froeble blocks led to the geometric approach to the space, which used intersecting grids. Frank Lloyd Wright's mother introduced Froebel blocks to him as a child, and he attributed much of his architectural success to his early experimentation with the blocks. The materials throughout the space include reclaimed lumber, painting the existing concrete, and low-VOC paints.

Molly Berman (eco-cultural, eco-technic)

I like the idea of arranging the inner structures of my buildings in a sequence of rooms that guide us, take us places, but also let us go and seduce us. Architecture is the art of space it is the art of time as well—between order and freedom, between flowing a path and discovering a path of our own, wandering, strolling, being seduced (Peter Zumthor, *Thinking Architecture*).

Figure 6.1 Stafford Benson, A. D. German Warehouse: Concept page

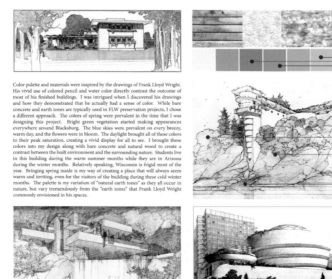

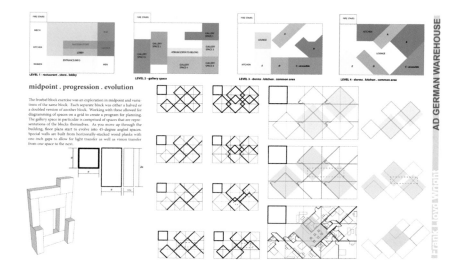

Figure 6.2 Stafford
Benson, A. D.
German Warehouse:
Froebel block
explorations

midpoint . progression . evolution

The froebel block exercise was an exploration in midpoint and variations of the same block. Each separate block was either a halved or
a doubled version of another block. Working with these allowed for
diagramming of spaces on a grid to create a program for planning.
The gallery space in particular is comprised of spaces that are repre-
sentations of the blocks themselves. As you move up through the
building, floor plans start to evolve into 45-degree angled spaces.
Special walls are built from horizontally-stacked wood planks with
one-inch gaps to allow for light transfer as well as vision transfer
from one space to the next.

Figure 6.3 Stafford
Benson, A. D.
German Warehouse:
Materials

Figure 6.4 Stafford
Benson, A. D.
German Warehouse:
Rendering

Figure 6.5 Stafford
Benson, A. D.
German Warehouse:
Rendering

Figure 6.6 Stafford
Benson, A. D.
German Warehouse:
Rendering

Figure 6.7 Stafford
Benson, A. D.
German Warehouse:
Gallery Plan

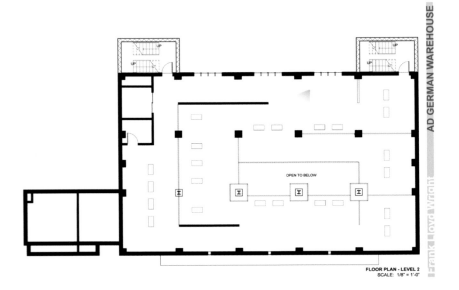

Inspired by a quote by architect Peter Zumthor, this project gradually turns from open and understandable at the first floor to more elusive at the upper levels (open-ended to allow for wandering). Sustainability is an integral part of the design with a central sky-lit atrium with large trees. Throughout the design, sustainable finishes are used. In addition to the existing concrete, reclaimed lumber has been used as an accent finish. Low-flow faucets are combined with dual flush toilets to improve water efficiency in the building. All lighting is either fluorescent or LED to enhance the energy efficiency.

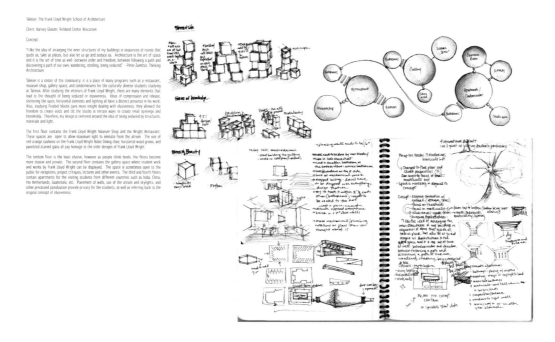

Figure 6.8 Molly Berman, A. D. German Warehouse: Concept page

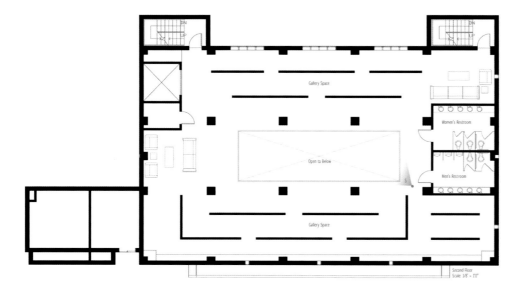

Figure 6.9 Molly Berman, A. D. German Warehouse: Gallery floor plan

Figure 6.10 Molly Berman, A. D. German Warehouse: Rendering

Liz Kulesza (eco-technic)

Taking a more traditional sustainable materials approach to the project, this design solution relies on the reuse of existing brick walls and concrete floors supplemented with reclaimed lumber and sustainable furnishings. The student design includes a LEED checklist of proposed credits.

Harmony House Home for Runaways

The Harmony House project included multiple space types in a shelter facility for runaway teens. The first floor includes office space, meeting rooms, and an organic café. The second floor has bedrooms and additional living facilities.

Figure 6.11 Liz Kulesza, A. D. German Warehouse: Gallery floor plan

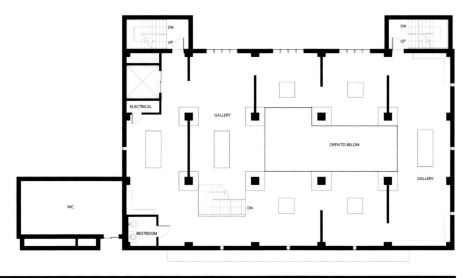

Figure 6.12 Liz Kulesza, A. D. German Warehouse: Rendering of museum

GALLERY

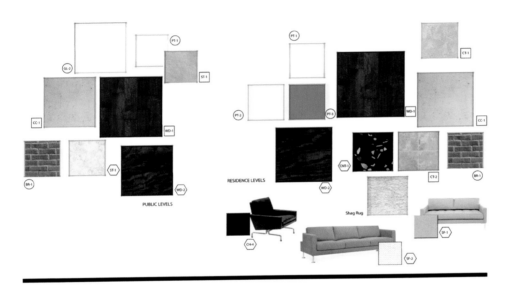

Figure 6.13 Liz Kulesza, A. D. German Warehouse: Materials and furniture

PUBLIC LEVELS

RESIDENCE LEVELS

Shag Rug

MATERIALS

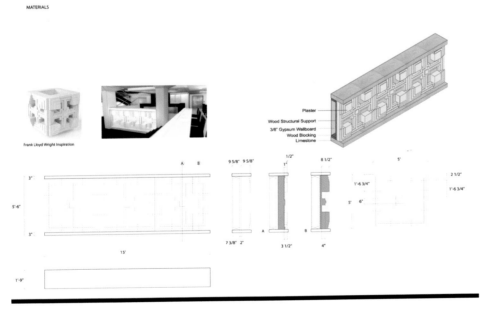

Figure 6.14 Liz Kulesza, A. D. German Warehouse: Millwork detail

Frank Lloyd Wright Inspiration

Plaster
Wood Structural Support
3/8" Gypsum Wallboard
Wood Blocking
Limestone

CUSTOM MILLWORK

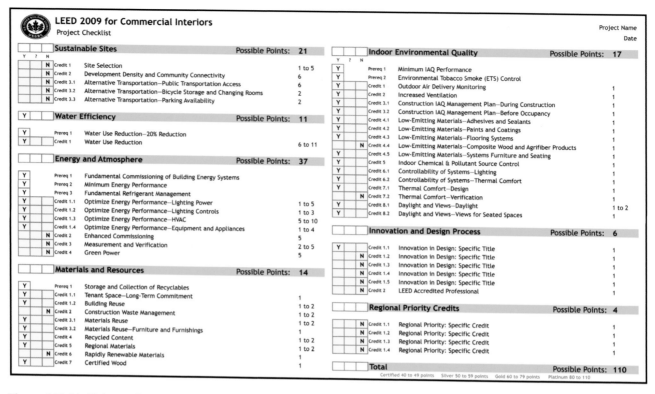

LEED 2009 for Commercial Interiors
Project Checklist

Project Name
Date

	Y	?	N			Sustainable Sites	Possible Points:	21
			N	Credit 1	Site Selection		1 to 5
			N	Credit 2	Development Density and Community Connectivity		6
			N	Credit 3.1	Alternative Transportation—Public Transportation Access		6
			N	Credit 3.2	Alternative Transportation—Bicycle Storage and Changing Rooms		2
			N	Credit 3.3	Alternative Transportation—Parking Availability		2

	Y				Water Efficiency	Possible Points:	11
	Y			Prereq 1	Water Use Reduction—20% Reduction	
	Y			Credit 1	Water Use Reduction	6 to 11

					Energy and Atmosphere	Possible Points:	37
	Y			Prereq 1	Fundamental Commissioning of Building Energy Systems	
	Y			Prereq 2	Minimum Energy Performance	
	Y			Prereq 3	Fundamental Refrigerant Management	
	Y			Credit 1.1	Optimize Energy Performance—Lighting Power	1 to 5
	Y			Credit 1.2	Optimize Energy Performance—Lighting Controls	1 to 3
	Y			Credit 1.3	Optimize Energy Performance—HVAC	5 to 10
	Y			Credit 1.4	Optimize Energy Performance—Equipment and Appliances	1 to 4
			N	Credit 2	Enhanced Commissioning	5
			N	Credit 3	Measurement and Verification	2 to 5
			N	Credit 4	Green Power	5

					Materials and Resources	Possible Points:	14
	Y			Prereq 1	Storage and Collection of Recyclables	
	Y			Credit 1.1	Tenant Space—Long-Term Commitment	1
	Y			Credit 1.2	Building Reuse	1 to 2
			N	Credit 2	Construction Waste Management	1 to 2
	Y			Credit 3.1	Materials Reuse	1 to 2
	Y			Credit 3.2	Materials Reuse—Furniture and Furnishings	1
	Y			Credit 4	Recycled Content	1 to 2
	Y			Credit 5	Regional Materials	1 to 2
			N	Credit 6	Rapidly Renewable Materials	1
	Y			Credit 7	Certified Wood	1

	Y	?	N			Indoor Environmental Quality	Possible Points:	17
	Y			Prereq 1	Minimum IAQ Performance	
	Y			Prereq 2	Environmental Tobacco Smoke (ETS) Control	
	Y			Credit 1	Outdoor Air Delivery Monitoring	1
	Y			Credit 2	Increased Ventilation	1
	Y			Credit 3.1	Construction IAQ Management Plan—During Construction	1
	Y			Credit 3.2	Construction IAQ Management Plan—Before Occupancy	1
	Y			Credit 4.1	Low-Emitting Materials—Adhesives and Sealants	1
	Y			Credit 4.2	Low-Emitting Materials—Paints and Coatings	1
	Y			Credit 4.3	Low-Emitting Materials—Flooring Systems	1
			N	Credit 4.4	Low-Emitting Materials—Composite Wood and Agrifiber Products	1
	Y			Credit 4.5	Low-Emitting Materials—Systems Furniture and Seating	1
	Y			Credit 5	Indoor Chemical & Pollutant Source Control	1
	Y			Credit 6.1	Controllability of Systems—Lighting	1
	Y			Credit 6.2	Controllability of Systems—Thermal Comfort	1
	Y			Credit 7.1	Thermal Comfort—Design	1
			N	Credit 7.2	Thermal Comfort—Verification	1
	Y			Credit 8.1	Daylight and Views—Daylight	1 to 2
	Y			Credit 8.2	Daylight and Views—Views for Seated Spaces	1

					Innovation and Design Process	Possible Points:	6
	Y			Credit 1.1	Innovation in Design: Specific Title	1
			N	Credit 1.2	Innovation in Design: Specific Title	1
			N	Credit 1.3	Innovation in Design: Specific Title	1
			N	Credit 1.4	Innovation in Design: Specific Title	1
			N	Credit 1.5	Innovation in Design: Specific Title	1
			N	Credit 2	LEED Accredited Professional	1

					Regional Priority Credits	Possible Points:	4
			N	Credit 1.1	Regional Priority: Specific Credit	1
			N	Credit 1.2	Regional Priority: Specific Credit	1
			N	Credit 1.3	Regional Priority: Specific Credit	1
			N	Credit 1.4	Regional Priority: Specific Credit	1

					Total	Possible Points:	110

Certified 40 to 49 points   Silver 50 to 59 points   Gold 60 to 79 points   Platinum 80 to 110

Figure 6.15 Liz Kulesza, A. D. German Warehouse: LEED CI checklist

Ross Johnson (eco-social, eco-medical)

The central concept for this design solution is to have each person who stays at the Harmony House make a unique contribution that will be left behind for others. Throughout the interior, this concept is reinforced through the use of customized interior walls made from FSC-certified wood painted with low-VOC paint. Energy-efficient lighting is used throughout the space to enhance the sustainability of the project solution.

Figure 6.16 Ross Johnson, Harmony House: Concept page

A PERSON IS AN AMALGAMATION OF EXPERIENCES, WHETHER BENEFICIAL OR DETRIMENTAL, EACH DAY, EACH CONVERSATION ADDS A FACET OF WHO SOMEONE IS, AND IN TURN HOW SHE REACTS TO HER ENVIRONMENT. ENTERING THE HARMONY HOUSE, NO TWO LIVES ARE SIMILAR, AND THROUGH THIS RICHNESS EACH LIFE MUST BE TOLD TO THOSE WHO WILL FOLLOW. THE MEDIUM IN WHICH THIS IS ACCOMPLISHED SHOULD ALSO VARY, BUT REGARDLESS IT BECOMES AN ARTIFACT, ONE OF A UNIQUE TIME AND DISPOSITION. SUCH OBJECTS ARE THE SOUL POURING ITSELF INTO A TANGIBLE FORM, AND SUCH PRODUCTIVITY CREATES CATHARSIS.

ONCE GRADUATING FROM THE HOUSE, THE USER WILL LEAVE BEHIND THE OBJECT TO CREATE A LIBRARY OF THOUGHT AND EXPERIENCES, INTO WHICH OTHERS CAN ESCAPE REALITY AND LEARN.

CARRYING THIS FORM OF THERAPY INTO THE TANGIBLE, IF EVERY PERSON CAN BE UNIQUE, WHY NOT THE FURNITURE?

HARMONY HOUSE

JOURNAL WRITTEN BY RESIDENT

SPACE BEFORE USE

BOOKSHELF AFTER RESIDENTS

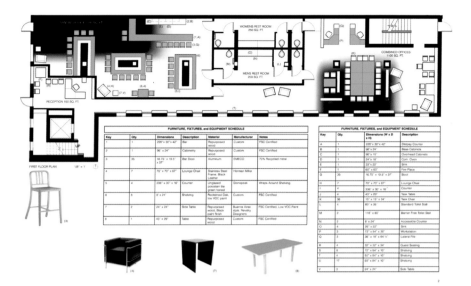

Figure 6.17 Ross Johnson, Harmony House: Deli

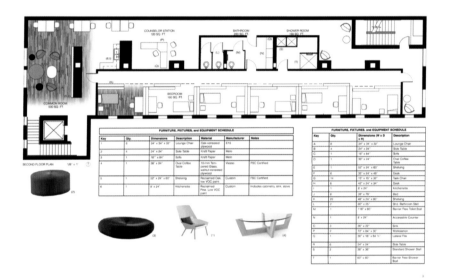

Figure 6.18 Ross Johnson, Harmony House: Materials

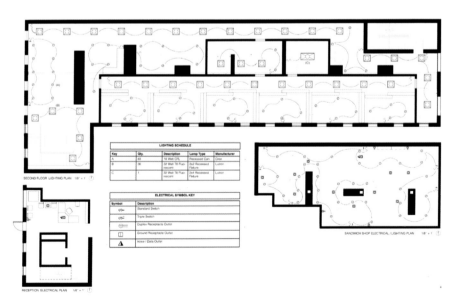

Figure 6.19 Ross Johnson, Harmony House: Lighting

Figure 6.20 Ross Johnson, Harmony House: Furniture

ROOM FINISHES SCHEDULE									
Room Name	Floor	Base	Walls				Ceiling		NOTES
			NORTH	EAST	SOUTH	WEST	MATERIAL	HT.	
Reception	Recycled Glazed Tile	Maple(FSC)	PT1	PT1	PT1	PT1	GWB	8'	1,2,3
Sandwich Shop	Recycled Glazed Tile	Maple (FSC)	PT1	PT1	PT1	PT1	GWB	8'	4,5,6
Triple Stall Women	Recycled Glazed Tile	Recycled Glazed Tile	TILE	TILE	TILE	TILE	GWB 2	8'	6,7,8
Triple Stall Men	Recycled Glazed Floor Tile	Recycled Glazed Tile	TILE	TILE	TILE	TILE	GWB 2	8'	6
Open Plan Offices	Recycled Glazed Tile	Wood	PT	PT	PT	PT	GWB	8'	6
Corridor 1	Recycled Glazed Tile	Maple (FSC)	PT1	PT1	PT1	PT1	GWB	9'	3,6
Corridor 2	Reclaimed Wood	Maple (FSC)	PT1	PT1	PT1	PT1	GWB	8'	2,9
Residence Room	Reclaimed Wood	Maple (FSC)	PT2	PT2	PT2	PT2	GBW	8'	2,9
Triple Stall Bathroom	Recycled Glazed Tile	Recycled Glazed Tile	TILE	TILE	TILE	TILE	GBW2	8'	6,7,8
Common Area	Reclaimed Wood	Maple (FSC)	PT1	PT1	PT1	PT1	GWB	8'	2,9

NOTES
1. CEILING—RECYCLED CONTENT FOR LEED
2. WALLS—NO VOC PAINTS FOR LEED
3. FSC CERTIFIED WOOD USED ON BASE FOR LEED
4. COUNTER AND CABINETS: COUNTERTOP STONEPEAK UNGLAZED PORCELAIN TILE GREEN HONED COLOR; CABINETS FSC CERTIFIED MAPLE WITH CLEAR WATER BASED FINISH, NO VOCS FOR LEED
5. GWB CEILING MADE WITH RECYCLED PAPER BACKING AND RECYCLES GYPSUM
6. ALL TILE COLOR BLACK PEARL GLAZED RECYCLED TILE BY DALTILE FOR LEED
7. COUNTERTOP AT 30" AFF WITH STONEPEAK UNGLAZED PORCELAIN TILE GREEN HONED FOR LEED
8. TOILET PARTITIONS, CREAM COLORED WITH SILVER HARDWARE BY TOILET PARTITION CO. LTD.
9. ELMWOOD RECLAIMED TIMBER CHERRY – PREMIUM SELECT

ABBREVIATIONS
PT1 PAINT 1: BENJAMIN MOORE NO VOC COLOR "WHITE" PREMIUM LATEX, SATIN FINISH
PT1 PAINT 2: BENJAMIN MOORE NO VOC COLOR "CREAM" PREMIUM LATEX, SATIN FINISH
GWB GYPSUM WALL BOARD
GWB2 WATER RESISTANT GYPSUM WALLBOARD

RECYCLED GLAZED TILE RECLAIMED OAK WHITE SATIN PAINT CREAM SATIN PAINT

Figure 6.21 Ross Johnson, Harmony House: Deli furniture

HARMONY DELI

THE SANDWICH SHOP COMBINES THE FLUX OF PUBLIC USERS INTERACTING WITH THE HARMONY HOUSE. WHILE THE PASSERBY MAY BUY FOOD AND BEVERAGES, SHE CAN ALSO PROVIDE CRUCIAL INTERACTION WITH RESIDENTS OF THE FACILITY. THE COMMON PUBLIC CUSTOMER REPRESENTS SOCIETY, TO WHERE THE RESIDENTS MUST EVENTUALLY RETURN.

WHILE EATING OR SPENDING TIME IN THE CAFE, USERS MAY READ JOURNALS AND SHORT STORIES WRITTEN BY THE RESIDENTS AS WELL WRITE LITERATURE OF THEIR OWN, CREATING AN ENVIRONMENT WHERE THOUGHT AND IMAGINATION ARE PRIORITIZED. IF EVERY CUSTOMER WERE TO LEAVE AN IDEA OR STORY, IMAGINE HOW MUCH THE RESIDENTS COULD GAIN IN TERMS OF PERSPECTIVE.

SECTION LEFT ELEV. FRONT ELEVATION 1/8" = 1' RIGHT ELEV

Figure 6.22 Ross Johnson, Harmony House: Common area

WHILE THE REST OF THE FACILITY IS DESIGNED FOR INTERACTION AND GROWTH, ALL RESIDENTS DO VARY IN TERMS OF PACE AND HOW MUCH PRIVACY THEY REQUIRE. THE BEDROOM IS THE SPACE WHERE EACH RESIDENT CAN FIND COMFORT AND SOLACE.

THE DOOR TO EACH BEDROOM IS DESIGNED TO APPEAR AS A BOOKSHELF ON A TRACK, SO THAT IT CAN BE PULLED CLOSED FOR WHEN THE RESIDENT WISHES TO BE ALONE, AND OPENED FOR LESS PRIVACY. ANOTHER ASPECT OF THE SLIDING DOOR IS THE SHELVES, THE RESIDENT MAY PLACE VALUABLES ON THE SHELVES WHEN IT IS PULLED OPEN, AND HIDE THEM WHEN HE WISHES LESS PRIVACY.

EACH RESIDENT IS TO FILL THE SPACES WITH PARTS OF HER LIFE, WHETHER THOUGH PEN AND PAPER OR OBJECTS VALUABLE TO HER.

PUBLIC STATS SEMI PRIVATE STATS PRIVACY STATS

Chelsea Buel (eco-technic, eco-medical)

The goal of this design solution was to provide a safe and stable shelter for runaway teens. Bands of color wrap from ceiling to floor and onto built-in surfaces and help to tie one space to the next. All sustainable furnishings and finishes are used throughout the design to create a healthy interior environment that will promote the health and well-being of the residents.

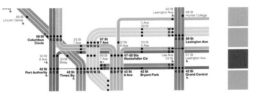

Harmony House | Seattle Washington

The goal of the Harmony House is to provide a secure and stable shelter for young runaway teens that are in crisis and are in need of help. The Harmony House exists to help the kids learn how to change and find their way through their own crisis. The kids are coming in lost, looking for something. This design is about helping kids find their way. The design is expressed through the idea of meandering paths. The paths are used as a way to guide and direct the kids throughout the Harmony House and life.

The floor plan expresses this concept with the paths that one person takes through the space. The paths are expressed by the halls on the first and second floor, and other implied paths. The implied paths are expressed by a change in the flooring material. Instead of being straight and direct, the paths allow a person to meander from one place to another. Throughout the space, bright colors and wrapped surfaces are used as a guide. The idea of wrapping is used with a touch of color indicating direction, leading from one space to the next.

These paths and wrapping can be found in the furniture, as well as shapes, finishes, and colors throughout the space. Bright colors are used as guidance to contrast with the darkness that the kids may be carrying within them; color and wrapping provide a positive and stable environment. Colors also show division throughout the space; each color represents a different place or part of the Harmony House. This provides a steady transition into the Harmony House, eliminating the feeling of confusion or of being lost within the space. This design helps the kids find their way through the physical space just as they are finding their way through their own personal life.

Figure 6.23 Chelsea Buel, Harmony House: Second floor views

Figure 6.24 Chelsea Buel, Harmony House: Sandwich shop millwork and FFE schedule

First Floor
Scale: 1/8" = 1'-0"

First Floor | FFE Schedule

Furniture, Fixtures & Equipment Schedule

Key	Quantity	Dimensions	Description
A	1	33" x 22"	Sink
B	1	24" x 18"	Commercial Toasking oven
C	1	14" x 18"	Cash Register
D	3	36" x 30"	Standard Toilet Stall
E	1	60" x 96"	Accessible Toilet Stall
F	1	120" x 24"	Accessible Barrier-Free Counter
G	3	72" x 82" x 30"	U-Shape Workstation
H	3	36" x 84" x 64 1/4"	Lateral File
I	4	32" x 32" x 34"	Guest seating
J	3	15" x 15" x 34"	Task Chair
K	2	42" x 29"	Conference Table
L	14	42" x 42" x 29"	Table
M	1	120" x 24"	Kitchenette
N	38	15" x 15" x 34"	Pull-Up chairs

Furniture, Fixture & Equipment Specification

Key	Quantity	Dimensions	Description	Manufacturer	Materials/ Finishes
1	3	16# x 19.25" x 36"	Stool	Blu Dot	White Oak, Chromed Steel
2	16	21.5" x 16.5" x 39"	Side Chair	Euro Style	Knoll Textiles Fabric: Topography, "Alpine", Chomed Steel
3	2	40" x 31" x 30"	Small Dining Table	Custom	Wood-Oak
4	4	40" x 64" x 30"	Large Dining Table	Custom	Wood-Oak
5	1	321" x 24"	Counter/ Cabinets	Custom	Wood-Oak and Maple, Icestone Countertop
6	1	336" x 30" x 42"	Serve-Over Counter	Custom	Wood-Oak and Maple, Icestone Countertop

Figure 6.25 Chelsea Buel, Harmony House: Finishes schedule

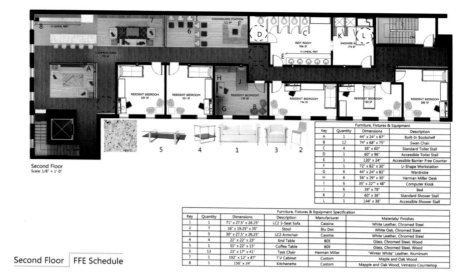

Second Floor
Scale: 1/8" = 1'-0"

Second Floor | FFE Schedule

Key	Quantity	Dimensions	Description
A	1	44" x 24" x 87"	Built-In Bookshelf
B	12	74" x 68" x 75"	Swan Chair
C	4	36" x 60"	Standard Toilet Stall
D	1	60" x 96"	Accessible Toilet Stall
E	1	120" x 24"	Accessible Barrier-Free Counter
F	1	72" x 82" x 30"	U-Shape Workstation
G	6	44" x 24" x 83"	Wardrobe
H	6	56" x 29" x 30"	Herman Miller Desk
I	6	35" x 22" x 48"	Computer Kiosk
J	6	39" x 78"	Bed
K	2	60" x 36"	Standard Shower Stall
L	1	144" x 36"	Accessible Shower Stall

Furniture, Fixtures & Equipment Specification

Key	Quantity	Dimensions	Description	Manufacturer	Materials/ Finishes
1	1	71" x 27.5" x 26.25"	LC2 3-Seat Sofa	Cassina	White Leather, Chromed Steel
2	7	16" x 19.25" x 35"	Stool	Blu Dot	White Oak, Chromed Steel
3	5	30" x 27.5" x 26.25"	LC2 Armchair	Cassina	White Leather, Chromed Steel
4	4	22" x 22" x 23"	End Table	BDI	Glass, Chromed Steel, Wood
5	1	55" x 22" x 15"	Coffee Table	BDI	Glass, Chromed Steel, Wood
6	13	23" x 17" x 41"	Task Chair	Herman Miller	"Winter White" Leather, Aluminum
7	1	192" x 12" x 87"	T.V Cabinet	Custom	Maple and Oak Wood
8	1	156" x 24"	Kitchenette	Custom	Mapple and Oak Wood, Vetrazzo Countertop

Figure 6.26 Chelsea Buel, Harmony House: Lighting and electrical plan

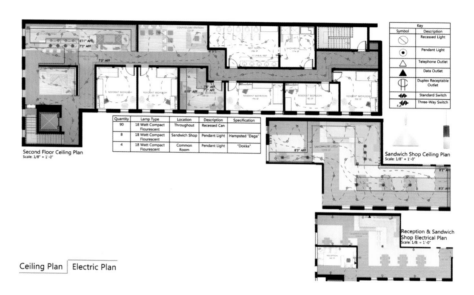

Second Floor Ceiling Plan
Scale: 1/8" = 1'-0"

Sandwich Shop Ceiling Plan
Scale: 1/8" = 1'-0"

Reception & Sandwich Shop Electrical Plan
Scale: 1/8" = 1'-0"

Quantity	Lamp Type	Location	Description	Specification
90	18 Watt Compact Flourescent	Throughout	Recessed Can	
8	18 Watt Compact Flourescent	Sandwich Shop	Pendant Light	Hampsted "Daga"
4	18 Watt Compact Flourescent	Common Room	Pendant Light	"Dokka"

Ceiling Plan | Electric Plan

Figure 6.27 Chelsea Buel, Harmony House: Material finish schedule

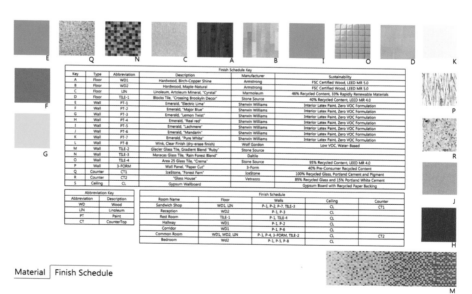

Material | Finish Schedule

Finish Schedule Key

Key	Type	Abbreviation	Description	Manufacturer	Sustainability
A	Floor	WD1	Hardwood, Birch-Copper Shine	Armstrong	FSC Certified Wood, LEED MR 5.0
B	Floor	WD2	Hardwood, Maple-Natural	Armstrong	FSC Certified Wood, LEED MR 5.0
C	Floor	LIN	Linoleum, Artoleum Mineral, "Crystal"	Marmoleum	46% Recycled Content, 33% Rapidly Renewable Materials
D	Floor	TILE-1	Blocks Tile, "Crossing Brooklyn Decor"	Stone Source	40% Recycled Content, LEED MR 4.0
E	Wall	PT-1	Emerald, "Electric Lime"	Sherwin Williams	Interior Latex Paint, Zero VOC Formulation
F	Wall	PT-2	Emerald, "Major Blue"	Sherwin Williams	Interior Latex Paint, Zero VOC Formulation
G	Wall	PT-3	Emerald, "Lemon Twist"	Sherwin Williams	Interior Latex Paint, Zero VOC Formulation
H	Wall	PT-4	Emerald, "Real red"	Sherwin Williams	Interior Latex Paint, Zero VOC Formulation
I	Wall	PT-5	Emerald, "Lachmere"	Sherwin Williams	Interior Latex Paint, Zero VOC Formulation
J	Wall	PT-6	Emerald, "Mandarin"	Sherwin Williams	Interior Latex Paint, Zero VOC Formulation
K	Wall	PT-7	Emerald, "Pure White"	Sherwin Williams	Interior Latex Paint, Zero VOC Formulation
L	Wall	PT-8	Wink, Clear Finish (dry-erase finish)	Wolf Gordon	Low VOC, Water-Based
M	Wall	TILE-2	Glacier Glass Tile, Gradient Blend "Ruby"	Stone Source	
N	Wall	TILE-3	Maracas Glass Tile, "Rain Forest Blend"	Daltile	
O	Wall	TILE-4	Area 25 Glass Tile, "Crema"	Stone Source	95% Recycled Content, LEED MR 4.0
P	Wall	3-FORM	Wall Panel, "Paper Cut"	3-Form	40% Pre-Consumer Recycled Content
Q	Counter	CT1	IceStone, "Forest Fern"	IceStone	100% Recycled Glass, Portland Cement and Pigment
R	Counter	CT2	"Glass House"	Vetrazzo	85% Recycled Glass and 15% Portland White Cement
S	Ceiling	CL	Gypsum Wallboard		Gypsum Board with Recycled Paper Backing

Abbreviation Key

Abbreviation	Description
WD	Wood
LIN	Linoleum
PT	Paint
CT	CounterTop

Finish Schedule

Room Name	Floor	Walls	Ceiling	Counter
Sandwich Shop	WD1, LIN	P-1, P-2, P-7, TILE-3	CL	CT1
Reception	WD2	P-1, P-3	CL	
Rest Room	TILE-1	P-1, TILE-4	CL	
Hallway	WD1	P-1, P-2	CL	
Corridor	WD1	P-1, P-6	CL	
Common Room	WD1, WD2, LIN	P-1, P-4, 3-FORM, TILE-2	CL	CT2
Bedroom	Wd2	P-1, P-5, P-8	CL	

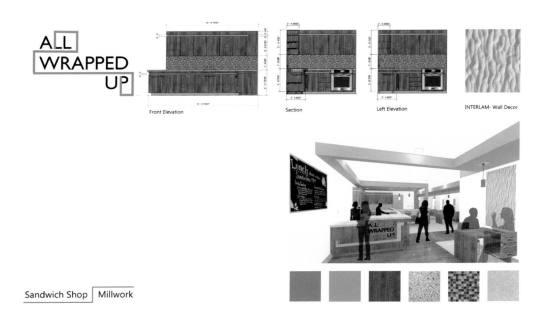

Figure 6.28 Chelsea Buel, Harmony House: Sandwich shop millwork

Front Elevation | Section | Left Elevation | INTERLAM- Wall Decor

Sandwich Shop | Millwork

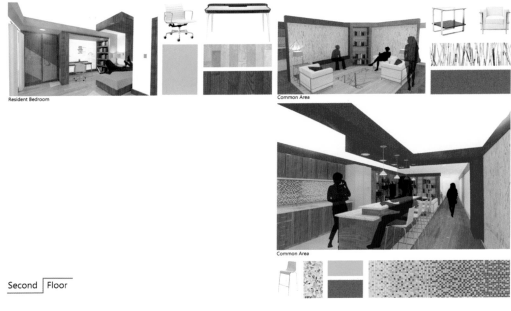

Figure 6.29 Chelsea Buel, Harmony House: Second floor

Resident Bedroom

Common Area

Common Area

Second | Floor

Lindsey Slough (eco-aesthetic, eco-social)

The power of ocean currents inspired this unique project solution. The Harmony House seeks to create sustainable lifestyles for the residents, spreading this out into the community through interaction. By working in the organic sandwich shop, residents learn responsibility and also where their food comes from. Cradle-to-cradle materials are used throughout to encourage environmental consciousness and sustainable behaviors. Energy monitors located throughout the facility encourage residents and staff to turn off lights and conserve.

Figure 6.30 Lindsey Slough, Harmony House: Concept statement page

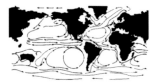

Figure 6.31 Lindsey Slough, Harmony House: First floor plan

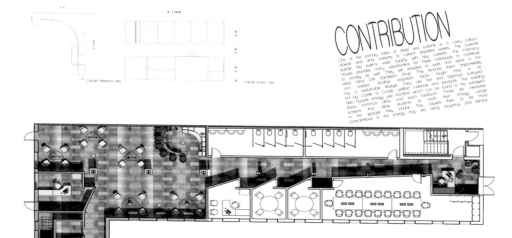

Figure 6.32 Lindsey Slough, Harmony House: Second floor plan

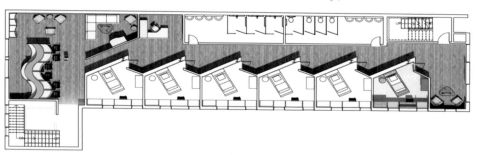

Figure 6.33 Lindsey Slough, Harmony House: Bedroom rendering

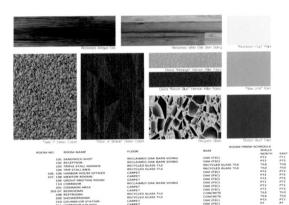

REDISTRIBUTE

An important characteristic of deep sea currents that is also found in the Harmony House is redistribution of nutrients and other important factors. The currents carry carbon dioxide into nutrient depleted water to restore and revitalize this area. From here the currents continue to carry them throughout the world. This same concept was applied to the materials and furniture placed in the space. The materials are renewable, recyclable and ultimately, Cradle to Cradle certified. The Harmony House works to mold and shape young people so that they can spread into the world creating a cycle of change. These materials also follow a cycle that can be reused and re-purposed throughout an entire life cycle.

Figure 6.34 Lindsey Slough, Harmony House: Materials

ROOM FINISH SCHEDULE

(Room finish schedule table — room numbers 101–211 with floor, base, walls (north/east/south/west), ceiling material, height, and notes)

FURNISHINGS

FURNITURE, FIXTURES, AND EQUIPMENT SCHEDULE

(Furnishings schedule table listing rooms 101–211 with quantity, dimensions, description, materials, and manufacturer)

Figure 6.35 Lindsey Slough, Harmony House: Furnishings

Figure 6.36 Lindsey
Slough, Harmony
House, West Wind
Café: Rendering

Learning Commons IDEC Competition Project

The Learning Commons competition project charges students with producing a 21st-century learning space within a university environment. This project was completed as a part of the Interior Design Educators Council (IDEC) Annual Student Design Competition. IDEC is a member organization of interior design educators that was formed in 1963.

Kelley O'Leary, Yuyu Schatz, and Alex Watt—"Chameleon" (biomimicry)

The Chameleon solution team used the rainforest for its conceptual approach to developing multiple levels within the space: understory, canopy, forest floor, and emergent. Sustainability was a driving force behind the solution, which uses a variety of environmentally friendly materials.

Ross Johnson, Kylie Gravlee, and Kathleen Barry—"Future of Design for Higher Education" (eco-social, eco-technic)

The approach of this team relied on a sensitivity to various learning styles, efficiency of space use, and growth. A custom-designed partition and easily movable furnishings allow for maximum flexibility in the space to adapt to varying needs and conditions. A customized food vendor station offers healthy snacks. A combination of Luccon (textured concrete) and polished concrete use fly ash and provide a sustainable finish palette.

Lindsey Slough, Rachel Russell, and Theresa Bartlett—"Stretch, Pull, Surround" (biomimicry)

Inspired by the amoeba, this organically arranged project solution responds to multiple learning styles, such as those listed previously by Howard Gardner. Natural light is used to bring in the outside and provide increased learning. Recent studies have shown the connection between the use of daylight and improved learning and test scores. (Cooper 1999). The classroom spaces are flexible and reconfigurable. Through the use of movable panels and furniture, the rooms can be reorganized as needed for the activity taking place.

CHAMELEON: "spaces that adapt for a purpose"

Our space aims to be highly customizable. Just as chameleons change color due to social conditions or temperature, our space will change based on the user. Through new technology, users will be able to program the space for their needs and store the settings for later use. This will include movable furniture, customizable lighting, and a variety of new technology. The concept of the chameleon will also influence our color palette, as their native habitat is the rain forest and a chameleon's "main" color is green. The 4 layers of the rainforest (from top to bottom) are the emergent layer, the canopy layer, the understory layer, and the forest floor. Our spaces have been divided based on the various layers, from which each space inherits a color palette and overall design idea.

Research Summary

The modern day student is a dynamic, transformative individual who is constantly moving, interacting with others and being thrown into new environments. Due to the vibrant pace students have, they must be engaged in educational environments that support this flexibility. When looking at learning spaces, the idea of a classroom has drastically transformed from that of the past. What used to be linear rows of desks neatly assembled in a partitioned and closed off space has now changed into a fluid and mobile space that generates collaboration. These new spaces are a product of how teachers facilitate a classroom and the change in mindset of the modern day student. Due to the rise in technology information systems, global communications and access to information has flourished. Teachers are no longer the only source of knowledge and they are able to integrate their own teachings with information technology. Students are more connected to each other and easily adaptable - learning spaces must now reflect these needs in them.

By moving away from the closed area of a traditional classroom, the college campus is able to encourage intellectual growth in different places. It's no longer merely a classroom that's a place of learning, but it can happen anywhere on campus. Each student is aware of what kind of environment is conducive to his or her own education, and learning spaces must be fluid enough to adapt and rearrange. Education is also no longer an individual activity, but a collaborative one as well. Learning spaces must be planned to accommodate a range of learning settings. Teachers and students need to be able to easily move and rearrange a space, as learning needs change throughout the day. Environments are planned to support various types of learners and these different styles of learning help students stay focused.

Successful learning environments not only must be able to easily adapt as needed but incorporate the technology of the future as well. Technology has been such a huge factor in paving student lifestyle and how people learn – it is now a tangible object that can be translated into a space. By allowing technology to guide access to information, education can be made so much more available. If learning spaces can be fluid enough to adapt to each individual student, technology can also be shaped based on a students needs. Information amongst students can be easily shared and understood through the sharing of ideas.

Through the incorporation of mobility physically throughout the space and through technology, higher education has transformed to become a place the supports the generation of new ideas and collaboration.

Design Goals

1. Higher education spaces of the future need to be flexible, mobile, and multipurpose.
2. The space needs to be able to integrate new technology so that it can be used for maximum benefit.
3. In order for students to get the most interactive learning experience, the space needs to allow for multiple furniture configurations.
4. Through new technology, users will be able to program the space for their needs and store the settings for later use.
5. The space needs to balance teaching, technology, and design in order to create an active classroom.

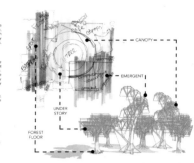

Figure 6.37 Kelley O'Leary, Yuyu Schatz, and Alex Watt: "Chameleon"

UNDERSTORY: MAIN LOUNGE

The main lounge contains an abstracted tree canopy. The spaces allows for casual gathering and interaciton. The form is placed in the center of the floor plan, from which concentric rings emanate. The concentric rings are used as boundaries for the floor materials, wall partitions, and ceiling interventions as well as allowing for circular movement through the space. Group rooms adjacent to the lounge act as private together workspaces. Visual transparency allows the users to feel a part of the surrounding lounge while still maintaining a level of privacy. The 3-form "Hint - Meadow" acrylic partitions mimic the natural environment of the rainforest, which the chameleon's habitat. In the background above the cafe seating, a circular media display is dropped from the ceiling. The display shows current time, weather forecasts, and any information relevant to students.

References

A Day Made of Glass . Made possible by Corning. (n.d.). Corning Incorporated Retrieved October 17, 2012, from http://www.youtube.com/watch?v=6Cf7IL_eZ38
(2012) Active Learning Spaces: Insights, Applications, & Solutions. Steelcase 360: 1, 1-67
Adaptable Futures >> Extending the Life of Our Built Environment. (n.d.). Adaptable Futures. Retrieved October 17, 2012, from http://adaptablefutures.com/
Berseghian, T. (2010, October 20). How Would You Design the Modern Classroom?. MindShift. Retrieved October 17, 2012, from http://blogs.kqed.org/mindshift/2010/10/how-would-you-design-the-modern-classroom/
Jilek, T. (2012, May 31). A Variety of Voices: Innovative Learning Spaces Transform the Hartland-Lakeside School District. DesignShare. Retrieved October 17, 2012, from http://www.designshare.com/index.php/a-variety-of-voices-innovative-learning-spaces-transform-the-hartland-lakeside-school-district/
Lippman, P. C. (n.d.). The L-Shaped Classroom. DesignShare. Retrieved October 17, 2012, from http://ldesignshare.com/index.php/articles/the-l-shaped-classroom
Newton, C. (2011, September 1). Innovative learning spaces. ArchitectureAU. â€" Architecture, Interiors and Landscape. Retrieved October 26, 2012, from http://architectureau.com/articles/innovative-learning-spaces/
Oblinger, D. (n.d.). Learning Spaces. Educause. Retrieved October 26, 2012, from http://www.educause.edu/research-and-publications/books/learning-spaces
Wenger, T., & Dobbin, G. (2009). Learning Environments: Where Space, Technology, and Culture Converge. Educause Learning Initiative: 1. Retrieved October 17, 2012, from http://net.educause.edu/ir/library/pdf/ELI3021.pdf

FOREST FLOOR: GROUP STUDY

The group study room is designed to accomodate active learning. The room itself responds to the user's needs via a wall control panel that can adjust lighting, the Corning Glass computer screen, and acoustics along with the mobile furniture.

CANOPY: CAFE

The cafe is built for community, comfort, and study. This space juxtaposes new and old with the existing brick walls adjacent to the DIRTT green wall. Various types of seating (booths, stools, and tables) allow for eating and learning.

UNDERSTORY: MEDIA LOUNGE

The media lounge is a casual presentation area where students can display information visually and collaborate on projects while resting on comfortable furniture. A custom designed charging station allows electronics to recharge while working.

FLOOR PLAN
SCALE: 1/16" = 1'-0"

Figure 6.38 Kelley O'Leary, Yuyu Schatz, and Alex Watt: "Chameleon"

EMERGENT: CLASSROOM

This revised L shaped classroom morphs into more fluid spaces. The tables can be used in a lecture orientation or together as group tables for collaboration. The large Corning Glass computer screens allow for student-teacher interaction.

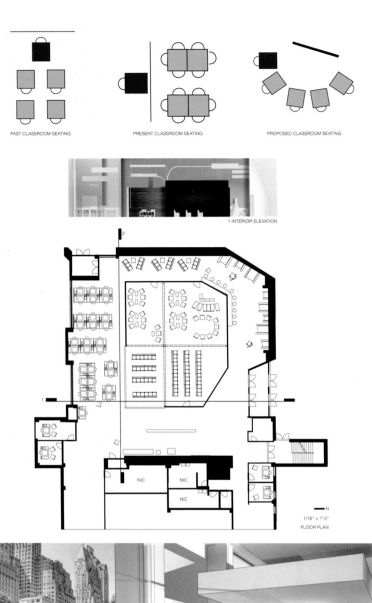

PAST CLASSROOM SEATING   PRESENT CLASSROOM SEATING   PROPOSED CLASSROOM SEATING

1 INTERIOR ELEVATION

NIC   NIC

NIC

N

1/16" = 1'-0"
FLOOR PLAN

THE FUTURE OF EDUCATION IS CONSOLIDATION, ONE OF SEAMLESSNESS & EFFICIENCY. A BLENDING OF TECHNOLOGY AND THE TANGIBLE WILL ALLOW STUDENTS TO REALIZE WHAT IS TRULY PIVOTAL TO LEARNING: RELATIONSIHPS - BIOPHILIC AND INTERPERSONAL.

ONE OF THE FIRST PROBLEMS WE HAVE CHOSEN TO ADDRESS IN OUR PROJECT IS DIFFERENT LEARNING TYPES. IN DOING SO, WE BEGAN TO HONE IN ON LEVELS OF DISTRACTION. SOME FIND IT EASIER TO FOCUS IN HIGHER ENERGY ENVIRONMENTS, WHILE OTHERS PREFER PLACES WITH VERY LOW ENERGY. IN CHAPTER SIX OF THE BOOK "LEARNING SPACES," THE AUTHOR DISCUSSES HOW PROVIDING DIFFERENT LEVELS OF DISTRACTION WITHIN THE LEARNING SPACE CAN POSITIVELY INFLUENCE THE PRODUCTIVITY OF THE STUDENTS INDIVIDUALLY. DEPENDING ON THE STUDENT AND THE TYPE OF TASK BEING PERFORMED, IT IS IMPORTANT THAT THERE ARE OPTIONS FOR HIGH OR LOW LEVEL OF DISTRACTION SO THAT THE STUDENT IS NOT BORED WITH THEIR SURROUNDINGS, BUT IS ALSO NOT UNABLE TO FOCUS. (1)

IN ORDER TO ACCOMMODATE VARIOUS LEVELS OF DISTRACTION, WE DECIDED TO INCORPORATE TRANSPARENCY INTO OUR SPACE. THE ARTICLE "THE DYSON BUILDING" BY HAWORTH TOMPKINS, SHOWCASES A PERFECT EXAMPLE OF USING TRANSPARENCY TO SPARK CREATIVITY AND LEARNING. NO MATTER WHERE A STUDENT MAY BE WITHIN THE BUILDING, THEY ARE ALWAYS ABLE TO PEER INTO ANOTHER SPACE. REFERRING TO THIS BUILDING, WHERE LEARNING AND PRODUCTIVITY IS OF THE UPMOST IMPORTANCE, ARCHITECT GRAHAM HAWORTH SAID, "WHAT'S MOST SUCCESSFUL IS THE WAY YOU CAN SEE EVERYWHERE." (2)

WHEN IT COMES TO ORGANIZING THE DIFFERENT AREAS WITHIN OUR SPACE, WE DEVELOPED A FLOOR PLAN THAT NOT ONLY WORKS TO COMPLIMENT THE EXTERIOR SHELL, BUT ALSO SPEAKS TO THE FUTURE OF LEARNING SPACES. ALTHOUGH PEOPLE OFTEN ASSOCIATE THE FUTURE WITH SHAPES THAT ARE ROUND, CIRCULAR OR CURVED, WE FEEL THESE OPTIONS ARE NOT THE ANSWER. IN THE ARTICLE "UK GOVERNMENT BANS CURVED SCHOOL BUILDINGS," WE FOUND PLENTY OF SUPPORT FOR OUR DECISION. NOT ONLY ARE CURVED BUILDINGS COSTLY AND IMPRACTICAL, THEY ALSO LACK "LONG-TERM SUSTAINABILITY AND VALUE." (3)

IN ADDITION TO AVOIDING CURVES, WE CREATED A LAYOUT THAT AGAIN REFERS BACK TO OUR GOAL TO ADDRESS THE DIFFERENT LEVELS OF FOCUS AND LEARNING BEHAVIOR IN A LEARNING ENVIRONMENT. NOT ONLY DID WE CREATE A SPACE THAT WILL AID TO EACH STUDENT'S PERSONAL NEEDS, WE ALSO ORGANIZED THE SPACE AS TO GRADUALLY TRANSFORM FROM AN INDIVIDUAL LEARNING ENVIRONMENT TO AN AREA FOR COLLABORATION. IN THE ARTICLE, "HOW DESIGN CAN FACILITATE BETTER EDUCATION," BY JEREMY WELU, THE SPACES ARE SPECIFIED AS "FOCUS," "SOCIALIZE" AND "COLLABORATE." THE ARTICLE EXPLAINS THAT A WELL-DESIGNED LEARNING ENVIRONMENT WOULD INCORPORATE ALL OF THESE SPACES INTO ONE IN A WAY THAT PROVIDES EASY ACCESS AND TRANSITIONING FROM ONE SETTING TO THE NEXT. (4)

(1)   FILE:///USERS/KYLIE92/LIBRARY/MAIL%20DOWNLOADS/PSYCHOLOGY%20OF%20LEARNING.PDF
(2)   HTTP://WWW.DEZEEN.COM/2012/09/28/THE-DYSON-BUILDING-BY-HAWORTH-TOMPKINS/
(3)   HTTP://WWW.DEZEEN.COM/2012/10/03/UK-GOVERNMENT-BANS-CURVED-SCHOOL-BUILDINGS/
(4)   HTTP://WWW.BSALIFESTRUCTURES.COM/BLOG/LEARNING-ENVIRONMENTS-OF-THE-FUTURE/HOW-DE
         SIGN-CAN-FACILITATE-BETTER-EDUCATION

FIVE PROPOSED DESIGN PRINCIPLES

1 - SENSITIVITY TO VARIOUS STYLES OF LEARNING

2 - SPECIALIZED ENVIRONMENTS FOR DIFFERENT LEVELS OF TASK

3 - GROWTH AS ONE MAJOR IN TERMS OF PROVIDING A SINGLE SPACE IN WHICH STUDENTS, PROFESSORS INTERACT WITH THE SAME ENVIRONMENT DAILY

4 - EFFICIENCY OF SPACE

5 - DESIGN WHICH GRACEFULLY BLENDS TECHNOLOGY WITH FURNITURE

EMECO BROOM CHAIR

WHY DOES THE INTIMACY OF A STUDENT WITH THE CLASS LESSEN AS ONE ADVANCES THROUGH SCHOOL. BEGINNING WITH PRIMARY LEVELS, EACH STUDENT IS ASSIGNED A DESK FOR THE YEAR, AND SHE IS ABLE TO KEEP BELONGINGS IN THIS DESK, CREATING A CLOSE RELATIONSHIP WITH THE LEARNING CONTEXT.

A COLLEGIATE STUDENT MUST NOT TRANSITION ENDLESSLY THROUGH DIFFERENT BUILDINGS AND HALLS, SPENDING TIME IN BETWEEN COURSES IN A LOUNGE. UNIVERSITIES IN THE FUTURE MUST BEGIN TO FOSTER A LOVE OF CONTEXT, WHERE STUDENTS AND FACULTY ROTATE CLASSES IN ONE BUILDING, ONE SPACE.

PAST DESK DESIGNS

THE FUTURE OF COLLEGIATE DESKS IS CONSOLIDATION AND COLLABORATION. WHEN EACH STUDENT CARRIES A PERSONAL TABLET, HE CAN PLUG THE DEVICE INTO THE TABLE, EASILY ABLE TO TRANSITION INFORMATION ONTO A TOUCH SCREEN WHERE HE CAN CONCURRENTLY WORK WITH OTHER STUDENTS ON THE SAME ASSIGNMENT.

- BUILT IN PRINTER
- TOUCH SCREEN
- TABLET DEVICE DOCK
- PEN/PENCILS STORAGE
- OTHER STORAGE BENEATH DESK
- WIRELESS NETWORK WITH OTHER DESKS

CUSTOM DESK AXON

1 WORKSPACE PERSPECTIVE

Figure 6.39 Ross Johnson, Kylie Gravlee, and Kathleen Barry: "Future of Design for Higher Education"

ANGULARITY IS THE FUTURE. ORGANIC FURNITURE AND DESIGN OFTEN IS TOO COSTLY IN RELATION TO PRODUCTIVITY. ONCE ANGLES HAVE BECOME THE DOMINANT INTERIOR DESIGN SHAPE, THE NEXT TREND WILL BE A LOVE OF MONOCHROME.

PEOPLE WILL EVENTUALLY BECOME OVER STIMULATED WITH COLORS AND WILL DESIRE THE GREY SCALE, WITH COLOR ONLY USED WHEN DESIGNATING AN ACTION OR WARNING.

IF ONE MAJOR WERE TO OCCUPY A SPACE, THEN FLEXIBILITY WILL BE A MAIN PRIORITY.

A SPACE MUST BE MOBILE, PARTITIONS WHICH RAISE TO OPEN SPACE ALLOW A ZERO TURNING RADIUS. IN LARGE INDUSTRIAL SPACES THE PARTITIONS, WHEN RAISED, WILL CREATE A MORE INTIMATE ATMOSPHERE RESEMBLING DROPPED CEILINGS.

SIMILAR TO THE LOACOON OF THE ANCIENT GREEKS, THE DESIRE OF TWISTING AND SHARP ANGULAR SHAPES WILL CREATE A DRAMATIC CONTRAST TO THE MONOCHROMATIC SPACE, ALLOWING OBJECTS OF FURNITURE TO BECOME OBJECTS OF VIRTUE.

WHAT IS THE DESIGN FOR THE NEXT GENERATION OF FOOD CONSUMERS?

A VENDING MACHINE WHICH CREATES, PREPARES, AND SERVES A MULTITUDE OF FOOD OPTIONS IN A SINGLE ENTITY. THIS WILL DECREASE THE COSTS OF SPACE FOR CHAIN FOOD BUSINESSES TO OCCUPY IN SCHOOLS.

THE ENTRANCE AND MAIN HALLWAY IN THE SPACE WILL BE VERY MINIMAL, SO THAT ALL ATTENTION MAY BE FOCUSED ON THE INFORMATION PANEL. WHERE VITAL ALERTS, MESSAGES FROM STAFF, AND VARIOUS OTHER MEDIA CAN BE SEEN.

THE ABILITY OF ANY STUDENT OR STAFF TO INTERACT WITH THE SCREEN WILL ALLOW SO THAT EVERY STUDENT MAY PERSONALIZE HIS ENVIRONMENT.

LUCCON IS A TEXTURED CONCRETE WITH A SOMEWHAT TRANSPARENT NATURE SO THAT LIGHT AND ACTIVITY MAY BE CARRIED THROUGH TO ANOTHER SPACE, CREATING STIMULI FOR STUDETNS AND STAFF IN THE CENTER CLASSROOMS

2 INTERIOR ELEVATION

WHEN DIVIDING SPACE

WHEN IN RAISED POSITION

INTERIOR PARTITION DIAGRAM

MOLO SOFT SEATING

TAKAHASI STOOL

DIESEL/MOROSO LAMP

FOOD VENDOR AXON

2 CAFE PERSPECTIVE

3 HALLWAY PERSPECTIVE

WHITE POLISHED CONRETE FLOORING

LUCCON PARTITIONS

Figure 6.40 Ross Johnson, Kylie Gravlee, and Kathleen Barry: "Future of Design for Higher Education"

Figure 6.41 Lindsey Slough, Rachel Russell, and Theresa Bartlett: "Stretch, Pull, Surround"

Figure 6.42 Lindsey Slough, Rachel Russell, and Theresa Bartlett: "Stretch, Pull, Surround"

Pro Bono Project

For this two-week project, students were asked to identify a social problem and design a response in a reused environment such as a shipping container, a train car, or a trailer.

Lindsey Slough—"Food and Hunger" (eco-social)

Using a single shipping container, this solution provides a mobile greenhouse that responds to the angle of the sun and can be used in communities as a communal garden where people learn to grow their own food. Using a hydroponic system (water-based growing), people work the gardens in exchange for some of the fruits and vegetables.

PROBLEM:
With a population growth rate of 75-80 million people annually, the world is constantly adjusting to the developing demands. With this growth comes new infrastructure to house all of the people and their needs (homes, Big Box stores, roads, etc.). Most of the population growth occurs in regions that are already impoverished like big cities. The cost of oil affects transportation of goods to these areas so they are continuously disconnected from resources. The problem of food scarcity lies in the social organization of food production and distribution. With 1.4 billion people living below the poverty line or $1.25 a day, its not hard to comprehend why so many go hungry.

Feeding America: Food Insecurity Rates
30% and above
25% - 29%
20% - 24%
15% - 19%
4% - 14%

COMMUNITY GARDENS

THE TRADITIONAL PROBLEM

THE FUTURE SOLUTION

By using a shipping container the community will not only provide for these impoverished communities, but will also reduce on the number of wasted containers around the world. Transportation costs are continuing to rise because of the cost of oil. Having a permanent location with on-site vegetation, resources, and learning opportunities is key. This system construct a new form of social organization that is capable of meeting the needs of the masses. It will reduce the reliance on national and international goods while creating a transition to focus on local goods. This will also encourage individuals to volunteer at these facilities to earn their sustenance when they are unable to afford the local goods.

Figure 6.43 Lindsey Slough: "Food and Hunger"

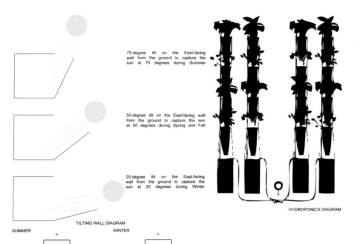

75-degree tilt on the East-facing wall from the ground to capture the sun at 75 degrees during Summer

50-degree tilt on the East-facing wall from the ground to capture the sun at 50 degrees during Spring and Fall

25-degree tilt on the East-facing wall from the ground to capture the sun at 25 degrees during Winter

TILTING WALL DIAGRAM

SUMMER   WINTER

SOLAR PATTERNS DIAGRAM

HYDROPONICS DIAGRAM

Each shipping container would be positioned based on an intensive sun study to ensure that this facility could function without relying on any other technology or energy source. With solar and hydro energy being the only means for growth and functionality, communities can ensure that all funds and time are spent towards the vegetation and sustenance growth. One of the main features in the space is a Hydroponic vegetation system that runs off of an air pump. With cone shaped canisters, nutrients and water that are pumped through can easily drain to each level to ensure all vegetation is receiving an adequate supply of nutrients. Along with the simply hydroponic system, the container will house a flexible wall that can move based on the season and weather conditions. This ensures that the plants that need sunlight will receive enough to continue growing and surviving. The ease of this system allows anyone in the community to assist in the success of the garden while also ensuring vegetation and sustenance regardless of the economic situation

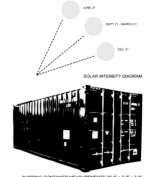

JUNE 21

SEPT 21 - MARCH 21

DEC 21

SOLAR INTENSITY DIAGRAM

SHIPPING CONTAINER MEASUREMENTS 20' 8" x 7' 8" x 7' 8"

Figure 6.44 Lindsey Slough: "Food and Hunger"

Maddie Potter—"What is Real Beauty?" (eco-social, eco-centric)

Responding to women's self-esteem issues, such as low self-esteem related to size, shape, complexion, and a variety of other issues, the real beauty mobile storage container unit provides a place for counseling women on body image. Counselors in the mobile unit provide guidance to the women who stop by the clinic.

Callie Reid—"Urban After School Help Center" (eco-social, eco-centric)

This shipping container provides a place for children in inner cities to complete their homework. Stocked with healthy snacks, computers, and worktables, this mobile unit allows for students to continue their education after the school day is over. The shipping container includes windows on all walls as well

Figure 6.45 Maddie Potter: "What is Real Beauty?"

Figure 6.46 Maddie Potter: "What is Real Beauty?"

After experiencing the informative area of the train car, students will experience the opportunity to partake in two activities. Students will be able to talk with real women who have their own insecurities. However, during these discussions - it will ONLY be positive. Talking about it negatively only makes it worse. 93% of college women engage in negative "fat talks" and those who do are more dissatisfied with their bodies. Having empowering talks about strength, beauty, and confidence will help turn around these incorrect depictions of beauty the media shows us.

The makeover area is another tool to be utilized in this workshop. Students will go through a natural makeover - one that enhances their natural beauty. However, the feature mirrors in the makeup area will be shattered. The students can't see themselves with natural makeup until their enhancement is complete. Objectives like this aim to promote confidence in outer appearance even though they won't have a crystal clear image of what they look like. It's important for the students to understand that no matter how much or how little makeup is applied, they are still beautiful. Our perception of beauty is distorted; we need to encourage the idea of being beautiful is being different. Beauty has been defined by a narrow stereotype, when in actuality, we need a broader, healthier, more positive view through encouraging a healthy relationship with the body. To be beautiful is to be confident.

THE HAND THAT ROCKS THE CRADLE RULES THE WORLD.
IF WE'RE GOING TO START SEEING DEVELOPMENT IN THE WORLD, OUR BEST INVESTMENT IS WOMEN.

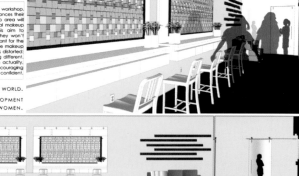

Figure 6.47 Maddie Potter: "What is Real Beauty?"

Back Elevation
Scale: 1/4" = 1'0"

Urban After School Help Center

1,489 highschool dropout already today, 1 student every 26 seconds

Figure 6.48 Callie Reid: "Urban After School Help Center"

Concept Inspiration

Many inner city children do not receive a proper education because of their irregular home life. If they do not have a place to do homework then they just won't do it. These repurposed shipping containers provide a safe and comfortable place for these children to get their work done.

The shipping containers will have computers with internet access, desks with supplies for doing projects, and even a lounging section with books to read.

A lot of these children need one on one attention that they cannot receive in a large classroom. So there is a teacher there at all times that can help the students with their work.

Many of these kids also do not receive proper nutrition. Without the proper nutrition, the brain does not develop fully. This could be a major contributor to why a lot of these kids cannot focus in school. The shipping container will be fully stocked with healthy snacks that the kids can eat while they work or bring home to eat later.

These repurposed shipping containers are easily transported. They can easily be placed in any large parking lot in cities all over the United States.

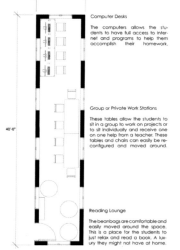

Computer Desks

The computers allows the students to have full access to internet and programs to help them accomplish their homework.

Group or Private Work Stations

These tables allow the students to sit in a group to work on projects or to sit individually and receive one on one help from a teacher. These tables and chairs can easily be reconfigured and moved around.

Reading Lounge

The beanbags are comfortable and easily moved around the space. This is a place for the students to just relax and read a book. A luxury they might not have at home.

Floor Plan

High School Drop-Out Disparities

The nation's graduation rate rose slightly from 1996 to 2005, but the already large gaps are continuing to widen between rates in urban and suburban districts of some metropolitan areas.

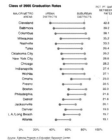

Figure 6.49 Callie Reid: "Urban After School Help Center"

Facts and Figures

The average high school graduation rate in the nation's 50 largest cities was 53 percent, compared with 71 percent in the suburbs. This gap is increasing every year. Only just over half the students in the United States' big cities are graduating from high school. The No Child Left Behind law, signed in 2002, did little to help this growing gap. This law was put in place to fix the urban schools, however that is only half the solution. Many of the kids growing up in urban areas do not have a good home life, or they may not even have a home at all. The fact of the matter is, if they do not have a place to do their homework, then they will not do it. The other growing issue is the quality of the teachers. Many of the teachers working in urban schools have given up. They do not think they get paid enough to deal with the students they are given to teach. But many of these students need one on one attention. They cannot focus in a class of twenty-five or thirty. Placing these repurposed shipping containers in all the major cities in the United States will begin to solve the half of the problem regarding after-school life.

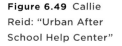

Haworth Very White Task Chair   Love Sac   Haworth Planes Flip-Top Tables

as skylights to give as much access to daylight and views as possible. The interior finishes are sustainable and include Interface Flor carpeting, low-VOC paint, Haworth sustainable furniture, and sustainable textiles.

Brittani Anderson—"Traveling the World by Storm" (eco-social, eco-centric)

The project takes a single shipping container and makes it into a mobile housing unit to be used in times of disaster. This temporary housing unit could be used by any number of relief organizations in times of need for semi-permanent, long-term post-disaster housing. The mobile unit contains a full bath with a shower, a small dining area for four, a living area, and sleeping for up to four people (a double bed and two twins in a bunk bed).

Jooyoung Hong—"Recycled Art After-School Program" (eco-social, eco-centric)

This shipping container is used to house an after-school art program and can be located in the parking lot of any school. Students learn about environmental

Figure 6.50 Brittani Anderson: "Traveling the World by Storm"

Figure 6.51 Jooyoung Hong: "Recycled Art After-School Program"

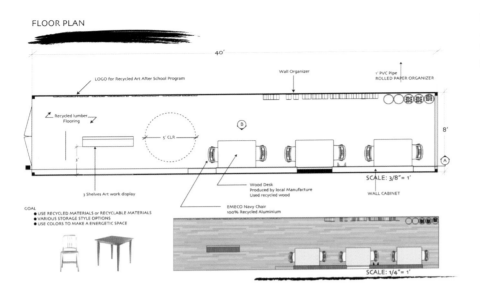

FLOOR PLAN

Figure 6.52
Jooyoung Hong:
"Recycled Art After-
School Program"

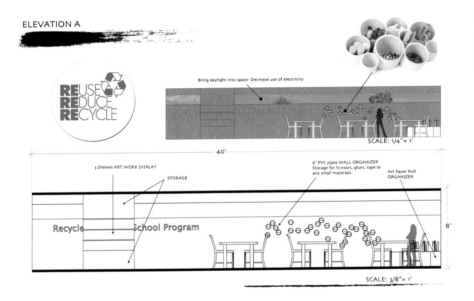

ELEVATION A

Figure 6.53
Jooyoung Hong:
"Recycled Art After-
School Program"

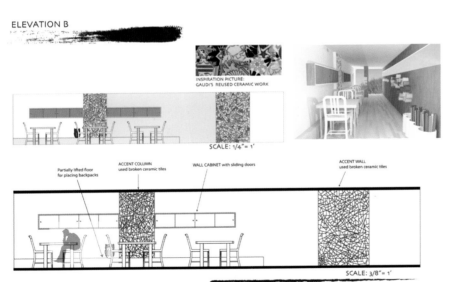

ELEVATION B

Figure 6.54
Jooyoung Hong:
"Recycled Art After-
School Program"

Figure 6.55
Jooyoung Hong:
"Recycled Art After-
School Program"

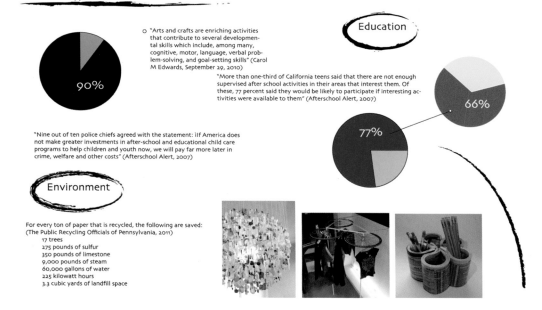

SOCIAL ISSUE- RESEARCH& DIAGRAMS

○ "Arts and crafts are enriching activities that contribute to several developmental skills which include, among many, cognitive, motor, language, verbal problem-solving, and goal-setting skills" (Carol M Edwards, September 29, 2010)

"More than one-third of California teens said that there are not enough supervised after school activities in their areas that interest them. Of these, 77 percent said they would be likely to participate if interesting activities were available to them" (Afterschool Alert, 2007)

90%

Education

66%

77%

"Nine out of ten police chiefs agreed with the statement: iIf America does not make greater investments in after-school and educational child care programs to help children and youth now, we will pay far more later in crime, welfare and other costs" (Afterschool Alert, 2007)

Environment

For every ton of paper that is recycled, the following are saved:
(The Public Recycling Officials of Pennsylvania, 2011)
17 trees
275 pounds of sulfur
350 pounds of limestone
9,000 pounds of steam
60,000 gallons of water
225 kilowatt hours
3.3 cubic yards of landfill space

issues and recycling as a part of this unique art program focused on making recycled art.

Christine Miller—"It Stops Here" (eco-social, eco-centric)

In response to increased incidents of bullying in many schools, this project creates a safe haven that students can go to after school to avoid bullying. The center provides a place for homework, counseling, and friendship. The shipping container includes a sitting area, a homework area, and a counseling area. Children can enter the sitting area where they can watch TV or do homework. The homework area includes four workstations and is sound-separated from the counseling area. A turquoise color scheme is used to create a relaxing yet fun and inviting area for the students. All of the finishes and furnishings are sustainable.

Figure 6.56
Christine Miller: "It
Stops Here"

IT STOPS HERE.

56% of students have personally felt some sort of bullying at school.
The most common reason or being harassed is **appearance or body size.**
1 in 4 teachers see nothing wrong with bullying and will only intervene 4% percent of the time.
A victim of bullying is **twice as likely** to take his or her **own life.**
1/10 students **drop out of school** because they are bullied.
57% of students who experience harassment **never report the incident** to the school.
more than a **1/4** of students feel that **school is an unsafe place to be.**

Inspiration

7'6"   40'   Shipping Container

Elevation 1

Anti-Bullying

Figure 6.57
Christine Miller: "It Stops Here"

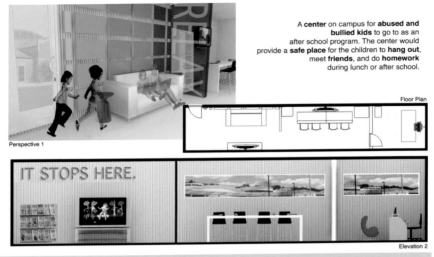

IT STOPS HERE.

A **center** on campus for **abused and bullied kids** to go to as an after school program. The center would provide a **safe place** for the children to **hang out**, meet **friends**, and do **homework** during lunch or after school.

Floor Plan

Perspective 1

IT STOPS HERE.

Elevation 2

Anti-Bullying

Firm Approaches to Cultural, Civic, and Institutional Design

As with many other types of design specialties, work in the public sphere is also an area of specialization. Some firms have entire offices or entire practices dedicated to specific types of design in order to maintain all the expertise required for a certain project type. The following examples depict two of these project areas—airport design and museum design. As very large and complex projects, these involved several consultants and designers over an extended period of time.

Fentress Architects— Raleigh-Durham International Airport (biophilic, eco-technic)

Designed to meet LEED Silver standards and opened in January 2011, the Raleigh-Durham International Airport is a 920,000-square-foot facility with 36

gates. Inspired by the undulating hills of the local area, the designers used a multitiered curved roof over the airport terminal. A primary requirement of the design solution included energy efficiency. In response, both the airport building and central energy plant incorporate a series of features to reduce energy use including a water-side economizer that offers free cooling of chilled water during certain times of the year, point-of-use hot water heaters, and an energy management system. Large spaces have digital controls with optimized settings, while smaller occupant rooms allow for occupants' control. Abundant windows and clerestories allow for natural daylighting.

Fentress Architects— Mineta San Jose International Airport, Terminal B (eco-technic)

Constructed in 2005, Terminal B meets LEED Silver certification and includes several sustainable components. As the chief transit airport (stopping point between two larger airports) for

Figure 6.58 Fentress Architects: Raleigh-Durham International Airport, exterior
Project Name: Raleigh-Durham International Airport Terminal 2
Location: Raleigh, North Carolina
Architect: Fentress Architects
Photo Credit: © Paul Dingman

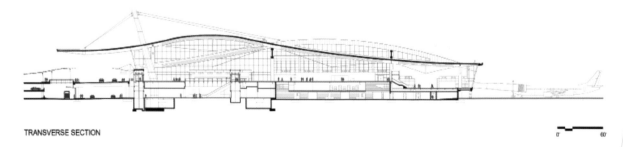

TRANSVERSE SECTION

Figure 6.59 Fentress Architects: Raleigh-Durham International Airport, exterior view and section
Project Name: Raleigh-Durham International Airport Terminal 2
Location: Raleigh, North Carolina
Architect: Fentress Architects
Drawing by Fentress Architects

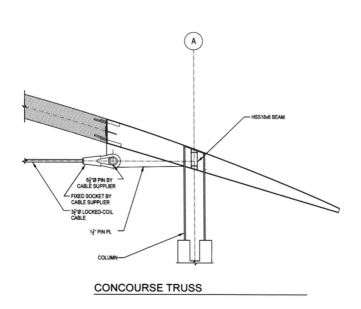

CONCOURSE TRUSS

A. Project Name: Raleigh-Durham International Airport Terminal 2
Location: Raleigh, North Carolina
Architect: Fentress Architects
Drawing: Fentress Architects

B. Project Name: Raleigh-Durham International Airport Terminal 2
Location: Raleigh, North Carolina
Architect: Fentress Architects
Photo Credit: Jason A. Knowles
© Fentress Architects

Figure 6.62 Fentress Architects: Raleigh-Durham International Airport, lenticular truss system

Figure 6.63
Fentress Architects:
Raleigh-Durham
International
Airport, glue-
laminated timbers
and steel cables
Project Name:
Raleigh-Durham
International
Airport Terminal 2
Location: Raleigh,
North Carolina
Architect:
Fentress Architects
Drawing:
Fentress Architects

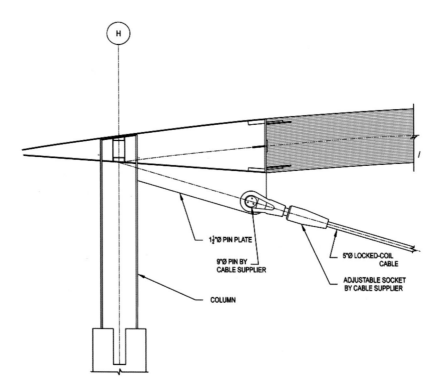

TERMINAL TRUSS @ H

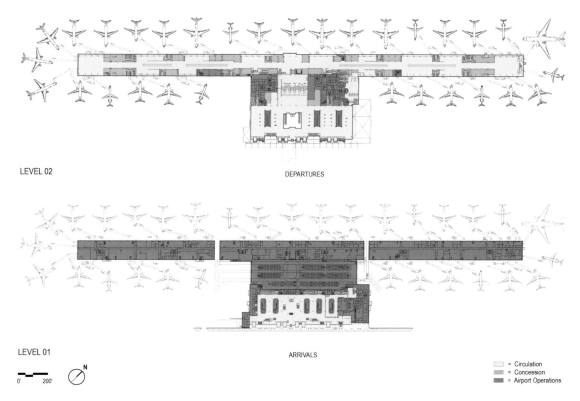

LEVEL 02

DEPARTURES

LEVEL 01

ARRIVALS

0'   200'   N

= Circulation
= Concession
= Airport Operations

Figure 6.64 Fentress Architects: Raleigh-Durham International Airport, plans
Project Name: Raleigh-Durham International Airport Terminal 2
Location: Raleigh, North Carolina
Architect: Fentress Architects
Drawing: Fentress Architects

Figure 6.65 Fentress Architects: Raleigh-Durham International Airport, wood trusses with clerestories
Project Name: Raleigh-Durham International Airport Terminal 2
Location: Raleigh, North Carolina
Architect: Fentress Architects
Photo Credit: © Brady Lambert

Figure 6.66
Fentress Architects:
Raleigh-Durham
International
Airport, public art
installation
Project Name:
Raleigh-Durham
International
Airport Terminal 2
Location: Raleigh,
North Carolina
Architect:
Fentress Architects
Photo Credit:
© Paul Dingman

Figure 6.67
Fentress Architects:
Raleigh-Durham
International
Airport, filtered
natural light
Project Name:
Raleigh-Durham
International
Airport Terminal 2
Location: Raleigh,
North Carolina
Architect:
Fentress Architects
Photo Credit:
© Brady Lambert

Silicon Valley in Northern California, the airport design takes its form from a deconstructed coaxial cable, thus reflecting the key economic driver of the area (the computer industry). The form of the coaxial cable shows up in the design of the airport. Water-conservation measures, recycled and reused construction waste, and energy-efficient glazing all contribute to the LEED design. Filtered daylight combined with high-performance glass and programmable lighting provides an energy-efficient interior that is full of natural light. Low-VOC materials contribute to good indoor environment for travelers and staff. Bicycle storage and changing rooms are provided for local workers, and 90 percent of spaces include daylighting and views. In addition to the airport's sustainable features, it is also designed to the latest earthquake-protection standards.

Figure 6.68
Fentress Architects: Mineta San Jose International Airport, Terminal B, exterior view
Project Name: Mineta San Jose International Airport Terminal B
Location: San Jose, California
Architect: Fentress Architects
Photo Credit: © Ken Paul

Figure 6.69
Fentress Architects: Mineta San Jose International Airport, Terminal B, façade details
Project Name: Mineta San Jose International Airport Terminal B
Location: San Jose, California
Architect: Fentress Architects
Photo Credit: Jason A. Knowles © Fentress Architects

A. Project Name:
Mineta San Jose
International
Airport Terminal B
Location: San Jose,
California
Architect:
Fentress Architects
Photo Credit:
© Ken Paul

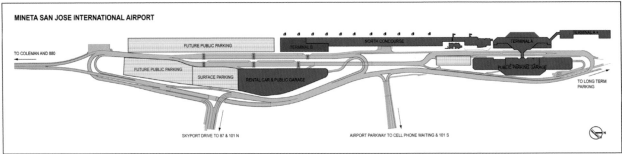

B. Project Name: Mineta San Jose International Airport Terminal B
Location: San Jose, California
Architect: Fentress Architects
Drawing Credit: Fentress Architects

Figure 6.70 Fentress Architects: Mineta San Jose International Airport, Terminal B, access

Figure 6.71
Fentress Architects:
Mineta San Jose
International
Airport, Terminal B,
section views
Project Name:
Mineta San Jose
International
Airport Terminal B
Location: San Jose,
California
Architect:
Fentress Architects
Drawing Credit:
Fentress Architects

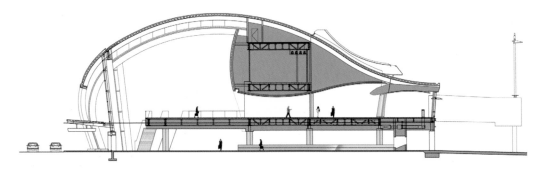

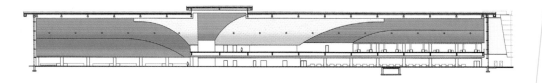

Figure 6.74

Fentress Architects: Mineta San Jose International Airport, Terminal B, finishes plans
Project Name: Mineta San Jose International Airport Terminal B
Location: San Jose, California
Architect: Fentress Architects
Drawing Credit: Fentress Architects

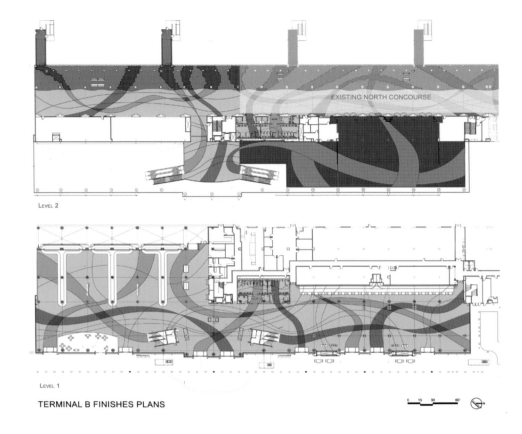

LEVEL 2

LEVEL 1

TERMINAL B FINISHES PLANS

EXISTING NORTH CONCOURSE

0   15   30   60'

Figure 6.75

Fentress Architects: Mineta San Jose International Airport, Terminal B, skylights and perforations
Project Name: Mineta San Jose International Airport Terminal B
Location: San Jose, California
Architect: Fentress Architects
Photo Credit: Nick Merrick
© Hedrich Blessing

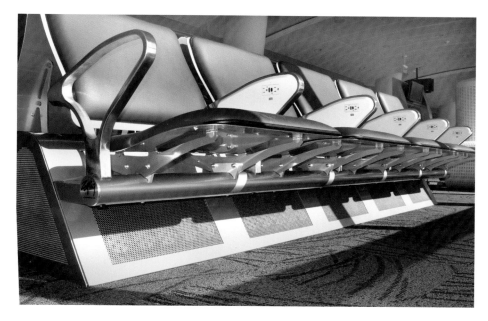

Figure 6.76
Fentress Architects:
Mineta San Jose
International
Airport, Terminal B,
The Air Chair

A. Project Name:
Mineta San Jose
International
Airport Terminal B
Location: San Jose,
California
Architect:
Fentress Architects
Photo Credit:
Mark Rothman ©
Fentress Architects

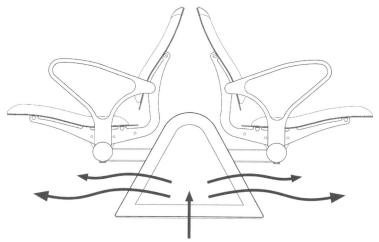

B. Project Name:
Mineta San Jose
International
Airport Terminal B
Location: San Jose,
California
Architect:
Fentress Architects
Drawing Credit:
Fentress Architects

C. Project Name:
Mineta San Jose
International
Airport Terminal B
Location: San Jose,
California
Architect:
Fentress Architects
Photo Credit:
Jason A. Knowles ©
Fentress Architects

Figure 6.77
Fentress Architects:
Mineta San Jose
International
Airport, Terminal B,
sustainable features
Project Name:
Mineta San Jose
International
Airport Terminal B
Location: San Jose,
California
Architect:
Fentress Architects
Photo Credit:
Fentress Architects

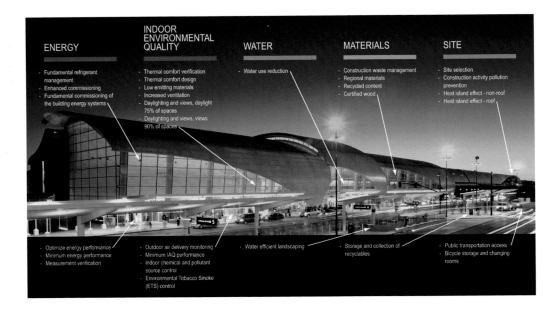

Figure 6.78
Fentress Architects:
Mineta San Jose
International
Airport, Terminal B,
exterior detail view
Project Name:
Mineta San Jose
International
Airport Terminal B
Location: San Jose,
California
Architect of Record:
Fentress Architects
Photo Credit:
Jason A. Knowles ©
Fentress Architects

Fentress Architects— Museum Design Project: Green Square Complex, Raleigh, NC (biophilic, eco-technic)

The Green Square Complex includes three buildings: a nature research center (105,000 square feet), an office building (146,250 square feet), and a parking structure (120,000 square feet). The office building (designed for LEED Platinum certification) and the research center (designed for LEED Gold certification) have a series of sustainable design features, including the collection and filtering of rainwater, a green roof, photovoltaics used to heat water and charge electric vehicle recharging stations, maximized daylighting with low-E glass, and exterior prismatic louvers that reflect daylight. All three buildings include salvaged materials from the site (marble, trees, and brick) as well as FSC-certified wood and locally manufactured furniture.

Figure 6.79 Fentress Architects: Museum Design Project: Green Square Complex, Raleigh, NC, exterior view
Project Name: Green Square Complex
Location: Raleigh, North Carolina
Architect of Record: O'Brien/Atkins
Design Architect: Fentress Architects
Photo Credit: Nick Merrick © Hedrich Blessing

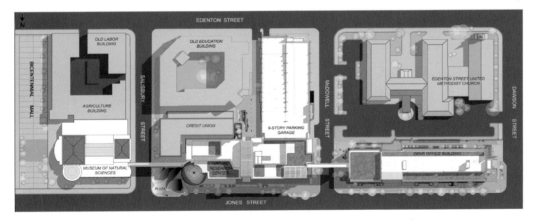

Project Name: Green Square Complex
Location: Raleigh, North Carolina
Architect of Record: O'Brien/Atkins
Design Architect: Fentress Architects
Drawing Credit: Fentress Architects

Figure 6.80 Fentress Architects: Museum Design Project: Green Square Complex, Raleigh, NC, elevation (A) and site plan (B)

A. Project Name: Green Square Complex
Location: Raleigh, North Carolina
Architect of Record: O'Brien/Atkins
Design Architect: Fentress Architects
Photo Credit: Jason A. Knowles © Fentress Architects

Figure 6.81 Fentress Architects: Museum Design Project: Green Square Complex, Raleigh, NC, exterior views showing aerial roof (A), green roof (B), water system (C), prismatic louvers (D)

B. Project Name: Green Square Complex
Location: Raleigh, North Carolina
Architect of Record: O'Brien/Atkins
Design Architect: Fentress Architects
Photo Credit: Nick Merrick © Hedrich Blessing

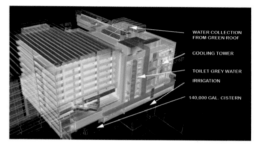

C. Project Name: Green Square Complex
Location: Raleigh, North Carolina
Architect of Record: O'Brien/Atkins
Design Architect: Fentress Architects
Drawing Credit: Fentress Architects

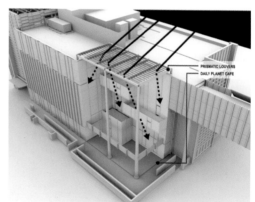

D. Project Name: Green Square Complex
Location: Raleigh, North Carolina
Architect of Record: O'Brien/Atkins
Design Architect: Fentress Architects
Drawing Credit: Fentress Architects

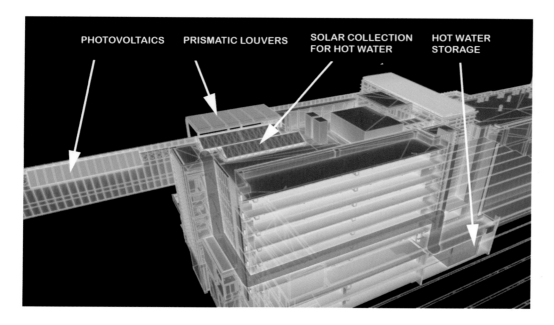

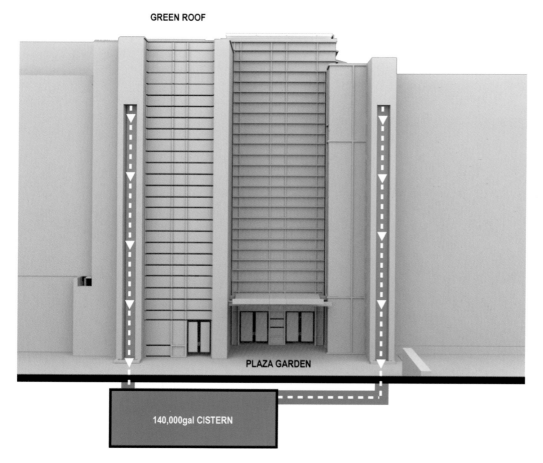

Figure 6.82 Fentress Architects: Museum Design Project: Green Square Complex, Raleigh, NC, Exterior views showing solar diagram (A), water system diagram (B)

Figure 6.83
Fentress Architects:
Museum Design
Project: Green
Square Complex,
Raleigh, NC, café
bridge (A),
overall elevation (B)
site plan (C)

A. Project Name: Green Square Complex
Location: Raleigh, North Carolina
Architect of Record: O'Brien/Atkins
Design Architect: Fentress Architects
Photo Credit: Nick Merrick © Hedrich Blessing

B. Project Name: Green Square Complex
Location: Raleigh, North Carolina
Architect of Record: O'Brien/Atkins
Design Architect: Fentress Architects
Drawing Credit: Fentress Architects

C. Project Name: Green Square Complex
Location: Raleigh, North Carolina
Architect of Record: O'Brien/Atkins
Design Architect: Fentress Architects
Drawing Credit: Fentress Architects

A. Project Name:
Green Square
Complex
Location: Raleigh,
North Carolina
Architect of Record:
O'Brien/Atkins
Design Architect:
Fentress Architects
Photo Credit:
Nick Merrick
© Hedrich Blessing

B. Project Name:
Green Square
Complex
Location: Raleigh,
North Carolina
Architect of Record:
O'Brien/Atkins
Design Architect:
Fentress Architects
Photo Credit:
Jason A. Knowles ©
Fentress Architects

Figure 6.84 Fentress Architects: Museum Design Project: Green Square Complex, Raleigh, NC, interior views of the Daily Planet

Resources for Students

The following plan prototypes provide guidance for museum display mounting heights for ADA, classroom layout and lighting, learning lab spaces, and library guidelines.

Applicable LEED Checklist

LEED for Schools

The LEED for School rating system is based on LEED NC, with several unique requirements based on K–12 education buildings. An extensive listing of resources and tools can be found at http://www.usgbc.org/DisplayPage. aspx?CMSPageID=1734.

The U.S. Green Building Council also has an online Center for Green Schools at http://www.centerforgreenschools.org/ home.aspx.

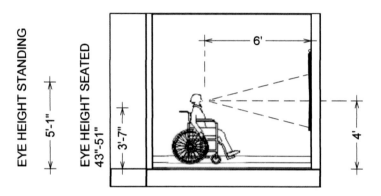

Figure 6.85 ADA museum exhibition heights

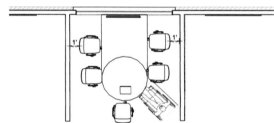

Figure 6.86 Learning lab prototype

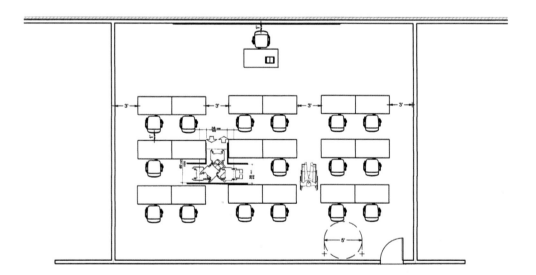

Figure 6.87 Traditional classroom layout

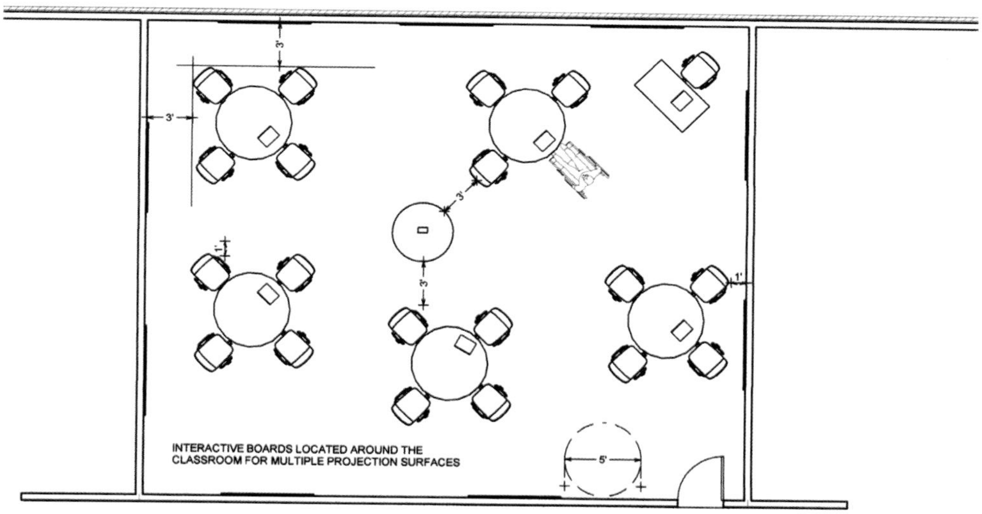

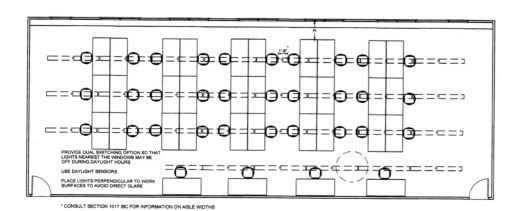

Figure 6.88
Contemporary
classroom layout

INTERACTIVE BOARDS LOCATED AROUND THE
CLASSROOM FOR MULTIPLE PROJECTION SURFACES

Figure 6.89
Classroom lighting
guidelines

PROVIDE DUAL SWITCHING OPTION SO THAT
LIGHTS NEAREST THE WINDOWS MAY BE
OFF DURING DAYLIGHT HOURS

USE DAYLIGHT SENSORS

PLACE LIGHTS PERPENDICULAR TO WORK
SURFACES TO AVOID DIRECT GLARE

* CONSULT SECTION 1017 IBC FOR INFORMATION ON AISLE WIDTHS

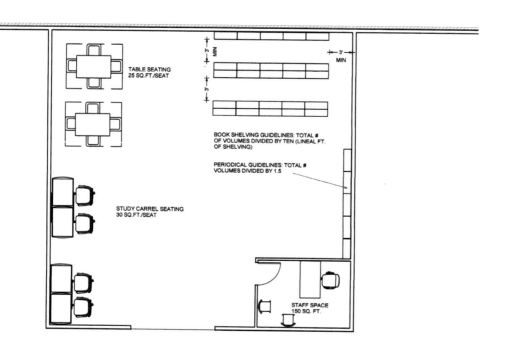

Figure 6.90 Library
space guidelines

TABLE SEATING
25 SQ.FT./SEAT

BOOK SHELVING GUIDELINES: TOTAL #
OF VOLUMES DIVIDED BY TEN (LINEAL FT.
OF SHELVING)

PERIODICAL GUIDELINES: TOTAL #
VOLUMES DIVIDED BY 1.5

STUDY CARREL SEATING
30 SQ.FT./SEAT

STAFF SPACE
150 SQ. FT.

Discussion Questions and Exercise

1. Ethical/philosophical question—Do we punish people through design? Do prisoners deserve good design?
2. What is a designer's role in designing for economically disadvantaged populations? In designing for populations who cannot afford design but would benefit from it?
3. Participate in the Annual "Make a Difference" Campaign (IDEC Social Responsibility Network).

Key Terms

Collaborative for High Performance Schools (CHPS)

cultural design

government design

Government Services Administration (GSA)

high security

learning commons

learning styles

low security

Sources

Bitgood, S., and D. Patterson. 1987. "Principles of Exhibit Design." *Visitor Behavior* Vol. 2 (Spring): 4.

Brown, J. S. 2005. "New Learning Environments for the 21st Century." Accessed July 1, 2013. http://www.johnseelybrown.com/Change%20article.pdf

Building Design and Construction Network. 2013. *Building Design and Construction.* Accessed July 1. www.bdcnetwork.com.

Cooper, K. 1999. "Study Says Natural Classroom Lighting Can Aid Achievement." *Washington Post*, November 26. Accessed July 1, 2013. http://www.h-m-g.com/projects/daylighting/publicity%20daylighting.htm#Study Says Natural Classroom Lighting Can Aid Achievement

Dittoe, W. (no date). "Creating the New Learning Environment: Enhancing Student Success through Principles Space Planning and Design." Published by KI: Green Bay, WI.

e.d|x. 2013. Accessed July 1. http://www.edxseattle.com/profile/philosophy/.

Fentress Architects. 2012. "An Airport Evolution: Edition 1.0" (unpublished study).

Gardner, H. 1983, 2004, 2011. *Frames of Mind: The Theory of Multiple Intelligences.* New York: Basic Books.

Kiefer, A. (no date). "Learning Per Square Foot: Shifting the Education Paradigm." Published by KI: Green Bay, WI.

PrisonDesign.org. 2012. "Peter Severin on the Latest Trends in Prison Design and Construction Rehabilitation." July 29. Accessed July 1, 2013. http://prisondesign.org/2012/07/29/peter-severin-on-the-latest-trends-in-prison-design-construction-rehabilitation/.

O'Brien, Sean. 2010. "Design Guidelines for Museums, Archives, and Art Storage Facilities." *Specialty Buildings Column Series*, Part 2 of 6. Accessed June 28, 2013. http://www.bdcnetwork.com/design-guidelines-museums-archives-and-art-storage-facilities.

Collaborative for High Performance Schools. Accessed June 28, 2013. http://www.chps.net/dev/Drupal/

Partnership for 21st Century Skills (P21). (no date). www.p21.org.

Thigpen, Morris, and Michael O'Toole. 1998."Jail Design Guide: A Resource for Small and Medium-Sized Jails." U.S. Department of Justice National Institute of Corrections: Washington, DC.

USGBC. 2012. Homepage. Accessed August 29. www.usbgc.org.

Webb, K. (no date). "Planet Library: The Center for Today's Learning, Experimentation, and Exploration." Published by KI: Green Bay, WI.

Whole Building Design Group (WBDG). www.wbdg.org

_____. 2010. Whole Building Design Guidelines for Libraries. Accessed July 1, 2013. http://www.wbdg.org/design/libraries.php

Additional Resources for Educational Facilities

AIA Committee on Architecture for Education
http://network.aia.org/committeeonarchitectureforeducation/home/

U.S. Department of Education National Clearinghouse for Educational Facilities (NCEF)
http://www.ncef.org/safeschools/

U.S. Department of Education
http://www.ed.gov/

U.S. Department of Energy
http://energy.gov/

ADAPTIVE REUSE PROJECTS

....

Objectives

- Students will be able to explain and describe the value of existing buildings as a sustainable choice.

- Students will know what to do when working with a historic building using sustainable methods.

- Students will understand how building codes apply to an existing building with and without a change in use.

- Students will understand the additional layers of meaning that should be addressed when working with a historically significant property.

Overview

The nature of interior design is that the interior designer focuses on the inside of the building. This can be either an existing building or a new one. Each building that is constructed uses a tremendous amount of energy and resources. One of the first questions that should be asked when designing for sustainability is whether an existing building could be rehabilitated to suit the needs of the client. Cities and suburbs are filled with empty buildings. The federal government alone has 55,000 to 77,000 vacant properties (Chumley, 2013). According to the 2010 U.S. Census, the estimated number of abandoned properties was 19 million. Because of the embodied energy (the sum of all the energy it takes to produce a material) in these existing materials and buildings, they often provide a suitable alternative to new, sustainable construction. An argument can be made that the most sustainable building is one that already exits.

Factors to Assess

Several factors must be taken into consideration when dealing with any existing building. An assessment of the conditions should include a complete evaluation of age, materials, structural soundness, the need for experts (to make sure the proper approach is ultimately taken), and historical significance. Generally speaking, buildings can be divided into two categories: those over 50 years old and those less than 50 years old. In the United States, this is the first criterion the National Register of Historic Places uses to determine whether a building may be considered historic. Since many of today's historic buildings predate World War II (the early to mid-1940s) and the mass production of building materials, the materials in many historic buildings can usually be categorized in a few basic ways: stone, brick, concrete, glass, plaster and stucco, and wood. Even interior finishes in many historic buildings are quite basic— wood, plaster, linoleum, paint, and the limited use of wallpaper. Materials from buildings constructed between the mid-1940s through the 1970s are much more varied and may contain lead or asbestos (materials now known to be harmful to human health). Any building with paint applied prior to the 1970s will have lead (a component in paints before that time). A complete investigation of the existing materials and their conditions will inform any possible demolition, encapsulation, or removal strategies that may be required (if there is lead paint or asbestos, depending on the condition). In most cases, an architect or structural engineer will need to determine the structural soundness of an older building before any subsequent planning or work can be initiated.

Historically Significant Buildings

Other expert opinions might also be needed. For example, if the project is historically significant and an addition is proposed, an archeological assessment might be required. The archeological survey is required to determine whether the site has the potential to reveal pertinent historical information. New construction should not damage any potential artifacts. Additionally, paint experts, historic finish experts, landscape architects, and others might also be part of an initial assessment. Architectural historians can often provide the historical rationale needed to have a property listed on the National Register if this is a project goal. Listing on the National Register has been shown to increase the value of a property. In addition, listing a property on the National Register also makes it potentially eligible for a 20 percent tax credit. There are currently more than 88,000 properties listed on the National Register of Historic Places.

Buildings Less Than 50 Years Old

Buildings less than 50 years old generally have plumbing, electrical, and mechanical systems that will require some updating. The construction methods will be relatively consistent with today's standards. As previously mentioned, a designer needs to be aware of is the potential for asbestos and lead-based paint with this age of construction (prior to the 1970s).

Buildings Over 50 Years of Age

The state of and approach to historic buildings varies around the world. In the United States and Canada, the majority of the building stock has been constructed within the past 250 years; whereas, in Europe, buildings may date back several centuries. Depending on the country and locale, the appreciation of older buildings may vary. Approximately 6 percent of buildings in the United States were constructed prior to 1920. An additional 11 percent of (non-residential) buildings were built prior to 1950. By

far, the majority of buildings (roughly 50 percent) in the United States were constructed between the 1950s and the 1980s (Elephante, 2005).

Thus, in many cases, an existing building will be over 50 years old. Often, such a building might be considered historic. As previously mentioned, historically significant buildings require a different approach than other existing buildings. First, an expert should assess the building to determine whether it has historic significance for its architectural, social, cultural standing or an association with important people or events in history. Each U.S. state has a **State Historic Preservation Officer (SHPO)** who can assist a designer with this process and who will be able to identify architectural historians in the region. Depending on the historical significance of the property, various levels of intervention may be deemed appropriate: rehabilitation, restoration, preservation, and in rare cases, reconstruction. It is normally the owner of the building or property who commissions this type of work.

Historic Building Assessment

There are some fairly standard and somewhat prescribed ways of dealing with the documentation and assessment of historic buildings.

Historic Structures Report

Preservation Brief 43, produced by the Secretary of the Interior's Office, outlines the typical components of a **historic structures report**. Included in this document are the Developmental History and Treatment and Work Recommendations.

Part 1: Developmental History

The developmental history of a property includes all known historic background and the context of the building as well as a chronology of use, physical description and condition assessment, and an evaluation of the significance of the property.

Measuring and Photographic Documentation

The first requirement when working with a significant historic site is to document the property as it was first found. This is done through the use of extensive photography, note-taking, and assessment and measured drawings. United States Geological Survey (USGS) maps are often used in the process of identifying possible historic properties (older buildings show up as black dots, while newer ones are purple). SHPOs and the National Park Service's National Register use USGS maps to show the precise boundaries of national register properties. **Photogrammetry** can also be used to accurately document the façade of historic building or structure. Photogrammetry is the science of using photographs to make precise measurements.

Measured Drawings: HABS/HAER

Prior work conducted as a part of the Works Progress Administration (WPA) resulted in the first documentation of many historic properties during the 1930s. Programs such as the Historic American Building Survey (HABS) and Historic American Engineering Record (HAER) produced hundreds of detailed, measured drawings and survey reports including black-and-white, large-format images. This is an excellent repository of information and should be checked for many of the most significant historic properties predating the 1930s. Both collections are stored in the Library of Congress and have online search engines.

In addition to the HABS work, many states have conducted extensive surveys of their historic resources—usually by county or city/town. These surveys tend to be updated over time on a roughly 20-year rotation. Thus, these survey records provide another excellent source of information about existing historic buildings that should be consulted to form an accurate assessment of the building and to assist in the establishment of preservation zones. **Preservation zones** are areas of a property or building, or individual features of a property or building, that have been singled out for a specific preservation approach. For example, all the woodwork in a building might be identified for preservation, while cracked plaster is deemed to require rehabilitation. Historic photographs and recorded recollections are often included in these files. Historic images and recollections can be located in local libraries, historical societies, the SHPO offices, and sometimes the Library of Congress's HABS/HAER collections.

Understanding the Historic Context

Understanding the construction sequence through survey records, photographic documentation, and a site assessment can assist in forming a thorough understanding of the historic context. Once all existing records have been reviewed, a clearer image of the building's history is often revealed. This, in turn, informs any future interventions. Based on the research, a designer would interpret the building's interiors.

Part 2: Treatment and Work Recommendations

The second part of the historic structures report includes the historic preservation objectives, the work requirements, and recommendations with alternate approaches. This could be diagrammed as a preservation zone plan.

Levels of Intervention

Working with a historic preservation consultant or your state's historic preservation officer, a designer can begin to determine the appropriate level of intervention for the historic building. The team should use a preservation zone overlay to guide the design decisions. For example, the exterior might be identified as a preservation zone while the interior is an adaptive reuse zone. Important historic character-defining features such as stairways and mantels might also fall under a preservation approach.

Preservation places a high premium on the retention of all historic fabric (materials in the building) through conservation, maintenance, and repair. It reflects a building's continuum over time, through successive occupancies, and the respectful changes and alterations that have been made thus far.

Rehabilitation/adaptive reuse projects are the most common. This is also the approach an interior designer is likely to take with a building located in a historic district, downtown Main Street community, or other historic building commonly found across the United States. With this approach, the historic fabric is retained as much as possible. The Secretary of the Interior's Standards recommend new uses that are deemed compatible with the existing building. New designs should maintain existing materials, features, spaces, and spatial relationships. The Secretary of the Interior oversees the National Park Service, the government agency that manages and holds the **National Register of Historic Places**. The National Register was authorized by the National Historic Preservation Act of 1966.

The Secretary of the Interior has 10 well-defined standards for all levels of intervention: preservation, stabilization, reconstruction, and rehabilitation. **Stabilization** is the act of keeping a building as it is while trying to resist further deterioration. **Reconstruction** involves rebuilding a history building for archeological evidence and archival records. In order to receive state or federal tax credits, designers must submit their work to show compliance with these standards. The documents are first reviewed by the SHPO and then forwarded to the national level if Federal Historic Tax Credits are requested. Some states offer their own historic tax credits in addition to those available at the federal level.

The complete **Standards for Rehabilitation** are as follows:

1. A property will be used as it was historically or be given a new use that requires minimal change to its distinctive materials, features, spaces, and spatial relationships.
2. The historic character of a property will be retained and preserved. The removal of distinctive materials or alteration of features, spaces, and spatial relationships that characterize a property will be avoided.
3. Each property will be recognized as a physical record of its time, place, and use. Changes that create a false sense of historical development, such as adding conjectural features or elements from other historic properties, will not be undertaken.
4. Changes to a property that have acquired historic significance in their own right will be retained and preserved.
5. Distinctive materials, features, finishes, and construction techniques or examples of craftsmanship that characterize a property will be preserved.
6. Deteriorated historic features will be repaired rather than replaced. Where the severity of deterioration requires replacement of a distinctive feature, the new feature will match the old in design, color, texture, and where possible, materials. Replacement of missing features will be substantiated by documentary and physical evidence.
7. Chemical or physical treatments, if appropriate, will be undertaken using the gentlest means possible. Treatments that cause damage to historic materials will not be used.
8. Archeological resources will be protected and preserved in place. If such

resources must be disturbed, mitigation measures will be undertaken.

9. New additions, exterior alterations, or related new construction will not destroy historic materials, features, and spatial relationships that characterize the property. The new work shall be differentiated from the old and will be compatible with the historic materials, features, size, scale and proportion, and massing to protect the integrity of the property and its environment.

10. New additions and adjacent or related new construction will be undertaken in such a manner that, if removed in the future, the essential form and integrity of the historic property and its environment would be unimpaired (NPS, 2011).

Guidelines

The National Park Service also provides extensive guidelines for how to apply the Secretary of the Interior's Standards for Rehabilitation. This guidance is divided into the following categories: choosing the rehabilitation treatment; identifying, retaining, and preserving historic materials and features; protecting and maintaining historic materials and features; repairing historic materials and features; replacing deteriorated historic materials and features; designing for the replacement of missing historic features; creating alterations or additions for the new use; and energy efficiency, accessibility considerations, and safety code considerations.

There are currently 47 preservation briefs available on the National Park Services website (nps.gov) that discuss many aspects of dealing with historic buildings and materials. The range of materials spans from exterior stone, brick, and clay tile roofs to interior finishes such as ceramic tile, historic plaster, and different kinds of windows and doors. Other preservation briefs discuss problems that are common to historic buildings, such as graffiti removal, paint problems, and the dangers of abrasive cleaning.

The Intersection of Sustainability and Historic Preservation Work

Sustainable preservation has received a great deal of attention in the past decade. The **Association for Preservation Technology (APT)** was originally founded in 1968 by preservationists from Canada and the United States. In 2004, several members of the APT formed a group to study the synergies and possible conflicts between sustainability and historic preservation as approaches toward building. These efforts resulted in several publications from 2005 to 2007, as well as a renewed interest in the topic by the National Trust for Historic Preservation. A list of many of these can be found at the end of this chapter. A recent publication produced by the Whole Building Design Guide Historic Preservation Subcommittee of the National Institute of Building Sciences (WBDG, 2010) outlines five arenas of sustainable preservation: sustainable sites, water efficiency, energy and atmosphere, materials and resources, and indoor environmental quality. These coincide with LEED Green Building Rating Systems categories and include several of the individual point indicators as contained in the LEED systems.

"Historic Preservation and Green Building: A Lasting Relationship," (Roberts, 2007), outlines the synergies between historic preservation and green building, again following the LEED Green Building Rating System model. The article addresses the question, "What's green about historic buildings?" According to the authors:

> Many historic buildings can contain materials and features that are valuable from several perspectives: the energy and materials expenditure that reuse of existing materials displaces; the architectural features and workmanship that

may be impossible to replace; and the societal value of maintaining artifacts.

Common benefits of reusing existing buildings include embodied energy, material reuse, societal value, artistic value, historic value, and high **thermal mass** (high volumetric heat capacity). Common problems cited by opponents of building reuse include leaky windows, energy-efficiency problems/high energy costs, roof problems (the addition of green roofs and solar panels), insulation concerns, and lead paint and asbestos content.

Several of the concerns about making historic buildings more sustainable were addressed by Santa Fe architect Victoria Jacobson at the 2007 American Institute of Architects Convention in San Antonio, Texas. In this presentation, Jacobson exploded three common myths: historic buildings cannot be made green, replacing historic windows will guarantee lower heating bills, and the Secretary's Standards are in direct conflict with green building guidelines such as LEED.

According to Jacobson, historic buildings can be made green by addressing several issues: building envelope, windows, plumbing fixtures, thermal comfort, historic light fixtures, appliances, and human behavior. The envelope can be sealed and insulated (appropriately with regard to historic fabric). Windows obviously contribute to natural ventilation and daylighting. Since many historic buildings did not contain plumbing fixtures, any existing ones can easily be retrofitted with low-water-use fixtures. Again, many historic buildings did not originally contain heating or air conditioning systems; these can therefore also be upgraded to efficient models. Historic light fixtures can be wired or rewired for LEDs or compact fluorescent lamps.

Replacing historic windows is in direct conflict with the Secretary of the Interior's Standards, as this removes historic fabric and potentially changes the appearance of the exterior of the building. More importantly, however, Jacobson points out that the majority of heat loss actually occurs through the ceiling in most buildings. Interior and historically sensitive exterior-type storm windows for historic buildings have been in use for many years and significantly reduce air infiltration around the windows. Preservation Brief 3 is dedicated to exploring energy efficiency in historic buildings.

Finally, the Secretary of the Interior's Standards serve as a reminder to designers and contractors to maintain historic fabric and spaces. Sustainable interventions can be made without significantly compromising these goals. Many historic materials already meet sustainability goals and should be left in place and cleaned with the gentlest means possible. Further, additional weather stripping and other nonintrusive measures can help make a building more energy efficient.

Building Code Considerations

The *International Building Code (IBC) 2009,* like its predecessors, includes a chapter dedicated to existing buildings, which addresses additions, alterations, and repairs to these structures. It also covers the use of fire escapes, changes in occupancy classification, historic buildings (defined as on the National Register of Historic Places or eligible for listing by some approved program), moved buildings, and most importantly, compliance alternatives. This allows for the health, safety, and welfare of the public through alternatives that might not meet the current wording of the IBC but that can help to preserve the historic fabric of a building. A series of tables and factors are provided for determining egress, dead-end corridors, sprinkler requirements and several other pertinent factors. Finally, the document also includes a summary sheet, Table 3412.7, which allows the building designer to demonstrate the safety of the existing building design renovation. The local building official is responsible for a complete review before issuing a building permit allowing construction to commence.

Benefits Associated with the Reuse of a Building

The most commonly cited benefit of using an existing building is the reduction of virgin material use and the capture of embodied energy contained by the existing materials. When approached from a life-cycle costing view, this makes building reuse economically attractive. Other reasons why building reuse is advantageous include the use of traditional building practices, a reduced carbon footprint, and the sustainable quality of the existing materials.

Life-Cycle Costing

Life-cycle costing is a relatively new way of looking at buildings and materials. Rather than looking simply at initial construction costs compared to one-time rehabilitation costs, the life-cycle approach takes into account all of the financial factors that go into making a building or renovating. According to businessdictionary.com, life-cycle costing is the "sum of all recurring and one-time (non-recurring) costs over the full life span or a specified period of a good, service, structure, or system. It includes purchase price, installation cost, operating costs, maintenance and upgrade costs, and remaining (residual or salvage) value at the end of ownership or its useful life."

A life-cycle assessment of a material seeks to account for the cost of a material during its entire life cycle. The cost of growing, harvesting, manufacturing,

installing, transporting, demolishing, and disposing of the material are all factored into the equation. An existing building has its materials in place—in other words, much of the life-cycle cost has already been expended and does not therefore need to be factored in anew. Furthermore, through continued use, the life cycle itself is extended.

Carbon Footprint

Attention to the carbon footprint of a building has resulted in several new measures in the building industry, such as the desire to produce carbon neutral buildings. According to the website Carbon Footprint, "A **carbon footprint** is a measure of the impact our activities have on the environment, and in particular climate change. It relates to the amount of greenhouse gases produced in our day-to-day lives through burning fossil fuels for electricity, heating, and transportation, etc."

The desire to reduce the carbon footprint also supports the reuse of an existing building and vice versa. According to preservation architect and director of Goody Clancy, Jean Caroon, renovation uses 70 percent less carbon than new construction (Caroon, 2010, 49).

Embodied Energy

According to Canadian Architect. com, there are two forms of **embodied energy**: **initial embodied energy** and **recurring bodied energy**. "The initial embodied energy in buildings represents the non-renewable energy consumed in the acquisition of raw materials, their processing, manufacturing, transportation to site, and construction." This includes both direct (energy to transport) and indirect (energy to manufacture) sources. By contrast, the recurring embodied energy in buildings is the energy used in the maintenance process once a building is constructed—-to maintain and repair it or replace materials during the building's lifetime. Embodied energy is measured in terms of the energy per unit of material (joules per weight). In a study by Cole and Kernan (1996), the amount of embodied energy associated with different parts of the building are as follows:

Envelope	26%
Structure	24%
Finishes	13%
Site Work	6%
Services	24%

Although low to begin with and as would be expected, the finishes account for the biggest recurring embodied energy increase over the life of the building.

By their very nature, existing buildings have a high embodied energy.

Sustainable, Locally Available Materials

As mentioned previously, most historic buildings were constructed from all-natural materials such as wood, stone, brick, plaster, and stucco. These materials were often harvested on-site, nearby, or made on-site. For example, bricks were often fired on-site from indigenous clay. Limekilns provided raw materials for plaster. Local stone was harvested for foundations and decorative work, and local timber was used for framing and floors.

Historic building traditions relied on local construction techniques and locally available materials. It was not until World War II that building materials were standardized and became widely available to be shipped anywhere. As such, historic buildings tend to contain a higher percentage of locally available materials.

Local Traditions

Historic buildings also relied on craftsmen to perform several of the tasks associated with construction. For example, stone masons and brick masons were responsible for masonry construction, woodcrafters made the trim work, plasterers did the plasterwork. As construction has become more streamlined, many of these craftsmen have disappeared and, with them, the art of their respective trades.

Step-by-Step Guide

The following step-by-step process describes some of the unique features that might be added to the design process when working with a historic building.

Inspiration and Conceptual Approach

The historic building itself often provides a great source of inspiration for a potential intervention. Character-defining features, spatial configurations, size, shape, and form can all contribute to a successful design sensitively executed.

Program
Ideally, the program of a historic building rehabilitation will be the same as or similar to the original use of the building.

Precedent Studies
Historic preservation has been used around the world for centuries; it has also been commonly practiced in the United States since the 1960s. Therefore, numerous examples and case studies can be used to guide a particular restoration project.

Evidence-Based Design/ Information Gathering/Research
Much of the evidence-based-design approach to sustainable design within a historic project should be guided by the Secretary of the Interior's Standards and recommendations for interpretation, the Association for Preservation Technology, and the National Trust for Historic Preservation. All three organizations have studied the compatibilities between historic preservation work and sustainability and provide guidelines

and useful case studies that can help to inform designers' decisions and subsequent work.

Schematic Design

The preservation zones already established during the initial project programming should guide initial studies in both plan and elevation. The preservation zones will have identified character-defining spaces, extant materials (existing) to be retained, and other key directions for any design intervention (design ideas).

Design Development: Entering the Existing Building Measurements into the Computer Model

One of the biggest challenges with many historic buildings is that the walls are not truly square. The primary reason for this was that builders did not have the same tools and technology as they do today and all work was being done by hand. Hence, once entered into the computer, field measurements can result in an out-of-square building. Additionally, ceiling heights, window sizes, doors, and other features might vary from the standard kit of parts available in a computer program requiring all to be custom drawn.

Production Drawings

In addition to the typically required construction documents and specifications that all projects require, work on a historic building usually entails many custom details. Detailed drawings about how new work will attach and impact the existing building is a key component of this type of project. Under the direction of the Secretary of the Interior's Standards, the preference for new work is that it be potentially reversible. The reason work should be reversible is that other interventions can then be taken in the future that might take a different approach. An example of this was the removal of a later addition to the Meyer May house by Frank Lloyd Wright during the most recent restoration. The lack of permanence in intervention requires a different level of detail than a more permanent solution might. All additions and changes need to be removable. A new ceiling for example, might simply adhere to the original and attached so that it could easily be removed at a later time. (It should be noted that changes in ceiling height are normally not recommended).

Student Approaches to Adaptive Reuse Design

The primary issue when students work with historically significant buildings is the understanding that this type of building is more than a simple building shell. The retention of historic fabric, character-defining spaces, and interior materials can pose a significant challenge to those who are accustomed to gutting the interior of the building.

Student Project Examples

The first project to be discussed is the A. D. German Warehouse. This project, designed by Frank Lloyd Wright (1914–1917; 1934), poses several challenges. First, the floor-to-ceiling height is 9 feet, without any plumbing or mechanical chases (boxed out areas to run supply and return) and limited surface-mounted electrical wiring. Second, the interior of the building, although designed by Wright, was never completed. A second design for the interior produced 20 years later gives some clues as to Wright's vision for the interior, but again, it was never built.

The second case study consists of a historic spa healing facility. Several extant historic structures contribute to the site including a ca. 1820 hotel and later hotel lodgings as well as several archeological sites (including the site of a second hotel built in 1890 hotel that burned to the ground). Of particular importance at this property is the former, albeit brief, association with African American history in the southern part of the United States following emancipation.

The final case study, Old Sweet Springs, like the first property, has little extant interior historic fabric. Designed in the style of Thomas Jefferson, the classically inspired building features three original porticoes and a fourth bay portico that was added in the 1970s. As was the case with Yellow Sulphur Springs, several buildings contribute to the historic complex, including four Italianate-era houses and a springhouse. During its 200-year history, the interior of the main building has been altered many times yet the fireplaces and some interior partitions remain.

All three properties provide a series of somewhat typical challenges presented to an interior designer by a historic building. These obstacles include how to integrate modern plumbing, electrical, and mechanical systems; how to work within the existing spatial configurations presented by the buildings; how to retain the sense of place for which the site is revered; and how to make a once-abandoned property vital again. On a more conceptual level, these projects provide a context for a rich conversation about society and culture, history and preservation, and the politics of the collective memory of a place.

All three buildings are listed on the National Register of Historic Places in the United States and should therefore follow the Secretary of the Interior's Standards for Historic Preservation: Adaptive Reuse when working on a historic building listed on the National Register if the desire is to retain the National Register listing. Further, if historic tax credits are desired, the Secretary's Standards must be followed. Overall, an understanding of the varying levels of intervention prefaced the approach to all these projects: stabilization, preservation, rehabilitation, and restoration. Thus students had to determine what the contributing historic features were and then establish preservation zones. The goal was to preserve important character-defining features while designing for a new use.

Project 1

Project Name: A. D. German Warehouse

Date: ca. 1917

Designer: Frank Lloyd Wright

Description: three-story brick warehouse with a poured concrete cornice

Although the building had been used strictly as a cold storage warehouse, Wright did complete designs that used the building as a restaurant on the first floor, gallery on the second floor, and apartments on the third and fourth floor. This was the program suggested to the students for this project. The program allowed for interpretation about how to best manage multiple functions within the space that might make the biggest contribution to Richland Center, Wisconsin, a town of 25,000 where the project was located.

The first design shows a typical way that a student approached the Wright building. Rather than engaging the building in a dramatically new aesthetic, most students chose to follow a Wright-style approach. For example, in this instance, there are several Wright-inspired artifacts such as lamps and accessories. However, when the programmatic requirements of the apartment require multiple smaller spaces, the student defaults to a more generic apartment design with little or no Wright references. The resulting design could be in any contemporary building. It is difficult to see that this might be a Frank Lloyd Wright building simply from the interior imagery. In order to let in more natural light, the student chose to cut through the building with a central atrium. This was also a default approach taken by most students to solve the problem of dark interior spaces with low ceilings and minimal windows. Despite the low ceiling height, this student chose

Figure 7.1 Natalie Brayley Long, A. D. German Warehouse: 3D view of café

Figure 7.2 Natalie Brayley Long, A. D. German Warehouse: 3D view of gallery

Figure 7.3 Natalie Brayley Long, A. D. German Warehouse: 3D view of museum shop

Figure 7.4 Natalie Brayley Long, A. D. German Warehouse: 3D view of apartment shared study area

to articulate the ceiling with lowered sections in wood and a coffered material.

Project 2

Project Name: Yellow Sulphur Springs

Date: ca. 1820

Designer: Unknown

Description:
The second project dates to the late 18th century and has received little attention in the past 75 years. As a result, it faces many issues of stabilization—windows need to be sealed and the roof needs to be repaired to prevent further leakage into the building prior to any potential use. Stabilizaton refers to making a building safe from further deterioration. Yet, most of the historic fabric still exists both on the interior and exterior, albeit in bad condition in many cases. The main challenge this project offers is demolition by neglect. The main hotel building—for which the site is listed on the National Register—is both abandoned and unused. The family that owns the property uses rooms that do not have leaks for storage.

A second important challenge posed by this project relates to its unique history. During the 18th and 19th centuries, the Yellow Sulphur Springs, in Christiansburg, VA, comprised one of the many stops along the historic springs tour. During the hot summer months many people would travel from spring to spring for the recreation and healing properties of the springs. Following the emancipation of slaves in the late 19th century, the Yellow Sulphur Springs became a destination for African Americans during segregation in the South. In 1926, a group of 10 prominent black businessmen purchased the Springs, which catered specifically to blacks between 1926 and 1929 (HALS NO. VA-55, 2011). Thus, it became a resort serving a clientele previously excluded from "taking the waters" (drinking or bathing in mineral waters from the springs for medicinal purposes). A major question for the students became how to resolve the contradiction embodied by this site, which housed officers of the Confederacy both during and following the Civil War and then later African Americans during segregation.

Does society (and consequently designers) have a responsibility to preserve this piece of early-20th-century African American history as well as a rare surviving example of a 19th century frame hotel? How does an intervention tell the history of the building?

The approach taken in this project was to contrast the new interiors with the old building. The materials, furnishings, light fixtures, and finishes project a contemporary spa interior that could be found almost anywhere. In the restaurant view, vestiges of the historic building show original two-panel double doors with transoms. Aside from an occasional piece of the original building, the interiors are entirely new and contemporary. This particular student chose to create a third

period of significance (contemporary) in the evolution of the building rather than to deal with the contradictory historical periods of the building's rich history. Although the interior solution is aesthetically pleasing, it does not capture the spirit of the Georgian building or the richness of the site's history.

Figure 7.5 Becca Crockett, Yellow Sulphur Springs: 3D view of restaurant

Figure 7.6 Becca Crockett, Yellow Sulphur Springs: 3D view of guest room

Figure 7.7 Becca Crockett, Yellow Sulphur Springs: 3D view of check-in

Figure 7.8 Becca Crockett, Yellow Sulphur Springs: 3D view of massage area hallway

Project 3

Project Name: Old Sweet Springs

Date: ca. 1823

Designer: Thomas Jefferson or one of Jefferson's workmen

Description:
This historic hotel building designed in the style of Thomas Jefferson and has been substantially altered during its 200-year history. Little, if any, of the interior historic fabric remains. The primary challenge of this project was to react to the heavy-handed renovations of the building; it could potentially be delisted from the National Register for these changes. In the 1970s, the State of West Virginia owned the building and added a fourth portico. In the 1980s, the Sweet Springs Water Company added additions to the rear of the building to accommodate the water bottling operations. The entire interior has been gutted, with some notable exceptions. Several interior fireplaces, one interior stair, and some interior doors remain.

Thus, students were challenged to answer the question, what is the value of the building as it stands today?

Oddly, the building with the least amount of interior materials and detail from which the students could work provided the most successful solutions in terms of working within the historic context. This student project demonstrates a clear blending of the historic building with both transitional and in some instances, modern whimsical furnishings. The proposal maintains the plaster walls, existing trim and mantels, and historic wood floors. The furnishings complement the space and include contemporary pieces such as a modernized four-poster bed and industrial designer, Phillipe Stark's "Ghost Chair" in the main dining room. Historically inspired new additions include the interior French doors and fanlights that are clearly new but are also compatible with the architecture.

Figure 7.9 Kelly Preston, Old Sweet Springs: 3D view of bathroom

Figure 7.10 Kelly Preston, Old Sweet Springs: 3D view of bedroom

Figure 7.11 Kelly Preston, Old Sweet Springs: 3D view of dining room

Discussion

The larger questions of the importance of history and the implications of the changing interior arise from these three examples. In the United States, the theory of historic preservation has largely been limited to a discussion about significance of the property and resulting levels of intervention on a very technical level. Bridging the gap between these two discussions has been less developed. On the preservationists' side, anything with the potential to reveal future significance might be retained. For example, it is not uncommon to require an archeological assessment of a historic property prior to allowing new additions or construction on the site. The State Historic Preservation Officers and National Park Service (keeper of the National Register) can threaten removal from the National Historic Landmarks and State Registers for failure to comply with the Secretary's Standards for Historic Preservation. On the design and construction side, the issues of use, building codes, accessibility, and detailing drive much of the design process. Where, then, are the larger questions about social and cultural meaning of the place and how a new intervention fits within this?

The intention of having students work with this project type is to explore the need for a deeper understanding of these issues. As a conceptual launching point, the historic building is not in a vacuum but rather provides a series of meanings, methods, and potential intervention approaches.

Firm Project Examples of Adaptive Reuse

While many firms design within existing buildings, there are a few firms that specialize in historic preservation and adaptive reuse projects.

SPECTRUM Design PC

Spectrum Design, located in Roanoke, Virginia, was incorporated in 2000, when Spectrum Engineers and Echols-Sparger Architects merged. This relatively small firm has 30 employees and focuses on several areas of practice including historic preservation and sustainability.

Meridium World Headquarters

Spectrum Design was retained for the adaptive reuse of a 100-year-old building located in Roanoke, Virginia, for Meridium, a global leader in software and consulting. The design solution emphasizes the historic warehouse materials including heavy timber framing, exposed brick walls, and wide plan wood flooring. New elements introduced into the space contrast with the old and are clearly new interventions such as the aluminum staircase.

Figure 7.12
Spectrum Design, Meridium World Headquarters: Plan

1 VESTIBULE/ RECEPTION
2 EXECUTIVE OFFICE
3 OFFICE
4 OFFICE SUITE
5 CONFERENCE
6 BREAK
7 COPY
8 SUPPORT

Figure 7.13
Spectrum Design,
Meridium World
Headquarters:
Exterior view

Figure 7.14
Spectrum Design,
Meridium World
Headquarters: Front
desk

Figure 7.15
Spectrum Design,
Meridium World
Headquarters:
Corridor

Figure 7.16
Spectrum Design, Meridium World Headquarters: Meeting space (existing elevator gate at the rear)

Figure 7.17
Spectrum Design, Meridium World Headquarters: Conference room showing existing brick walls and wood flooring

Figure 7.18
Spectrum Design, Meridium World Headquarters: Lounge area

Figure 7.19
Spectrum Design,
Meridium World
Headquarters: View
into conference
room showing
retained historic
doors

Figure 7.20
Spectrum Design,
Meridium World
Headquarters:
Employee café area

Access Advertising

A Streamline Moderne building once
used as a car dealership provided the
new building for Access Advertising.
Located in downtown Roanoke, the
one-story brick building was retrofitted
with HVAC and interior energy-efficient
lighting while the original storefront and
architecture were retained.

Blacksburg Municipal Annex Building

Like the advertising agency building,
the Blacksburg annex used a former car
dealership, in this case the 1925 home
of the Blacksburg Motor Company.
In addition to retaining the historic
character of the building and respecting
the Secretary of the Interior's Standards,

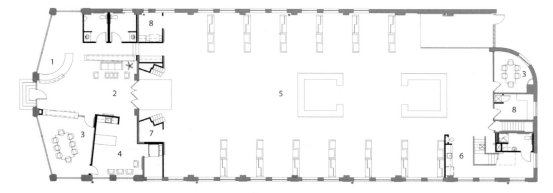

Figure 7.21 Spectrum Design, Access, Floor Plan

1 RECEPTION
2 LOBBY
3 CONFERENCE
4 LOUNGE
5 OPEN OFFICE
6 BREAK
7 STORAGE
8 SUPPORT

Figure 7.22
Spectrum Design,
Access, "Bullpen"
(open office area)
view

Figure 7.23
Spectrum Design,
Access: Lobby

Figure 7.24
Spectrum Design,
Access: Mezzanine

Figure 7.25
Spectrum Design,
Access: Lounge area

Figure 7.26
Spectrum Design,
Access: Conference
room

the project has also received a LEED Platinum rating from the U.S. Green Building Council. The exterior of the building underwent a careful restoration including the reconstruction of original window mullion patterns.

Archdale Hall

Archdale Hall, located on the campus of Guilford College in Greensboro, North Carolina, provides a more historically inspired interior renovation than the previous examples. For this project, the 120-year-old building was renovated to be more energy efficient and maintained its original historic interior. All interior walls and doors, including the transoms above them, were retained. One connecting doorway was enclosed and a shower was added to the bathroom. All historic

woodwork, stairs, and flooring were painted and refinished.

Discussion

As with the student examples, this range of projects show a variety of elements integrated into the sustainable design and historic building design process. The LEED Green Building Rating Systems figured prominently into providing guidelines for energy efficiency, reduced water use, and improved lighting efficiencies. The projects exhibit a sensitive approach to the historic fabric wherein character-defining spaces, materials, and methods were retained to the largest extent possible. New materials are clearly distinguished from the old and most of the work is potentially reversible.

Figure 7.27
Spectrum Design, Blacksburg Municipal Annex Building: Plan

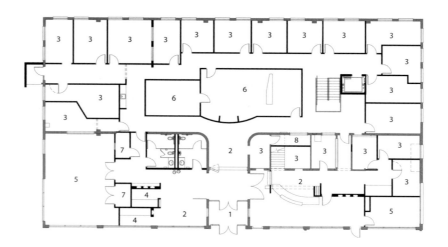

1 VESTIBULE
2 RECEPTION/LOBBY
3 OFFICE
4 TOUCHDOWN
5 CONFERENCE
6 WORKROOM
7 STORAGE
8 SUPPORT

Figure 7.28
Spectrum Design, Blacksburg Municipal Annex Building: Exterior ciew

Figure 7.29
Spectrum Design,
Blacksburg
Municipal Annex
Building: Entry area

Figure 7.30
Spectrum Design,
Blacksburg
Municipal Annex
Building: Front desk

Figure 7.31
Spectrum Design,
Blacksburg
Municipal Annex
Building: Conference
room

Figure 7.32
Spectrum Design,
Blacksburg
Municipal Annex
Building: Stairway

Figure 7.33
Spectrum Design,
Archdale Building:
Plan

1 LOBBY
2 OFFICE
3 STORAGE
4 SUPPORT
5 RECYCLING

Figure 7.34
Spectrum Design,
Archdale Building:
Main stair hall

Figure 7.35
Spectrum Design,
Archdale Building:
Office

Discussion Questions and Exercises

1. What are the key considerations you must first deal with prior to beginning design work on a historic building?
2. What types of consultants might you need to work on an art deco-era theater rehabilitation? And why?

Key Terms

adaptive reuse

Association for Preservation Technology (APT)

carbon footprint

embodied energy: initial and recurring

historic structures report

life-cycle cost

National Register of Historic Places

photogrammetry

preservation

preservation zone

reconstruction

rehabilitation

State Historic Preservation Officer (SHPO)

stabilization

Standards for Rehabilitation

thermal mass

Sources

Business Dictionary. Accessed on January 11, 2011. http://www.businessdictionary.com/definition/life-cycle-cost.html.

Carbon Footprint. Accessed on March 26, 2014, http://www.nature.org/greenliving/carboncalculator/.

Caroon, J. 2010. Sustainable Preservation. Hoboken, NJ: John Wiley and Sons.

Chumley, C. 2013. "Federal Government spends $8 billion—on empty buildings," Washington Times, March 27. Accessed July 1. http://www.washingtontimes.com/news/2013/mar/27/federal-government-spends-8-billion-empty-building/.

Cole, R. and O. Kernan. 1996. "Life-Cycle in Office Buildings." Building and Environment 31 (4): 307–17.

Dictionary Babylon. Accessed January 11, 2011. http://dictionary.babylon.com/embodied%20energy/.

Elefante, C. 2005. "Historic Preservation and Sustainable Development: Lots to Learn, Lots to Teach," APT Bulletin 34(4): 53–54.

Environmental Building News. 2007. "Historic Preservation and Green Building: A Lasting Relationship." Environmental Building News, January. Accessed July 1. www.preservationnation.org.

Frey, P. 2007. "Making the Case: Historic Preservation as Sustainable Development" (draft white paper, unpublished). Accessed July 1. www.preservationnation.org.

"Green Building Practices and the Secretary of the Interior's Standards for Historic Preservation: A White Paper prepared in advance of the 2008 Pocantico Symposium," http://www.mdf.org/documents/HistoricPreservationasSustainableDevelopment.pdf.

Jackson, V. 2007. "Is Historic Preservation Green?" Presented at the 2007 AIA Convention. San Antonio, TX.

National Park Service. 2011. "Guidelines for Rehabilitation," Accessed January 11. http://www.nps.gov/history/hps/tps/standguide/rehab/rehab_standards.htm

National Park Service Website on Sustainability. Accessed January 11 http://www.nps.gov/tps/sustainability.htm.

National Trust for Historic Preservation. 2013. "Position Statement: Deconstruction." Accessed July 1. http://www.preservationnation.org/information-center/sustainable-communities/additional-resources/Deconstruction-Position-Paper-NTHP.pdf

National Trust for Historic Preservation. 2009. "Position Statement: Fostering Renewable Energy Development and Historic Preservation as All Scales." Accessed July 1, 2013. http://www.preservationnation.org/information-center/sustainable-communities/additional-resources/Deconstruction-Position-Paper-NTHP.pdf

National Trust for Historic Preservation. 2013. "Position Statement: Weatherizing Existing Windows." Accessed July 1. http://www.preservationnation.org/information-center/sustainable-communities/buildings/weatherization/windows/#.UzMFd_aitZE.

National Trust for Historic Preservation. 2007. "The Greenest Building Is... One That Is Already Built." *Forum Journal* 1(4): 26–38.

Nelson, A. 2006. "The Boom To Come: America Circa 2030," *Architect* 95(11): 93–97.

Roberts, Tristan. 2007. "Historic Preservation and Green Building: A Lasting Relationship," *Environmental Building News*. Accessed July 1, 2013. http://www.buildinggreen.com/auth/article.cfm/2007/1/2/Historic-Preservation-and-Green-Building-A-Lasting-Relationship/.

Slaton, D. *Preservation Brief 43: The Preparation and Use of Historic Structures Reports*. Available at http://www.nps.gov/tps/how-to-preserve/briefs/43-historic-structure-reports.htm

WBDG Historic Preservation Subcommittee. 2010 "Sustainable Historic Preservation." WBDG.org. Last updated Dec. 2, 2013. www.wbdg.org/resources/sustainable_hp.php.

Additional Resources

Sustainable Preservation

Cavallo, J. 2005. "Capturing Energy-Efficient Opportunities in Historic Homes," *APT Bulletin* 34(4): 19–24.

Jackson, M. 2005 "Embodied Energy and Historic Preservation," *APT Bulletin* 34(4): 347–52.

Lesak, J. 2005. "APT and Sustainability: The Halifax Symposium," *APT Bulletin* 34(4): 3–4.

SINGLE-FAMILY RESIDENTIAL PROJECTS

Objectives

- Students will be able to identify the latest sustainable design trends impacting single-family house design.

- Students will understand the issues designers must confront in the single-family house design market.

- Students will have knowledge of common programs for sustainable houses.

- Students will learn how others have approached the design of the single-family house.

Overview

Single-family house design is often outside the realm of the professionally trained designer in the United States. According to recent accounts, trained professionals design fewer than 10 percent of single-family houses in the United States. There are many reasons for this, not the least of which is that in a capitalist society, there is not money to be made through the custom design of every home. The rise of the National Homebuilder's Association beginning in the 1940s coupled with the demand for single-family houses led to a housing market driven by non-designer individuals. Regardless, designers can impact this market in many ways. Interior designers specifically have the knowledge to assist people in using their space more efficiently, thus reducing the need for additions and larger houses. Designers can also provide universal design for clients, making homes more accessible to all. The need for accessible spaces expands well beyond the aging, to the many returning military veterans with war-related disabilities. A designer must now ask, how can I make living spaces for all people of all sizes, ages, and abilities?

Current Issues in Single-Family Residential Design

Single-family houses in the United States face several issues: an aging population, the need for smaller and more affordable houses, and the need for more accessible housing.

Aging in Place

The U.S. population is aging. The most recent census (2010) indicated that approximately 13 percent of the 281,421,906 people in the United States were over 65 years of age. The U.S. Department of Health and Human Services Administration on Aging's (AOA) has developed a complete profile of older Americans, which is available on the organization's website. The over-65 population has increased by 15.3 percent since 2000, and those who will reach 65 in the next two decades will result in a 31-percent increase. Additionally, the average life expectancy of this group's members is 83.8 years. This has profound implications for housing, including the need for living all on one-level, ramps, larger accessible bathrooms, and accessible doors throughout the house. The AOA found that almost half of women age 75 and older live alone.

The current aging population is different from their predecessors. According to transgenerational.org, baby boomers (those born between 1946 and 1964) exercise twice as much as their parents did and will continue to do so as they age. This is relevant because, as a result, they are in better shape and will live on their own longer, possibly even until death. Further, 40 percent of the members of this age group have their own computer and are expected to continue to work at home following retirement. The combination of a more active lifestyle coupled with the tendency to continue working at home demonstrates a need for independence and a desire to age at home rather than in an institutional setting. It also has implications for specific spatial needs in the design of the home. The standard size of interior door is 30 inches wide and bathrooms can be as small as 5 feet x 8 feet—neither of these can accommodate a person in a wheelchair. Standard house construction in the United States is rarely accessible to those with a disability without some modification.

Accessibility and Military Veterans

As previously mentioned, the need for accessible housing extends beyond the elderly. One organization dedicated to helping former members of the military with their housing needs is Homes for Our Troops, a nonprofit founded in 2004. Returning soldiers face many health challenges—severe brain trauma, lost limbs, and psychiatric issues.

Smaller, More Efficient Housing

The size of the average house in the United States has risen fairly consistently from 1,500 square feet in the early 1970s to more than 2,000 square feet in 2010. Across the nation, the largest homes tend to be in the Northeast (2,336 square feet) and the most compact in the Midwest (2,001 square feet). Despite a decrease in size between 2007 and 2009, the median square footage was again on the rise in 2010, according to the U.S. Census. Concurrently, the size of the average family and household has gone down. ("Family" refers to household members that are related, while "households" include non-related people living together.) In 1949, the average family had 2.39 members, and the average household 3.42. As of 2003, these numbers were down to 2.18 family members and 2.57 household members. Although up slightly in the 2010 census, (2.58 people in a household) the numbers remain at an all time low. (U.S. Census 2003, Table HH).

Despite these trends, some designers have started to focus on reducing the size of the house, as seen in the work of Minnesota Architect, Sarah Susanka with the *Not So Big House*. Trained designers know how to reduce square footage through better and more efficient layouts.

Sustainability

As consumers seek to lower their own global footprint and do their part to reduce global warming, several programs have been developed to assist them. Consumers want to have houses that are more energy efficient, as evidenced by the increased number of energy audits, energy-efficient window replacements, and energy-efficient appliances. A few different programs—including Energy Star and LEED for Homes—specifically address sustainability issues related to single-family houses.

Energy Star

As a joint program of the U.S. Environmental Protection Agency and U.S. Department of Energy, Energy Star (established in 1992) provides homeowners with resources to help them save energy. The website, www. energystar.gov, provides information on home improvement and new home construction as well as products. The Energy Star label signals to consumers that that specific appliance will save energy. According to Energy Star, replacing an older heating and cooling system with Energy Star-rated equipment will save the average homeowner $115 or more a year.

LEED for Homes

As is the case with the other LEED Green Building Rating Systems, LEED for Homes provides a checklist of energy-saving and green building techniques that can assist the builder and homeowner in creating a more sustainable house design. All the LEED rating systems include points for a sustainable site, water use, materials and resources, energy and atmosphere, indoor environmental quality, and innovation. The most current version of LEED for

Homes is 2008. LEED for Neighborhood Development (2009) addresses the single-family house on the subdivision scale of development. Both rating systems can be found on the usgbc.org website under the LEED tab.

Rethinking How We Live

One of the most significant issues that has not been readily addressed by today's homebuilding industry is the changing demographics of the family. There are more single-parent families in the United States than ever in history. Further, recent economic challenges (for example, an estimated 4 million home foreclosures between 2008 and 2012 and high unemployment among recent college graduates—as much as 50 percent) have resulted in **multigenerational housing**, where as many as three or four generations of a family might share one home. The implications for designers are significant. Rather than designing for a traditional family with two adults and children, multiple adults might be living together. They will, in turn, have different privacy and space requirements that a traditional family might have.

Multigenerational Housing

According to the National Association of Homebuilders, multigenerational housing is a top trend in 2012. This situation commonly results in the addition of an in-law apartment. The **in-law apartment** is creating an apartment within the house for an elderly parent. The inclusion of two master bedroom suites is also common.

Co-Housing

Cohousing is a collaborative neighborhood approach to housing. The co-housing concept groups people in single-family units with shared cooperative spaces such as kitchens, gardens, and recreational areas. Those living within the co-housing development are committed to the community experience. Six characteristics define cohousing: it is a participatory process,

the neighborhood is designed for a sense of community, there are shared facilities, there is a nonhierarchical structure and decision-making process, and there is no shared economy (cohousing.org). Most communities contain anywhere from 20 to 40 households. Legally, cohousing communities are usually set up like condominiums. Cohousing communities can be found in about half the states in the United States with the largest number located in California.

Industry Trends

As with many design sectors, industry trends help to shape new directions in house design. Some of these trends relate to the integration of new technologies while others relate to sustainability goals.

Smart Home Design

Smart home design includes a series of handheld devices, sensors, and wireless technologies that allow an occupant to control lighting and temperature, as well as the position of doors, windows, shades, and multiple other items. Researchers have shown that people think of their homes as distinctly different from their work environments and thus require a "homier" technology than might be found in a typical office (Saizmaa and Kim, 2008). Examples include the need to integrate technology so that it is not overpowering. A central control panel might be located in a built-in shelf area or touch screens located where light switches would normally be. "The study shows that home evokes safe, relaxing, and comfortable feelings while technology [raises] opposite emotions such as fear, reservation, inevitability, and stress" (Saizmaa and Kim, 2008, 146). Therefore, it is important that integrating technology take into account the need to maintain a sense of home or feeling of "**hominess**." "Hominess is defined as 'the spatial quality that make built environments feel residential'" (Shin, Maxwell, and Eshelman, 2004). Digital touch screen devices can be used to control lighting scenarios, temperature, sprinkler systems, ceiling fans, window treatments, and other home amenities. The goal is to make the house as efficient as possible but in an aesthetically pleasing way that does not change the character of the home.

U.S. Department of Energy: Solar Decathlon

First held in 2002, the solar decathlon focuses almost entirely on energy use and technology. This competition challenges college teams to create a solar-powered house that can also charge a small vehicle along with other tasks during the weeklong competition period.

Since its conception, many schools have participated in the Solar Decathlon. Unfortunately, instead of providing a viable and affordable option, many of the solar house designs have cost significantly more than a standard home, placing them well outside the affordable range for most people. Despite this, the Department of Energy lists as its first goal for the competition to have houses that are affordable, attractive, and easy to live in.

Research in Single-Family Residential Design

Although most residential design is done outside of trained architectural and interior design circles (designed by contractors, developers, and home designers), a plethora of research studies and theories about the home have been conducted and developed over the past 40 to 50 years. Both high-style architecturally designed houses and local building customs provide housing samples for historians to research. The quantity of the U.S. housing stock coupled with the promise of the American Dream during the 20th century led to many books and articles about the differences between house and home and the home as a venue for self-expression. Homeowners' efforts to improve their own houses fund such retail giants as Lowe's and Home Depot.

Despite the multiple studies and millions of residences, little has been written about the design process for residential work as a typology. Books on the subject tend to take a traditional approach using tract housing examples or they focus on specific rooms like the kitchen and bathroom. These texts present conventional construction methods and materials with very little innovation or integration of the research done in the past 50 years.

Books and Essays

More recent books focus on guidelines for how to create more of what already exists. One exception that focuses on the language of design is 2007's *Get Your House Right: Architectural Elements to Use and Avoid*, by Cusato and Pentreath. The book shares the same premise as design programs around the world: that people can be taught to see proper scale, proportions, relationships, and what makes a pleasing design. Some of the other how-to books would benefit from the integration of these "avoid" and "use" guidelines.

Rapoport

Amos Rapoport's seminal work, *House Form and Culture* (1969), took a historical approach to understanding vernacular house forms and linked these house forms to the way in which the occupant lived. By considering materials, sites, economics, and a variety of other factors, Rapoport sought to connect cultural beliefs and house forms. He concluded that housing needed to meet four requirements to be considered successful:

1. It needs to be socially and culturally valid.
2. It should be sufficiently economical to ensure that the greatest number can afford it.

3. It should ensure the maintenance of the health of the occupants.
4. There should be a minimum of maintenance over the life of the building. (129)

The conclusion then implies that function is not the primary driver of house form, rather that cultural need might be more important.

Almost 40 years later, Rapoport revisited the nature and definition of the modern house. According to this essay, tradition in American housing has disappeared and with this, a shared cultural image of the house (2007). In its place, codes, regulations, plan books, and zoning have resulted in the typology suited toward a typical middle-class family with two children as promoted in advertising and other forms of media. This model simultaneously disenfranchises all those falling outside the model (which millions of people do).

Arguably many of today's houses not only fail to be culturally relevant but also fail to be economical, healthy, and easy to maintain. The recent housing market destabilization (high housing prices, bad loans, and the subsequent collapse of the housing market) underscored the lack of affordability in the market, although this situation is undergoing an adjustment in response to the excesses of the period 2004 to 2007. Multiple indoor air quality issues such as off-gassing of chemicals and increased dust allergens have been identified related to common indoor materials such as particleboard, carpeting, paint, and drywall. Particleboard often includes formaldehyde, a known carcinogen. Carpeting, paint, and drywall can release volatile organic compounds into the air. Rethinking the house is a significant and important design problem and designers could benefit from integrating vernacular knowledge.

Barbara Miller Lane's 2007 anthology, *House and Dwelling: Perspectives on Modern Domestic Architecture*, poses several questions about tract housing and designers. The most basic challenge posed by Lane is "...do the ideals of those who select and remodel their dwellings come from the 'great minds' of the era, or is the reverse true?" (2) Lane, professor emeritus of history and Mellon Emeritus Fellow at Bryn Mawr College, implies that many of the house designs of today have not benefited from deep thinking or from trained designers. By presenting many theoretical and practical points of view in her book, she has compiled thoughts from some of the best thinkers on the subject in a single volume.

The National Association of Homebuilders

The **National Association of Home Builders (NAHB)** conducts much of the research about the homebuilding industry in the United States. This research serves manufacturers, builders, and government agencies. The four component areas of the research agenda are market research, product testing and certification, technology field evaluation, and Green Building certification. The NAHB produces a quarterly newsletter for consumers and offers educational resources to educators, builders, and consumers.

Center for Universal Design, North Carolina State University

First established in 1989 at North Carolina State, the Center for Universal Design has developed a series of guidelines for universal design and is the repository of the most current research, guidelines, and information about universal design. The center provides technical assistance and resources to those interested in the topic, a significant amount of which is available at http://www.ncsu.edu/ncsu/design/cud/. Since compliance with the Americans with Disabilities Act (ADA) is not required in single-family residences, **universal design** provides a way in which houses can be made to meet the needs of all people regardless of their age, gender, or physical abilities.

Bournemouth University Sustainable Design Research Centre

The Sustainable Design Research Centre focuses on the physical deterioration of surfaces in order to understand the energy consumption and durability associated with products. Its areas of research are lean manufacturing, tribology and environmental design, ceramics tribology (**tribology** is the science of interacting surfaces in relative motion), and sustainable design. Information about the center is available at http://research.bournemouth.ac.uk/centre/sustainable-design-research-centre/. Although the center is located in the United Kingdom, its findings are applicable anywhere.

Sustainable Single-Family Residential Design

The process used to design a sustainable single-family house differs from the standard approach to a subdivision. For example, the placement of the dwelling on the site should take advantage of the orientation for sun and prevailing breezes, as opposed to facing a traditional neighborhood street. The materials and construction techniques will often use local or regional materials and follow local building customs. Thus, a house in San Diego would be radically different than one in Virginia Beach. For example, vernacular houses in Virginia would recommend the following: Using porches (which provide shade) and natural cooling (for example, cross ventilation) can greatly reduce the need for air-conditioning in many areas and can eliminate it entirely in others. Open stair halls can serve as a cooling tower, allowing hot air to rise out of the first floor.

Maximizing the square footage with a minimum allocated toward circulation will reduce the overall square footage of a house. Some ways to maximize square footage include designing dual-purpose spaces (dens that double as guest rooms or great room–type spaces), providing built-ins, and condensing circulation to a minimum. Eliminating long hallways and large stair halls reduces circulation.

The use of grey water to flush toilets and to irrigate landscaping can result in the reduction of water consumption. Grey water is the water produced by showers, sinks, and washing machines. Using local plants and those requiring no irrigation—**xeriscaping**—also reduces water usage.

While many of these interventions are common sense, the cumulative effect can create a much more sustainable house than those typically found in today's subdivisions. Other sustainable additions might include solar panels, tankless hot water heaters (also known as "on-demand"), and improved weather stripping around doors and other openings.

Max Jacobson, Murray Silverstein, and Barbara Winslow describe another approach to sustainable design in their 2002 book, *Patterns of the Home: The Ten Essentials of Enduring Design*. The book was based upon Berkeley Professor of Architecture Christopher Alexander's *Pattern Language* research (Jacobsen and Silverstein studied with Alexander). The patterns the group identified for successful house design include inhabiting the site; creating rooms outside and in; having a sheltering roof; capturing light; using parts in proportion; careful attention to the flow through rooms; private edges, common core; refuge and outlook; places in between; and composing with materials.

The premise of a pattern language approach (as developed by Christopher Alexander) is that people react to certain patterns in the built environment that afford them desirable experiences. For example, private edges and a common core describe the need for large open rooms and small intimate spaces on the periphery.

Common spaces such as the kitchen, dining room, and living room can flow into one another when accompanied by private spaces such as an intimate eating alcove. Each of the patterns described customized features within the home that people might find appealing and engaging.

Such multipurpose spaces allow for a reduction in square footage. Architect Sarah Susanka has made a successful career through her work with *The Not So Big House* phenomenon, focusing on smaller, more efficient houses. The work reinforces the customization seen in the enduring patterns based on pattern language. Through customized and carefully detailed accoutrements, the overall square footage is reduced. Bookcases, built-in shelves and cabinets, as well as built-in furniture make the house more user-friendly and customized.

Cusato, Pentreath, Susanka, Jacobson, Silverstein, and Winslow all emphasize design principles in successful house design. Although, to designers, the notion of design principles as applied to single-family house design may seem obvious, it has been largely lacking in many (if not most) houses in the United States.

Student Approaches to Single-Family Residential Design

It is not at all uncommon for students to initially approach residential design using the images they see around them. Unfortunately, in many cases this might consist of developer-designed tract housing lacking in both design excellence and sustainability. Large luxury housing has traditionally been a sign of status. Building upon the tradition of the American Dream, wherein all are entitled to a single-family house and yard, a more recent emphasis has been placed on demonstrating one's wealth, position, and success through the physical construct of the home. Following the recent housing

bubble and subsequent market collapse, a renewed interest in smaller and more affordable dwellings seems to be on the rise based on the consumer interest in Susanka's books of small house ideas, which have sold over 1.5 million copies.

Another common student approach to the single-family house is to review shelter/professional magazines such as *Architectural Digest*, *Dwell*, and *Metropolis* or perhaps even *Architectural Record's* housing issue. While these resources can provide visual inspiration, the majority of these projects are for wealthy clientele.

Perhaps a more useful and fruitful approach might be to ask the bigger design questions related to the house. How do people live in the 21st century? What are the new demands being placed on the house that have never seen before? Is the American Dream itself sustainable? Are we willing to let most people live in non-designer-produced house designs? How can we successfully impact this market?

Case Studies

The following three case studies show three different student approaches to the Cradle-to-Cradle House Design competition (originally conducted in 2005), which was given as a class project at Virginia Tech in 2012.

Project 1 (biophilic, eco-cultural)

The student focused on blurring the line between the inside and outside for this project. Following multiple schematic diagrams to explore the geometry of the site and resulting house, the student used a series of slices through the house to allow for outside penetrations into the massing of the house itself. The plan shows that the house is centered on a central tree atrium. Thus the site and the concept of blurring inside and outside drove the approach to sustainability. All wood used in the house is FSC certified and has water-based finishes. The other primary material used in the construction of the home is fly-ash concrete. Area rugs are made of a rapidly renewable sisal.

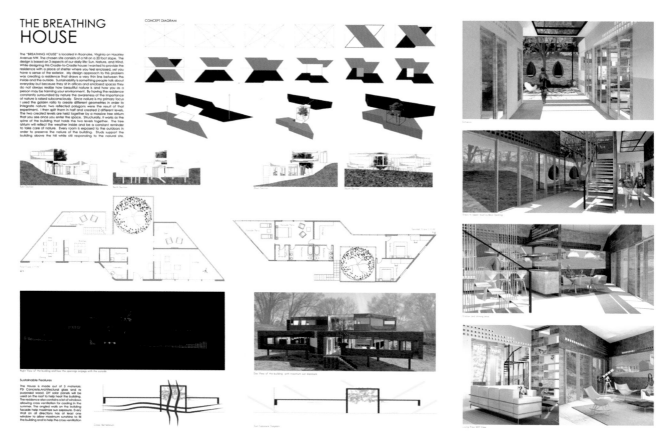

Figure 8.1 Yasmin Hamza, "The Breathing House": Design poster

Figure 8.2 Yasmin Hamza, "The Breathing House": 3D view of entrance

Figure 8.3
Yasmin Hamza,
"The Breathing
House": 3D view of
kitchen and dining
areas

Figure 8.4
Yasmin Hamza,
"The Breathing
House": 3D view of
living room

Figure 8.5
Yasmin Hamza,
"The Breathing
House": 3D view of
living space with
den beyond

Project 2 (eco-technic, eco-centric)

The conceptual approach used for the second design focused on the use of recycled industrial byproducts: shipping containers. The design used a series of four shipping containers to respond to the topography of the site and the design intent: Small is beautiful. In addition to the use of shipping containers, wood pallets are repurposed and used for flooring. All interior textiles are sustainable and meet cradle-to-cradle product certification. The sloped roof system is used to collect rainwater for irrigation and toilet flushing.

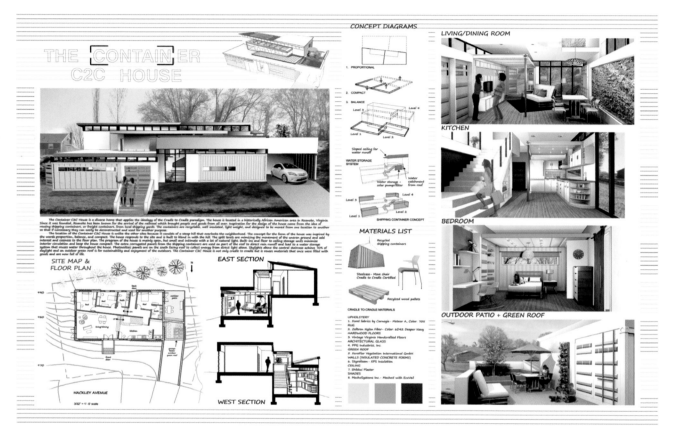

Figure 8.6 Cathleen Campbell, "The Container House": Design poster

Figure 8.7
Cathleen Campbell, "The Container House": 3D view of front of house

Figure 8.8 Cathleen Campbell, "The Container House": 3D view of living room

Project 3 (eco-cultural)

The third project is nestled within the topography of the site. The multilevel house is cut into the hillside and features a green roof (made of sod), which allows it to blend with the hill upon which it rests. The use of the green roof attracts local flora and fauna, reduces the heat island effect, and collects rainwater back into the site. The house is situated such that the constant earth temperature is used to keep it cool in the summer and warm in the winter.

LEED Rating Systems

The two LEED Rating systems applicable to the single-family house include LEED for Homes and LEED for Neighborhoods. Both can be found on the usgbc.org website along with examples and commentary.

Planning Guidelines

Although it is not legally required, it is good practice to design for people of all sizes and abilities. Universal design and accessibility principles can be easily integrated into a design. The following plan prototypes address many of the major spaces in a residence including kitchens, bathrooms, bedrooms, laundry rooms, and eating areas. These designs include universal design clearances.

Figure 8.9
Loren Heslep,
"The Hidden House":
Design poster

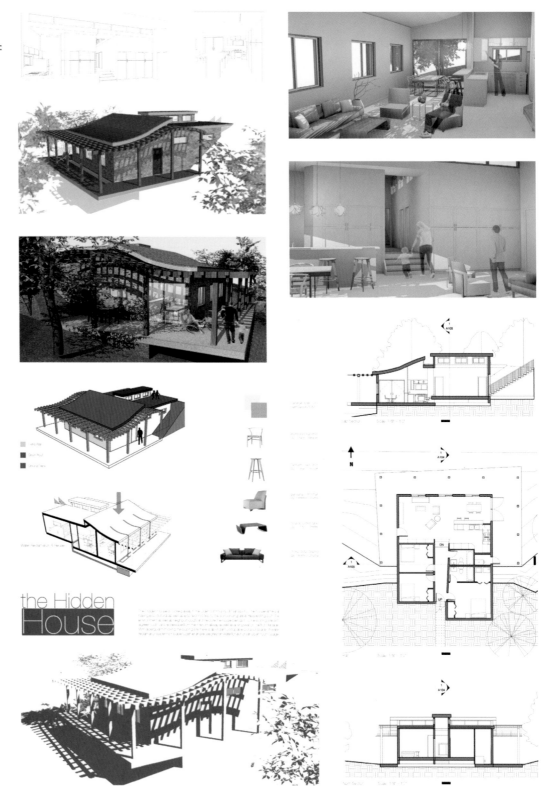

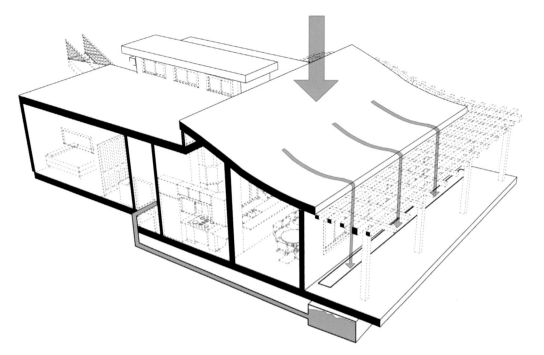

Figure 8.10
Loren Heslep,
"The Hidden House":
Water reclamation
section

Figure 8.11
Loren Heslep,
"The Hidden House":
3D view of interior

Figure 8.12
Loren Heslep,
"The Hidden House":
3D view of outdoor
space

Figure 8.13
Accessible kitchen
clearances

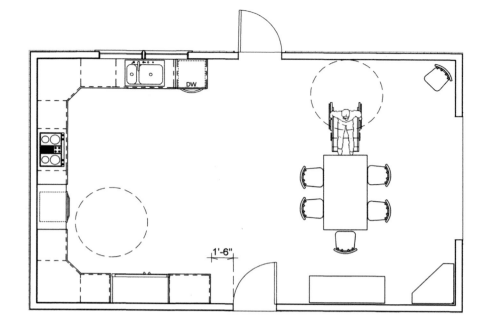

1'-6"

Figure 8.14
Elevation of
accessible kitchen
pointing out
universal design
features

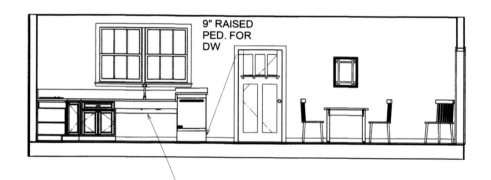

9" RAISED
PED. FOR
DW

ADJUSTABLE HEIGHT SINK

NOTE: BACKSPLASH IS
CONTRASTING COLOR TO
ASSIST THE VISUALLY
IMPAIRED

Figure 8.15
Elevation of
accessible kitchen
pointing out
universal design
features

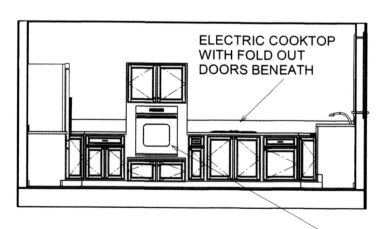

ELECTRIC COOKTOP
WITH FOLD OUT
DOORS BENEATH

PULL OUT COUNTER
BELOW SINGLE WALL
OVEN

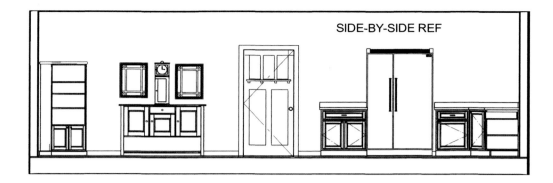

Figure 8.16
Elevation of accessible kitchen pointing out universal design features

SIDE-BY-SIDE REF

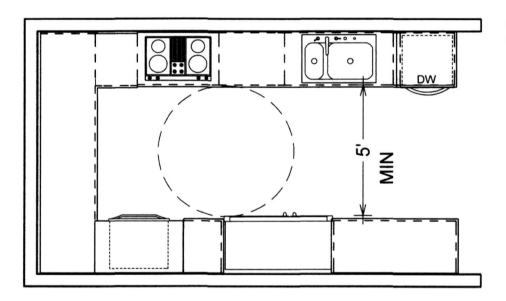

Figure 8.17 U-shape accessible kitchen

5' MIN

DW

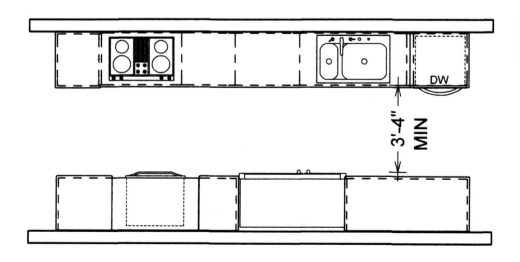

Figure 8.18
Pass-through accessible kitchen

3'-4" MIN

DW

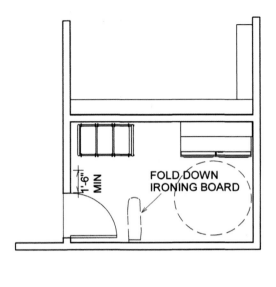

LIVING AREA
116 sq ft

Figure 8.19 Accessible laundry room

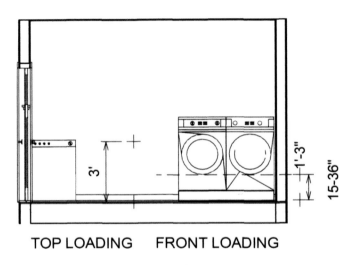

TOP LOADING   FRONT LOADING

Figure 8.20 Elevation of accessible laundry room

Figure 8.21
Accessible bedroom

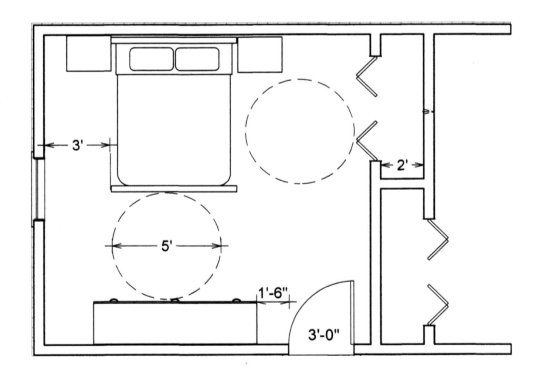

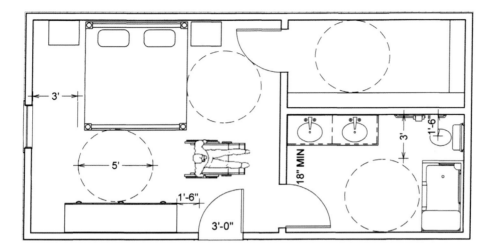

Figure 8.22
Accessible master bedroom and bath

Figure 8.23
Rendering of accessible master bath with features

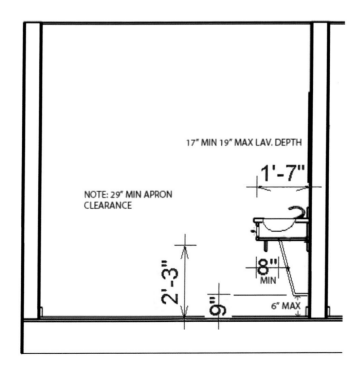

Figure 8.24
Section at accessible bathroom counter

Discussion Questions and Exercises

1. Visit a local housing development and collect a brochure for a possible house to purchase; make sure a floor plan is included. Study the plan, noting issues such as the efficiency of the circulation. Check door swings and codes to make sure the building is ADA compliant (and to see what might need to be changed). Try to analyze the underlying elements and principles of design. How is proportion used? Is there a center of emphasis in the design? A sense of hierarchy? How might you improve the design? How might you make it more sustainable? Is the house designed for universal design?

2. Discuss in groups whether you think designers and architects should be the only ones allowed to produce single-family house design. Why? Why not? Create a 5-minute presentation to express your group's position to the class.

Key Terms

co-housing

hominess

in-law apartment

multigenerational housing

National Association of Home Builders (NAHB)

smart home

tribology

universal design

xeriscaping

Sources

Bournemouth University Sustainable Design Research Centre. Homepage. Accessed June 28, 2013. http://www.bournemouth.ac.uk/sdrc/.

———. 2013. Homepage. Accessed June 28. http://www.ncsu.edu/ncsu/design/cud/.

Cohousing Organization. 2013. Homepage. Accessed June 28. http://www.cohousing.org/.

Cusato, Marianne, and Ben Pentreath. 2007. *Get Your House Right: Architectural Elements to Use and Avoid.* New York: Sterling Publishing.

Homes for Our Troops. 2013. Accessed June 28. http://www.homesforourtroops.org/site/PageServer.

Lane, Barbara Miller. 2007. *Housing and Dwelling: Perspectives on Modern Domestic Architecture.* London: Routledge.

Maleska, K. 2012. "Multigenerational Housing," Central Minnesota Builder's Association. Accessed June 28, 2013. http://blog.cmbaonline.org/?p=270.

Rapoport, Amos. 1969. *House, Form and Culture.* England Cliffs, NJ: Prentice-Hall, Inc.

———. 2007. "The Nature and Definition of the Field." In *Housing and Dwelling: Perspectives on Modern Domestic Architecture*, edited by Barbara Miller Lane, 26–32. London: Routledge.

Saizmaa, Tsogzolmaa, and Hee-Cheol Kim. 2008. "Smart Home Design: Home or House?" Third International Conference of Convergence and Hybrid Information Technology. 143–48. IEE Computer Society DOI 10.1109/ICCIT.2008.26.

Shin, Jung-Hye, Lorraine E. Maxwell, and Paul Eshelman. 2004. "Hospital Birthing Room Design: A Study of Mothers' Perceptions of Hominess." *Journal of Interior Design*, 30(1): 23–36.

U.S. Census. 2004. "Table HH-6: Average Population Per Household and Family: 1940-present." *Census.gov*, Sept. 15. Accessed June 28, 2013. http://www.census.gov/population/socdemo/hh-fam/tabHH-6.pdf

———. 2010. "Age and Sex Composition: 2010." Accessed June 28, 2013. http://www.census.gov/prod/cen2010/briefs/c2010br-03.pdf.

———. 2010. "Median and Average Square Feet of Floor Area in New Single-Family Houses Completed by Location." Accessed June 28, 2013. www.census.gov/const/C25Ann/sftotalmedavgsqft.pdf.

U.S. Department of Health and Human Services Administration on Aging. 2012. "Profile of Older Americans." Accessed June 28, 2013. http://www.aoa.gov/AoARoot/Aging_Statistics/Profile/index.aspx

9

HOUSING PROJECTS

··

Objectives

- Students will understand the other types of residences besides single-family houses.

- Students will be able to describe common issues facing housing including sustainability concerns.

- Students will be able to apply the basic guidelines for accessible housing including ADA and universal design principles.

Overview

Although we tend to live in single-family houses in the United States, many other types of residences are also found here and around the world. In some countries, the single-family, freestanding house is rarely, if ever, found. In some parts of the world, multifamily housing is the norm. Multifamily housing describes the condition where several unrelated people are occupying the same building. Oftentimes, this is a multi-story building containing many individual housing units.

Types of Housing

There are many forms of multifamily housing found around the world and in the United States. While some of these were mentioned in the last chapter on the freestanding single-family house (multigenerational housing and co-housing), there are several other forms.

Apartment

A unit located in a building with multiple units rented for living space is an **apartment**. It is self-contained, with its own kitchen, bath, and sleeping, and living areas. If all of these are located in a single room, this is described as a **studio apartment**.

Condominium

A **condominium** is like an apartment, but the occupants own their living spaces. Often, the owner also pays fees to contribute to the common areas, outdoor upkeep, and any personnel that might be required to run the facility.

Row Houses

Much like condominiums, the occupant often owns the **row house**, but it still shares sidewalls with the other houses in the row. In this case, the owner cares for the yards or grounds directly in front and back of the particular vertical unit. Row houses most commonly occur in urban environments across Europe and in large cities in the United States such as New York, Baltimore, and San Francisco.

Cluster Houses

The **cluster house** includes a group of houses that are attached to one another. There are many forms of the cluster house depending on where in the world it is located.

Duplex

The **duplex** is a form of cluster house that includes only two residences attached by a common wall. Because of the size of these facilities, architects must be involved.

Public Housing Projects

The U.S. government subsidizes public housing **projects**. This type of housing often consists of multi-story apartment units for low-income occupants. As a result, these types of residences have had more architectural intervention in their design than the freestanding house. As such, some have been used to further the utopian vision of the architect at various times in history. Well-known historic examples include Pruitt-Igoe, St. Louis, Missouri; Queensbridge Houses, Queens, New York; Robert Taylor Homes, Chicago, Illinois; and Jordan Downs, Watts, California. In a 2007 article for the *Wall Street Journal*, journalist Ben Casselman describes the many recent efforts of architects to design for affordable housing in multifamily complexes.

Emergency Housing

Another form of housing of great interest to many, including celebrities and high profile architects, is the design of housing for disaster relief. In the wake of Hurricane Katrina, actor and producer Brad Pitt engaged in an effort to have well-known architects from around the world create designs for new houses in New Orleans. Similar efforts have followed the earthquakes in Haiti and Hurricane Sandy in the Northeastern United States.

Design Considerations for Multifamily Housing

As a way of housing many unrelated people, multifamily housing poses many issues not found in single-family housing. Several of these issues stem from putting multiple people together in a confined footprint.

Privacy

The need for privacy places some limitations on the design of multifamily units. Privacy varies culturally and because of this, the needs will vary depending on where the project is located. In the United States, there are expectations for privacy in living units that include a buffer zone between public spaces such as corridors and outside walkways and personal spaces. This can be created using a visual separation, such as an entry

foyer. Bathrooms also need to be screened from entry doors and ideally from more public living spaces such as living and dining rooms and kitchens. Some other cultures are less concerned with some of these privacy requirements and are more accustomed to living communally.

Ownership of Communal Spaces

One of the major concerns in multifamily housing buildings is the lack of ownership by residents of communal spaces. When this occurs, these spaces tend to accumulate trash and graffiti and begin to look neglected.

Accessibility Requirements

In single-family housing there is no requirement to follow Americans with Disabilities Act (ADA) requirements unless federal funding is involved. As mentioned in the last chapter, this has led to the rise of universal design guidelines for the home. In a multifamily housing complex, there are legal requirements in place to require accessibility features. For example, in a project built after 1991, when there are four or more units and all other buildings with ground level units (containing four or more units), accessible units must be provided. This is also true in the case in all federally assisted housing.

The specific requirements for accessibility extend to all public spaces and to those units required for accessibility purposes. Elevators (where provided) must meet minimum ADA requirements. All public spaces including entrances and common areas must have accessible doors, accessible passages, controls, and signage.

Within the individual unit, at least one entry door, storage spaces, all controls (thermostats, switches, alarms), at least one full bathroom, the living and dining areas, at least one bedroom, and all patios, terraces, carports, and garages (if provided) must be accessible.

Latest Best Practices-HUD

The **U.S. Department of Housing and Urban Development Office (HUD)** publishes the latest success stories in affordable housing across the Unites States. The U.S. Housing Act of 1937 created HUD, which was elevated to a cabinet-level agency in 1965. The agency's mission is to "create strong, sustainable, inclusive communities and quality affordable homes for all." As affordable housing, each project includes a social justice component. Sustainability is also central to HUD's mission.

Sustainable Community Development

The St. Luke's Manor building located in Cleveland, Ohio, sat empty for 12 years before it was rehabilitated into

Figure 9.1
St. Luke's Manor: Exterior view, before
Photo credit: © Artography Studios, Lauren R. Pacini, Photographer

Figure 9.2
St. Luke's Manor: Exterior view, after
Photo credit: © Artography Studios, Lauren R. Pacini, Photographer

137 affordable apartment units for local seniors. Listed on the National Register in 2005, the project provided a perfect opportunity to combine green design and historic preservation. The entire neighborhood around the building was also being developed so that the whole project is LEED for Neighborhood Development (LEED ND) certified. The neighborhood relies on green infrastructure and buildings as well as its links to public transportation to achieve its sustainable footprint. In addition to being LEED ND, the project also provides affordable for housing for seniors in an important historic building.

Excellence for Homelessness

Architecture firm Michael Maltzan Architecture created the New Carver Apartments, a 97-single-room homeless facility within a six-story cylinder

Figure 9.3
St. Luke's Manor:
Interior view, before
Photo credit:
© Artography
Studios, Lauren
R. Pacini,
Photographer

Figure 9.4
St. Luke's Manor:
Interior view, after
Photo credit:
© Artography
Studios, Lauren
R. Pacini,
Photographer

structure with onsite medical and mental health care located two miles southwest of skid row in Los Angeles. The design was based on the **Housing First Model** that seeks to provide permanent housing for the homeless. A shared kitchen and community area with laundry facilities are located on the first floor with rooms on the upper levels. The primary emphasis of this project is on social justice and providing housing for those who would not otherwise have a place to stay. Sustainability features include extensive access to daylight through the interior courtyard and accessibility to public transportation.

Figure 9.5 New Carver Apartments: Exterior view
Photo credit: Courtesy of Iwan Baan

Figure 9.6 New Carver Apartments: Interior view
Photo credit: Courtesy of Iwan Baan

Street Green and Revitalization

Congo Street, located in Jubilee Park (Dallas, Texas), is a historically and economically segregated neighborhood that had long been ignored. Through the efforts of a nonprofit group, the Jubilee Park and Community Center helped owners and occupants to revitalize the community. A holding house was constructed to model sustainable building practices, and then individual families moved into the holding house while their own homes were rehabilitated using sustainable materials and practices. The emphasis on energy and resource efficiency worked well with the 17 single family and duplex homes that averaged around 600 square feet each.

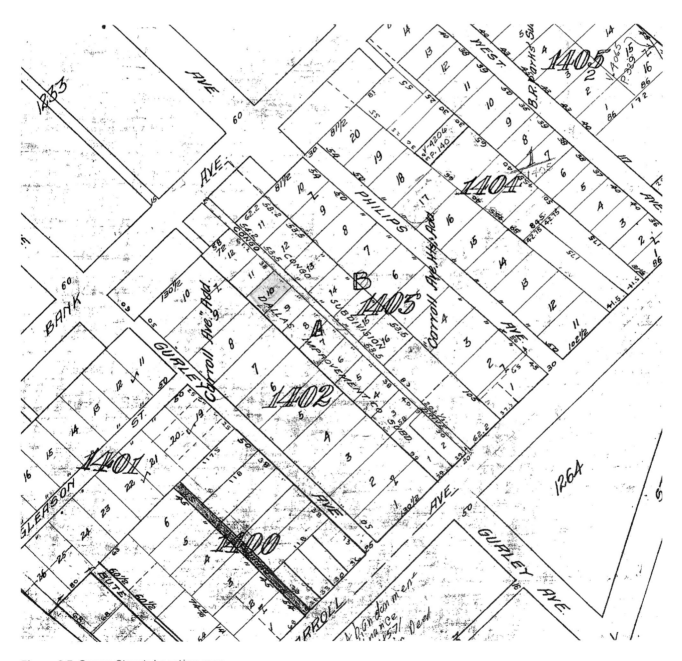

Figure 9.7 Congo Street: Location map
Drawing courtesy: © bcWORKSHOP

Figure 9.8 Congo
Street: Before,
looking toward
Carroll Street
Photo credit:
© bcWORKSHOP

Figure 9.9 Congo
Street: Now, looking
toward Carroll Street
Photo credit:
© bcWORKSHOP

Figure 9.10 Congo Street: Interior view of stair and loft area
Photo credit:
© bcWORKSHOP

Figure 9.11 Congo Street: Interior view of kitchen showing reclaimed and recycled interior finishes
Photo credit:
© bcWORKSHOP

Figure 9.12 Congo
Street: Interior view
living room showing
reclaimed wood
slats on wall
Photo credit:
© bcWORKSHOP

Figure 9.13 Congo
Street: Interior view
looking toward
kitchen
Photo credit:
© bcWORKSHOP

Figure 9.14 Congo Street: Interior view looking toward kitchen
Photo credit:
© bcWORKSHOP

Figure 9.15 Congo Street: Interior view living area
Photo credit:
© bcWORKSHOP

Figure 9.16 Congo
Street: Exterior
walkway detail
Photo credit:
© bcWORKSHOP

Figure 9.17 Congo
Street: Street view
Photo credit:
© bcWORKSHOP

Figure 9.18 Congo
Street: Exterior view
Photo credit:
© bcWORKSHOP

Figure 9.19 Congo
Street: Exterior view
Photo credit:
© bcWORKSHOP

Figure 9.20 Congo Street composite photo
Photo credit: © bcWORKSHOP

Figure 9.21 Congo Street resident posing in front of construction Photo credit: © bcWORKSHOP

Figure 9.22 Congo Street residents in front of newly remodeled home Photo credit: © bcWORKSHOP

Design Guidelines for Multifamily Housing

The Fair Housing Act Design Manual (1996) published by HUD focuses on assisting builders and designers in fulfilling the accessibility requirements of the Fair Housing Act. The 334-page document is divided into three sections with seven design requirements. The laws that mandate accessibility in housing include the Architectural Barriers Act of 1968, Section 504 of the Rehabilitation Act of 1973, the Fair Housing Act of 1968 (as amended), and the Americans with Disabilities Act of 1990.

Accessibility Statistics

One in five Americans aged 15 or older has a disability of some type, the most common of which relate to lifting or walking. In the 1994 report, "Statistical Report: the Status of People with Disabilities," the following statistics were reported:

- 48.9 million Americans have disabilities.
- There are 32 million Americans over 65.
- 70 percent of all Americans will have temporary or permanent disability at some point in their lifetime.
- 8.1 million Americans have visual disabilities.
- 27 million Americans have heart disease and limited mobility (HUD, 1996, 18).

The types of disabilities taken into account in the guidelines include ambulatory mobility, visual, hearing, and cognitive.

Requirement 1: Accessible Building Entrance on an Accessible Route

This requirement asks designers to consider factors such as placing floor levels as close as possible to ground levels, providing passenger drop-off locations that are covered, and creating clear paths of travel to outdoor amenities such as mailboxes, disposal areas, clubhouses, and other site features. When creating an accessible route, the designer should consider the width and slope of the route, the ground surfaces, ramps, headroom cross slope, and any protruding objects. Stairs cannot be included in an accessible route. Accessible routes must occur at site arrival points, walks between buildings, and all site amenities (gazebos, playgrounds, etc.)

An accessible entrance should have no (or only a low) threshold, clear maneuvering space, require little force to open the door, accessible hardware, and a safe closing speed on the door. Any call boxes, doorbells, signage, or illumination must meet ADA guidelines.

All buildings must have one or more elevators and one or more entrances. If a building does not have an elevator, only the ground floor units require an accessible route. If this is the case, at least 20 percent of the units must be ground floor units.

Requirement 2: Accessible and Usable Public and Common Use Areas

A **common use area** is any space intended for the use of residents, while **public use** refers to those areas for use by the general public. If there is more than one recreational facility or other common features, only one must be accessible, providing they are all the same. Examples of common spaces include passenger loading areas, toilet rooms, bathing facilities, shower rooms, exercise rooms, performance areas, laundry rooms, trash collection areas, and outside seating areas. Elements that must be accessible in a common clubhouse include sinks, walkways around pool tables, seating areas, vending machines, countertops, and windows that are operable.

When a common laundry facility is included, all appliances, utility sinks, routes, folding tables, and vending machines must comply with ADA guidelines.

Requirement 3: Usable Doors

Accessible doors (32 inches minimum clear) must be provided at all common and public use spaces. **Usable doors** (nominal 32 inches clear width—this allows for ¼-inch to 3/8-inch variance) must be provided within the living unit on the entry door, bathroom and powder room doors, doors to decks, balconies, and patios, into walk-in closets, and utility/ storage or laundry rooms. The depth for all cased openings cannot exceed 24 inches unless the clear opening is expanded to 36 inches clear. Hinged single doors are recommended. When a double-leaf door is used (one with two smaller parts hinged on each side), a clear opening of 32 inches must be maintained with one leaf open. When pocket or folding doors are used, a door opening that is a minimum of 36 inches wide should be used. With a sliding door, a minimum clear passage of 32 inches must be maintained when open. Loop handles are recommended for ease of use.

Requirement 4: Accessible Route into and through the Covered Unit

A 36-inch clear accessible route should exist through the entire dwelling unit. No more than a maximum vertical floor level change of ¼ inch should occur unless there is a tapered threshold. Split levels, sunken rooms, steps up, and other level changes should be avoided. If they are included, they must not contain the entire functional living space—for example, only part of a living room could be sunken while the rest is accessible. If a loft is included, it need not be accessible as long as it not a primary living space. A **loft** is defined as less then one-third of the floor area and open to the room below.

Requirement 5: Light Switches, Electrical Outlets, Thermostats, and Other Environmental Controls in Accessible Locations

All light switches and controls should be located a maximum of 48 inches above the finished floor, while outlets should be a minimum of 15 inches above the finished floor. A clear floor space of 30 inches x 48 inches allows access to all wall-mounted controls. The controls covered by the guidelines include light switches for controlling all room lights, electrical outlets, and environmental controls (thermostats and other heating and air-conditioning controls.) Those controls not covered by the ADA guidelines include appliance controls, outlets for specific appliances, and circuit breakers. When designing for a forward reach to controls, allow 20 to 25 inches (with the recommended clear floor space of 30 inches by 48 inches). When a side approach is used, 24 inches in the maximum side reach permitted.

The most easily operated types of switches include rocker switches, toggle switches, and touch-sensitive switches. Lever handles, although rarely found, are ideal for appliances. When not available a central blade on the knob makes operation easier.

Requirement 6: Reinforced Walls for Grab Bars

Although grab bars are not required, reinforcing for their eventual installation is required. At the toilet location, the minimum grab bar reinforcement area required is a 24-inch-wide area centered on the back of the toilet and locate between 32 and 38 inches above the finished floor. This is for when the toilet is located next to a sidewall. On the sidewall, the minimum reinforced area should be 24-inches wide to 42-inches wide and set 12 inches from the face of the back wall and installed between 32 inches and 38 inches above the finished floor. When the toilet is located in the middle of the room (not next to a sidewall), reinforcing for folding grab bars is required. This requires the sides without the grab bar to have 15 inches of reinforcing from the centerline of the toilet out and 18 inches of reinforcing on the grab bar side from the centerline of the toilet. Fixed floor grab bars are not recommended since they block access to other controls.

Bathtub reinforcing is installed at the same height as toilet reinforcing and should be placed extending from the outside edge of the bathtub and extending in 24 inches toward the back wall. Longitudinally, blocking should be provided that extends within 6 inches of either end of the bathtub and at the same height (between 30 inches and 38 inches above finished floor).

Requirement 7: Usable Kitchens and Bathrooms

For the **usable kitchen**, standard cabinets may be used (36-inch-high counter height). Although levered handled faucets are recommended, they are not required.

In order to be usable, a clear floor space of 30 inches x 48 inches should be provided in front of each fixture and appliance. Outlets and switches should be placed per the previous guidelines. A side approach is recommend at the range/cooktop. In kitchens with a center island, a 40-inch walkway around the island is recommended, and in a U-shaped kitchen, a turning radius of 5 feet is required. Removable base cabinets should be provided beneath the kitchen sink with retractable doors located beneath the cooktop—both for wheelchair access. The maximum height for wall-mounted oven controls is 54 inches. A pantry door can be less than 32 inches clear as long as it swings open 180 degrees, although for walk-in pantries, the door must be 32 inches clear to be used.

According to the HUD guidelines, a **bathroom** contains a toilet, sink, and bathtub and/or shower, while a **powder room** contains a toilet and sink. All bathrooms and powder rooms must be on an accessible route. All switches, outlets, and controls in both must be accessible, and all fixtures in both must include proper reinforcing for grab bars. In a bathroom, additional inaccessible outlets can be included, and, while level handles are recommended, they are not required. A clear floor space of 30 inches x 48 inches is required in front of all fixtures and cannot overlap with the door swing except at the sink. In order to provide clear space for a front approach to a toilet located next to the lavatory, a minimum 48-inches wide x 66-inches deep should be included. When a side approach is used, the required clear space is 56-inches deep x 48-inches wide. The recommended height for the toilet seat is 18 inches for ease of transfer from a wheelchair. The lavatory base cabinet should be removable for use with a wheelchair. These same requirements cover powder rooms.

Discussion Questions and Exercises

1. What are key differences between single-family houses and multifamily residences?
2. What are five things a designer can do to make an existing residence more accessible?

Key Terms

accessible doors

apartment

bathroom

common use area

condominium

cluster house

duplex

Housing First Model

U.S. Department of Housing and Urban Development Office (HUD)

loft

powder room

public use

row house

studio apartment

usable doors

usable kitchen

Sources

ACT Planning and Land Authority. 2005. "Apartment Guidelines: For Mixed Use and High-Density Residential Environments." Accessed July 1, 2013. http://apps. actpla.act.gov.au/tplan/planning_ register/register_docs/apartments. pdf.

Casselman, Ben. 2007. "High Design for Low-Income Housing." *Wall Street Journal,* December 28. Accessed July 1. http://online.wsj.com/article/ SB119876732563552709.html.

U.S. Department of Housing and Urban Development. 1996. *Fair Housing Act Design Manual: A Manual to Assist Designers and Builders in Meeting the Accessibility Requirements of the Fair Housing Act.* Accessed July 2, 2013. http://www.huduser.org/ Publications/PDF/FAIRHOUSING/ fairfull.pdf.

———. 2013. "Best Practices." Accessed July 1. http://www. huduser.org/portal/bestpractices/ study_02282013_1.html.

———. 2013. "Mission." Accessed July 2. http://portal.hud.gov/ hudportal/HUD?src=/about/ mission.

APPENDIX: PROJECT CHECKLISTS

This appendix includes a variety of checklists for students to use on the numerous design project types mentioned in this book. These checklists include information based on advice from firms. Some are geared toward thinking on project design, such as the biophilic checklist, while others are more detail oriented and to be used during product selection, like the plumbing and lighting checklists. The value of these checklists is to keep sustainability on the forefront while working through the various details of a project.

Design Checklists
1. Checklist for a Sustainable Design Process
2. Checklist for Biophilic Design
3. Checklist Based on HOK's Design Process
4. Checklist for Local Strategies

Detailed Checklists (Design Development)
5. Checklist for Materials
6. Checklist for Plumbing
7. Checklist for Lighting
8. Checklist for Furnishings
9. Evidence-Based Design Furniture Checklist (Healthcare)

Code and Guidelines Checklists
10. Building Code Checklist
11. Checklist for Universal Design

LEED Checklists
12. LEED 2009 CI
13. LEED 2009 Retail: CI
14. LEED 2009 Retail: NC and MR
15. LEED 2009 Schools: NC and MR
16. LEED 2009 for Healthcare: NC and MR
17. LEED for Homes
18. LEED 2009 for NC and MR
19. LEED 2.2 for NC (2013)

1. Checklist for a Sustainable Design Process

Programming

Information gathering
> Case studies
> Relevant research for project type
> Relevant trends
> Code information
> Plan prototypes

Client information
> Program requirements
> Space needs
> Interviews/surveys
> Behavioral mapping of existing space use

Schematic Design

Concept development (from Tucker and Baker, *C2C Home Design: Process and Experience*)
> Simile/metaphor
> Analogy
> Direct response
> Essence
> Ideals

Diagramming
Bubble diagrams
Block diagrams
Circulation proposals
Schematic plans (minimum of three options in response to concept)
Schematic sketches: 1- and 2-point perspective sketches (sketching for ideation)
Revised proposals

Preliminary Systems Selections

Plumbing
> Greywater systems
> Composting toilets
> Low-/no-water use fixtures
> Low-flow faucets

Mechanical
> Renewable Power Sources

Solar power
> Wind power
> Hydropower
> Biomass

System Selections
> Geothermal
> Integrated solar
> High-efficiency system

Electrical

Electrical
> Lighting
>> LEDS
>> Fluorescents
>> Controls/sensors
>> Double switching for energy reduction
> Building controls

Preliminary Material Selections

Green certifications for products (third party)
> Green Seal
> Green Globes
> C2C

Low- or no-VOC content
Recycled content
> Post-consumer
> Post-industrial

Recyclable content
> Locally obtained
> Locally manufactured
> Locally abstracted (taken from, example stone)
> Life-cycle analysis
> Avoid items on known toxins list (See Perkins + Will Transparency website.)

Design Development

Finalized plans, elevations, and sections
Code check
Materials selections
> See guidance on materials selection above.

Furniture, fixture, and equipment selection.
> See guidance on furniture selection above.

Lighting design (using calculations)
> Lighting power density as regulated by applicable building code
> Do not "over" light.
> Plan for controls and sensors.
> Provide for individual occupant controls.

Construction Documents

F, F and E and materials specifications
Final drawings with dimensions and notes
Cover sheet with all applicable codes, location map, abbreviations, etc.
Follow LEED checklist (at a minimum).

2. Checklist for Biophilic Design

Check any of the following guiding elements that you plan to use in your design to express a biophilic approach to your project. Indicate where in nature you found the inspiration.

Environmental Features

Color
Water
Air
Sunlight
Plants
Animals
Natural materials
Views and vistas
Façade greening
Geology and landscape
Habitats and ecosystems
Fire

Natural Shapes and Forms

Botanical motifs
Tree and columnar supports
Animal motifs
Shells and spirals
Egg, oval, and tubular forms
Arches, vaults, and domes
Shapes resisting straight lines and right angles
Simulation of natural features
Biomorphy
Geomorphy
Biomimicry

Natural Patterns and Processes

Sensory variability
Information richness
Age, change, and the patina of time
Growth and efflorescence
Central focal point
Patterned wholes
Bounded spaces
Transitional spaces
Linked series and chains
Integration of parts to wholes
Complementary contrasts
Dynamic balance and tension
Fractals
Hierarchically organized ratios and scales

Light and Space

Natural light
Filters and diffused light
Light and shadow
Reflected light
Light pools
Warm light
Light as shape and form
Spaciousness
Spatial variability
Spaces as shape and dorm
Spatial harmony
Inside-outside spaces

Place-Based Relationships

Geographic connection to place
Historic connection to place
Ecological connection to place
Cultural connection to place
Indigenous materials
Landscape orientation
Landscape features that define building form
Integration of culture and ecology
Spirit of place
Avoiding placelessness

Evolved Human—Nature Relationships

Prospect and refuge
Order and complexity
Curiosity and enticement
Change and metamorphosis
Security and protection
Mastery and control
Affection and attachment
Attraction and beauty
Exploration and discovery
Information and cognition
Fear and awe
Reverence and spirituality

Source: Stephen Kellert's *Biophilic Design*

3. Checklist Based on HOK's Design Process

A New Design Process: 10 Key Steps

1. Project definition
2. Team building
3. Education and goal setting
4. Site evaluation
5. Baseline analysis
6. Design concept
7. Design optimization
8. Documents and specifications
9. Bidding and construction
10. Postoccupancy

Source: The HOK Checklist from *The HOK Guidebook to Sustainable Design,* 2nd Edition

Checklist for Interior Designers

____ Be a part of the multidisciplinary team.

____ Be a part of the project goal-setting process.

____ Help identify sustainable strategies.

____ Participate in the programming process.

____ Participate in the design concept stage.

____ Explore opportunities to enhance flexibility and future adaptability.

____ Seek out environmentally preferable options for primary building materials and systems.

____ Promote health and wellness through daylighting, views, and connection to the natural environment.

____ Consider the use of ultra low-flow or waterless plumbing fixture alternatives.

____ Develop integrated daylighting and sun-control strategies with architects.

____ Develop a lighting concept using a holistic approach considering daylighting, heat gain and loss, lighting quality, and reduced reliance on electric lighting.

____ Integrate digital controls for energy management.

____ Specify water-efficient plumbing fixtures.

____ Specify water-efficient appliances.

____ Document detailed environmental performance criteria for materials specified.

____ Specify reuse of on-site materials to the greatest extent possible.

____ Develop materials specifications to protect the IAQ in the facility.

____ Educate users on the use and maintenance of the indoor materials and systems.

____ Schedule periodic review of recycling programs.

Source: Abstracted from the 10 detailed checklists for each of the steps in the design process; based on information in Chapter 2, "Process Guidance," *The HOK Guidebook to Sustainable Design,* 2nd Edition

4. Checklist for Local Strategies

Check any of the following guiding elements that you plan to use in your design that are based on the locale where the design is being done.

Site Conditions

Sun studies
Prevailing wind studies
Nearby bodies of water
Micro-climate information
Weather averages
Building orientation response

Local Materials

Stone
Wood
Clay
Other?

Local traditions

Trades (plaster work)
Trades (masons)
Other?

5. Checklist for Materials

- Life-cycle assessment.
- Avoid known toxins.
- Design for disassembly.
- Use durable materials.
- Use products where sections can be easily replaced and matched.
- Consider material packaging.
- Look at the product certifications.
- Check for off-gassing and VOCs.
- Use modular sizes.
- Detail for least waste.
- Avoid mixed materials that cannot be recycled.
- Use FSC wood.
- Use formaldehyde free products.
- Use low-VOC paints and stains.
- Use ceiling tiles with a minimum 65% recycled content.
- Consider using salvaged materials.
- Use low-VOC adhesives for flooring installation.
- Seek carpets with recycled content that are also recyclable; specify green label or green label-plus.
- Consider cork, linoleum, or rubber resilient flooring.
- Use tiles over sheet goods for ease of piece replacement.

Source: The HOK Checklist from *The HOK Guidebook to Sustainable Design,* 2nd Edition, Chapter 2

6. Checklist for Plumbing

Planning Stage

Consider rainwater harvesting.

Consider a green roof.

Consider xeriscaping.

Consider pervious paving.

Consider on-site wastewater treatment.

Consider solar hot water.

Selection Stage

Select low-water or no-water use fixtures.

Plan for greywater reuse.

Select low-flow faucets.

Specify on-demand hot water heaters.

Specify water-sense products.

Specify dual-flush toilets.

7. Checklist for Lighting

Planning Stage

- Calculate specific lighting needs to meet the required foot-candle levels and do not exceed these.
- Keep within the maximum watts per square foot allowable by code and strive to be below this.
- Design for light that goes where the light is needed and not where it is not needed.

Selection

- Select energy-efficient fixtures.
- Specify EnergyStar-rated fixtures.
- Use LEDs where possible.
- When specifying LEDs, make sure the lamp and fixture are separate.
- Specify fluorescent lamps for general lighting when LEDs are not used.
- Avoid incandescent lamps if possible.
- Use low-voltage lighting minimally and for specific accent purposes, if at all.
- Use HID lighting in place of incandescent in retail environments.
- Use energy-efficient ballasts.
- Provide dimming capability.
- Provide automatic sensors on light fixtures (daylight sensors, movement sensors, etc).
- Provide dual switching where light levels can be reduced to account for daylight.

8. Checklist for Furnishings

- Consider refurbished over new.
- Choose easily disassembled pieces that can be broken into component parts for recycling.
- Consider specifying furniture with recycled content.
- Choose casegoods made with FSC wood.
- Select low-toxicity fabrics.
- Consider natural fibers such as organically grown cotton.
- Avoid plastic laminates and wood veneers if possible.

9. Evidence-Based Design Furniture Checklist

Findings EBD Goals and Furniture Features

1. **Reduce surface contamination linked to healthcare associated infections.**
   a) Surfaces are easily cleaned, with no surface joints or seams.
   b) Materials for upholstery are impervious (nonporous).
   c) Surfaces are nonporous and smooth.

2. **Reduce patient falls and associated injuries.**
   a) Chair seat height is adjustable.
   b) Chair has armrests.
   c) Space beneath the chair supports foot position changes.
   d) Chair seat posterior tilt angle and seat back recline facilitate patient egress.
   e) Chairs are sturdy, stable, and cannot be easily tipped over.
   f) Rolling furniture includes locking rollers or casters.
   g) Chairs have no sharp or hard edges that can injure patients who fall or trip.

3. **Decrease medication errors.**
   a) Lighting fixtures should provide 90 to 150 foot-candle illumination and an adjustable 50-watt high intensity task lamp for furniture with built-in lighting that is used in a medication safety zone.
   b) Furniture is configurable to create a sense of privacy to minimize visual distractions and interruptions from sound and noise during medication transcription, preparation, dispensing, and administration activities.

4. **Improve communication and social support for patients and family members.**
   a) Furniture can be configured into small, flexible groupings that are easily adjusted to accommodate varying numbers of individuals in a variety of healthcare settings.
   b) Wide size and age variations are supported.
   c) Acoustic and visual patient privacy are supported.

5. **Decrease patient, family member, and staff stress and fatigue.**
   a) Materials suggest a link to nature.
   b) Appearance is attractive and noninstitutional.
   c) Furniture is tested for safe and comfortable use by all, including morbidly obese individuals.

6. **Improve staff effectiveness, efficiency, and communication.**
   a) Furniture is easily adjustable to individual worker's ergonomic needs.
   b) Design enables care coordination and information sharing.
   c) Materials are sound absorbing.

7. **Improve environmental safety.**
   a) Materials do not contain volatile organic compounds (VOC), such as formaldehyde and benzene.

8. **Represent the best investment.**
   a) Reflect and reinforce the organizational mission, strategic goals, and brand.
   b) Integrate new with existing furniture and objects for facility renovation projects.
   c) Pieces can be flexibly reconfigured and moved to support changing and emerging missions.
   d) Provide casters or glides to reduce floor damage.
   e) Check that there are no protuberances that may damage walls; check chair rail heights.
   f) Manufacturer provides results of safety and durability testing.
   g) Manufacturer describes the specific evidence that has been used to design the product.
   h) Manufacturer includes a warranty appropriate to use, such as furniture used all day, every day.
   i) Replacement parts are available.
   j) Repairs can be done in the healthcare facility.
   k) Manufacturer or local dealer can assist with furniture repair and refurbishing.
   l) Environmental services (housekeeping) staff can easily maintain furniture.
   m) A group purchasing organization (GPO) can be used when purchasing furniture.

Additional information about each checklist variable:

1a Joints and seams complicate effective cleaning, creating organism reservoirs that can further the spread of contact transmitted healthcare associated infections. A space between the chair back and seat can facilitate cleaning.

1b Contaminated body fluids soak into porous upholstered furniture complicating effective cleaning

1c Nonporous, smooth solid surfaces such as laminate or poly resin products facilitate effective cleaning.

Note: Hard metal surfaces like copper and surface antimicrobial treatment claims presently lack sufficient evidence for efficacy.

2a/b/c/d Chair seat heights sized to individual needs, armrests, and space beneath a chair to support posterior foot placement facilitate safer sit-to-stand movements.

2e Increased chair posterior seat tilt and increased chair back recline interferes with egress, especially in older adults.

2f Tipped-over-furniture-caused injuries for children are increasing.

2g Locking rollers and casters prevent unwanted furniture movement.

2h Sharp furniture edges, such as wooden chair arms with corners, can injure vulnerable patients or children who bump into them.

3a For systems and built-in furniture used in an area where medications are prescribed, medication orders are entered into a computer, or onto paper documents, and where medications are prepared and administered that includes lighting, brighter illumination results in fewer visual medication errors.

3b Distractions and interruptions are associated with more medication errors.

4a Smaller, more intimate furniture groupings foster communication.

4b/c Systems furniture should include acoustical panels with a minimum noise-reduction coefficient of 0.65.

5a Humans have a genetic propensity to positively respond to nature.

5b Perception of quality, service, and waiting time are linked to physical environment attractiveness. Noninstitutional environments are associated with less patient stress.

5c Sixty-eight percent of Americans are either overweight or obese and require furniture safely designed for their comfort.

6a OSHA recommends furniture that can be tailored to worker ergonomic requirements.

6b Quality healthcare delivery depends on informal interactions by the healthcare team, facilitated by furniture design.

6c Noise distracts and stresses staff, resulting in more time needed to complete procedures, as well as in-staff burnout.

7a Furniture made with VOCs is a source of indoor air pollution.

8a Furniture provides important visual cues about the healthcare organization.

8b Furniture color, material, and style contribute to an image.

8c Emergency preparedness and response situations require furniture that can be easily moved and reconfigured.

8d Some soft flooring products used to reduce noise, fatigue, and injury are more vulnerable to furniture-caused damage.

8e Hard furniture protuberances can damage walls.

8f Manufacturer-conducted furniture testing for safety and durability is required; ask for the results.

8g Manufacturers engage in significant product design and research; ask for the results.

8h Some furniture is used 24 hours a day, every day.

8i The availability of replacement furniture parts, especially for those components exposed to more wear and tear can prolong the life of the object.

8j Furniture that can be repaired in the healthcare facility will be potentially out of use for a shorter period of time.

8k Manufacturer or dealer-supported furniture repair and refurbishing will prolong the life of the object.

8l The environmental services team must be able to easily clean, disinfect, and maintain the furniture; involve them!

8m Group purchasing organizations are used to lower costs.

Source: Checklist by E.B. Malone and B.A. Dellinger. 2011. *Furniture Design Features and Healthcare Outcomes.* Concord, CA: The Center for Health Design. See Center for Health Design Website for full 73-page report.

10. Building Code Checklist

1. Determine your occupancy classification(s) and list in the space provided:

2. Determine your occupancy factor (gross or net) for each of the occupancy classifications listed in Number 1.

Occupancy	Factor	Gross/Net?

3. Calculate your occupant load for each space.

Occupancy	Factor	Sq. Footage	# occupants permitted
TOTAL number of occupants			

4. What is the diagonal for egress? _____
5. How far apart must your fire-rated stair towers/exits be (minimum)? _____
6. How many of each of the following do you need for your design?
   a) WC   M_____ F _____
   b) Lavatory   M _____ F_____
   c) Water fountains _____
   d) Service sinks   _____

7. What is the maximum travel distance to an exit (common path of travel) for each floor?
   a) First _____
   b) Second _____
   c) Third _____
   d) Fourth _____
8. All doors MUST swing in the direction of EGRESS. Verify that your doors are swinging the correct direction and check this box that you have verified this: ☐
9. According to your use group, what is the minimum egress corridor width you can use? _____
10. Verify all your egress corridor widths. Check this box indicating that you have verified this: ☐
11. What is the maximum dead-end corridor width you are permitted for this use group? _____ Check this box indicating that you have verified this: ☐
12. What is the required clear distance on the PUSH side of an accessible door? _____
13. What is the required clear distance on the PULL side of an accessible door? _____
14. What size door is required to comply with ADA requirements? _____
15. For 12–14, verify that you have checked your door sizes, push and pull clearances by checking this box: ☐
16. Where should exit signs be placed in your Reflected Ceiling Plan? Describe in the space provided below:

11. Checklist for Universal Design

Principle One: Equitable Use

Provide the same means of use for all users: identical when possible; equivalent when not possible.

Avoid segregating or stigmatizing any user.

Provide for privacy, security, and safety equally for all users.

Make the design appealing to all users.

Principle Two: Flexibility in Use

Provide choice in methods of use.

Accommodate right- and left-handed access and use.

Facilitate the user's accuracy and precision.

Provide adaptability to the user's pace.

Principle Three: Simple and Intuitive Use

Eliminate unnecessary complexity.

Be consistent with user expectations and intuition.

Accommodate a wide range of literacy and language skills.

Arrange information consistent with its importance.

Provide effective prompting and feedback during and after task.

Principle Four: Perceptible Information

Use different modes for redundant presentation of essential information (pictorial, verbal, tactile).

Provide adequate contrast between essential information and its surroundings.

Maximize legibility of essential elements.

Differentiate elements in ways that can be described (give instruction or directions).

Provide compatibility with a variety of techniques of devices used by people with sensory limitations.

Principle Five: Tolerance for Error

Arrange elements to minimize hazards and errors; most-used elements, most accessible; hazardous elements eliminated, isolated, or shielded.

Provide warnings of hazards and errors.

Provide fail-safe features.

Discourage unconscious action in tasks that require vigilance.

Principle Six: Low Physical Effort

Allow user to maintain a neutral body position.

Use reasonable operating forces.

Minimize repetitive actions.

Minimize sustained physical effort.

Principle Seven: Size and Space for Approach and Use

Provide a clear line of sight to important elements for any seated or standing user.

Make reach to all components comfortable to any seated or standing user.

Accommodate variations in hand and grip size.

Provide adequate space for the use of assistive devices or personal assistance.

Source: Adapted from the Principles of Universal Design (version 2.0, 1997). http://www.ncsu.edu/ncsu/design/cud/

LEED 2009 for Commercial Interiors
Project Checklist

			Sustainable Sites	Possible Points:	**21**
Y	?	N			
			Credit 1	Site Selection	1 to 5
			Credit 2	Development Density and Community Connectivity	6
			Credit 3.1	Alternative Transportation—Public Transportation Access	6
			Credit 3.2	Alternative Transportation—Bicycle Storage and Changing Rooms	2
			Credit 3.3	Alternative Transportation—Parking Availability	2

			Water Efficiency	Possible Points:	**11**
Y			Prereq 1	Water Use Reduction—20% Reduction	
			Credit 1	Water Use Reduction	6 to 11

			Energy and Atmosphere	Possible Points:	**37**
Y			Prereq 1	Fundamental Commissioning of Building Energy Systems	
Y			Prereq 2	Minimum Energy Performance	
Y			Prereq 3	Fundamental Refrigerant Management	
			Credit 1.1	Optimize Energy Performance—Lighting Power	1 to 5
			Credit 1.2	Optimize Energy Performance—Lighting Controls	1 to 3
			Credit 1.3	Optimize Energy Performance—HVAC	5 to 10
			Credit 1.4	Optimize Energy Performance—Equipment and Appliances	1 to 4
			Credit 2	Enhanced Commissioning	5
			Credit 3	Measurement and Verification	2 to 5
			Credit 4	Green Power	5

			Materials and Resources	Possible Points:	**14**
Y			Prereq 1	Storage and Collection of Recyclables	
			Credit 1.1	Tenant Space—Long-Term Commitment	1
			Credit 1.2	Building Reuse	1 to 2
			Credit 2	Construction Waste Management	1 to 2
			Credit 3.1	Materials Reuse	1 to 2
			Credit 3.2	Materials Reuse—Furniture and Furnishings	1
			Credit 4	Recycled Content	1 to 2
			Credit 5	Regional Materials	1 to 2
			Credit 6	Rapidly Renewable Materials	1
			Credit 7	Certified Wood	1

Source: www.usgbc.com

Indoor Environmental Quality — Possible Points: 17

	Y	?	N			
	Y			Prereq 1	Minimum IAQ Performance	
	Y			Prereq 2	Environmental Tobacco Smoke (ETS) Control	
				Credit 1	Outdoor Air Delivery Monitoring	1
				Credit 2	Increased Ventilation	1
				Credit 3.1	Construction IAQ Management Plan—During Construction	1
				Credit 3.2	Construction IAQ Management Plan—Before Occupancy	1
				Credit 4.1	Low-Emitting Materials—Adhesives and Sealants	1
				Credit 4.2	Low-Emitting Materials—Paints and Coatings	1
				Credit 4.3	Low-Emitting Materials—Flooring Systems	1
				Credit 4.4	Low-Emitting Materials—Composite Wood and Agrifiber Products	1
				Credit 4.5	Low-Emitting Materials—Systems Furniture and Seating	1
				Credit 5	Indoor Chemical & Pollutant Source Control	1
				Credit 6.1	Controllability of Systems—Lighting	1
				Credit 6.2	Controllability of Systems—Thermal Comfort	1
				Credit 7.1	Thermal Comfort—Design	1
				Credit 7.2	Thermal Comfort—Verification	1
				Credit 8.1	Daylight and Views—Daylight	1 to 2
				Credit 8.2	Daylight and Views—Views for Seated Spaces	1

Innovation and Design Process — Possible Points: 6

				Credit 1.1	Innovation in Design: Specific Title	1
				Credit 1.2	Innovation in Design: Specific Title	1
				Credit 1.3	Innovation in Design: Specific Title	1
				Credit 1.4	Innovation in Design: Specific Title	1
				Credit 1.5	Innovation in Design: Specific Title	1
				Credit 2	LEED Accredited Professional	1

Regional Priority Credits — Possible Points: 4

				Credit 1.1	Regional Priority: Specific Credit	1
				Credit 1.2	Regional Priority: Specific Credit	1
				Credit 1.3	Regional Priority: Specific Credit	1
				Credit 1.4	Regional Priority: Specific Credit	1

Total — Possible Points: 110

Certified 40 to 49 points   Silver 50 to 59 points   Gold 60 to 79 points   Platinum 80 to 110

LEED 2009 for Retail: Commercial Interiors
Project Checklist

					Possible Points:	21
Sustainable Sites						

Y	?	N				
			Credit 1	Site Selection	1 to 5
			Credit 2	Development Density and Community Connectivity	6
			Credit 3	Alternative Transportation	1 to 10

					Possible Points:	11
Water Efficiency						

Y			Prereq 1	Water Use Reduction—20% Reduction	
			Credit 1	Water Use Reduction	6 to 11

					Possible Points:	37
Energy and Atmosphere						

Y			Prereq 1	Fundamental Commissioning of Building Energy Systems	
Y			Prereq 2	Minimum Energy Performance	
Y			Prereq 3	Fundamental Refrigerant Management	
			Credit 1.1	Optimize Energy Performance—Lighting Power	1 to 5
			Credit 1.2	Optimize Energy Performance—Lighting Controls	1 to 3
			Credit 1.3	Optimize Energy Performance—HVAC	5 to 10
			Credit 1.4	Optimize Energy Performance—Equipment and Appliances	1 to 4
			Credit 1.5	Optimize Energy Performance—Building Envelope	1
			Credit 2	Enhanced Commissioning	5
			Credit 3	Measurement and Verification	2 to 5
			Credit 4	Green Power	2
			Credit 5	On-Site Renewable Energy	1 to 2

					Possible Points:	14
Materials and Resources						

Y			Prereq 1	Storage and Collection of Recyclables	
			Credit 1.1	Tenant Space—Long-Term Commitment	1
			Credit 1.2	Building Reuse—Maintain Interior Nonstructural Components	1 to 2
			Credit 2	Construction Waste Management	1 to 2
			Credit 3.1	Materials Reuse	1 to 2
			Credit 3.2	Materials Reuse—Furniture and Furnishings	1
			Credit 4	Recycled Content	1 to 2
			Credit 5	Regional Materials	1 to 2
			Credit 6	Rapidly Renewable Materials	1
			Credit 7	Certified Wood	1

Source: www.usgbc.com

Y	?	N		**Indoor Environmental Quality**	Possible Points:	**17**
Y			Prereq 1	Minimum IAQ Performance		
Y			Prereq 2	Environmental Tobacco Smoke (ETS) Control		
			Credit 1	Outdoor Air Delivery Monitoring	1	
			Credit 2	Increased Ventilation	1	
			Credit 3.1	Construction IAQ Management Plan—During Construction	1	
			Credit 3.2	Construction IAQ Management Plan—Before Occupancy	1	
			Credit 4.1	Low-Emitting Materials—Adhesives and Sealants	1	
			Credit 4.2	Low-Emitting Materials—Paints and Coatings	1	
			Credit 4.3	Low-Emitting Materials—Flooring Systems	1	
			Credit 4.4	Low-Emitting Materials—Composite Wood and Agrifiber Products	1	
			Credit 4.5	Low-Emitting Materials—Furniture	1	
			Credit 4.6	Low-Emitting Materials—Ceiling and Wall Systems	1	
			Credit 5	Indoor Chemical & Pollutant Source Control	1	
			Credit 6	Controllability of Systems—Lighting and Thermal Comfort	1	
			Credit 7.1	Thermal Comfort—Design	1	
			Credit 7.2	Thermal Comfort—Employee Verification	1	
			Credit 8.1	Daylight and Views—Daylight	1 to 2	
			Credit 8.2	Daylight and Views—Views	1	

				Innovation and Design Process	Possible Points:	**6**
			Credit 1.1	Innovation in Design: Specific Title	1	
			Credit 1.2	Innovation in Design: Specific Title	1	
			Credit 1.3	Innovation in Design: Specific Title	1	
			Credit 1.4	Innovation in Design: Specific Title	1	
			Credit 1.5	Innovation in Design: Specific Title	1	
			Credit 2	LEED Accredited Professional	1	

				Regional Priority Credits	Possible Points:	**4**
			Credit 1.1	Regional Priority: Specific Credit	1	
			Credit 1.2	Regional Priority: Specific Credit	1	
			Credit 1.3	Regional Priority: Specific Credit	1	
			Credit 1.4	Regional Priority: Specific Credit	1	

				Total	Possible Points:	**110**

Certified 40 to 49 points   Silver 50 to 59 points   Gold 60 to 79 points   Platinum 80+ points

LEED 2009 for Retail: New Construction and Major Renovations
Project Checklist

Sustainable Sites — Possible Points: 26

Y	?	N			
Y			Prereq 1	Construction Activity Pollution Prevention	
			Credit 1	Site Selection	1
			Credit 2	Development Density and Community Connectivity	5
			Credit 3	Brownfield Redevelopment	1
			Credit 4	Alternative Transportation	1 to 10
			Credit 5.1	Site Development—Protect or Restore Habitat	1
			Credit 5.2	Site Development—Maximize Open Space	1
			Credit 6.1	Stormwater Design—Quantity Control	1
			Credit 6.2	Stormwater Design—Quality Control	1
	.		Credit 7.1	Heat Island Effect—Nonroof	1 to 2
			Credit 7.2	Heat Island Effect—Roof	1
			Credit 8	Light Pollution Reduction	2

Water Efficiency — Possible Points: 10

Y	?	N			
Y			Prereq 1	Water Use Reduction—20% Reduction	
	..		Credit 1	Water Efficient Landscaping	2 to 4
	.		Credit 2	Innovative Wastewater Technologies	2
			Credit 3	Water Use Reduction	2 to 4

Energy and Atmosphere — Possible Points: 35

Y	?	N			
Y			Prereq 1	Fundamental Commissioning of Building Energy Systems	
Y			Prereq 2	Minimum Energy Performance	
Y			Prereq 3	Fundamental Refrigerant Management	
			Credit 1	Optimize Energy Performance	1 to 19
			Credit 2	On-Site Renewable Energy	1 to 7
			Credit 3	Enhanced Commissioning	2
			Credit 4	Enhanced Refrigerant Management	2
			Credit 5	Measurement and Verification	3
			Credit 6	Green Power	2

Materials and Resources — Possible Points: 14

Y	?	N			
Y			Prereq 1	Storage and Collection of Recyclables	
			Credit 1.1	Building Reuse—Maintain Existing Walls, Floors, and Roof	1 to 3
			Credit 1.2	Building Reuse—Maintain Interior Nonstructural Elements	1
			Credit 2	Construction Waste Management	1 to 2
			Credit 3	Materials Reuse	1 to 2

Source: www.usgbc.com

Materials and Resources, Continued

Y	?	N			
			Credit 4	Recycled Content	1 to 2
			Credit 5	Regional Materials	1 to 2
			Credit 6	Rapidly Renewable Materials	1
			Credit 7	Certified Wood	1

Indoor Environmental Quality　　Possible Points:　15

Y			Prereq 1	Minimum Indoor Air Quality Performance	
Y			Prereq 2	Environmental Tobacco Smoke (ETS) Control	
			Credit 1	Outdoor Air Delivery Monitoring	1
			Credit 2	Increased Ventilation	1
			Credit 3.1	Construction IAQ Management Plan—During Construction	1
			Credit 3.2	Construction IAQ Management Plan—Before Occupancy	1
			Credit 4	Low-Emitting Materials	1 to 5
			Credit 5	Indoor Chemical and Pollutant Source Control	1
			Credit 6	Controllability of Systems—Lighting and Thermal Comfort	1
			Credit 7.1	Thermal Comfort—Design	1
			Credit 7.2	Thermal Comfort—Employee Verification	1
			Credit 8.1	Daylight and Views—Daylight	1
			Credit 8.2	Daylight and Views—Views	1

Innovation and Design Process　　Possible Points:　6

			Credit 1.1	Innovation in Design: Specific Title	1
			Credit 1.2	Innovation in Design: Specific Title	1
			Credit 1.3	Innovation in Design: Specific Title	1
			Credit 1.4	Innovation in Design: Specific Title	1
			Credit 1.5	Innovation in Design: Specific Title	1
			Credit 2	LEED Accredited Professional	1

Regional Priority Credits　　Possible Points:　4

			Credit 1.1	Regional Priority: Specific Credit	1
			Credit 1.2	Regional Priority: Specific Credit	1
			Credit 1.3	Regional Priority: Specific Credit	1
			Credit 1.4	Regional Priority: Specific Credit	1

Total　　Possible Points:　110

Certified 40 to 49 points　　Silver 50 to 59 points　　Gold 60 to 79 points　　Platinum 80+ points

LEED 2009 for Schools New Construction and Major Renovations
Project Checklist

			Sustainable Sites	Possible Points:	24
Y	?	N			
Y			Prereq 1 Construction Activity Pollution Prevention		
Y			Prereq 2 Environmental Site Assessment		
			Credit 1 Site Selection		1
			Credit 2 Development Density and Community Connectivity		4
			Credit 3 Brownfield Redevelopment		1
			Credit 4.1 Alternative Transportation—Public Transportation Access		4
			Credit 4.2 Alternative Transportation—Bicycle Storage and Changing Rooms		1
			Credit 4.3 Alternative Transportation—Low-Emitting and Fuel-Efficient Vehicles		2
			Credit 4.4 Alternative Transportation—Parking Capacity		2
			Credit 5.1 Site Development—Protect or Restore Habitat		1
			Credit 5.2 Site Development—Maximize Open Space		1
			Credit 6.1 Stormwater Design—Quantity Control		1
			Credit 6.2 Stormwater Design—Quality Control		1
			Credit 7.1 Heat Island Effect—Non-roof		1
			Credit 7.2 Heat Island Effect—Roof		1
			Credit 8 Light Pollution Reduction		1
			Credit 9 Site Master Plan		1
			Credit 10 Joint Use of Facilities		1

			Water Efficiency	Possible Points:	11
Y			Prereq 1 Water Use Reduction—20% Reduction		
			Credit 1 Water Efficient Landscaping		2 to 4
			Credit 2 Innovative Wastewater Technologies		2
			Credit 3 Water Use Reduction		2 to 4
			Credit 3 Process Water Use Reduction		1

			Energy and Atmosphere	Possible Points:	33
Y			Prereq 1 Fundamental Commissioning of Building Energy Systems		
Y			Prereq 2 Minimum Energy Performance		
Y			Prereq 3 Fundamental Refrigerant Management		
			Credit 1 Optimize Energy Performance		1 to 19
			Credit 2 On-Site Renewable Energy		1 to 7
			Credit 3 Enhanced Commissioning		2
			Credit 4 Enhanced Refrigerant Management		1
			Credit 5 Measurement and Verification		2
			Credit 6 Green Power		2

			Materials and Resources	Possible Points:	13
Y			Prereq 1 Storage and Collection of Recyclables		
			Credit 1.1 Building Reuse—Maintain Existing Walls, Floors, and Roof		1 to 2
			Credit 1.2 Building Reuse—Maintain 50% of Interior Non-Structural Elements		1
			Credit 2 Construction Waste Management		1 to 2

Source: www.usgbc.com

Materials and Resources, Continued

Y	?	N			
			Credit 3	Materials Reuse	1 to 2
			Credit 4	Recycled Content	1 to 2
			Credit 5	Regional Materials	1 to 2
			Credit 6	Rapidly Renewable Materials	1
			Credit 7	Certified Wood	1

Indoor Environmental Quality — Possible Points: 19

Y	?	N			
Y			Prereq 1	Minimum Indoor Air Quality Performance	
Y			Prereq 2	Environmental Tobacco Smoke (ETS) Control	
Y			Prereq 3	Minimum Acoustical Performance	
			Credit 1	Outdoor Air Delivery Monitoring	1
			Credit 2	Increased Ventilation	1
			Credit 3.1	Construction IAQ Management Plan—During Construction	1
			Credit 3.2	Construction IAQ Management Plan—Before Occupancy	1
			Credit 4	Low-Emitting Materials	1 to 4
			Credit 5	Indoor Chemical and Pollutant Source Control	1
			Credit 6.1	Controllability of Systems—Lighting	1
			Credit 6.2	Controllability of Systems—Thermal Comfort	1
			Credit 7.1	Thermal Comfort—Design	1
			Credit 7.2	Thermal Comfort—Verification	1
			Credit 8.1	Daylight and Views—Daylight	1 to 3
			Credit 8.2	Daylight and Views—Views	1
			Credit 9	Enhanced Acoustical Performance	1
			Credit 10	Mold Prevention	1

Innovation and Design Process — Possible Points: 6

Y	?	N			
			Credit 1.1	Innovation in Design: Specific Title	1
			Credit 1.2	Innovation in Design: Specific Title	1
			Credit 1.3	Innovation in Design: Specific Title	1
			Credit 1.4	Innovation in Design: Specific Title	1
			Credit 2	LEED Accredited Professional	1
			Credit 3	The School as a Teaching Tool	1

Regional Priority Credits — Possible Points: 4

Y	?	N			
			Credit 1.1	Regional Priority: Specific Credit	1
			Credit 1.2	Regional Priority: Specific Credit	1
			Credit 1.3	Regional Priority: Specific Credit	1
			Credit 1.4	Regional Priority: Specific Credit	1

Total — Possible Points: 110

Certified 40 to 49 points   Silver 50 to 59 points   Gold 60 to 79 points   Platinum 80 to 110

LEED 2009 for Healthcare: New Construction

Project Checklist

					Possible Points:	
Sustainable Sites					**18**	
Y	?	N				
Y			Prereq 1	Construction Activity Pollution Prevention		
Y			Prereq 2	Environmental Site Assessment		
			Credit 1	Site Selection	1	
			Credit 2	Development Density and Community Connectivity	1	
			Credit 3	Brownfield Redevelopment	1	
			Credit 4.1	Alternative Transportation—Public Transportation Access	3	
			Credit 4.2	Alternative Transportation—Bicycle Storage and Changing Rooms	1	
			Credit 4.3	Alternative Transportation—Low-Emitting and Fuel-Efficient Vehicles	1	
			Credit 4.4	Alternative Transportation—Parking Capacity	1	
			Credit 5.1	Site Development—Protect or Restore Habitat	1	
			Credit 5.2	Site Development—Maximize Open Space	1	
			Credit 6.1	Stormwater Design—Quantity Control	1	
			Credit 6.2	Stormwater Design—Quality Control	1	
			Credit 7.1	Heat Island Effect—Non-roof	1	
			Credit 7.2	Heat Island Effect—Roof	1	
			Credit 8	Light Pollution Reduction	1	
			Credit 9.1	Connection to the Natural World—Places of Respite	1	
			Credit 9.2	Connection to the Natural World—Direct Exterior Access for Patients	1	

					Possible Points:	
Water Efficiency					**9**	
Y			Prereq 1	Water Use Reduction—20% Reduction		
Y			Prereq 2	Minimize Potable Water Use for Medical Equipment Cooling		
			Credit 1	Water Efficient Landscaping—No Potable Water Use or No Irrigation	1	
			Credit 2	Water Use Reduction: Measurement & Verification	1 to 2	
			Credit 3	Water Use Reduction	1 to 3	
			Credit 4.1	Water Use Reduction—Building Equipment	1	
			Credit 4.2	Water Use Reduction—Cooling Towers	1	
			Credit 4.3	Water Use Reduction— Food Waste Systems	1	

					Possible Points:	
Energy and Atmosphere					**39**	
Y			Prereq 1	Fundamental Commissioning of Building Energy Systems		
Y			Prereq 2	Minimum Energy Performance		
Y			Prereq 3	Fundamental Refrigerant Management		
			Credit 1	Optimize Energy Performance	1 to 24	
			Credit 2	On-Site Renewable Energy	1 to 8	
			Credit 3	Enhanced Commissioning	1 to 2	
			Credit 4	Enhanced Refrigerant Management	1	
			Credit 5	Measurement and Verification	2	
			Credit 6	Green Power	1	
			Credit 7	Community Contaminant Prevention—Airborne Releases	1	

Source: www.usgbc.com

and Major Renovations

Project Name

Date

				Materials and Resources	Possible Points:	16

Y	?	N			
Y			Prereq 1	Storage and Collection of Recyclables	
Y			Prereq 2	PBT Source Reduction—Mercury	
			Credit 1.1	Building Reuse—Maintain Existing Walls, Floors, and Roof	1 to 3
			Credit 1.2	Building Reuse—Maintain Interior Non-Structural Elements	1
			Credit 2	Construction Waste Management	1 to 2
			Credit 3	Sustainably Sourced Materials and Products	1 to 4
			Credit 4.1	PBT Source Reduction—Mercury in Lamps	1
			Credit 4.2	PBT Source Reduction—Lead, Cadmium, and Copper	2
			Credit 5	Furniture and Medical Furnishings	1 to 2
			Credit 6	Resource Use—Design for Flexibility	1

			Indoor Environmental Quality	Possible Points:	18

Y			Prereq 1	Minimum Indoor Air Quality Performance	
Y			Prereq 2	Environmental Tobacco Smoke (ETS) Control	
Y			Prereq 3	Hazardous Material Removal or Encapsulation	
			Credit 1	Outdoor Air Delivery Monitoring	1
			Credit 2	Acoustic Environment	1 to 2
			Credit 3.1	Construction IAQ Management Plan—During Construction	1
			Credit 3.2	Construction IAQ Management Plan—Before Occupancy	1
			Credit 4	Low-Emitting Materials	1 to 4
			Credit 5	Indoor Chemical and Pollutant Source Control	1
			Credit 6.1	Controllability of Systems—Lighting	1
			Credit 6.2	Controllability of Systems—Thermal Comfort	1
			Credit 7	Thermal Comfort—Design and Verification	1
			Credit 8.1	Daylight and Views—Daylight	2
			Credit 8.2	Daylight and Views—Views	1 to 3

			Innovation in Design	Possible Points:	6

Y			Prereq 1	Integrated Project Planning and Design	
			Credit 1.1	Innovation in Design: Specific Title	1
			Credit 1.2	Innovation in Design: Specific Title	1
			Credit 1.3	Innovation in Design: Specific Title	1
			Credit 1.4	Innovation in Design: Specific Title	1
			Credit 2	LEED Accredited Professional	1
			Credit 3	Integrated Project Planning and Design	1

			Regional Priority Credits	Possible Points:	4

			Credit 1.1	Regional Priority: Specific Credit	1
			Credit 1.2	Regional Priority: Specific Credit	1
			Credit 1.3	Regional Priority: Specific Credit	1
			Credit 1.4	Regional Priority: Specific Credit	1

			Total	Possible Points:	110

Certified 40 to 49 points   Silver 50 to 59 points   Gold 60 to 79 points   Platinum 80 to 110

17. LEED for Homes

LEED for Homes Simplified Project Checklist

for Homes

Builder Name:	
Project Team Leader (if different):	
Home Address (Street/City/State):	

Project Description:

Building type:

# of bedrooms: **0**

Project type:

Floor area: **0**

Adjusted Certification Thresholds

Certified: **45.0**	Gold: **75.0**
Silver: **60.0**	Platinum: **90.0**

Project Point Total		Final Credit Category Total Points			
Prelim: **0 + 0 maybe pts**	Final: **0**	ID: **0** SS: **0**	EA: **0**		EQ: **0**
Certification Level		LL: **0** WE: **0**	MR: **0**		AE: **0**
Prelim: **Not Certified**	Final: **Not Certified**	Min. Point Thresholds Not Met for Prelim. OR Final Rating			

date last updated :

last updated by :

				Max Points	Y/Pts	Maybe	No	Y/Pts
Innovation and Design Process (ID)		(No Minimum Points Required)		Max				
1. Integrated Project Planning	1.1	Preliminary Rating		Prereq				
	1.2	Integrated Project Team		1	0	0		0
	1.3	Professional Credentialed with Respect to LEED for Homes		1	0	0		0
	1.4	Design Charrette		1	0	0		0
	1.5	Building Orientation for Solar Design		1	0	0		0
2. Durability Management Process	2.1	Durability Planning		Prereq				
	2.2	Durability Management		Prereq				
	2.3	Third-Party Durability Management Verification		3	0	0		0
3. Innovative or Regional Design	3.1	Innovation #1 _____		1	0	0		0
	3.2	Innovation #2 _____		1	0	0		0
	3.3	Innovation #3 _____		1	0	0		0
	3.4	Innovation #4		1	0	0		0
		Sub-Total for ID Category:		**11**	0	0		**0**
Location and Linkages (LL)		(No Minimum Points Required)	OR	Max	Y/Pts	Maybe	No	Y/Pts
1. LEED ND	1	LEED for Neighborhood Development	LL2-6	10	0	0		0
2. Site Selection	2	Site Selection		2	0	0		0
3. Preferred Locations	3.1	Edge Development	LL 3.2	1	0	0		0
	3.2	Infill		2	0	0		0
	3.3	Previously Developed		1	0	0		0
4. Infrastructure	4	Existing Infrastructure		1	0	0		0
5. Community Resources/ Transit	5.1	Basic Community Resources / Transit	LL 5.2, 5.3	1	0	0		0
	5.2	Extensive Community Resources / Transit	LL 5.3	2	0	0		0
	5.3	Outstanding Community Resources / Transit		3	0	0		0
6. Access to Open Space	6	Access to Open Space		1	0	0		0
		Sub-Total for LL Category:		**10**	0	0		**0**
Sustainable Sites (SS)		(Minimum of 5 SS Points Required)	OR	Max	Y/Pts	Maybe	No	Y/Pts
1. Site Stewardship	1.1	Erosion Controls During Construction		Prereq				
	1.2	Minimize Disturbed Area of Site		1	0	0		0
2. Landscaping	2.1	No Invasive Plants		Prereq				
	2.2	Basic Landscape Design	SS 2.5	2	0	0		0
	2.3	Limit Conventional Turf	SS 2.5	3	0	0		0
	2.4	Drought Tolerant Plants	SS 2.5	2	0	0		0
	2.5	Reduce Overall Irrigation Demand by at Least 20%		6	0	0		0
3. Local Heat Island Effects	3	Reduce Local Heat Island Effects		1	0	0		0
4. Surface Water Management	4.1	Permeable Lot		4	0	0		0
	4.2	Permanent Erosion Controls		1	0	0		0
	4.3	Management of Run-off from Roof		2	0	0		0
5. Nontoxic Pest Control	5	Pest Control Alternatives		2	0	0		0
6. Compact Development	6.1	Moderate Density	SS 6.2, 6.3	2	0	0		0
	6.2	High Density	SS 6.3	3	0	0		0
	6.3	Very High Density		4	0	0		0
		Sub-Total for SS Category:		**22**	0	0		**0**

Source: www.usgbc.com

LEED for Homes Simplified Project Checklist (continued)

				Max Points	Project Points Preliminary			Final
					Y/Pts	Maybe	No	Y/Pts
Water Efficiency (WE)		(Minimum of 3 WE Points Required)	OR	Max	Y/Pts	Maybe	No	Y/Pts
1. Water Reuse	1.1	Rainwater Harvesting System	WE 1.3	4	0	0		0
	1.2	Graywater Reuse System	WE 1.3	1	0	0		0
	1.3	Use of Municipal Recycled Water System		3	0	0		0
2. Irrigation System	2.1	High Efficiency Irrigation System	WE 2.3	3	0	0		0
	2.2	Third Party Inspection	WE 2.3	1	0	0		0
	2.3	Reduce Overall Irrigation Demand by at Least 45%		4	0	0		0
3. Indoor Water Use	3.1	High-Efficiency Fixtures and Fittings		3	0	0		0
	3.2	Very High Efficiency Fixtures and Fittings		6	0	0		0
		Sub-Total for WE Category:		**15**	0	0		**0**
Energy and Atmosphere (EA)		(Minimum of 0 EA Points Required)	OR	Max	Y/Pts	Maybe	No	Y/Pts
1. Optimize Energy Performance	1.1	Performance of ENERGY STAR for Homes		Prereq				
	1.2	Exceptional Energy Performance		34	0	0		0
7. Water Heating	7.1	Efficient Hot Water Distribution		2	0	0		0
	7.2	Pipe Insulation		1	0	0		0
11. Residential Refrigerant Management	11.1	Refrigerant Charge Test		Prereq				
	11.2	Appropriate HVAC Refrigerants		1	0	0		0
		Sub-Total for EA Category:		**38**	0	0		**0**
Materials and Resources (MR)		(Minimum of 2 MR Points Required)	OR	Max	Y/Pts	Maybe	No	Y/Pts
1. Material-Efficient Framing	1.1	Framing Order Waste Factor Limit		Prereq				
	1.2	Detailed Framing Documents	MR 1.5	1	0	0		0
	1.3	Detailed Cut List and Lumber Order	MR 1.5	1	0	0		0
	1.4	Framing Efficiencies	MR 1.5	3	0	0		0
	1.5	Off-site Fabrication		4	0	0		0
2. Environmentally Preferable Products	2.1	FSC Certified Tropical Wood		Prereq				
	2.2	Environmentally Preferable Products		8	0	0		0
3. Waste Management	3.1	Construction Waste Management Planning		Prereq				
	3.2	Construction Waste Reduction		3	0	0		0
		Sub-Total for MR Category:		**16**	0	0		**0**
Indoor Environmental Quality (EQ)		(Minimum of 6 EQ Points Required)	OR	Max	Y/Pts	Maybe	No	Y/Pts
1. ENERGY STAR with IAP	1	ENERGY STAR with Indoor Air Package		13	0	0		0
2. Combustion Venting	2.1	Basic Combustion Venting Measures	EQ 1	Prereq				
	2.2	Enhanced Combustion Venting Measures	EQ 1	2	0	0		0
3. Moisture Control	3	Moisture Load Control	EQ 1	1	0	0		0
4. Outdoor Air Ventilation	4.1	Basic Outdoor Air Ventilation	EQ 1	Prereq				
	4.2	Enhanced Outdoor Air Ventilation		2	0	0		0
	4.3	Third-Party Performance Testing	EQ 1	1	0	0		0
5. Local Exhaust	5.1	Basic Local Exhaust	EQ 1	Prereq				
	5.2	Enhanced Local Exhaust		1	0	0		0
	5.3	Third-Party Performance Testing		1	0	0		0
6. Distribution of Space Heating and Cooling	6.1	Room-by-Room Load Calculations	EQ 1	Prereq				
	6.2	Return Air Flow / Room by Room Controls	EQ 1	1	0	0		0
	6.3	Third-Party Performance Test / Multiple Zones	EQ 1	2	0	0		0
7. Air Filtering	7.1	Good Filters	EQ 1	Prereq				
	7.2	Better Filters	EQ 7.3	1	0	0		0
	7.3	Best Filters		2	0	0		0
8. Contaminant Control	8.1	Indoor Contaminant Control during Construction		1	0	0		0
	8.2	Indoor Contaminant Control		2	0	0		0
	8.3	Preoccupancy Flush	EQ 1	1	0	0		0
9. Radon Protection	9.1	Radon-Resistant Construction in High-Risk Areas	EQ 1	Prereq				
	9.2	Radon-Resistant Construction in Moderate-Risk Areas	EQ 1	1	0	0		0
10. Garage Pollutant Protection	10.1	No HVAC in Garage	EQ 1	Prereq				
	10.2	Minimize Pollutants from Garage	EQ 1, 10.4	2	0	0		0
	10.3	Exhaust Fan in Garage	EQ 1, 10.4	1	0	0		0
	10.4	Detached Garage or No Garage	EQ 1	3	0	0		0
		Sub-Total for EQ Category:		**21**	0	0		**0**
Awareness and Education (AE)		(Minimum of 0 AE Points Required)		Max	Y/Pts	Maybe	No	Y/Pts
1. Education of the Homeowner or Tenant	1.1	Basic Operations Training		Prereq				
	1.2	Enhanced Training		1	0	0		0
	1.3	Public Awareness		1	0	0		0
2. Education of Building Manager	2	Education of Building Manager		1	0	0		0
		Sub-Total for AE Category:		**3**	0	0		**0**

LEED 2009 for New Construction and Major Renovations
Project Checklist

			Sustainable Sites	Possible Points:	26
Y	?	N			
Y			Prereq 1 Construction Activity Pollution Prevention		
			Credit 1 Site Selection		1
			Credit 2 Development Density and Community Connectivity		5
			Credit 3 Brownfield Redevelopment		1
			Credit 4.1 Alternative Transportation—Public Transportation Access		6
			Credit 4.2 Alternative Transportation—Bicycle Storage and Changing Rooms		1
			Credit 4.3 Alternative Transportation—Low-Emitting and Fuel-Efficient Vehicles		3
			Credit 4.4 Alternative Transportation—Parking Capacity		2
			Credit 5.1 Site Development—Protect or Restore Habitat		1
			Credit 5.2 Site Development—Maximize Open Space		1
			Credit 6.1 Stormwater Design—Quantity Control		1
			Credit 6.2 Stormwater Design—Quality Control		1
			Credit 7.1 Heat Island Effect—Non-roof		1
			Credit 7.2 Heat Island Effect—Roof		1
			Credit 8 Light Pollution Reduction		1

			Water Efficiency	Possible Points:	10
Y			Prereq 1 Water Use Reduction—20% Reduction		
			Credit 1 Water Efficient Landscaping		2 to 4
			Credit 2 Innovative Wastewater Technologies		2
			Credit 3 Water Use Reduction		2 to 4

			Energy and Atmosphere	Possible Points:	35
Y			Prereq 1 Fundamental Commissioning of Building Energy Systems		
Y			Prereq 2 Minimum Energy Performance		
Y			Prereq 3 Fundamental Refrigerant Management		
			Credit 1 Optimize Energy Performance		1 to 19
			Credit 2 On-Site Renewable Energy		1 to 7
			Credit 3 Enhanced Commissioning		2
			Credit 4 Enhanced Refrigerant Management		2
			Credit 5 Measurement and Verification		3
			Credit 6 Green Power		2

			Materials and Resources	Possible Points:	14
Y			Prereq 1 Storage and Collection of Recyclables		
			Credit 1.1 Building Reuse—Maintain Existing Walls, Floors, and Roof		1 to 3
			Credit 1.2 Building Reuse—Maintain 50% of Interior Non-Structural Elements		1
			Credit 2 Construction Waste Management		1 to 2
			Credit 3 Materials Reuse		1 to 2

Source: www.usgbc.com

Materials and Resources, Continued

Y	?	N			
			Credit 4	Recycled Content	1 to 2
			Credit 5	Regional Materials	1 to 2
			Credit 6	Rapidly Renewable Materials	1
			Credit 7	Certified Wood	1

Indoor Environmental Quality — Possible Points: 15

Y	?	N			
Y			Prereq 1	Minimum Indoor Air Quality Performance	
Y			Prereq 2	Environmental Tobacco Smoke (ETS) Control	
			Credit 1	Outdoor Air Delivery Monitoring	1
			Credit 2	Increased Ventilation	1
			Credit 3.1	Construction IAQ Management Plan—During Construction	1
			Credit 3.2	Construction IAQ Management Plan—Before Occupancy	1
			Credit 4.1	Low-Emitting Materials—Adhesives and Sealants	1
			Credit 4.2	Low-Emitting Materials—Paints and Coatings	1
			Credit 4.3	Low-Emitting Materials—Flooring Systems	1
			Credit 4.4	Low-Emitting Materials—Composite Wood and Agrifiber Products	1
			Credit 5	Indoor Chemical and Pollutant Source Control	1
			Credit 6.1	Controllability of Systems—Lighting	1
			Credit 6.2	Controllability of Systems—Thermal Comfort	1
			Credit 7.1	Thermal Comfort—Design	1
			Credit 7.2	Thermal Comfort—Verification	1
			Credit 8.1	Daylight and Views—Daylight	1
			Credit 8.2	Daylight and Views—Views	1

Innovation and Design Process — Possible Points: 6

Y	?	N			
			Credit 1.1	Innovation in Design: Specific Title	1
			Credit 1.2	Innovation in Design: Specific Title	1
			Credit 1.3	Innovation in Design: Specific Title	1
			Credit 1.4	Innovation in Design: Specific Title	1
			Credit 1.5	Innovation in Design: Specific Title	1
			Credit 2	LEED Accredited Professional	1

Regional Priority Credits — Possible Points: 4

Y	?	N			
			Credit 1.1	Regional Priority: Specific Credit	1
			Credit 1.2	Regional Priority: Specific Credit	1
			Credit 1.3	Regional Priority: Specific Credit	1
			Credit 1.4	Regional Priority: Specific Credit	1

Total — Possible Points: 110

Certified 40 to 49 points   Silver 50 to 59 points   Gold 60 to 79 points   Platinum 80 to 110

19. LEED for New Construction version 2.2 (LEED-NC v2.2)

Sustainable Sites

- SSp1Construction Activity Pollution Prevention
- SSc1Site Selection
- SSc2Development Density & Community Connectivity
- SSc3Brownfield Redevelopment
- SSc4.1Alternative Transportation— Public Transportation Access
- SSc4.2Alternative Transportation— Bicycle Storage & Changing Rooms
- SSc4.3Alternative Transportation— Low-Emitting & Fuel-Efficient Vehicles
- SSc4.4Alternative Transportation— Parking Capacity
- SSc5.1Site Development— Protect or Restore Habitat
- SSc5.2Site Development—Maximize Open Space
- SSc6.1Stormwater Design—Quantity Control
- SSc6.2Stormwater Design—Quality Control
- SSc7.1Heat Island Effect—Non-Roof
- SSc7.2Heat Island Effect—Roof
- SSc8Light Pollution Reduction

Water Efficiency

- WEc1.1-1.2Water Efficient Landscaping
- WEc2Innovative Wastewater Technologies
- WEc3.1-3.2Water Use Reduction

Energy and Atmosphere

- EAp1Fundamental Commissioning of the Building Energy Systems
- EAp2Minimum Energy Performance
- EAp3Fundamental Refrigerant Management
- EAc1Optimize Energy Performance
- EAc2On-Site Renewable Energy
- EAc3Enhanced Commissioning
- EAc4Enhanced Refrigerant Management
- EAc5Measurement & Verification
- EAc6Green Power

Materials and Resources

- MRp1Storage & Collection of Recyclables
- MRc1.1-1.2Building Reuse
- MRc1.3Building Reuse—Non-Structural
- MRc2Construction Waste Management
- MRc3Materials Reuse
- MRc4Recycled Content
- MRc5Regional Materials
- MRc6Rapidly Renewable Materials
- MRc7Certified Wood

Indoor Environmental Quality

- EQp1Minimum IAQ Performance
- EQp2Environmental Tobacco Smoke (ETS) Control
- EQc1Outdoor Air Delivery Monitoring
- EQc2Increased Ventilation
- EQc3.1Construction IAQ Management Plan— During Construction
- EQc3.2Construction IAQ Management Plan— Before Occupancy
- EQc4.1Low-Emitting Materials— Adhesives & Sealants
- EQc4.2Low-Emitting Materials—Paints & Coatings
- EQc4.3Low-Emitting Materials—Carpet Systems
- EQc4.4Low-Emitting Materials— Composite Wood & Agrifiber Products
- EQc5Indoor Chemical and Pollutant Source Control
- EQc6.1Controllability of Systems—Lighting
- EQc6.2Controllability of Systems— Thermal Comfort
- EQc7.1Thermal Comfort—Design
- EQc7.2Thermal Comfort—Verification
- EQc8.1Daylight and Views—Daylight 75% of Spaces
- EQc8.2Daylight and Views— Views for 90% of Spaces

Innovation in Design

- IDc1Innovation in Design
- IDc2LEED Accredited Professional

Source: www.leeduser.com

INDEX

Water conservation, site analysis example, 33–34
WATG (design firm), 177–181
Watt, Alex, 210, 211
"What is Real Beauty?" counseling unit, 216–217
Wheelchair accessible homes, 272, 281, 284–287
Wheelchair ramps, multi-family housing, 303
Whole Building Design Guidelines, 193
      Historic Preservation Subcommittee, 246
Wilmot Sanz, 97, 100–104
Wind energy, site analysis example, 24, 28–29
Winds, prevailing, site analysis example, 23
Winslow, Barbara, 276
Women shoppers, 46–47
Wood, sustainable forestry, 13
Works Progress Administration (WPA), 244

Workstation ergonomics
    in healthcare design, 82
    in offices, 123–124
Wright, Frank Lloyd, museum, 66–72, 185–202, 250, 251–252

X
Xeriscaping, 276

Y
Yellow Sulphur Springs resort, 250–251, 253–255
Youth rehabilitation center, 94–96

Z
Zero-carbon buildings, 4–5
Zero-energy buildings, 5–6